contents

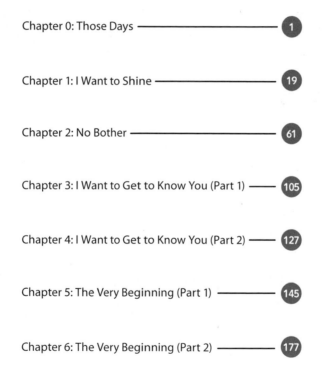

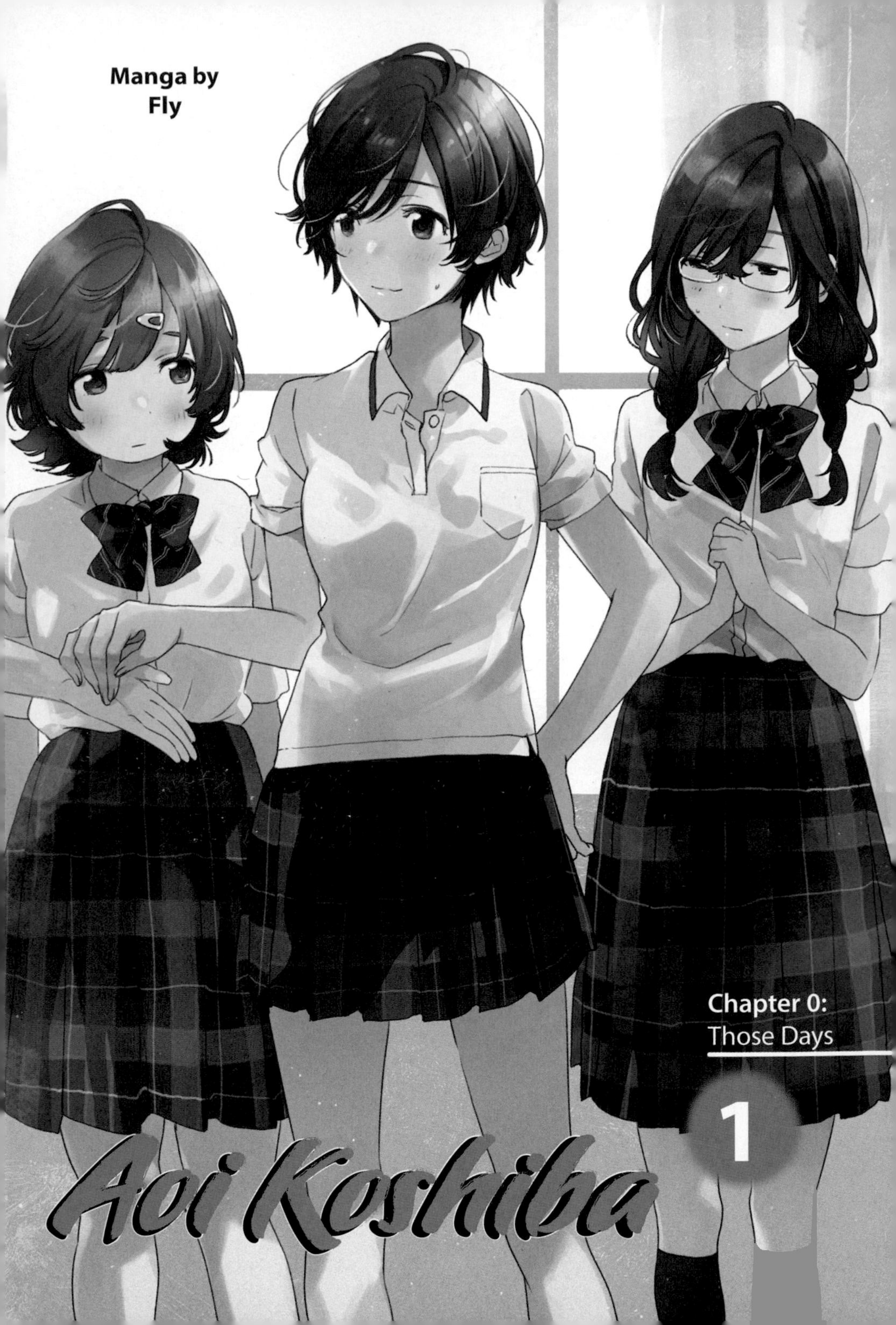

Manga by
Fly
Chapter 0:
Those Days
1
Aoi Koshiba

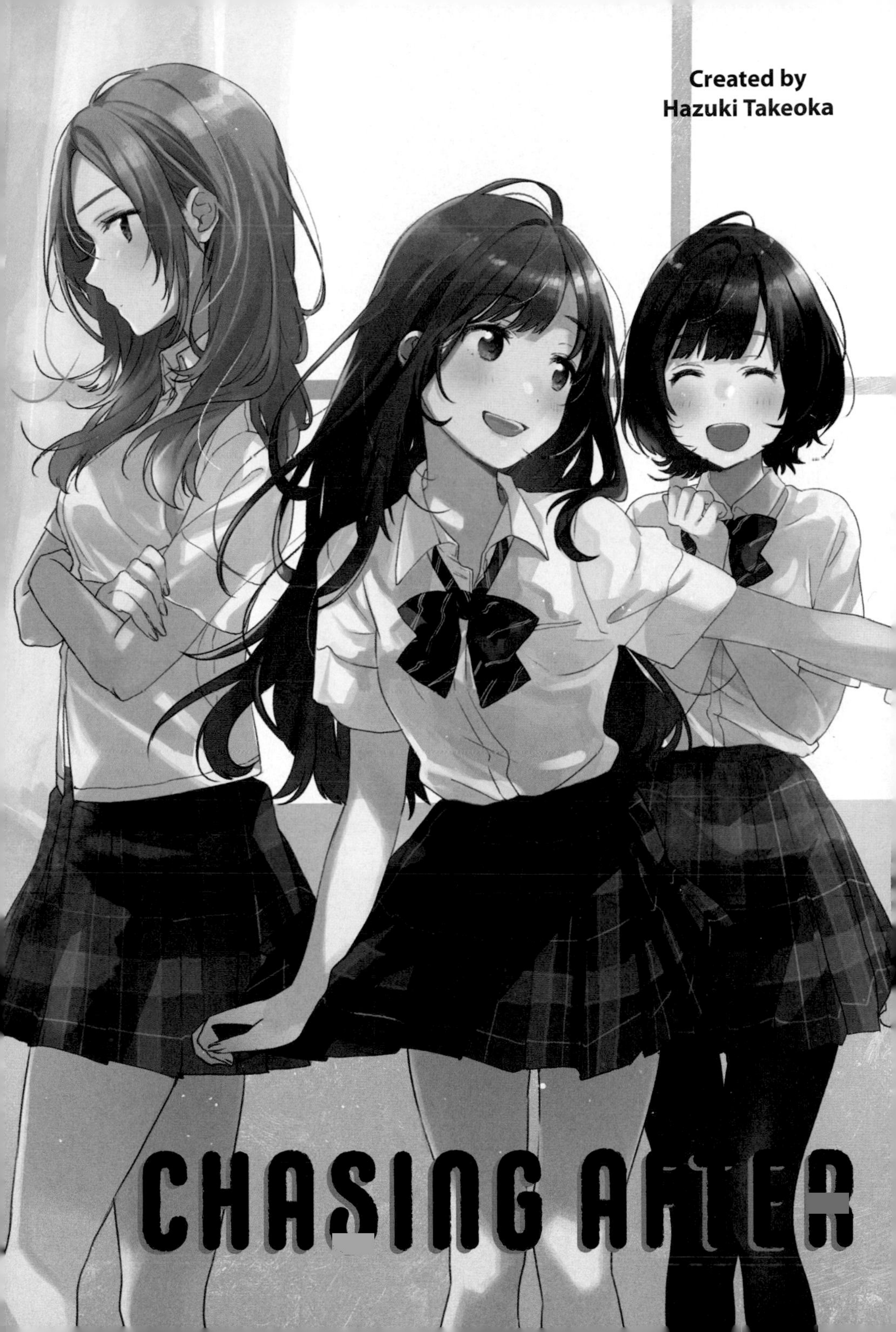
Created by
Hazuki Takeoka
CHASING AFTER

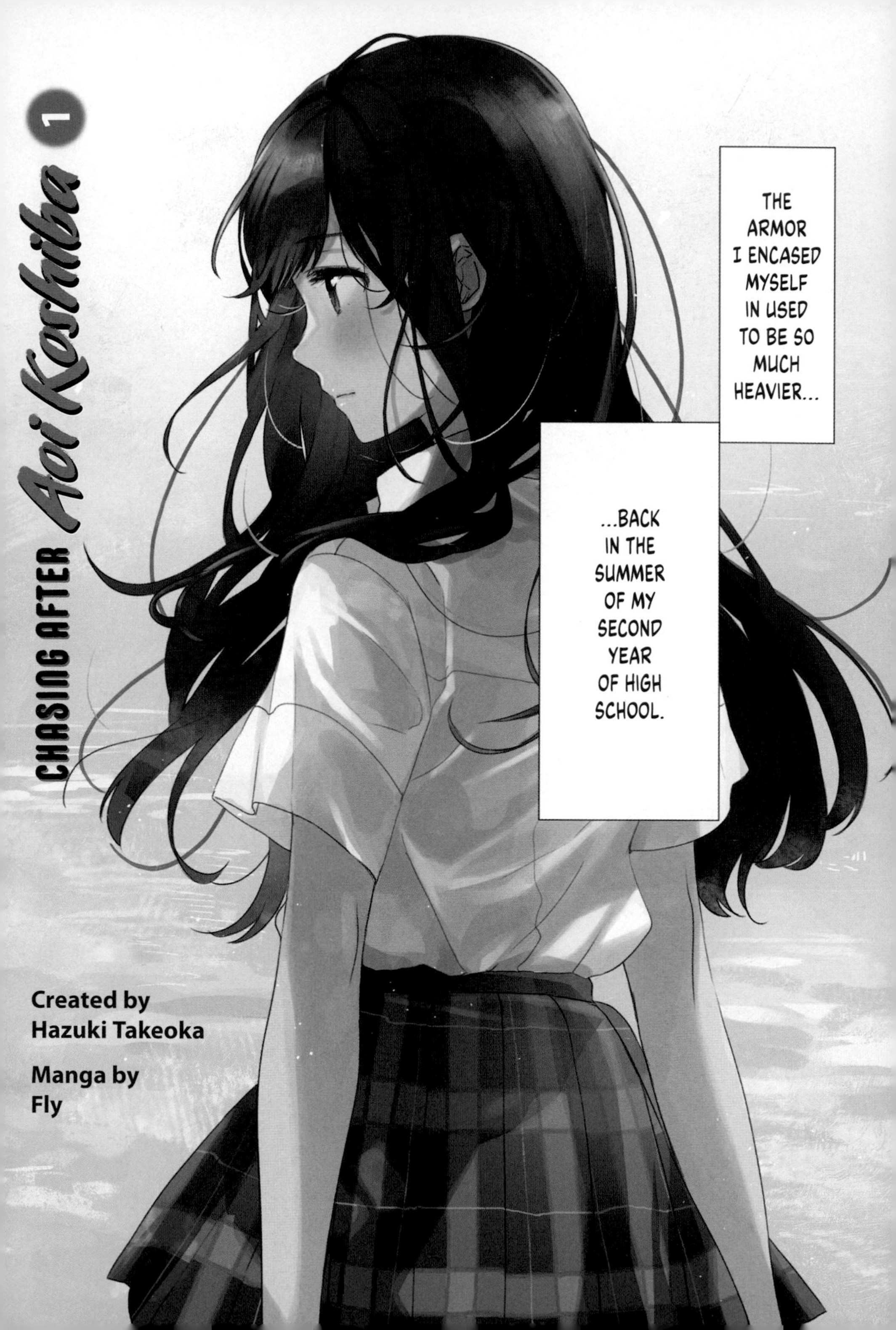
CHASING AFTER Aoi Koshiba 1
THE ARMOR I ENCASED MYSELF IN USED TO BE SO MUCH HEAVIER...
...BACK IN THE SUMMER OF MY SECOND YEAR OF HIGH SCHOOL.

Created by
Hazuki Takeoka

Manga by
Fly

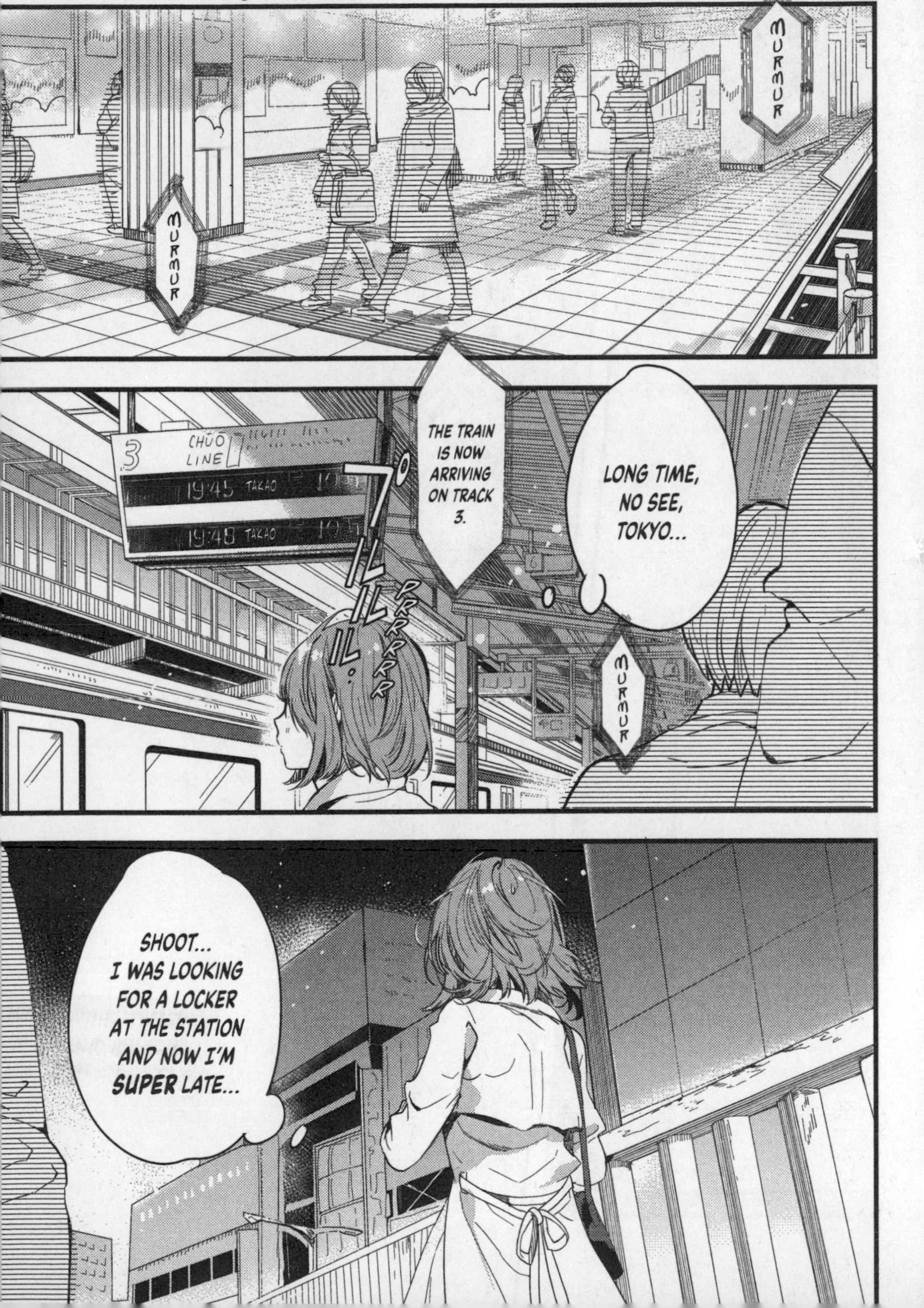
MURMUR
MURMUR
LONG TIME, NO SEE, TOKYO...
THE TRAIN IS NOW ARRIVING ON TRACK 3.
MURMUR
3 CHŪO LINE
19:45 TAKAO
19:48 TAKAO
SHOOT... I WAS LOOKING FOR A LOCKER AT THE STATION AND NOW I'M SUPER LATE...

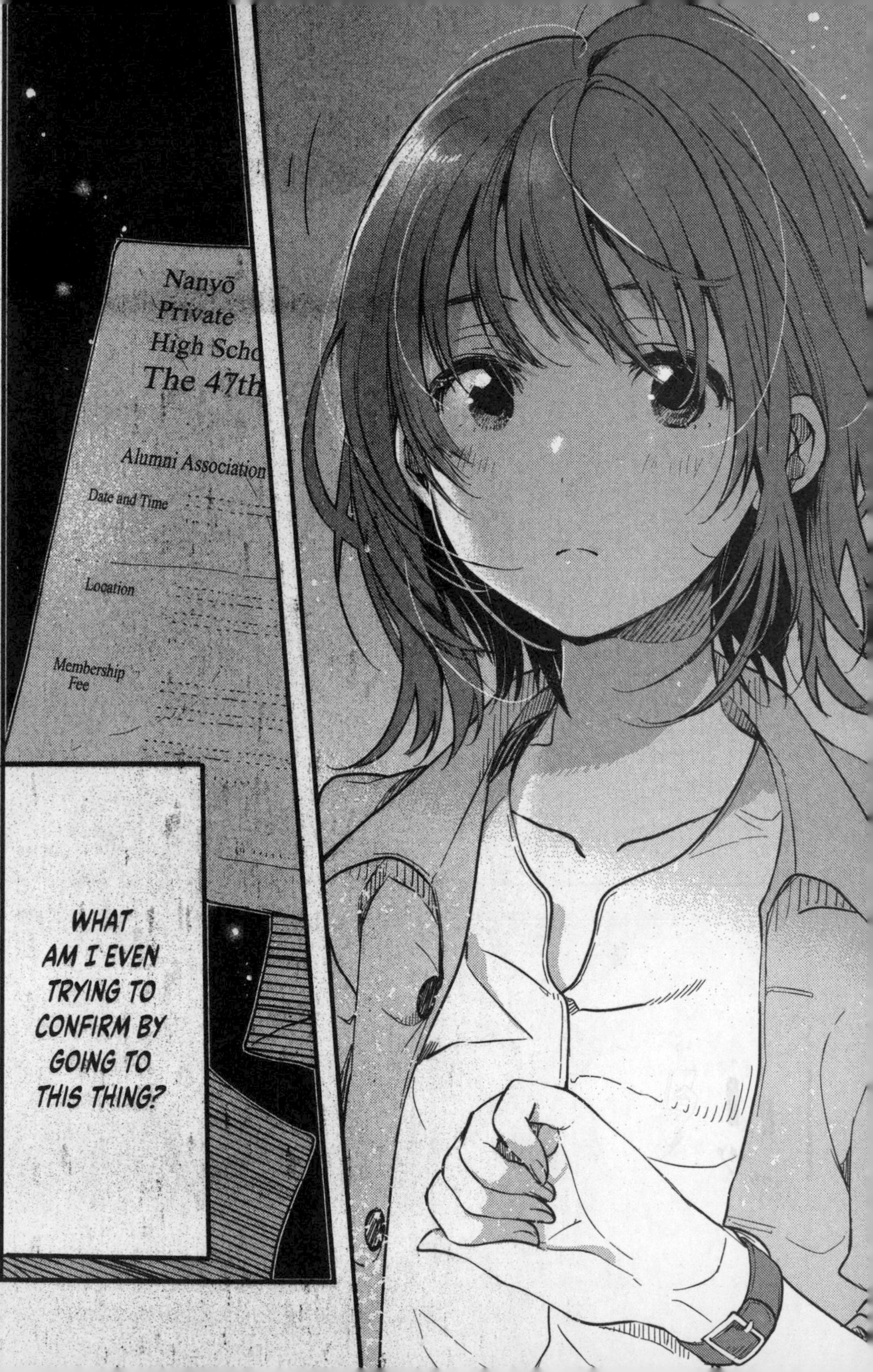
Nanyō
Private
High Scho
The 47th
Alumni Association
Date and Time
Location
Membership
Fee
WHAT AM I EVEN TRYING TO CONFIRM BY GOING TO THIS THING?

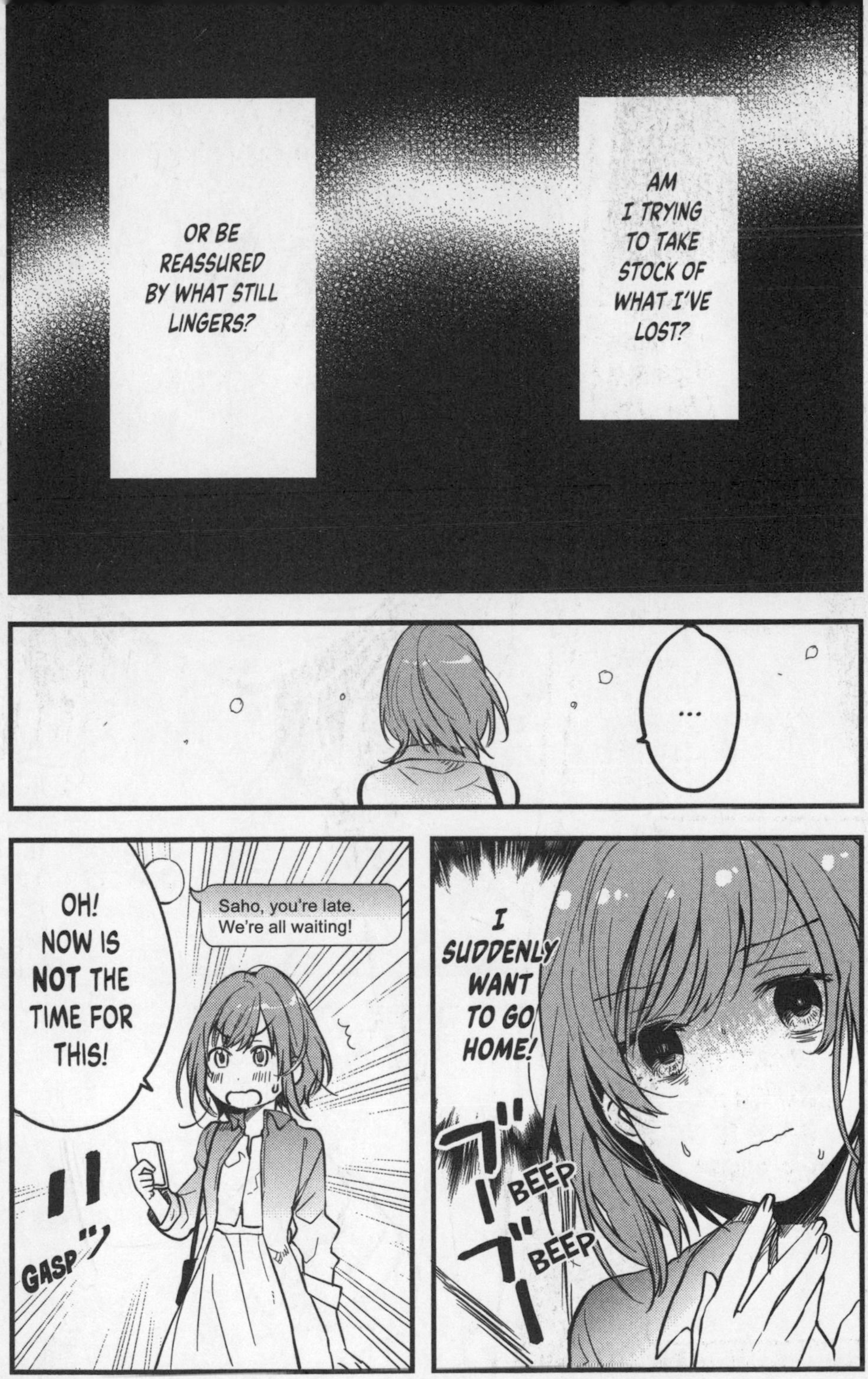
AM I TRYING TO TAKE STOCK OF WHAT I'VE LOST?
OR BE REASSURED BY WHAT STILL LINGERS?
...
I SUDDENLY WANT TO GO HOME!
BEEP
BEEP
Saho, you're late. We're all waiting!
OH! NOW IS NOT THE TIME FOR THIS!
GASP

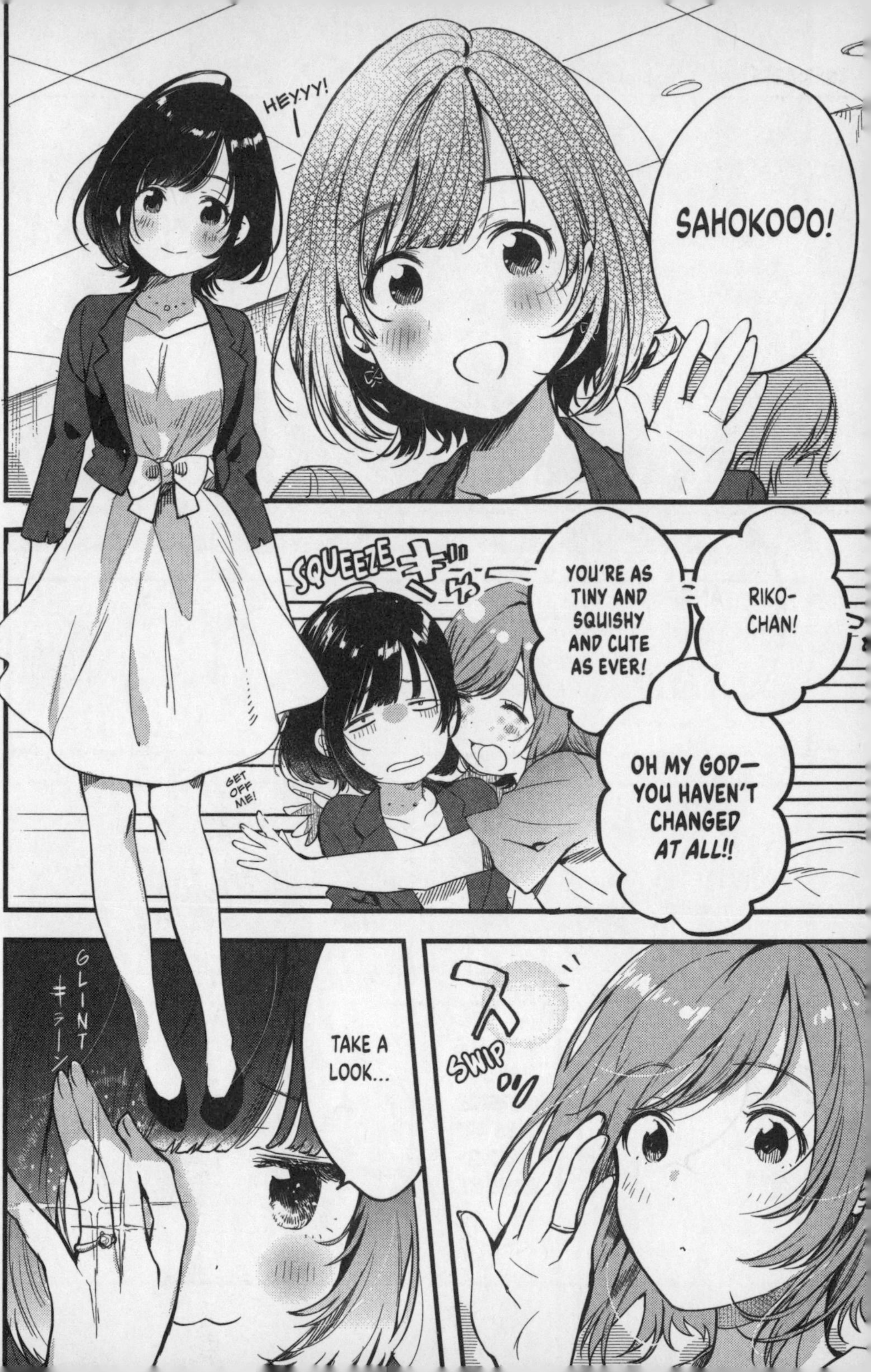
SAHOKOOO!
HEYYY!
RIKO-CHAN!
YOU'RE AS TINY AND SQUISHY AND CUTE AS EVER!
OH MY GOD— YOU HAVEN'T CHANGED AT ALL!!
SQUEEZE
GET OFF ME!
SWIP
TAKE A LOOK...
GLINT
キラーン

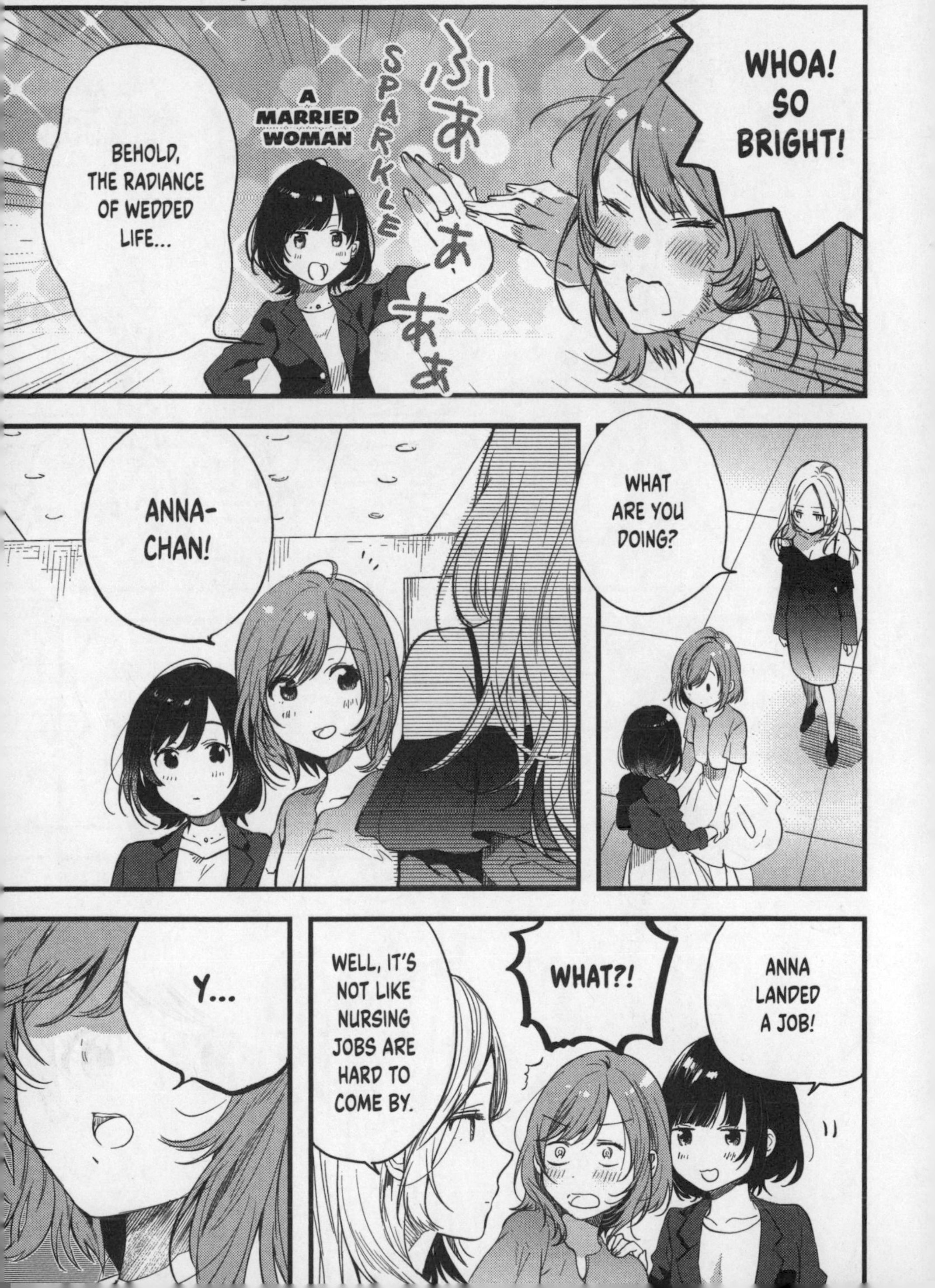
WHOA! SO BRIGHT!
ふあああ
SPARKLE
A MARRIED WOMAN
BEHOLD, THE RADIANCE OF WEDDED LIFE...
WHAT ARE YOU DOING?
ANNA-CHAN!
ANNA LANDED A JOB!
WHAT?!
WELL, IT'S NOT LIKE NURSING JOBS ARE HARD TO COME BY.
Y...

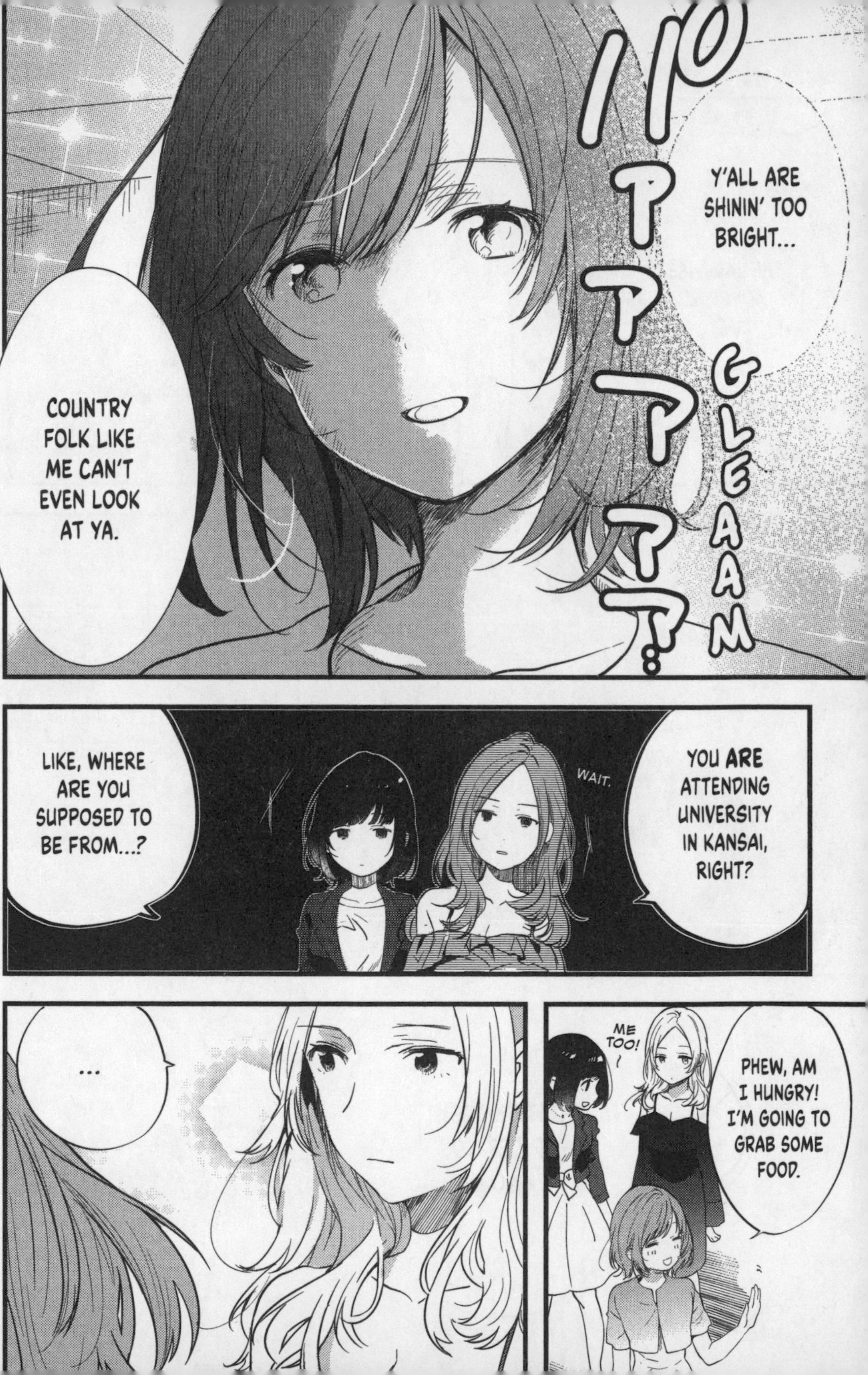
Y'ALL ARE SHININ' TOO BRIGHT...
パアアアア
GLEAM
COUNTRY FOLK LIKE ME CAN'T EVEN LOOK AT YA.
YOU ARE ATTENDING UNIVERSITY IN KANSAI, RIGHT?
WAIT.
LIKE, WHERE ARE YOU SUPPOSED TO BE FROM...?
PHEW, AM I HUNGRY! I'M GOING TO GRAB SOME FOOD.
ME TOO!
...

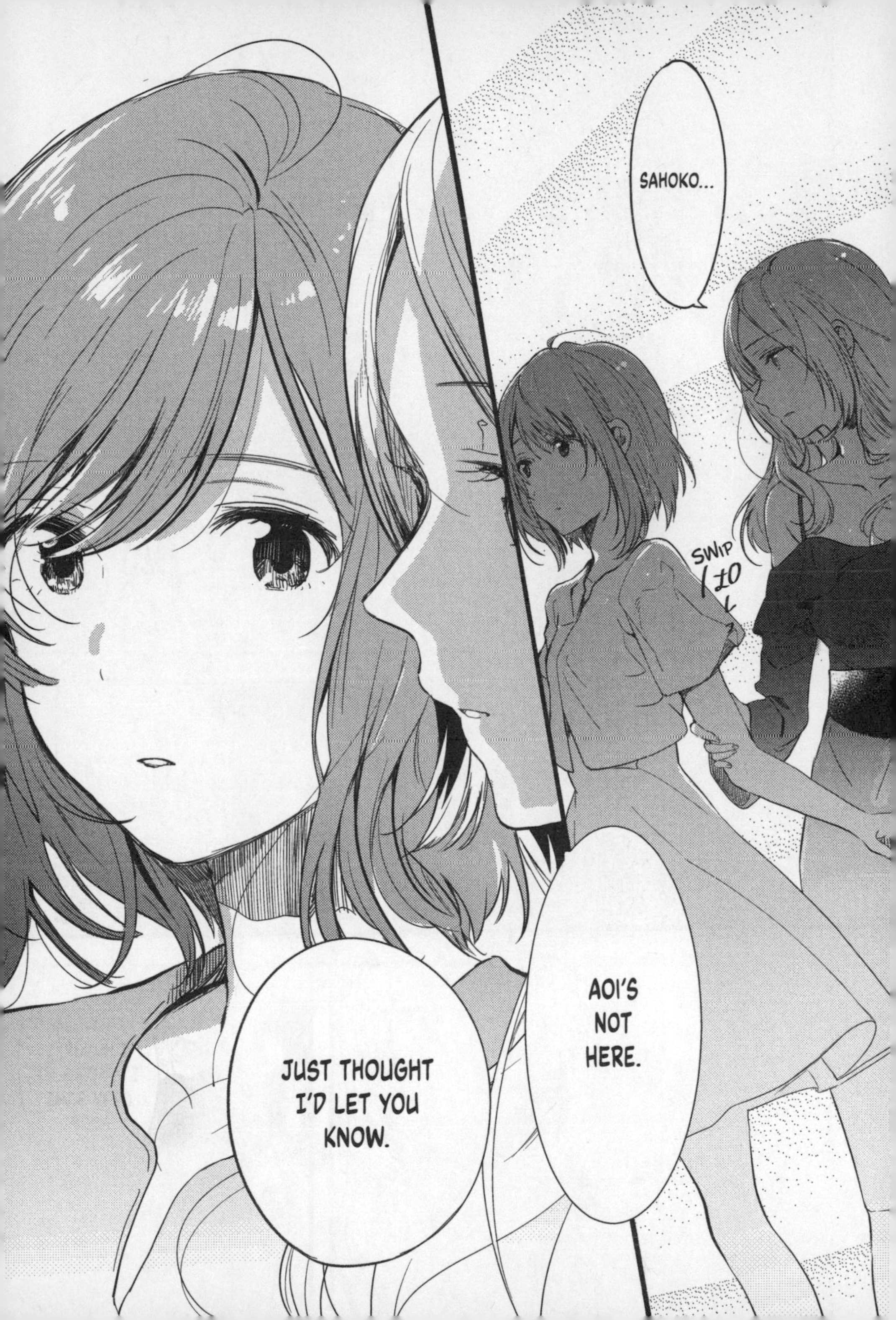
SAHOKO...
SWIP
AOI'S NOT HERE.
JUST THOUGHT I'D LET YOU KNOW.

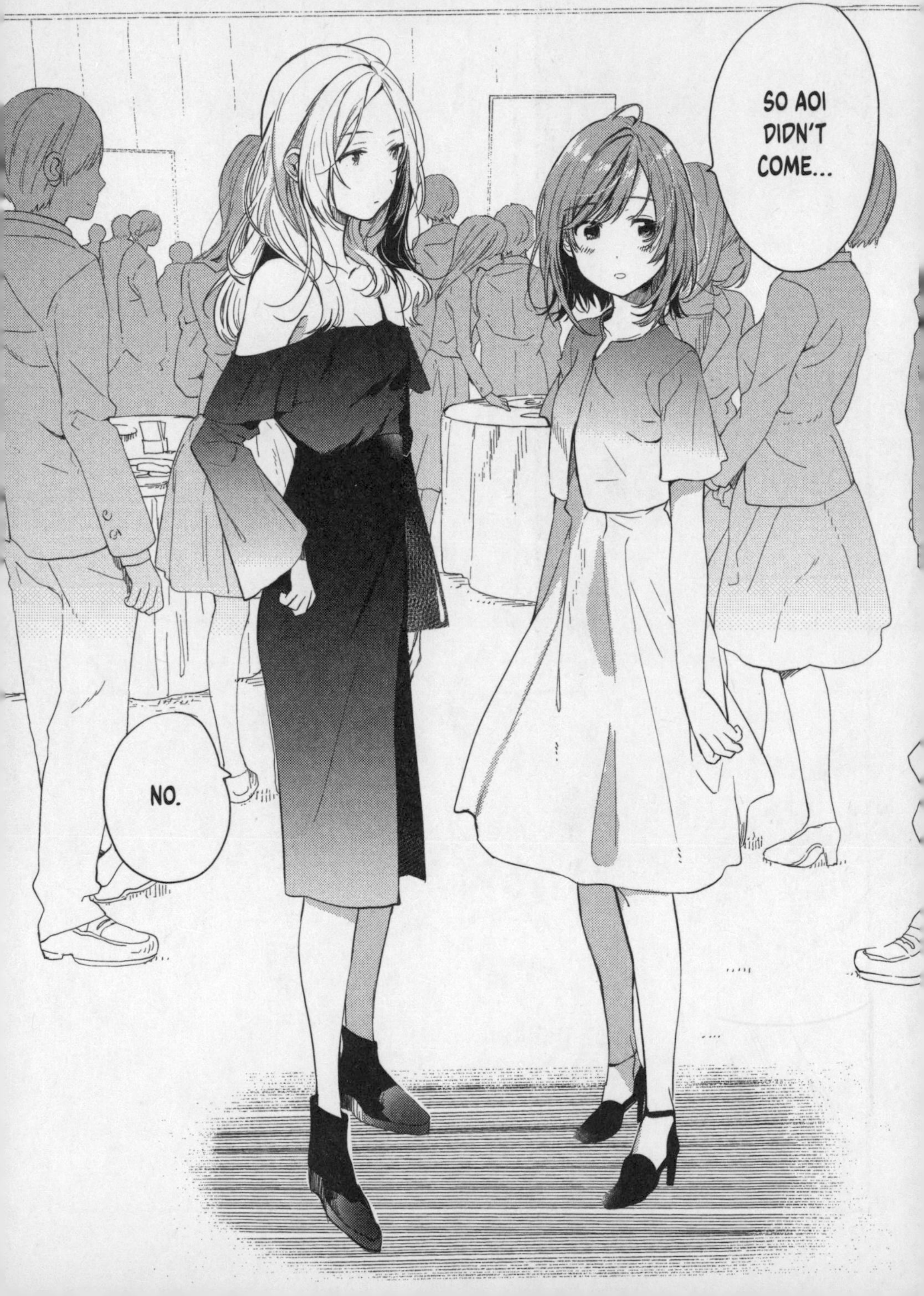
SO AOI DIDN'T COME...
...
...
NO.

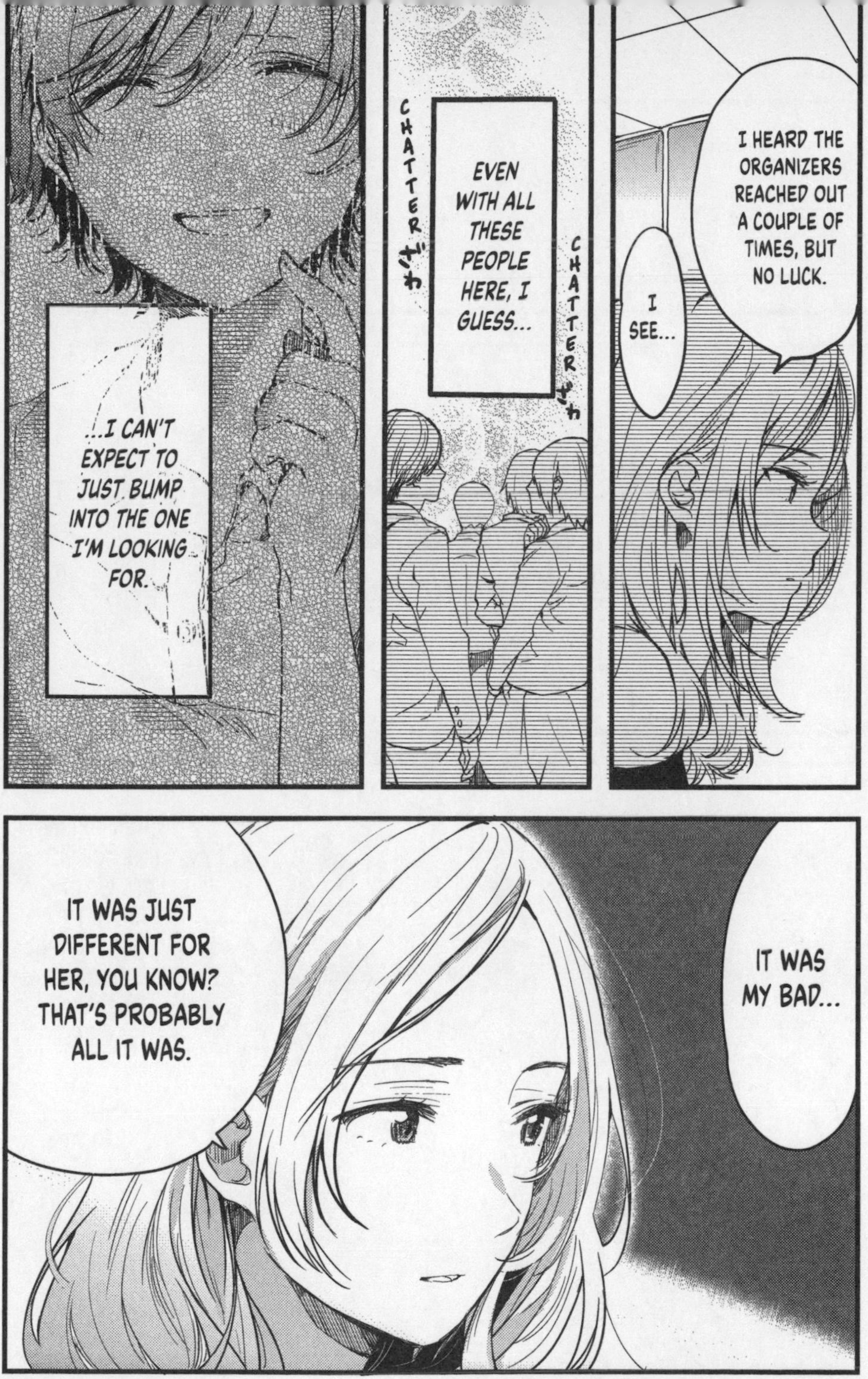
I HEARD THE ORGANIZERS REACHED OUT A COUPLE OF TIMES, BUT NO LUCK.
I SEE...
CHATTER ざわ
EVEN WITH ALL THESE PEOPLE HERE, I GUESS...
CHATTER ざわ
...I CAN'T EXPECT TO JUST BUMP INTO THE ONE I'M LOOKING FOR.
IT WAS MY BAD...
IT WAS JUST DIFFERENT FOR HER, YOU KNOW? THAT'S PROBABLY ALL IT WAS.

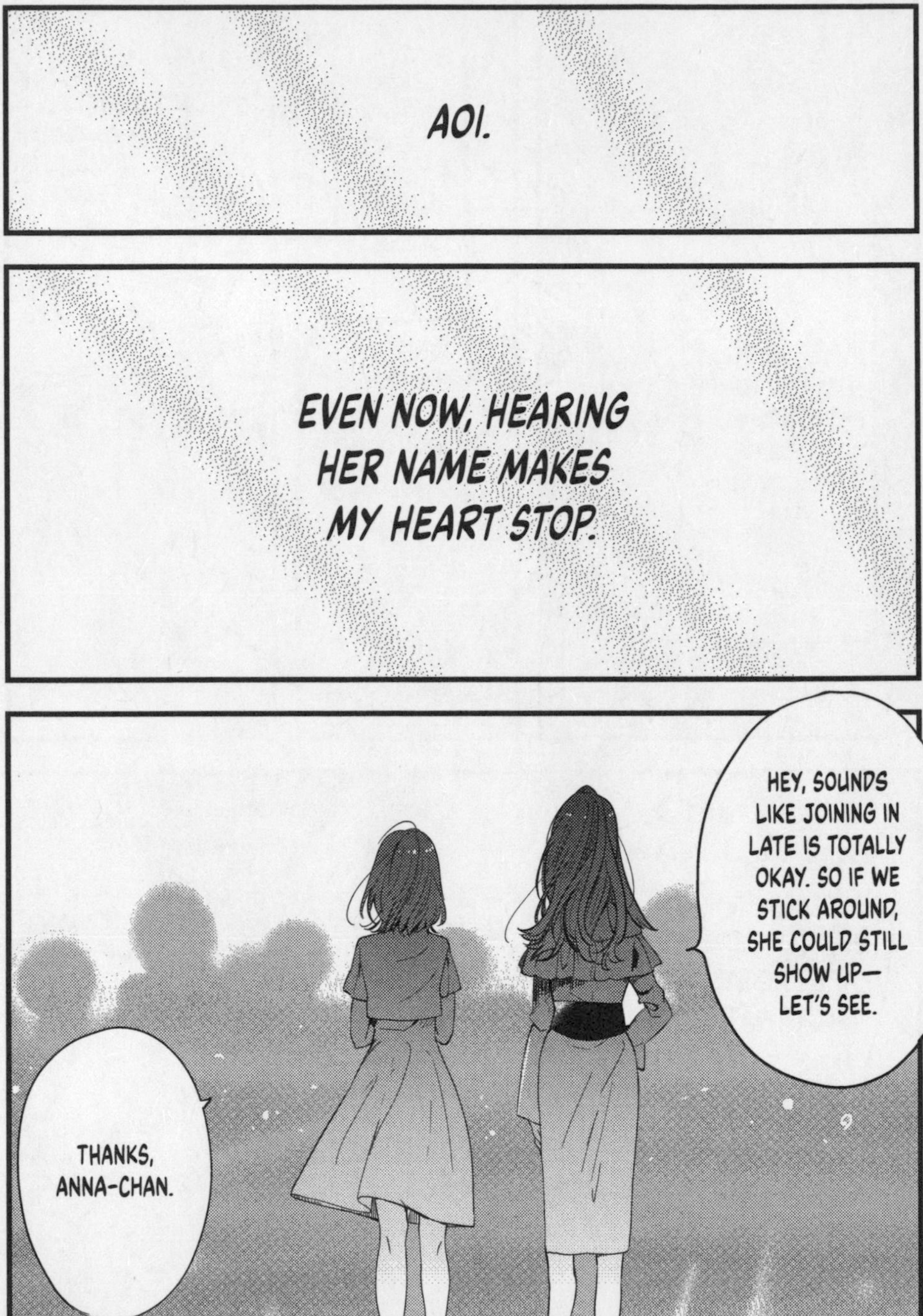
AOI.
EVEN NOW, HEARING HER NAME MAKES MY HEART STOP.
HEY, SOUNDS LIKE JOINING IN LATE IS TOTALLY OKAY. SO IF WE STICK AROUND, SHE COULD STILL SHOW UP— LET'S SEE.
THANKS, ANNA-CHAN.

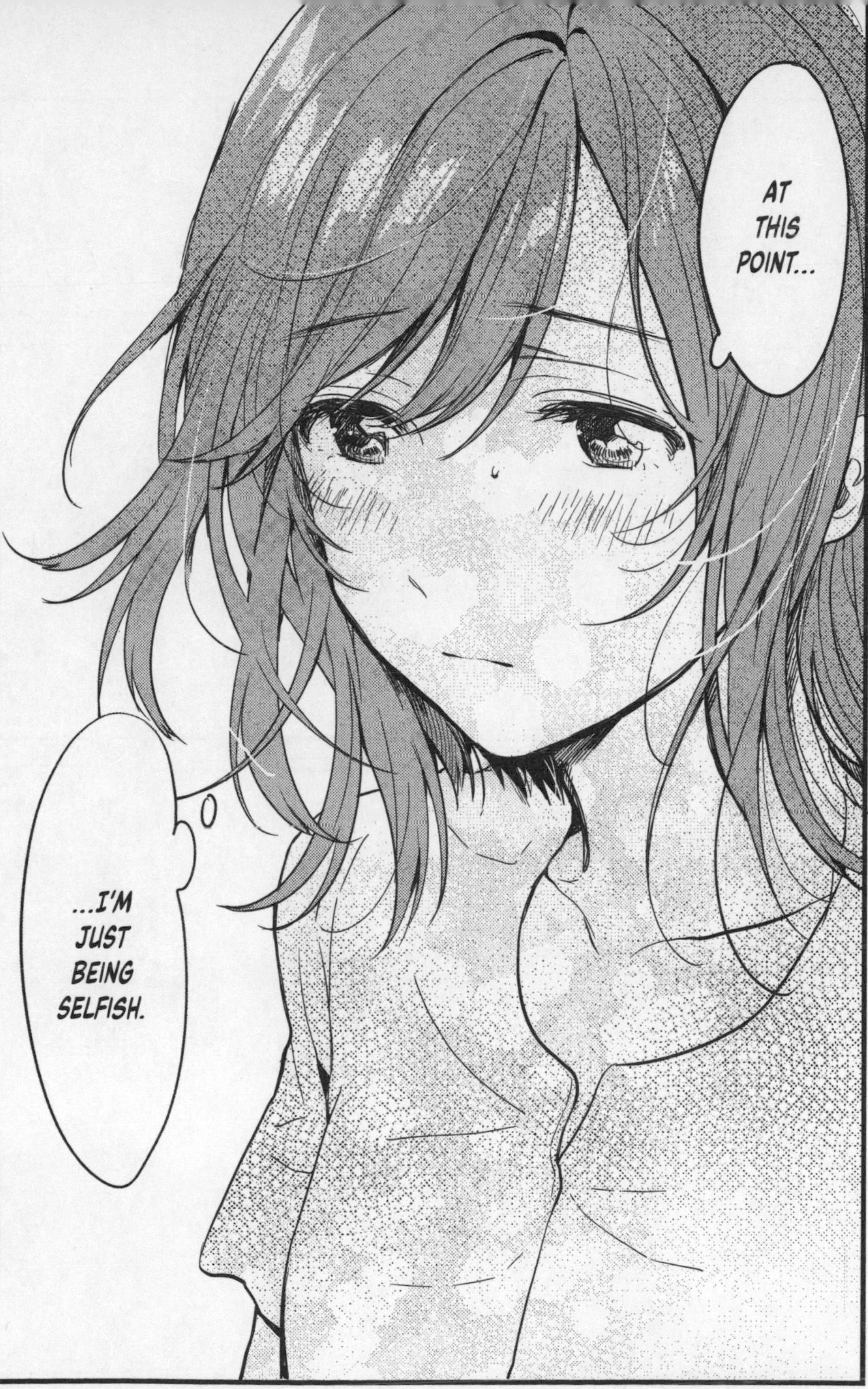
AT THIS POINT...
...I'M JUST BEING SELFISH.

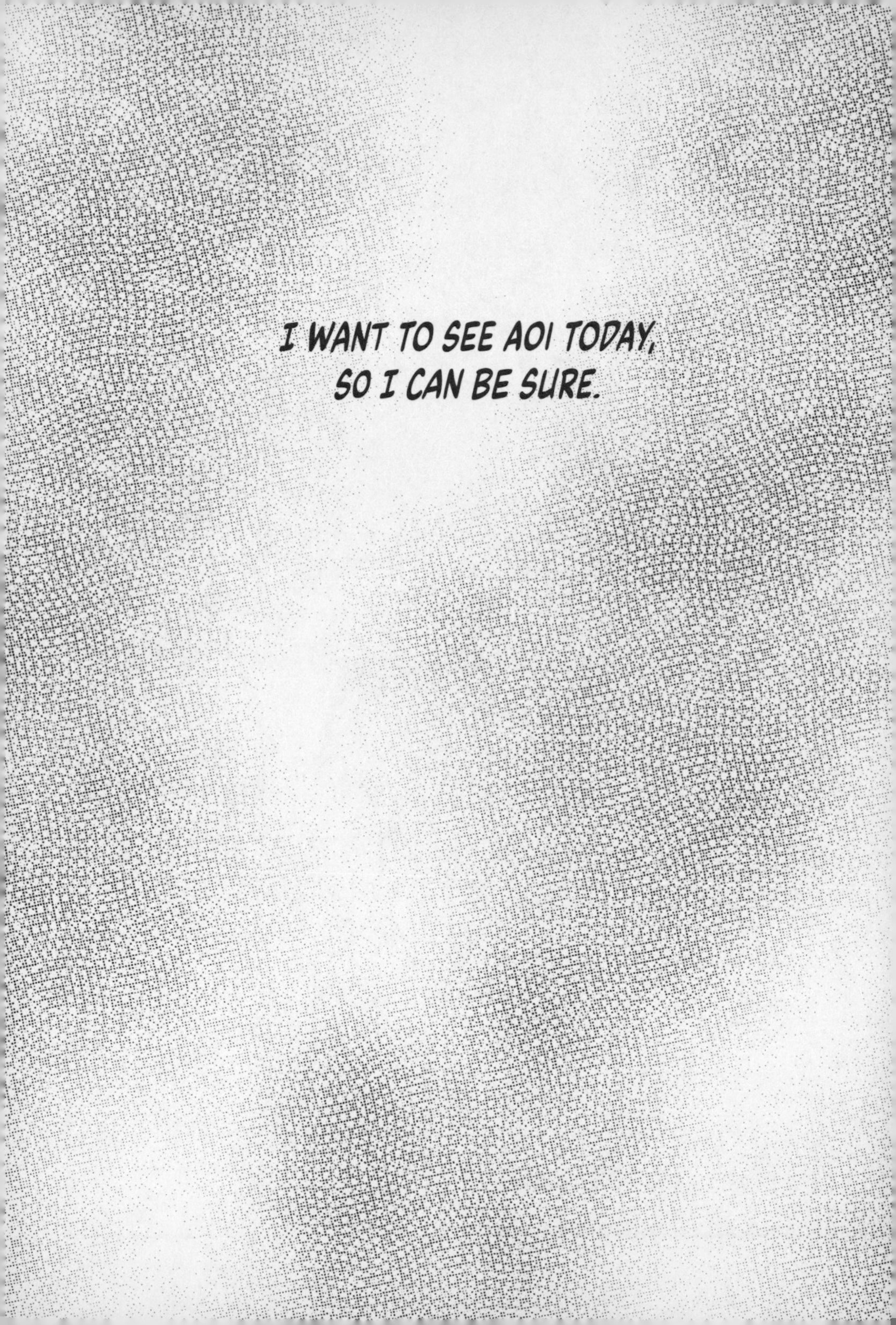
I WANT TO SEE AOI TODAY, SO I CAN BE SURE.

CHASING AFTER Aoi Koshiba

Winter, Third Year of University

CHASING AFTER *Aoi Koshiba*

Summer, Second Year of High School

Chapter 1: I Want to Shine

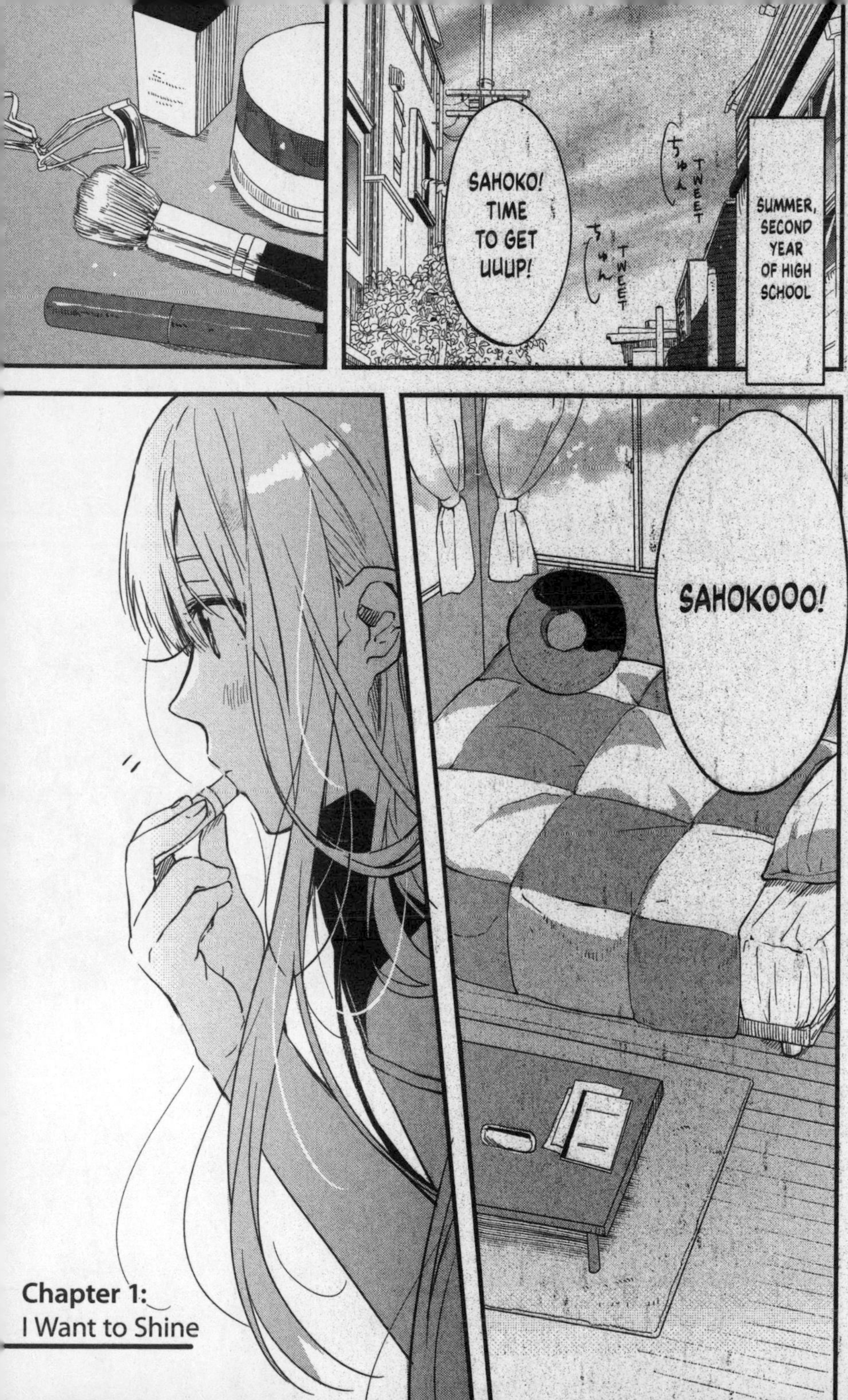
SUMMER, SECOND YEAR OF HIGH SCHOOL
ちゅん TWEET
ちゅん TWEET
SAHOKO! TIME TO GET UUUP!
SAHOKOOO!

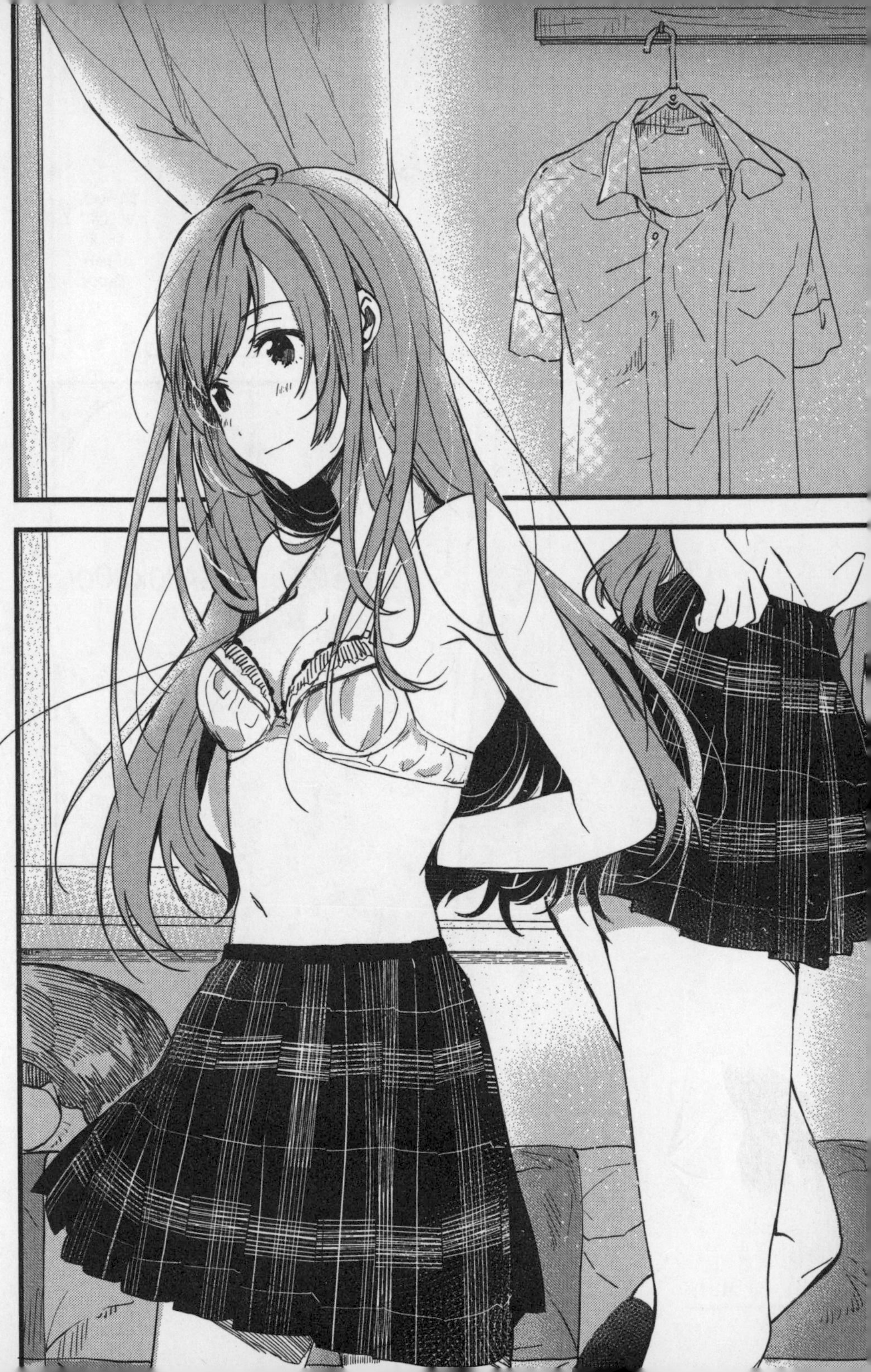

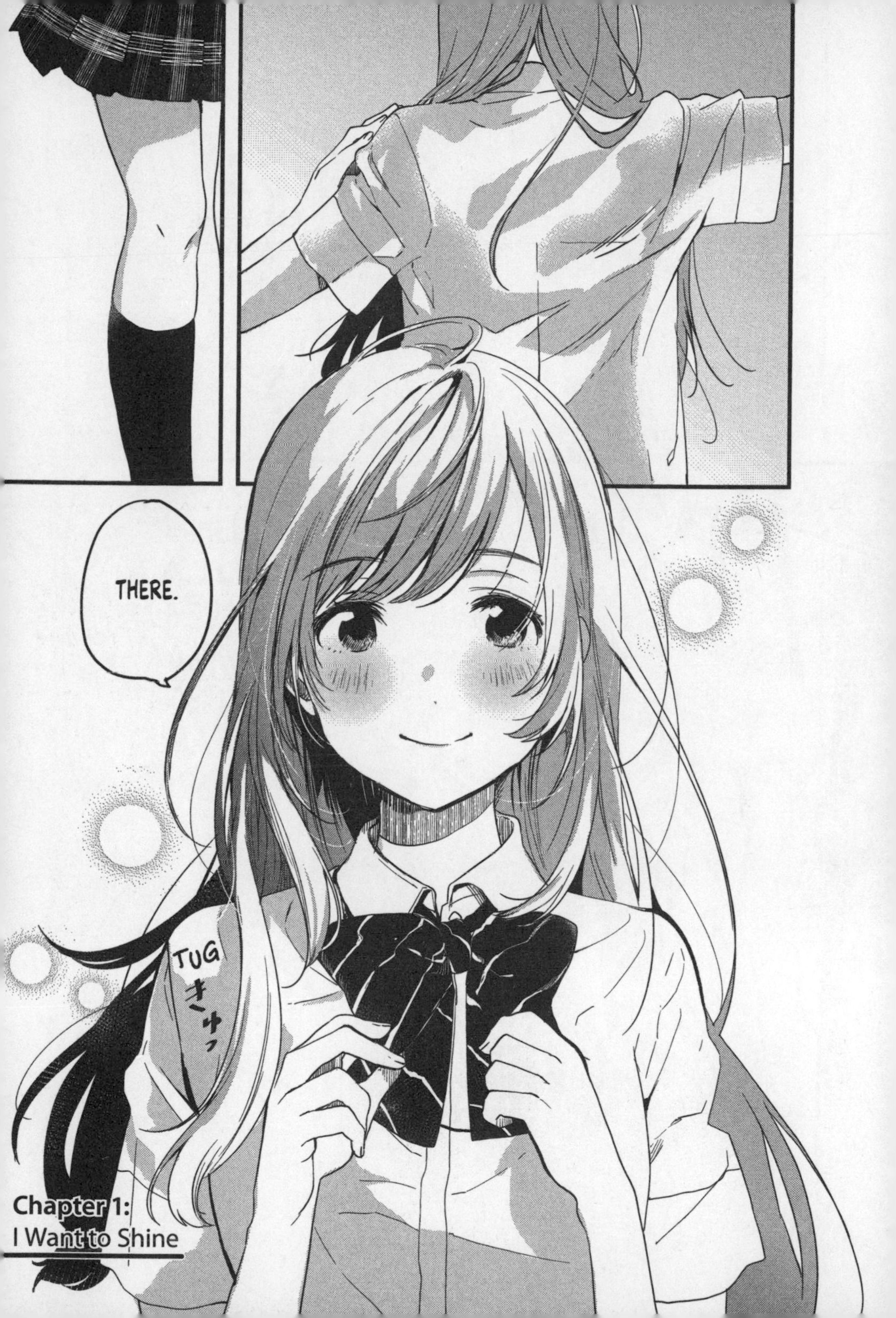
THERE.
TUG
きゅっ
Chapter 1:
I Want to Shine

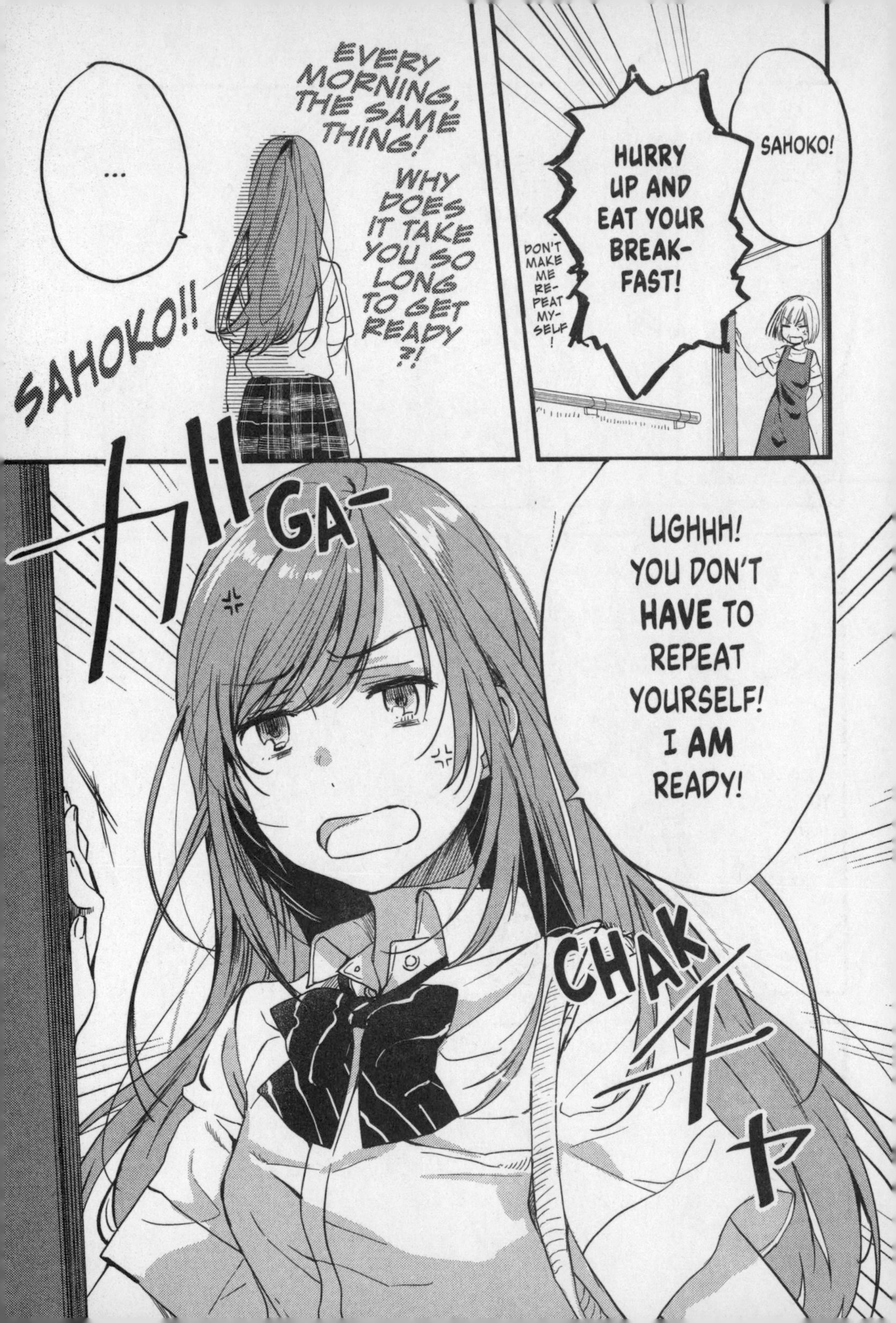
SAHOKO!
HURRY UP AND EAT YOUR BREAKFAST!
DON'T MAKE ME REPEAT MYSELF!
EVERY MORNING, THE SAME THING!
WHY DOES IT TAKE YOU SO LONG TO GET READY?!
...
SAHOKO!!
GA-
UGHHH! YOU DON'T HAVE TO REPEAT YOURSELF! I AM READY!
CHAK

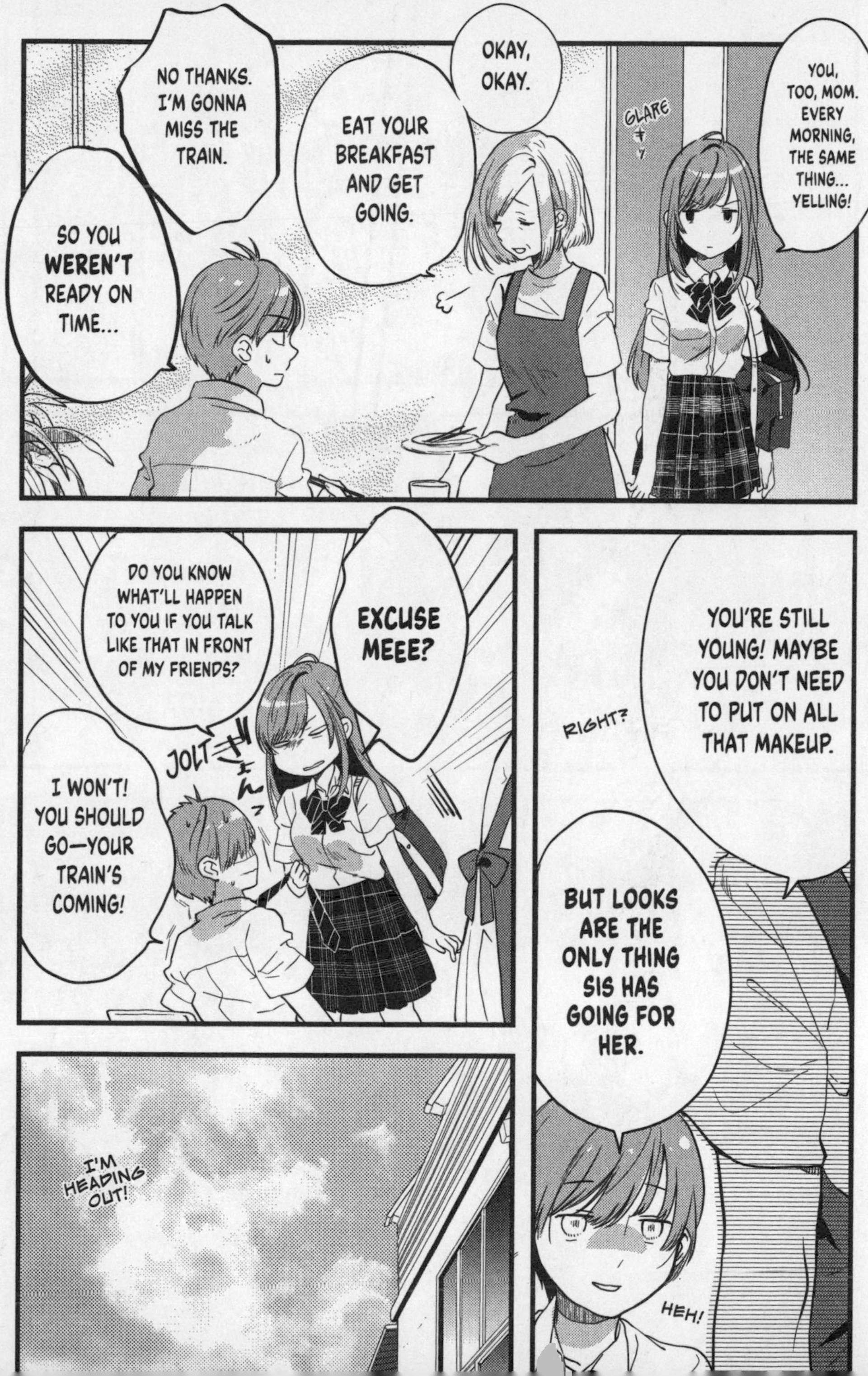
YOU, TOO, MOM. EVERY MORNING, THE SAME THING... YELLING!
GLARE
OKAY, OKAY.
EAT YOUR BREAKFAST AND GET GOING.
NO THANKS. I'M GONNA MISS THE TRAIN.
SO YOU WEREN'T READY ON TIME...
YOU'RE STILL YOUNG! MAYBE YOU DON'T NEED TO PUT ON ALL THAT MAKEUP.
RIGHT?
BUT LOOKS ARE THE ONLY THING SIS HAS GOING FOR HER.
HEH!
EXCUSE MEEE?
DO YOU KNOW WHAT'LL HAPPEN TO YOU IF YOU TALK LIKE THAT IN FRONT OF MY FRIENDS?
JOLT
I WON'T! YOU SHOULD GO—YOUR TRAIN'S COMING!
I'M HEADING OUT!

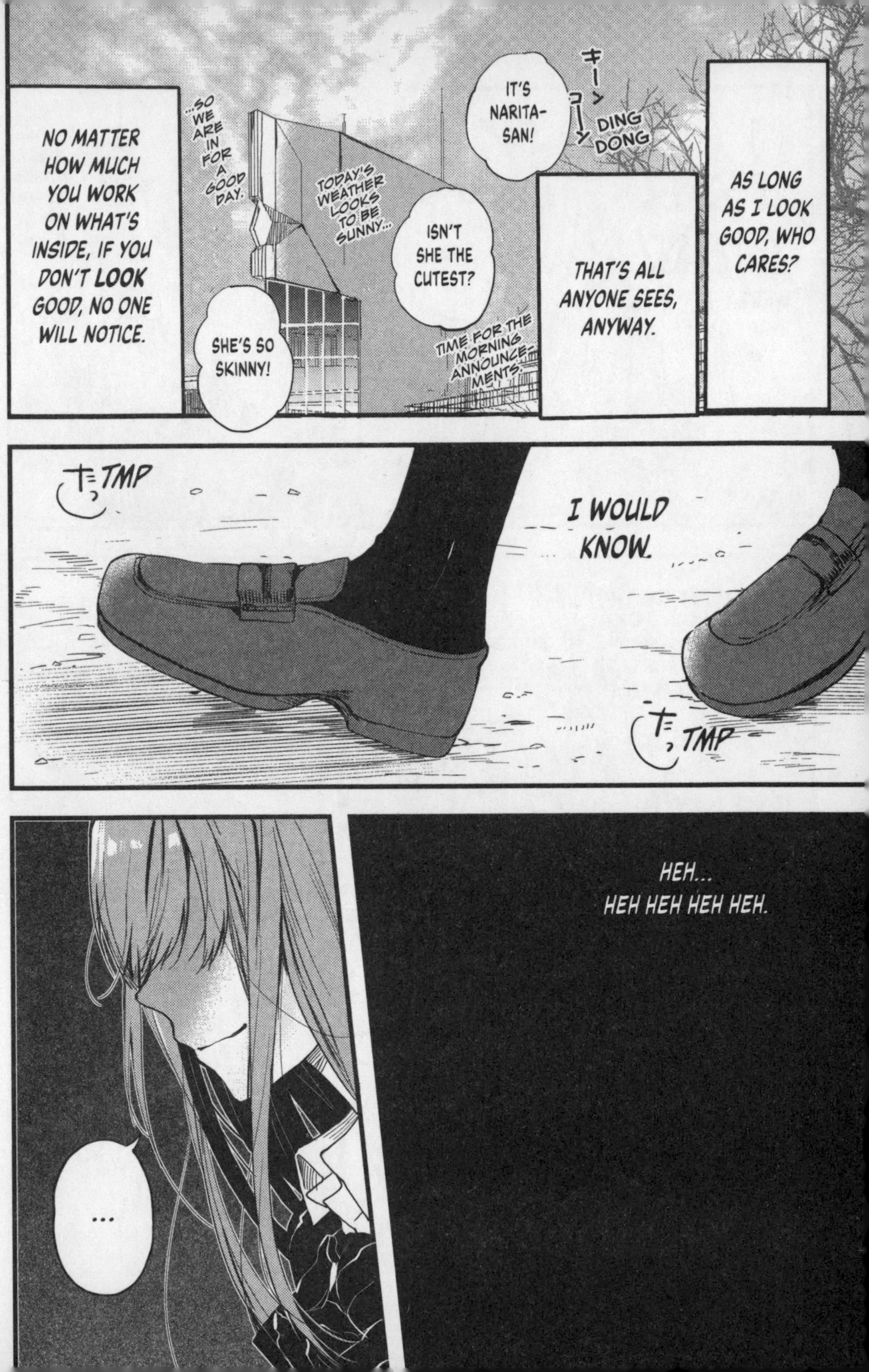
AS LONG AS I LOOK GOOD, WHO CARES?
THAT'S ALL ANYONE SEES, ANYWAY.
キーンコーン
DING DONG
IT'S NARITA-SAN!
ISN'T SHE THE CUTEST?
TIME FOR THE MORNING ANNOUNCEMENTS.
TODAY'S WEATHER LOOKS TO BE SUNNY...
...SO WE ARE IN FOR A GOOD DAY.
SHE'S SO SKINNY!
NO MATTER HOW MUCH YOU WORK ON WHAT'S INSIDE, IF YOU DON'T LOOK GOOD, NO ONE WILL NOTICE.
I WOULD KNOW.
TMP
TMP
HEH... HEH HEH HEH HEH.
...

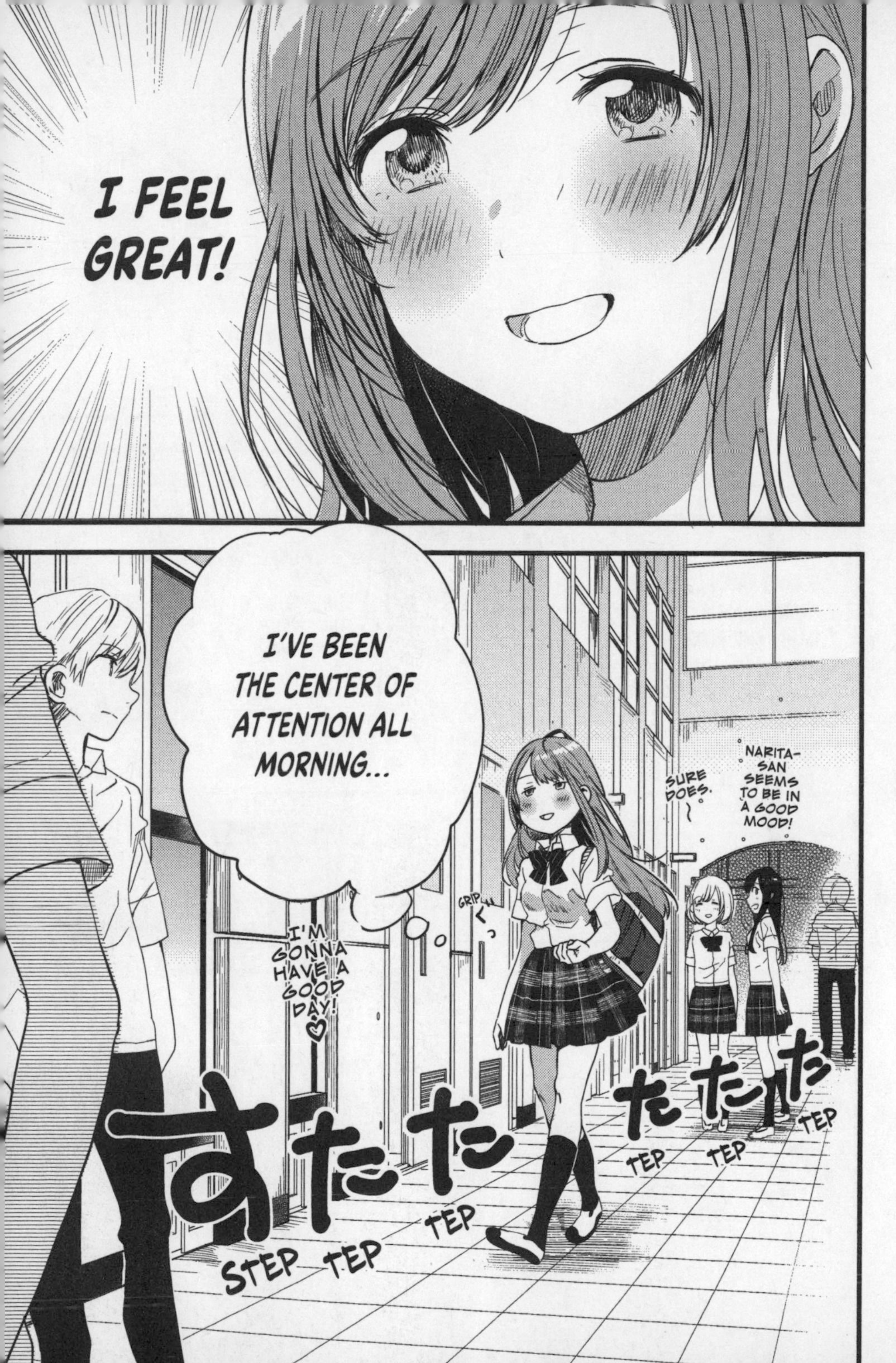
I FEEL GREAT!
NARITA-SAN SEEMS TO BE IN A GOOD MOOD!
SURE DOES.
I'VE BEEN THE CENTER OF ATTENTION ALL MORNING...
GRIP
I'M GONNA HAVE A GOOD DAY!
TEP TEP TEP
STEP TEP TEP

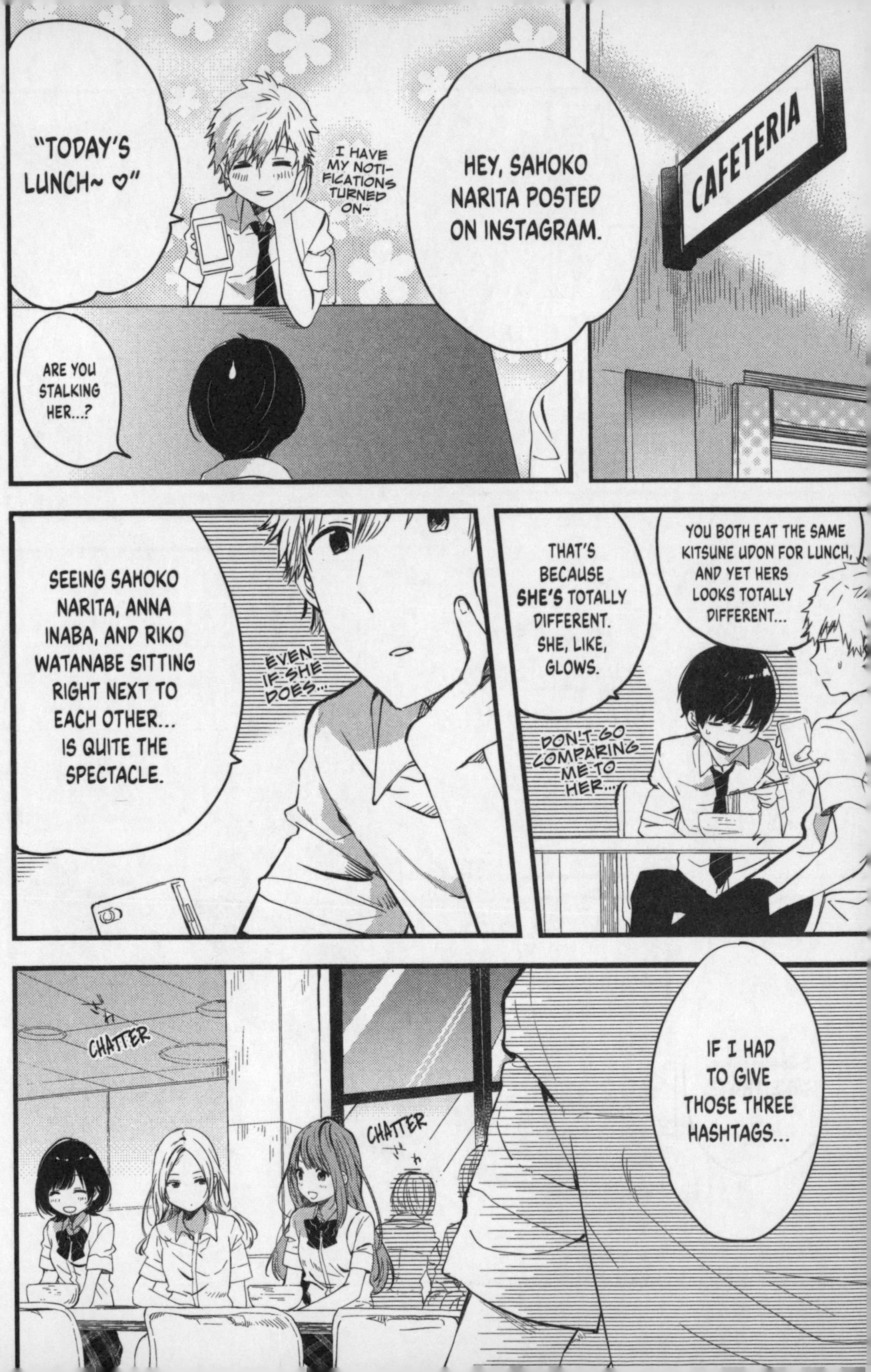
CAFETERIA
HEY, SAHOKO NARITA POSTED ON INSTAGRAM.
I HAVE MY NOTI-FICATIONS TURNED ON~
"TODAY'S LUNCH~ ♡"
ARE YOU STALKING HER...?
YOU BOTH EAT THE SAME KITSUNE UDON FOR LUNCH, AND YET HERS LOOKS TOTALLY DIFFERENT...
THAT'S BECAUSE SHE'S TOTALLY DIFFERENT. SHE, LIKE, GLOWS.
DON'T GO COMPARING ME TO HER...
EVEN IF SHE DOES...
SEEING SAHOKO NARITA, ANNA INABA, AND RIKO WATANABE SITTING RIGHT NEXT TO EACH OTHER... IS QUITE THE SPECTACLE.
IF I HAD TO GIVE THOSE THREE HASHTAGS...
CHATTER
CHATTER

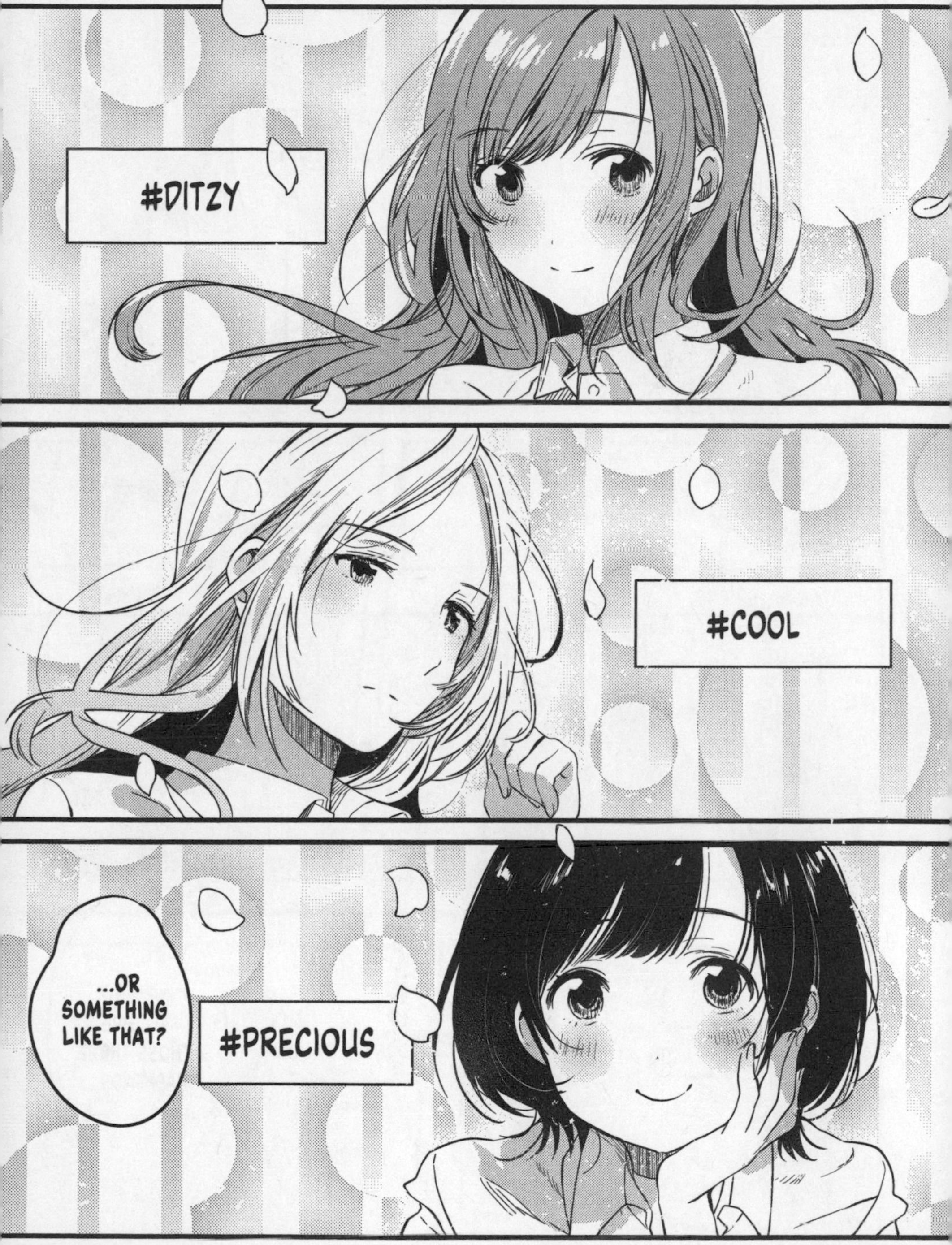
#DITZY
#COOL
#PRECIOUS
...OR SOMETHING LIKE THAT?

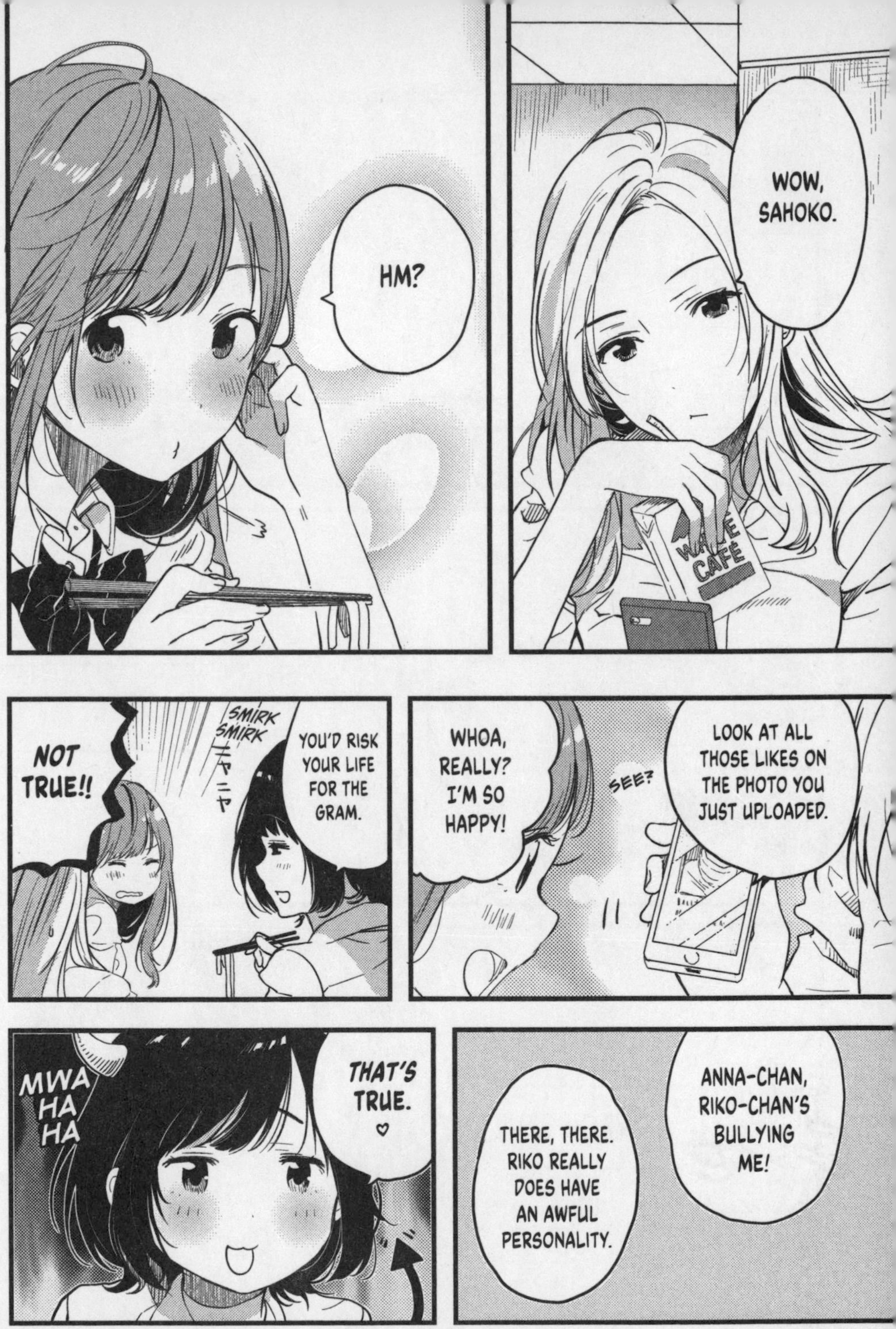
WOW, SAHOKO.
HM?
SEE?
LOOK AT ALL THOSE LIKES ON THE PHOTO YOU JUST UPLOADED.
WHOA, REALLY? I'M SO HAPPY!
SMIRK SMIRK
ニヤ
YOU'D RISK YOUR LIFE FOR THE GRAM.
NOT TRUE!!
ANNA-CHAN, RIKO-CHAN'S BULLYING ME!
THERE, THERE. RIKO REALLY DOES HAVE AN AWFUL PERSONALITY.
THAT'S TRUE. ♡
MWA HA HA

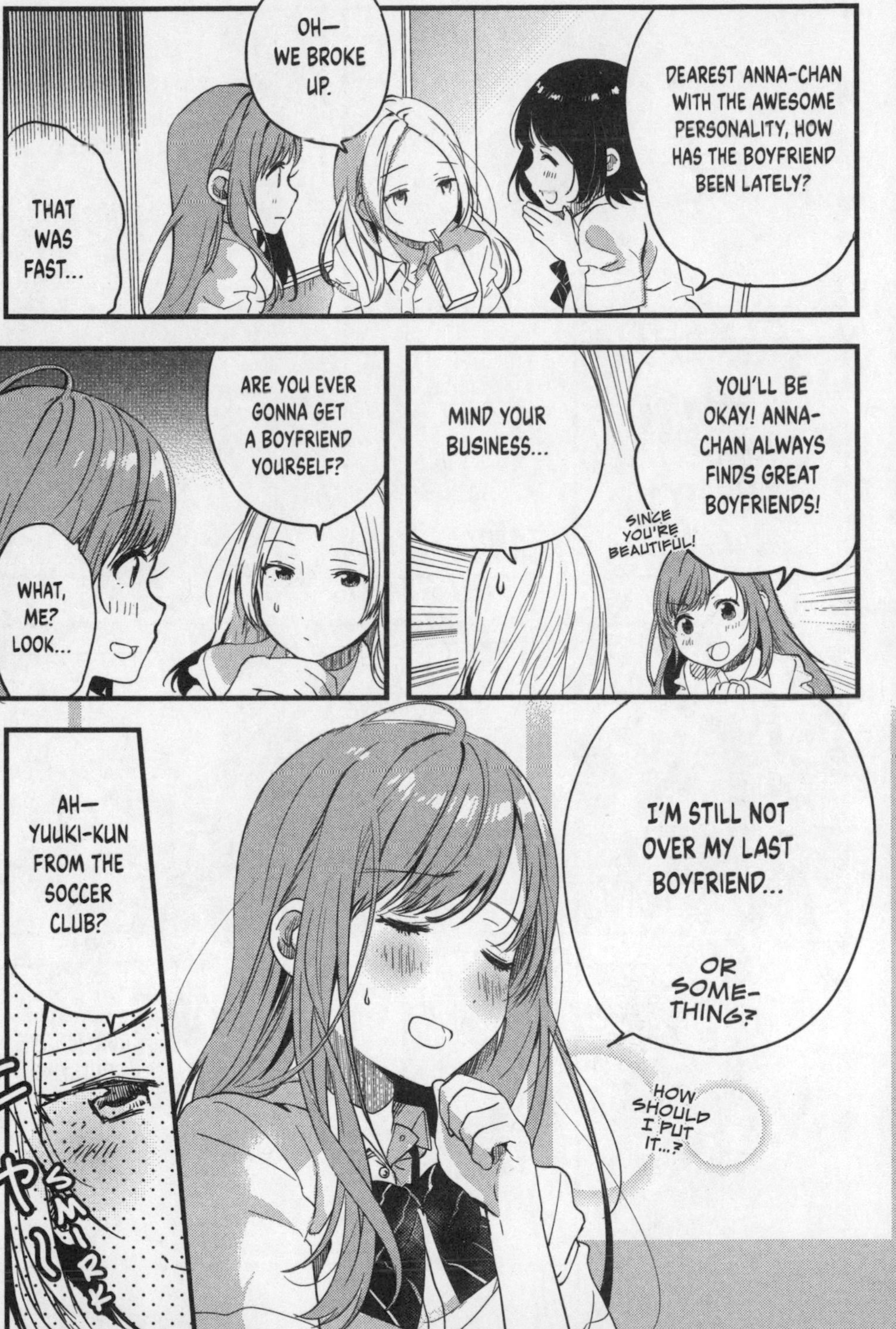
DEAREST ANNA-CHAN WITH THE AWESOME PERSONALITY, HOW HAS THE BOYFRIEND BEEN LATELY?
OH— WE BROKE UP.
THAT WAS FAST...
YOU'LL BE OKAY! ANNA-CHAN ALWAYS FINDS GREAT BOYFRIENDS!
SINCE YOU'RE BEAUTIFUL!
MIND YOUR BUSINESS...
ARE YOU EVER GONNA GET A BOYFRIEND YOURSELF?
WHAT, ME? LOOK...
I'M STILL NOT OVER MY LAST BOYFRIEND...
OR SOME-THING?
HOW SHOULD I PUT IT...?
AH— YUUKI-KUN FROM THE SOCCER CLUB?
ニヤ〜
SMIRK

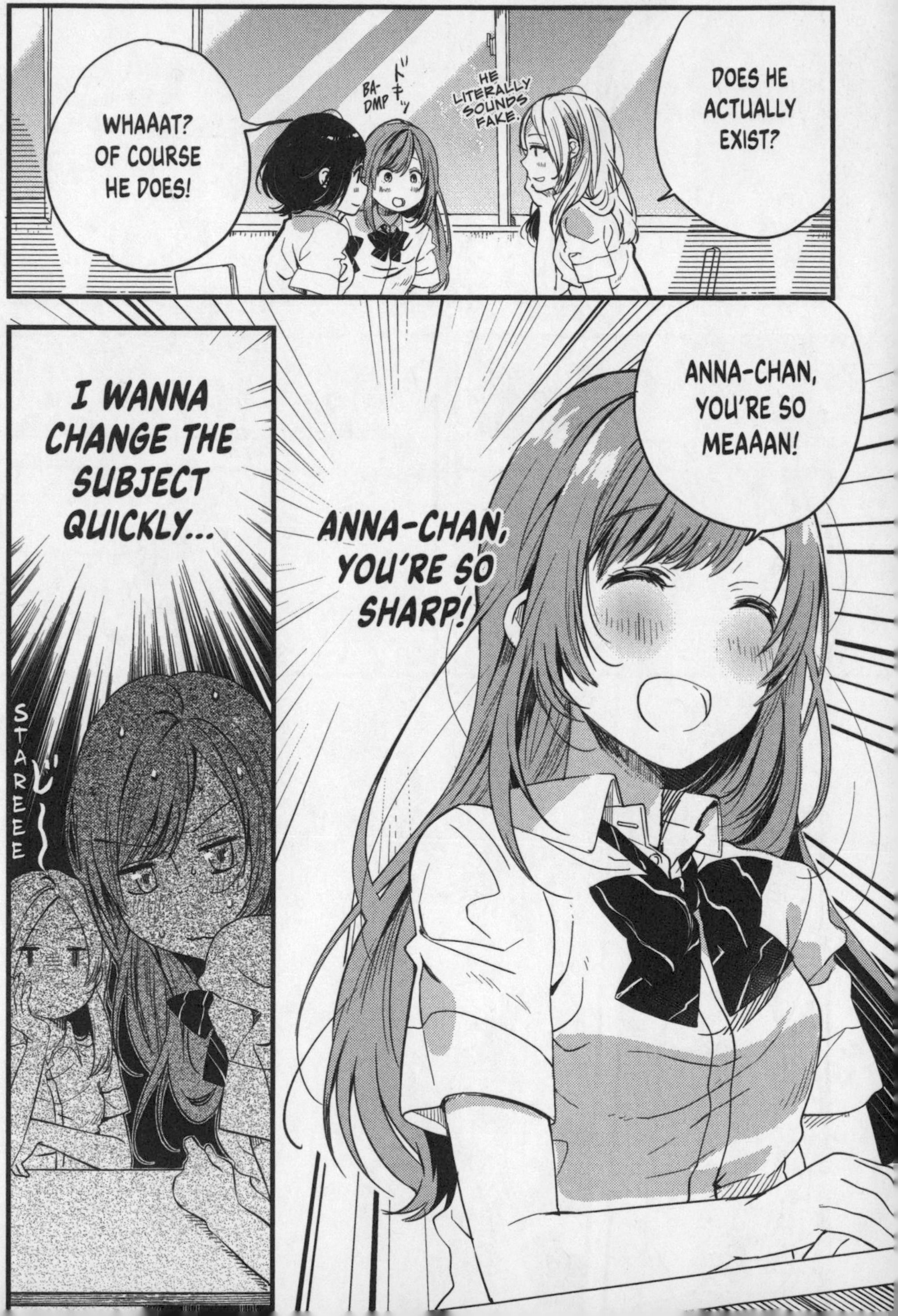
DOES HE ACTUALLY EXIST?
HE LITERALLY SOUNDS FAKE.
BA-DMP
WHAAAT? OF COURSE HE DOES!
ANNA-CHAN, YOU'RE SO MEAAAN!
ANNA-CHAN, YOU'RE SO SHARP!
I WANNA CHANGE THE SUBJECT QUICKLY...
STAREEE

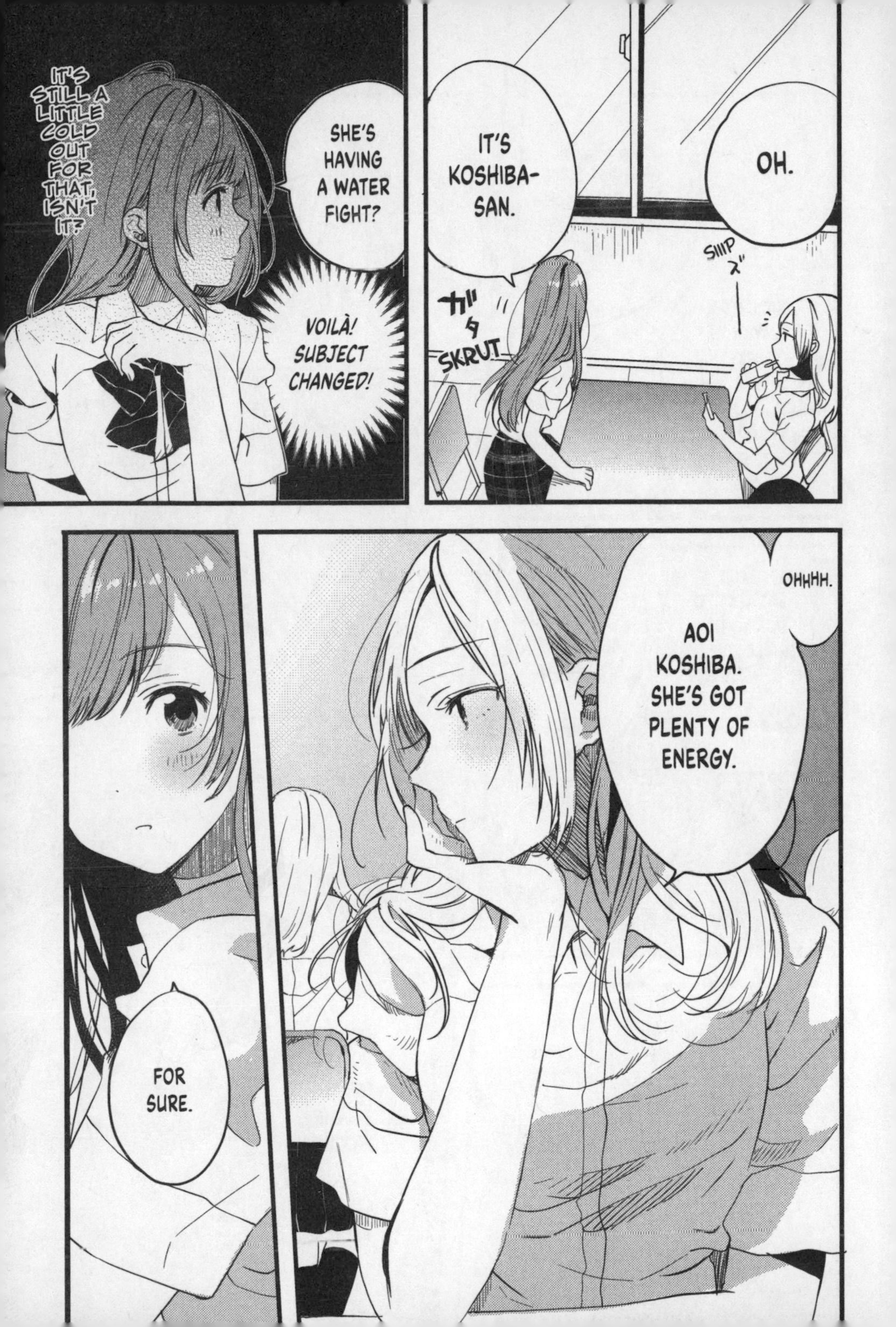
OH.
SIIIP
ズ
IT'S KOSHIBA-SAN.
ガタ
SKRUT
SHE'S HAVING A WATER FIGHT?
VOILÀ! SUBJECT CHANGED!
IT'S STILL A LITTLE COLD OUT FOR THAT, ISN'T IT?
OHHHH.
AOI KOSHIBA. SHE'S GOT PLENTY OF ENERGY.
FOR SURE.

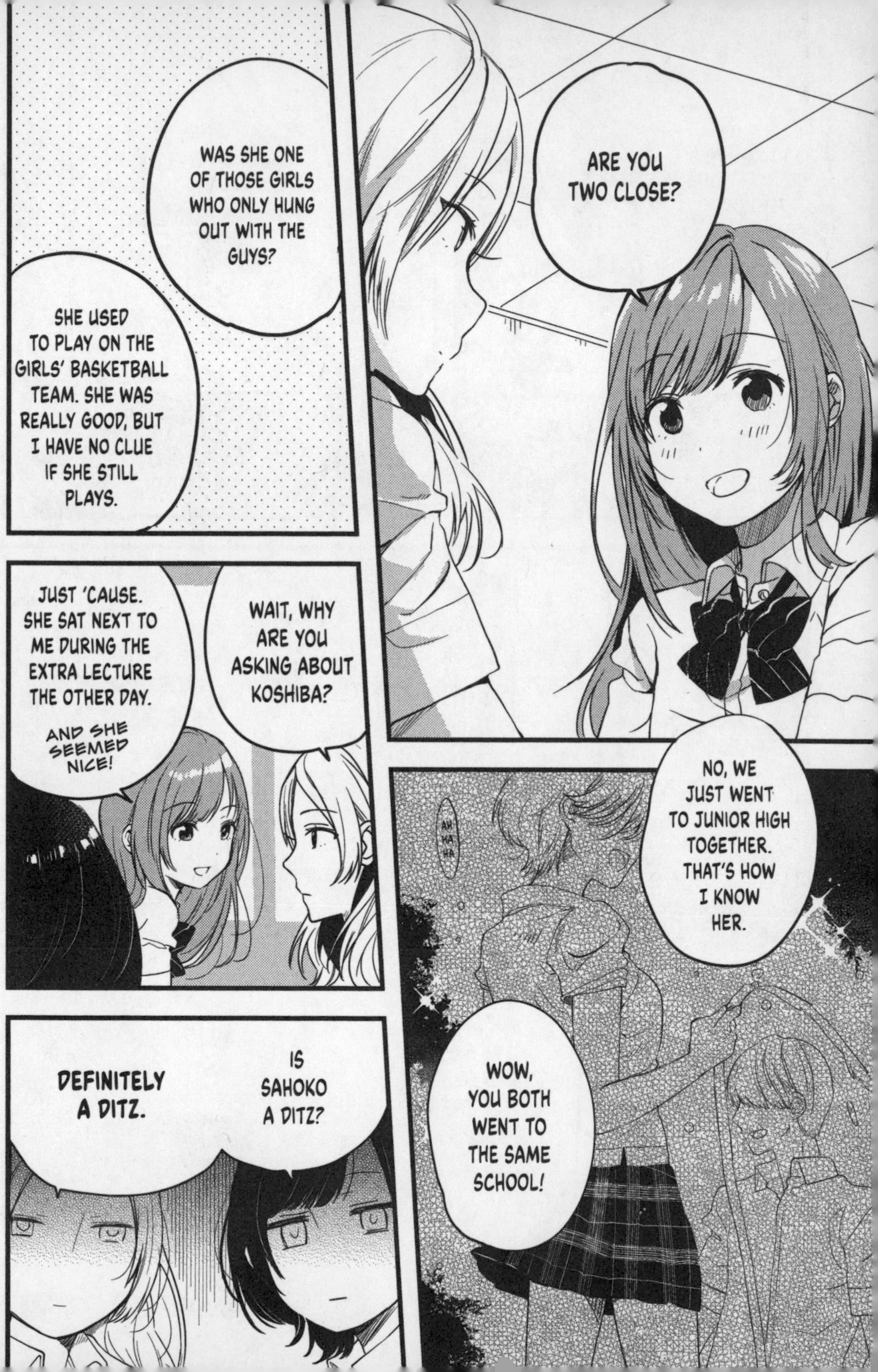
ARE YOU TWO CLOSE?
WAS SHE ONE OF THOSE GIRLS WHO ONLY HUNG OUT WITH THE GUYS?
SHE USED TO PLAY ON THE GIRLS' BASKETBALL TEAM. SHE WAS REALLY GOOD, BUT I HAVE NO CLUE IF SHE STILL PLAYS.
WAIT, WHY ARE YOU ASKING ABOUT KOSHIBA?
JUST 'CAUSE. SHE SAT NEXT TO ME DURING THE EXTRA LECTURE THE OTHER DAY.
AND SHE SEEMED NICE!
NO, WE JUST WENT TO JUNIOR HIGH TOGETHER. THAT'S HOW I KNOW HER.
AH HA HA
WOW, YOU BOTH WENT TO THE SAME SCHOOL!
IS SAHOKO A DITZ?
DEFINITELY A DITZ.

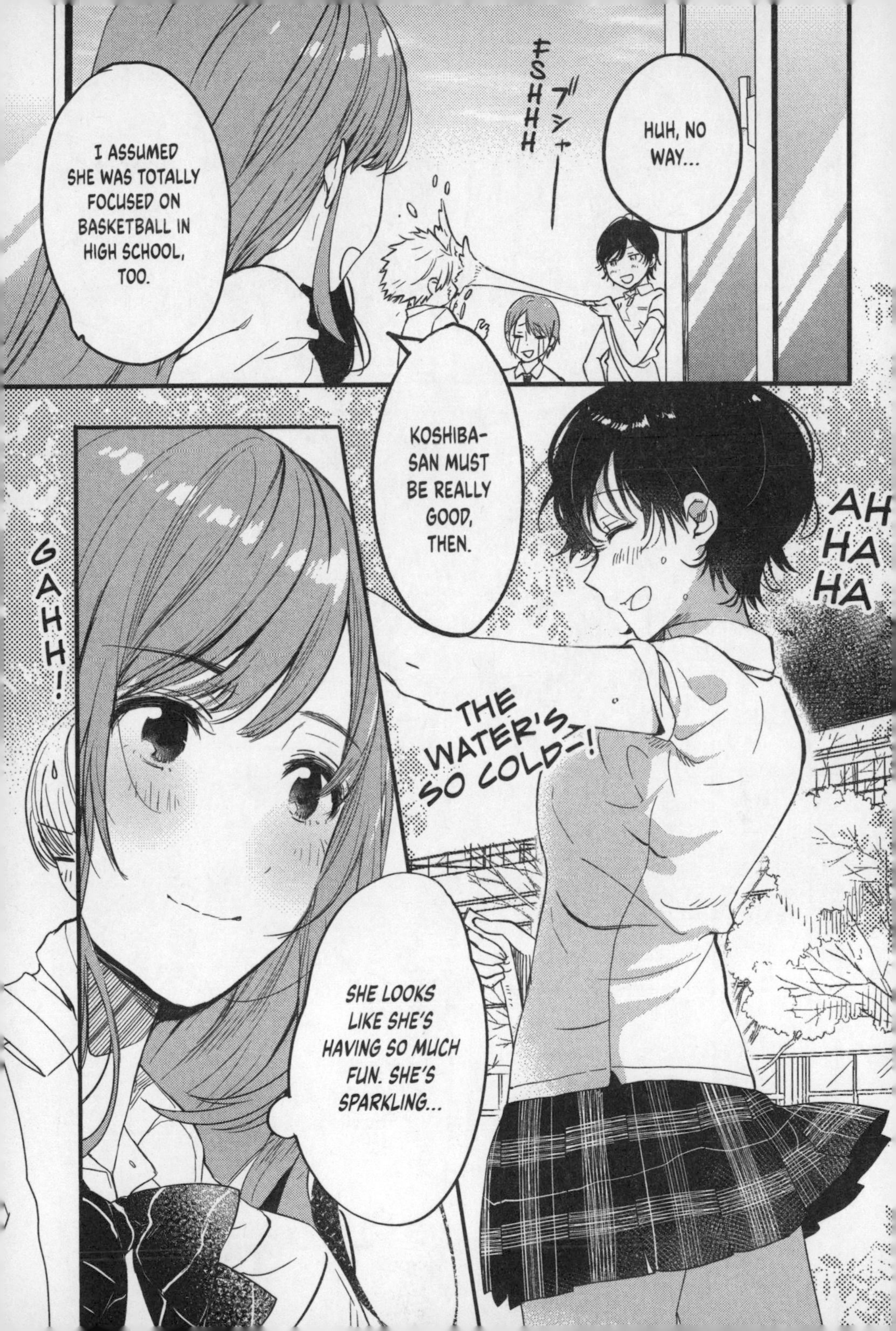
HUH, NO WAY...
ブシャー
FSHHH
I ASSUMED SHE WAS TOTALLY FOCUSED ON BASKETBALL IN HIGH SCHOOL, TOO.
KOSHIBA-SAN MUST BE REALLY GOOD, THEN.
AH HA HA
THE WATER'S SO COLD—!
GAHH!
SHE LOOKS LIKE SHE'S HAVING SO MUCH FUN. SHE'S SPARKLING...

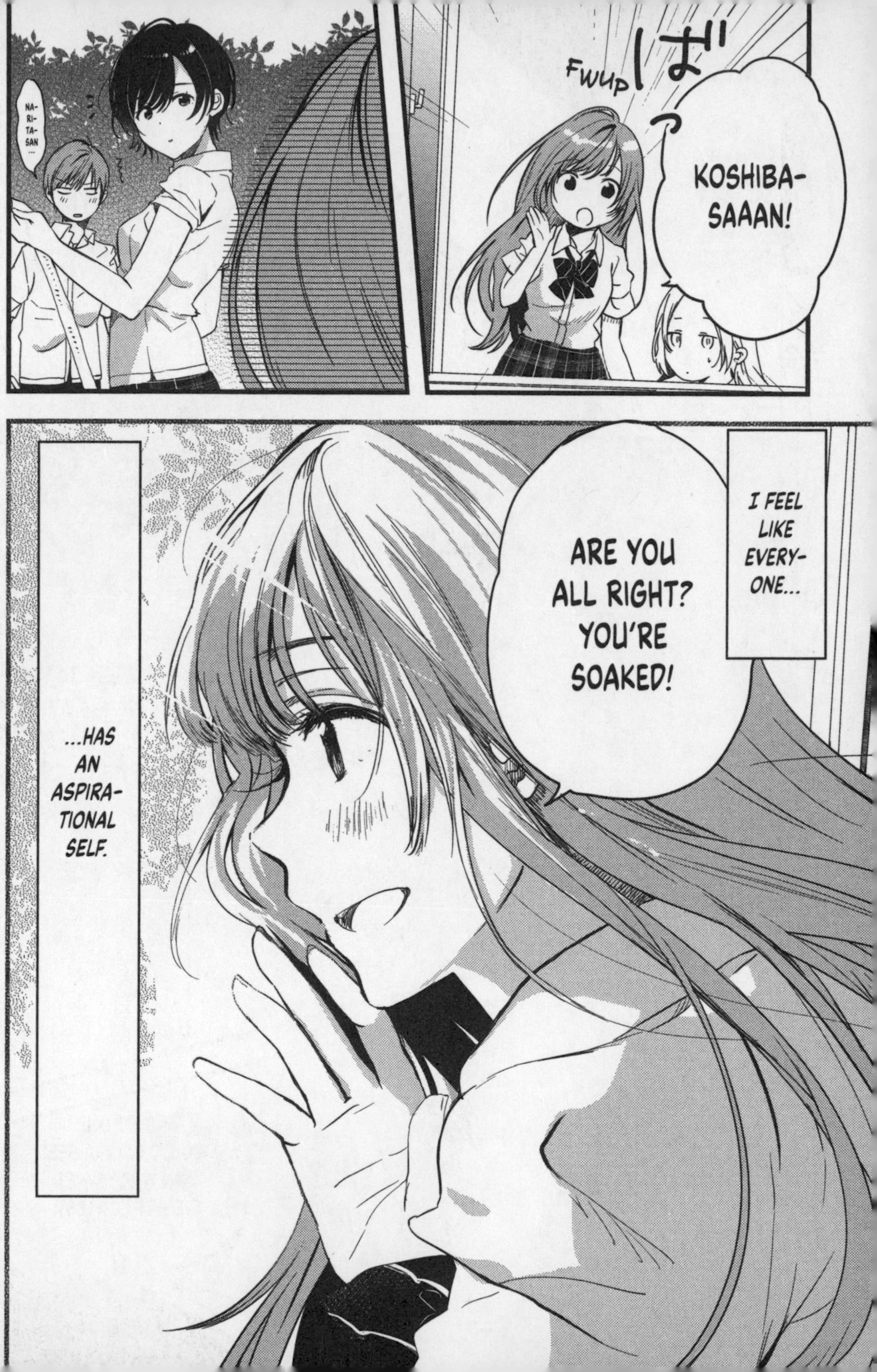
ばっ
FWUP
KOSHIBA-SAAAN!
NARITA-SAN...
I FEEL LIKE EVERYONE...
ARE YOU ALL RIGHT? YOU'RE SOAKED!
...HAS AN ASPIRATIONAL SELF.

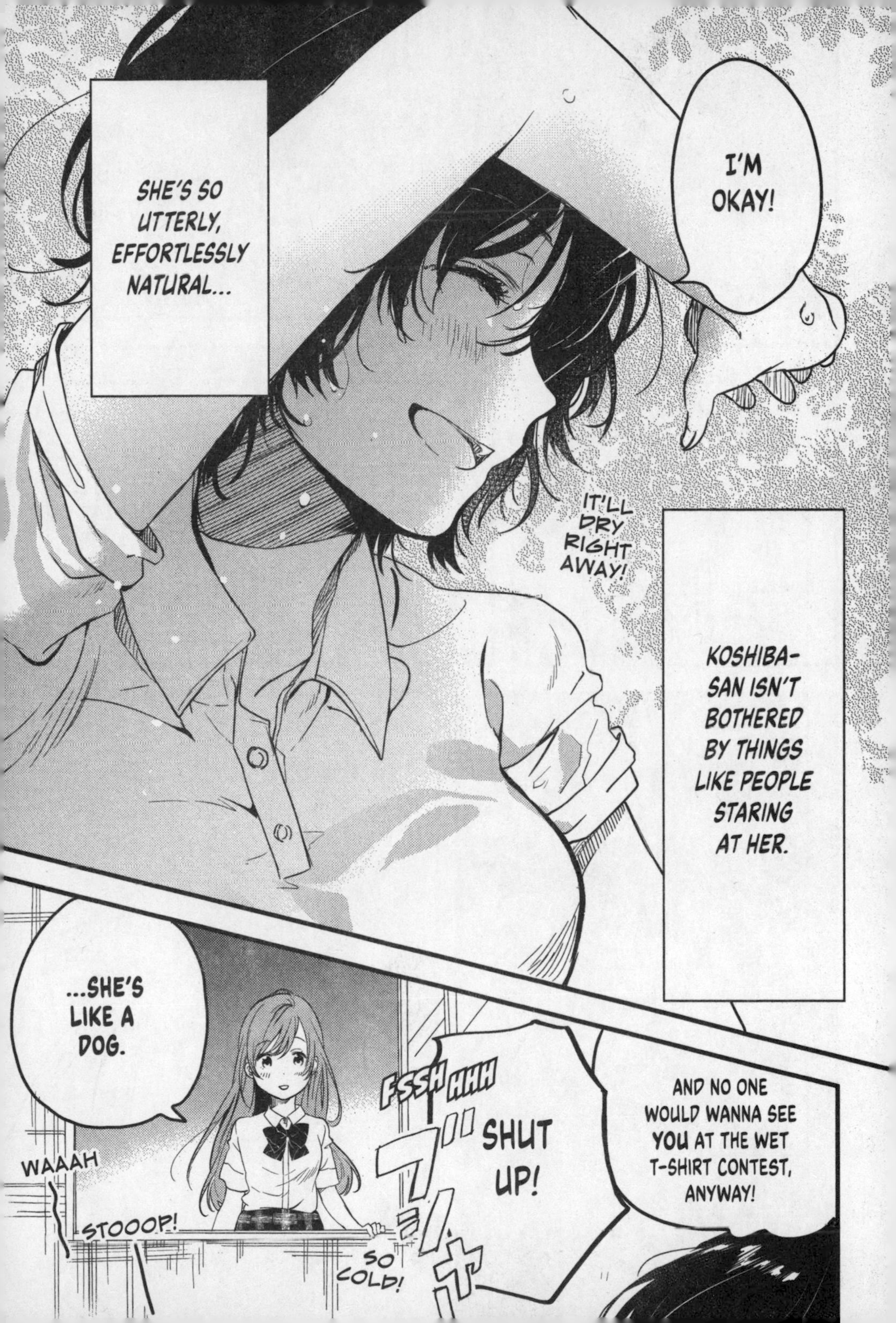
I'M OKAY!
IT'LL DRY RIGHT AWAY!
SHE'S SO UTTERLY, EFFORTLESSLY NATURAL...
KOSHIBA-SAN ISN'T BOTHERED BY THINGS LIKE PEOPLE STARING AT HER.
AND NO ONE WOULD WANNA SEE YOU AT THE WET T-SHIRT CONTEST, ANYWAY!
SHUT UP!
FSSHHHH
...SHE'S LIKE A DOG.
WAAAH
STOOOP!
SO COLD!

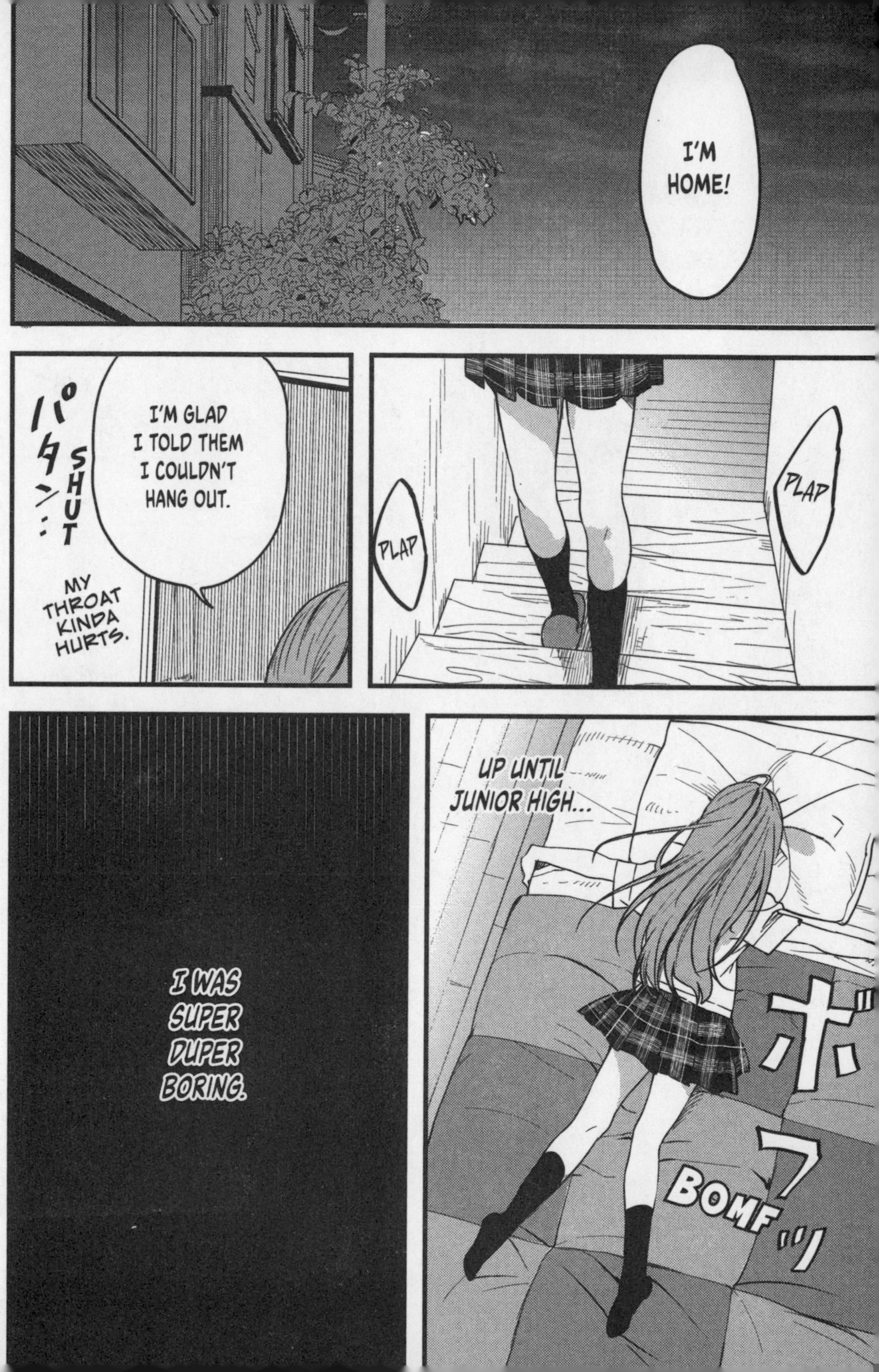
I'M HOME!
PLAP
PLAP
パタン…
SHUT
I'M GLAD I TOLD THEM I COULDN'T HANG OUT.
MY THROAT KINDA HURTS.
UP UNTIL JUNIOR HIGH...
ボフッ
BOMF
I WAS SUPER DUPER BORING.

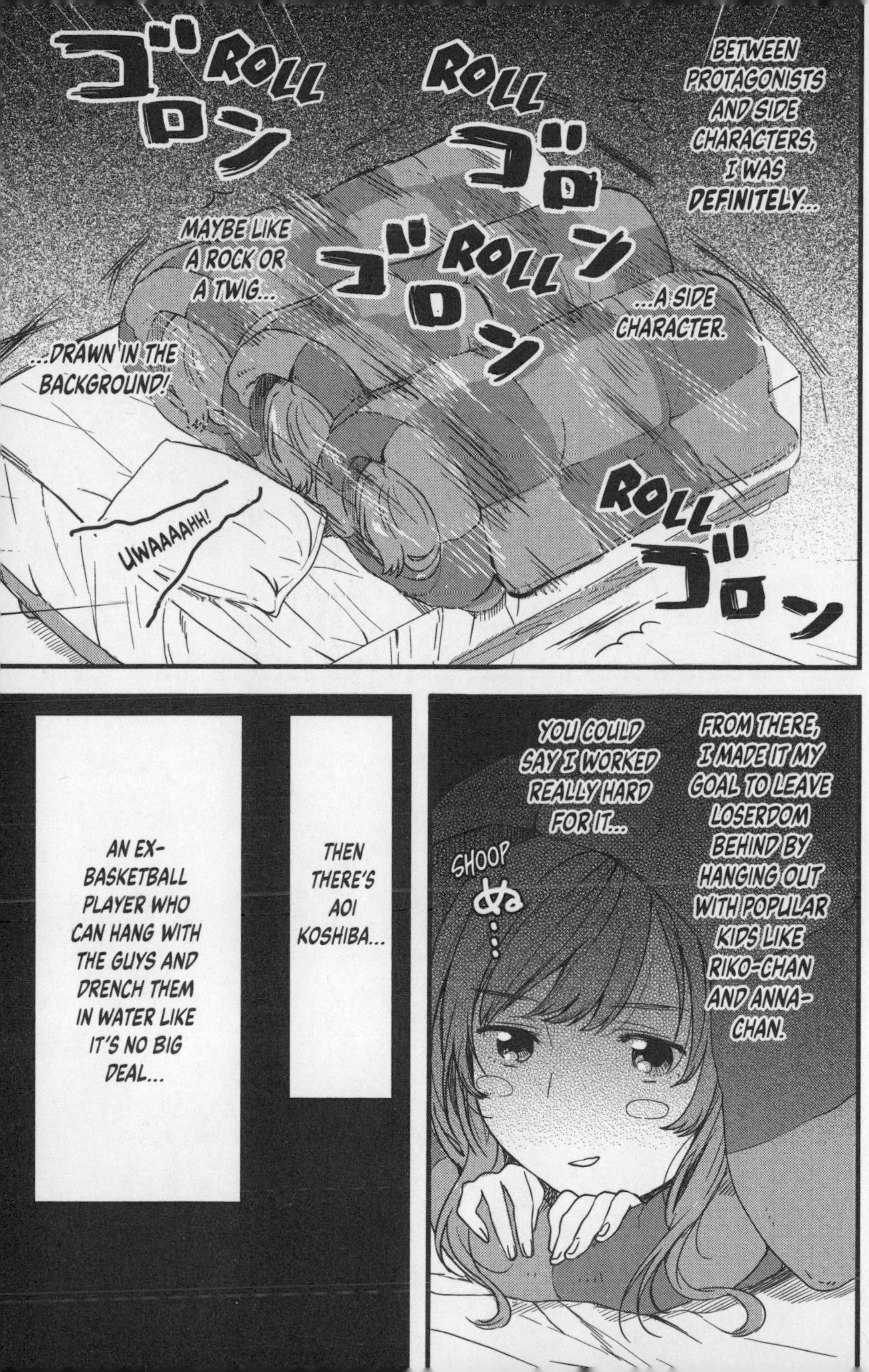
BETWEEN PROTAGONISTS AND SIDE CHARACTERS, I WAS DEFINITELY...
ROLL
ゴロン
ROLL
ゴロン
...A SIDE CHARACTER.
ROLL
ゴロン
MAYBE LIKE A ROCK OR A TWIG...
ROLL
ゴロン
...DRAWN IN THE BACKGROUND!
ROLL
ゴロン
UWAAAAHH!
FROM THERE, I MADE IT MY GOAL TO LEAVE LOSERDOM BEHIND BY HANGING OUT WITH POPULAR KIDS LIKE RIKO-CHAN AND ANNA-CHAN.
YOU COULD SAY I WORKED REALLY HARD FOR IT...
SHOOP
ぬ...
THEN THERE'S AOI KOSHIBA...
AN EX-BASKETBALL PLAYER WHO CAN HANG WITH THE GUYS AND DRENCH THEM IN WATER LIKE IT'S NO BIG DEAL...

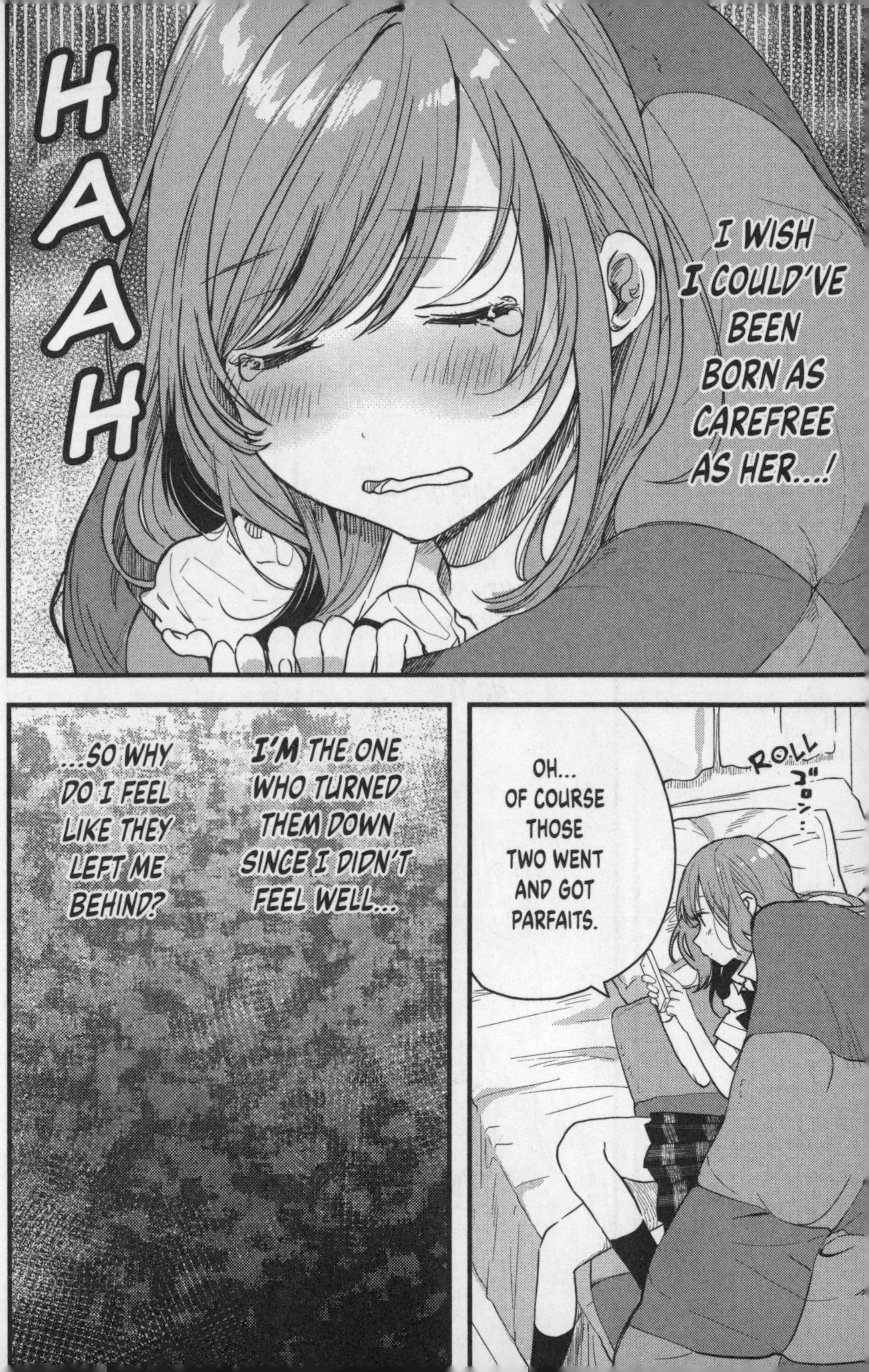
I WISH I COULD'VE BEEN BORN AS CAREFREE AS HER...!
HAAH
ROLL
ゴロン…
OH... OF COURSE THOSE TWO WENT AND GOT PARFAITS.
I'M THE ONE WHO TURNED THEM DOWN SINCE I DIDN'T FEEL WELL...
...SO WHY DO I FEEL LIKE THEY LEFT ME BEHIND?

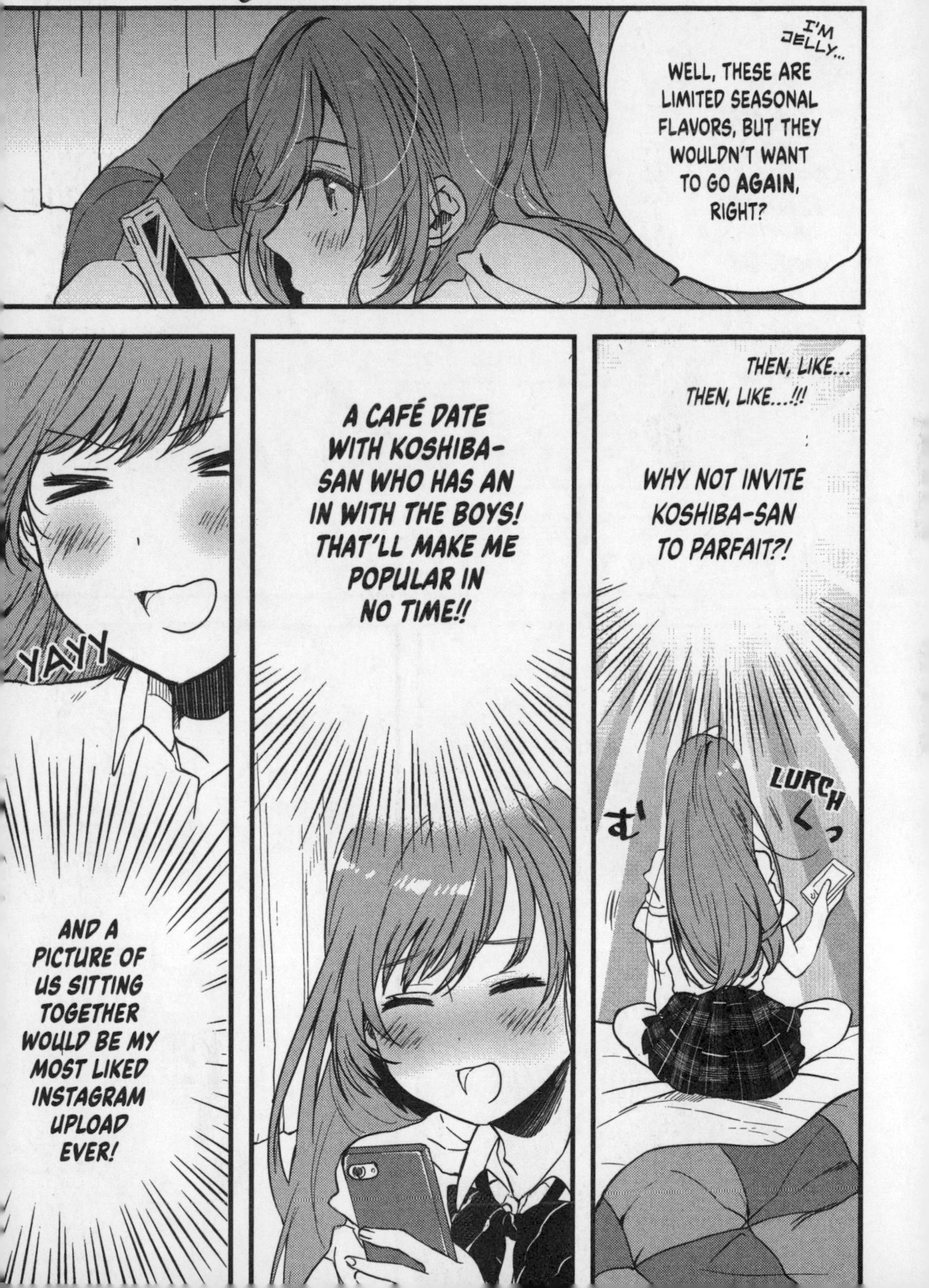
I'M JELLY...
WELL, THESE ARE LIMITED SEASONAL FLAVORS, BUT THEY WOULDN'T WANT TO GO AGAIN, RIGHT?
THEN, LIKE...
THEN, LIKE...!!!
WHY NOT INVITE KOSHIBA-SAN TO PARFAIT?!
LURCH
くっ
む
A CAFÉ DATE WITH KOSHIBA-SAN WHO HAS AN IN WITH THE BOYS! THAT'LL MAKE ME POPULAR IN NO TIME!!
YAYY
AND A PICTURE OF US SITTING TOGETHER WOULD BE MY MOST LIKED INSTAGRAM UPLOAD EVER!

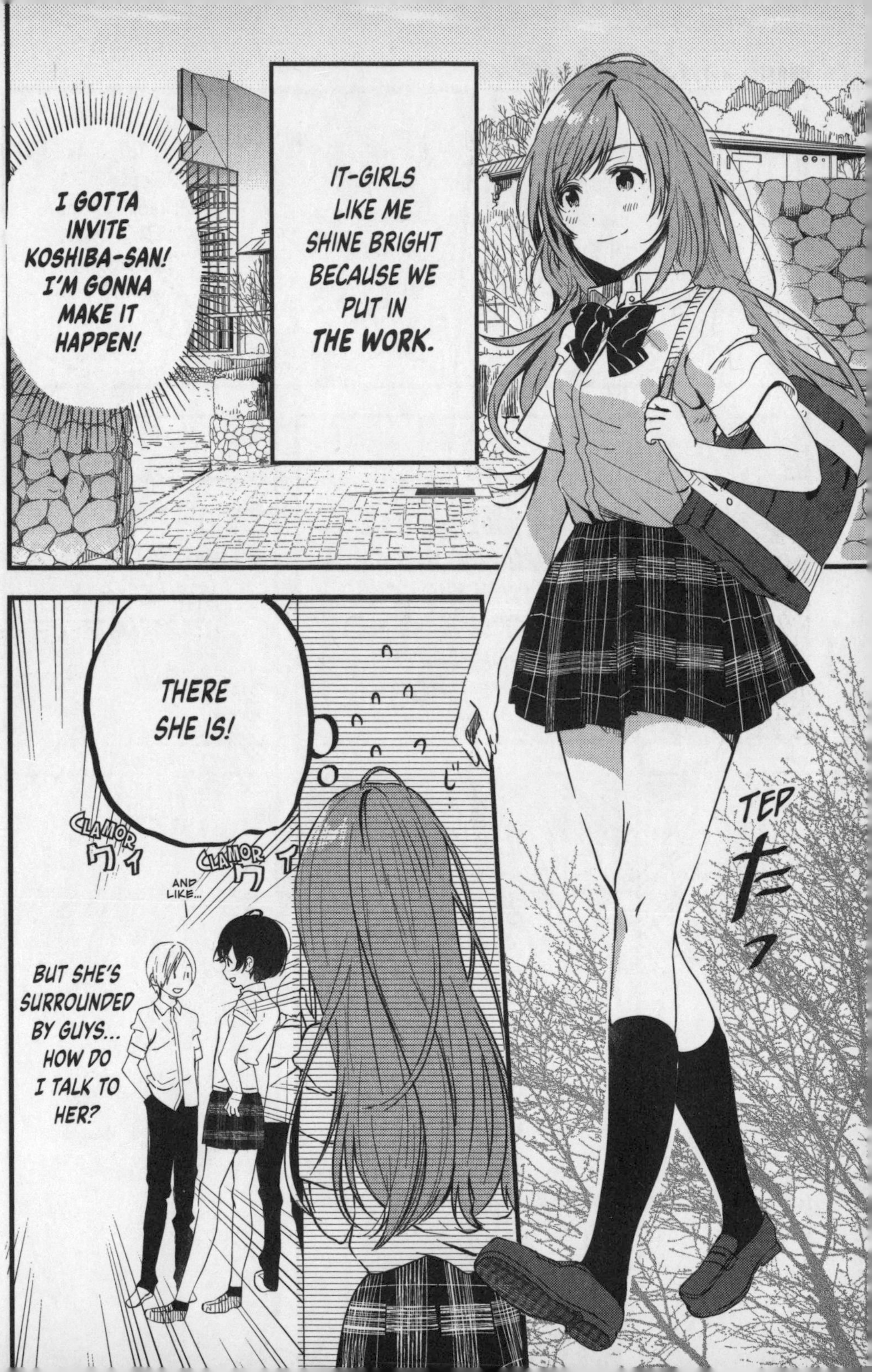
IT-GIRLS LIKE ME SHINE BRIGHT BECAUSE WE PUT IN THE WORK.
I GOTTA INVITE KOSHIBA-SAN! I'M GONNA MAKE IT HAPPEN!
TEP
THERE SHE IS!
CLAMOR
CLAMOR
AND LIKE...
BUT SHE'S SURROUNDED BY GUYS... HOW DO I TALK TO HER?

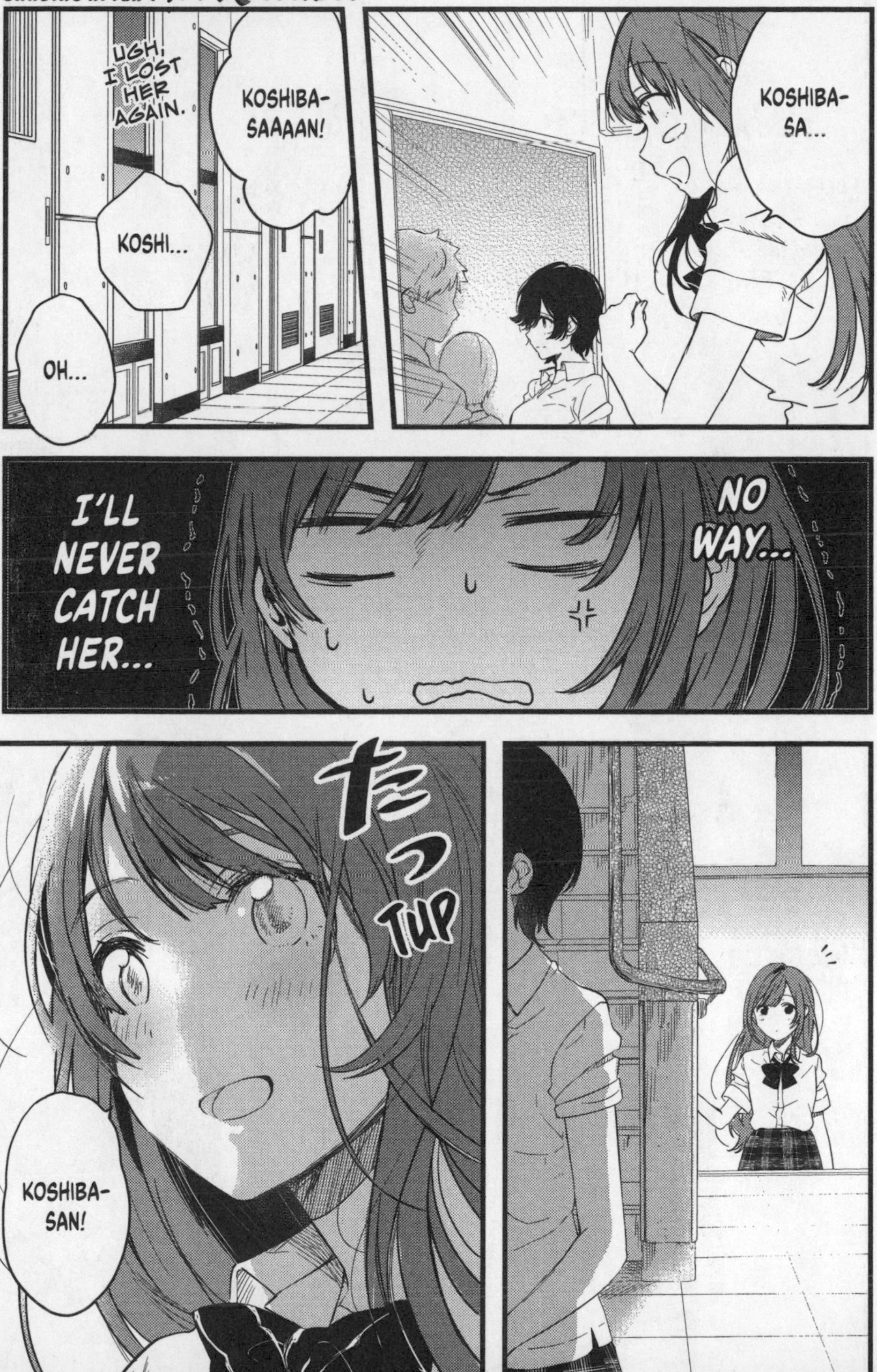
KOSHIBA-SA...
KOSHIBA-SAAAAN!
UGH, I LOST HER AGAIN.
KOSHI...
OH...
NO WAY...
I'LL NEVER CATCH HER...
たっ
TUP
KOSHIBA-SAN!

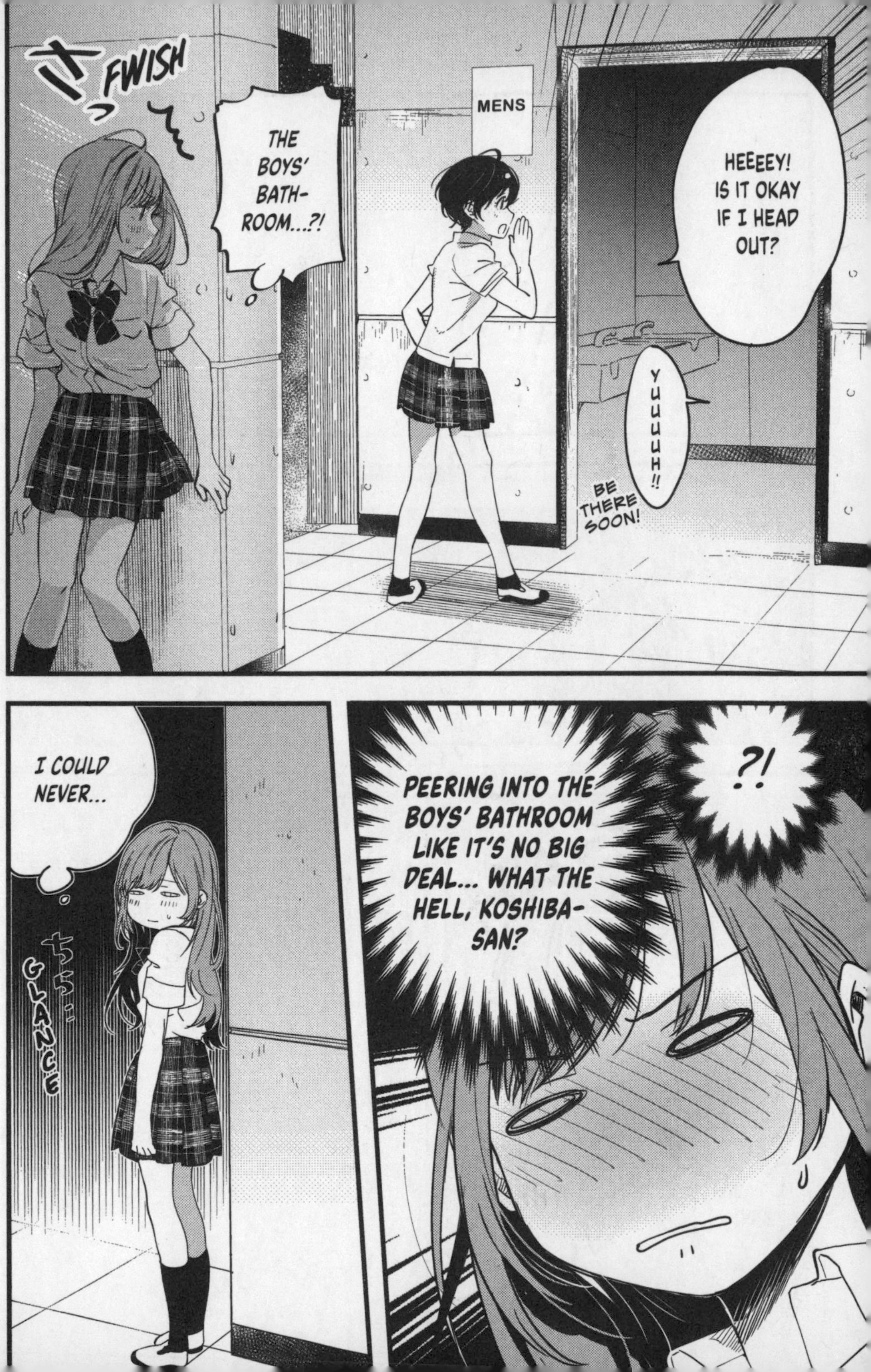
HEEEEY! IS IT OKAY IF I HEAD OUT?
YUUUUH!!
BE THERE SOON!
MENS
THE BOYS' BATH-ROOM...?!
さっ FWISH
?!
PEERING INTO THE BOYS' BATHROOM LIKE IT'S NO BIG DEAL... WHAT THE HELL, KOSHIBA-SAN?
I COULD NEVER...
ちら… GLANCE

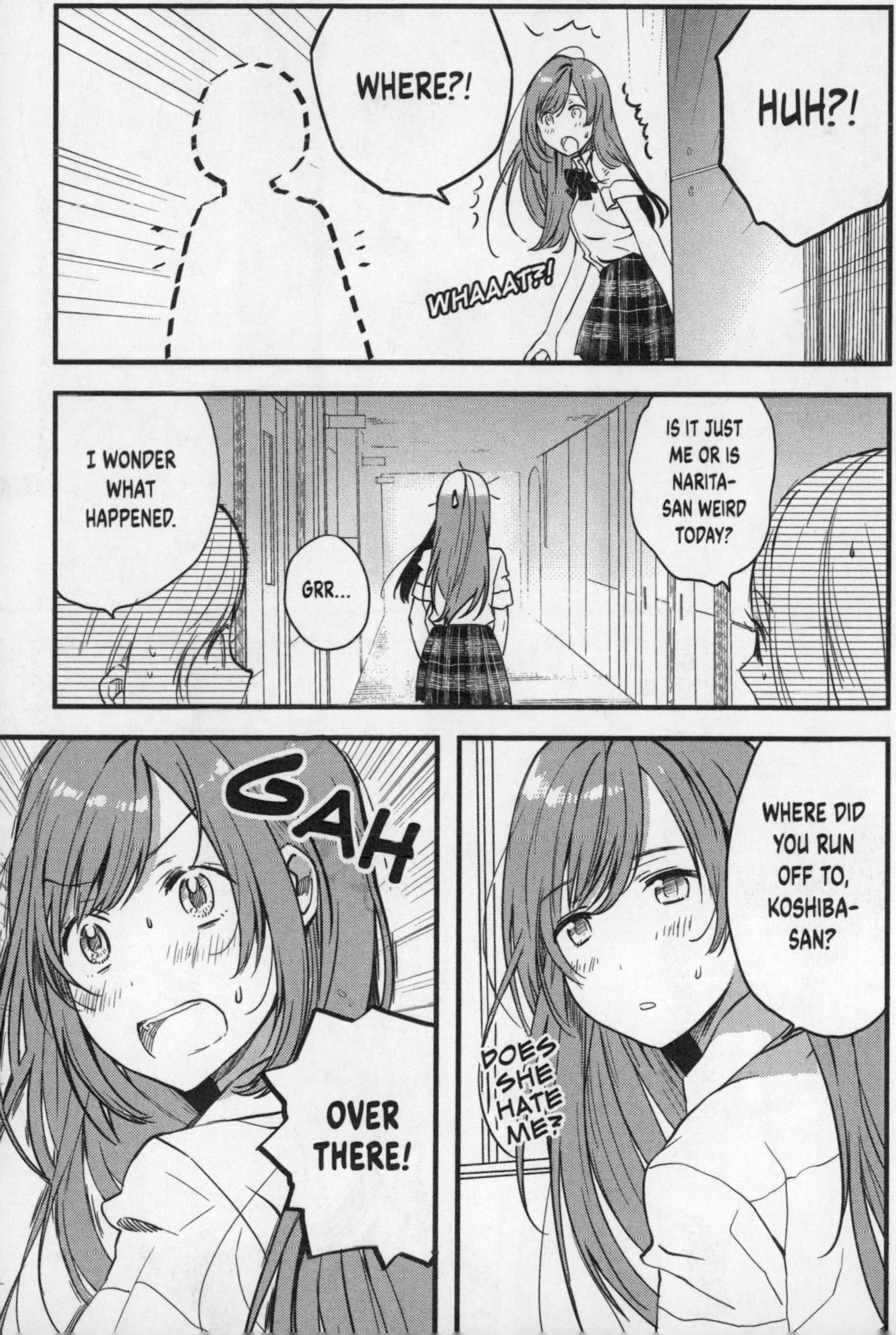
HUH?!
WHERE?!
WHAAAT?!
IS IT JUST ME OR IS NARITA-SAN WEIRD TODAY?
GRR...
I WONDER WHAT HAPPENED.
WHERE DID YOU RUN OFF TO, KOSHIBA-SAN?
DOES SHE HATE ME?
GAH
OVER THERE!

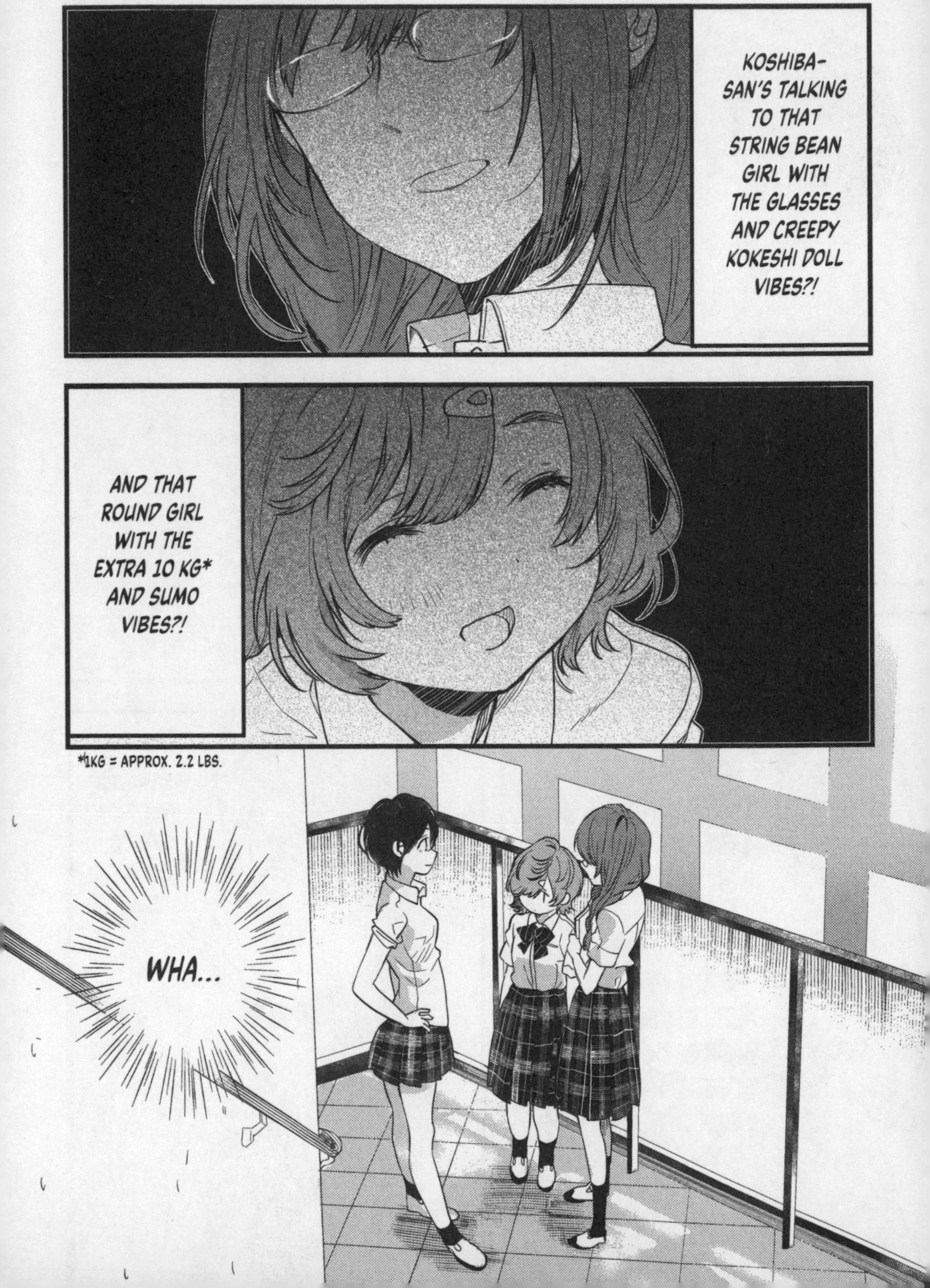
KOSHIBA-SAN'S TALKING TO THAT STRING BEAN GIRL WITH THE GLASSES AND CREEPY KOKESHI DOLL VIBES?!
AND THAT ROUND GIRL WITH THE EXTRA 10 KG* AND SUMO VIBES?!
WHA...
*1KG = APPROX. 2.2 LBS.

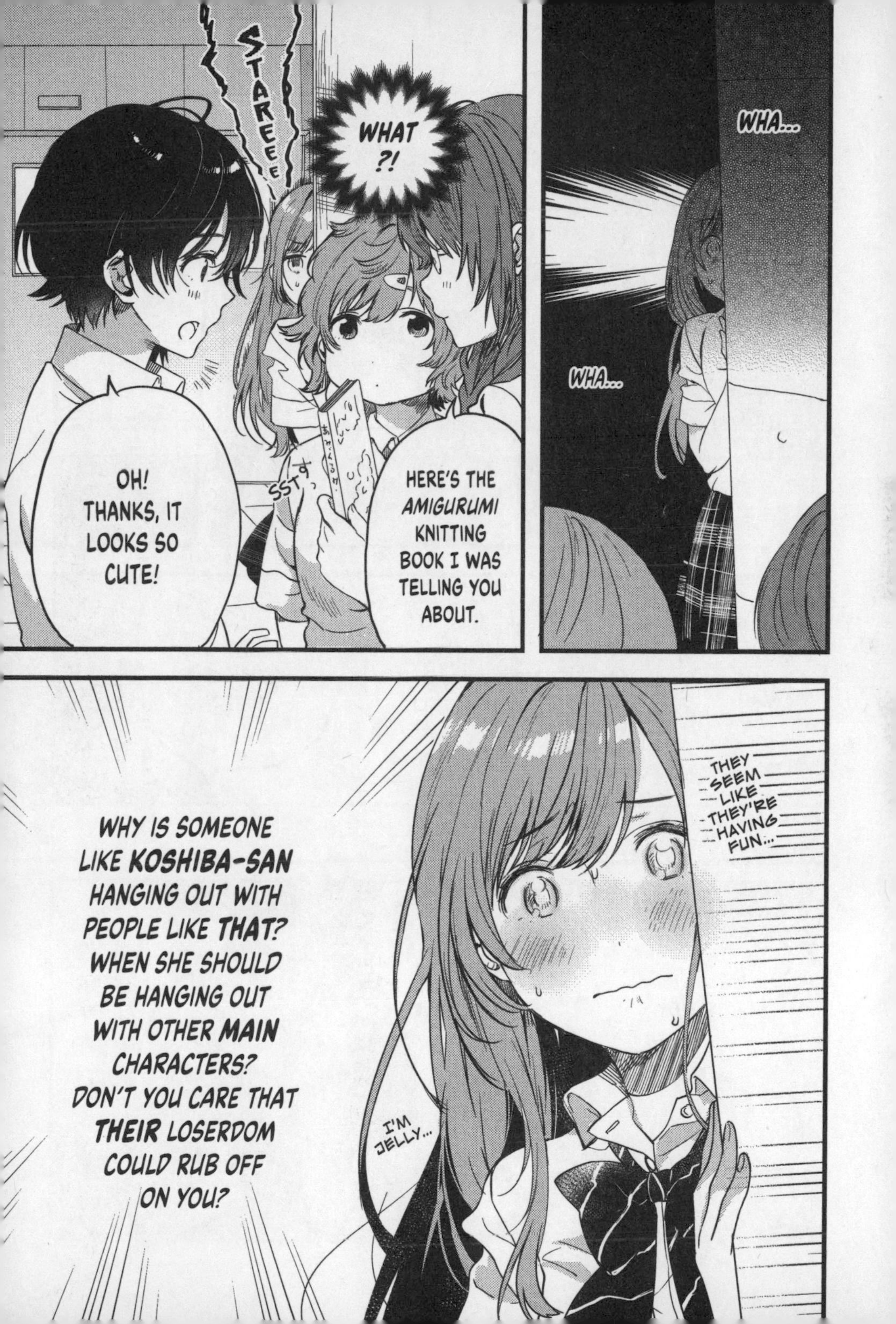
WHA...
WHA...
WHAT ?!
STAREEE
HERE'S THE AMIGURUMI KNITTING BOOK I WAS TELLING YOU ABOUT.
SST
OH! THANKS, IT LOOKS SO CUTE!
THEY SEEM LIKE THEY'RE HAVING FUN...
WHY IS SOMEONE LIKE KOSHIBA-SAN HANGING OUT WITH PEOPLE LIKE THAT? WHEN SHE SHOULD BE HANGING OUT WITH OTHER MAIN CHARACTERS? DON'T YOU CARE THAT THEIR LOSERDOM COULD RUB OFF ON YOU?
I'M JELLY...

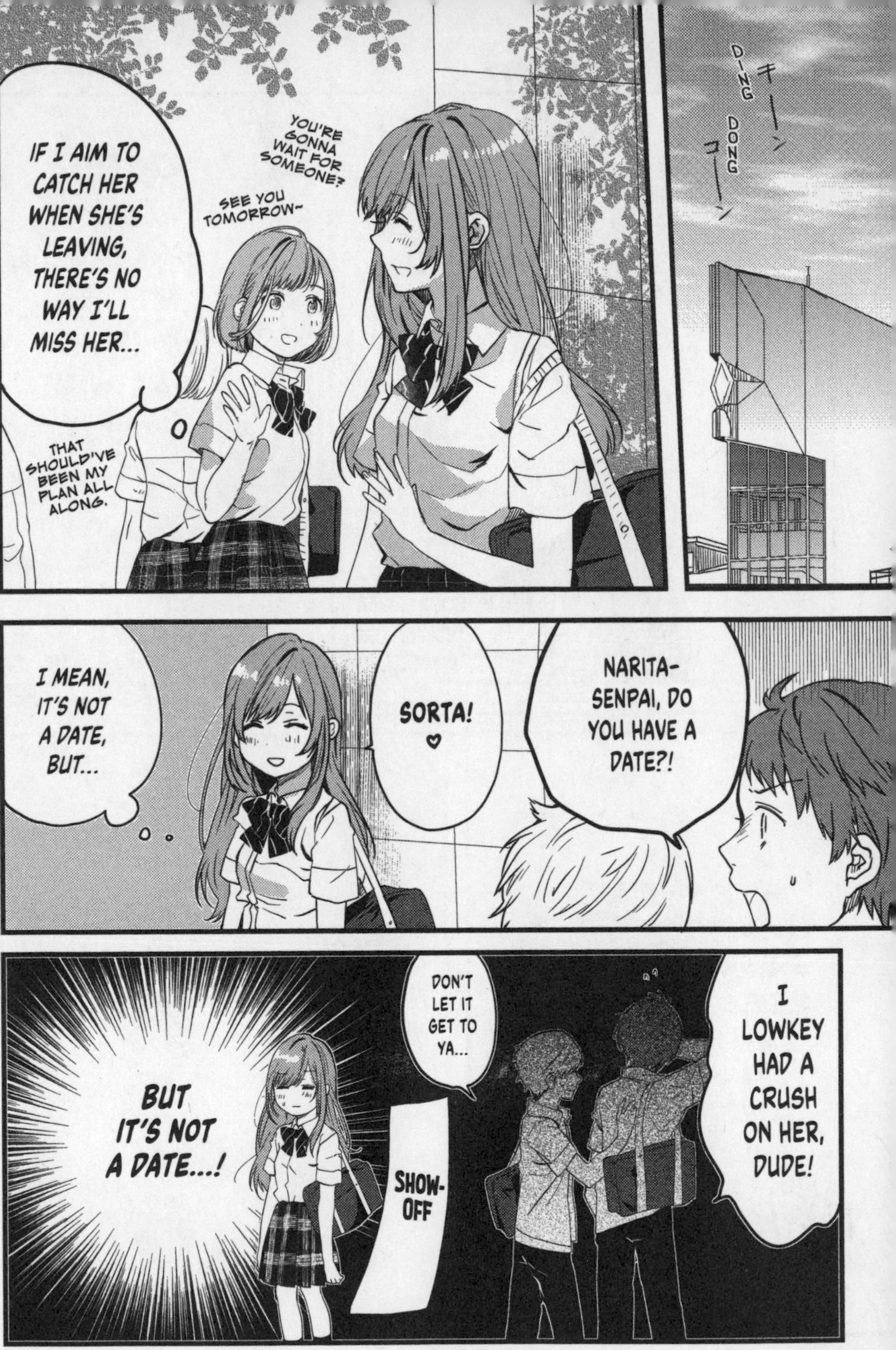
DING DONG
YOU'RE GONNA WAIT FOR SOMEONE?
SEE YOU TOMORROW~
IF I AIM TO CATCH HER WHEN SHE'S LEAVING, THERE'S NO WAY I'LL MISS HER...
THAT SHOULD'VE BEEN MY PLAN ALL ALONG.
NARITA-SENPAI, DO YOU HAVE A DATE?!
SORTA! ♡
I MEAN, IT'S NOT A DATE, BUT...
I LOWKEY HAD A CRUSH ON HER, DUDE!
DON'T LET IT GET TO YA...
SHOW-OFF
BUT IT'S NOT A DATE...!

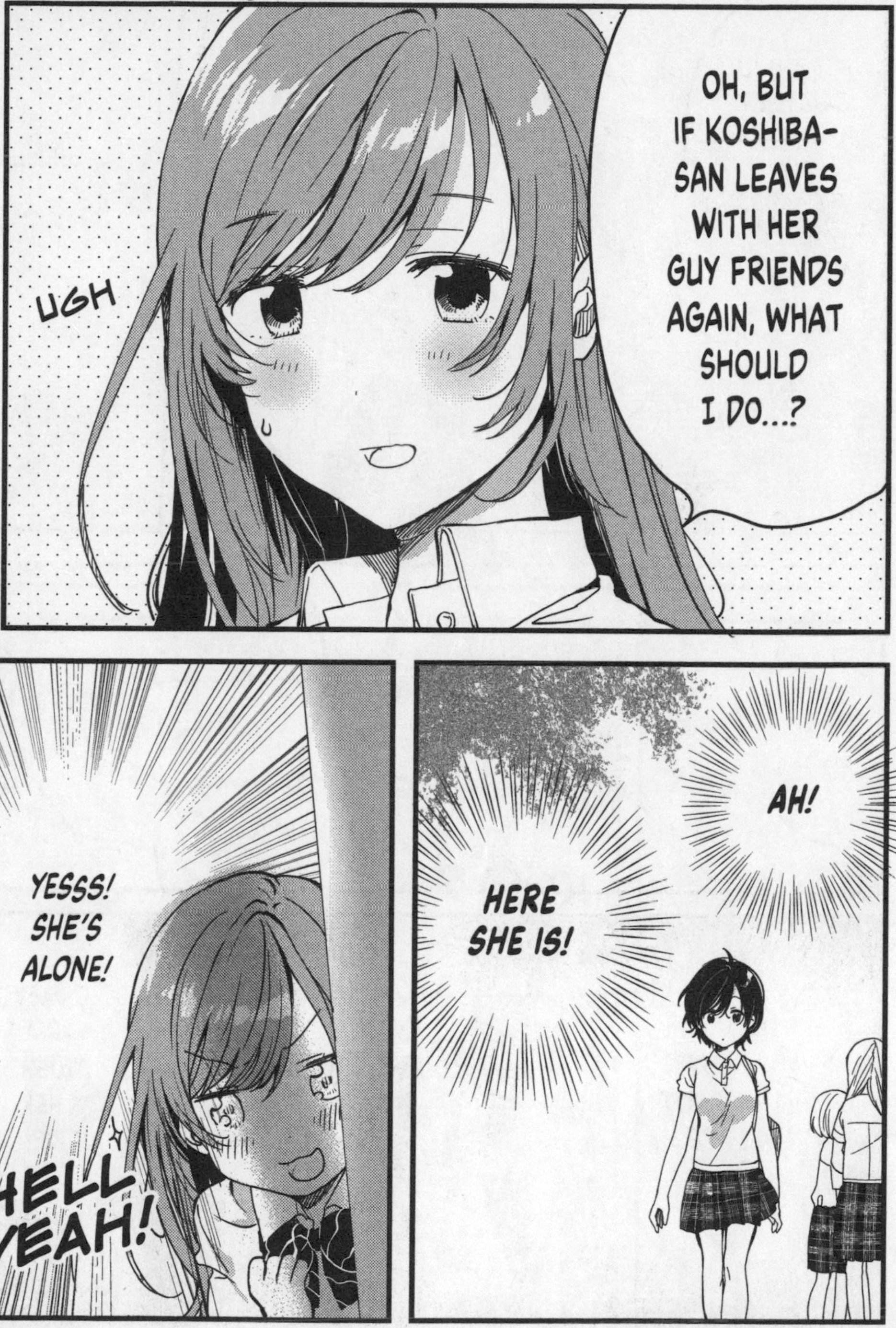
OH, BUT IF KOSHIBA-SAN LEAVES WITH HER GUY FRIENDS AGAIN, WHAT SHOULD I DO...?
UGH
AH!
HERE SHE IS!
YESSS! SHE'S ALONE!
HELL YEAH!

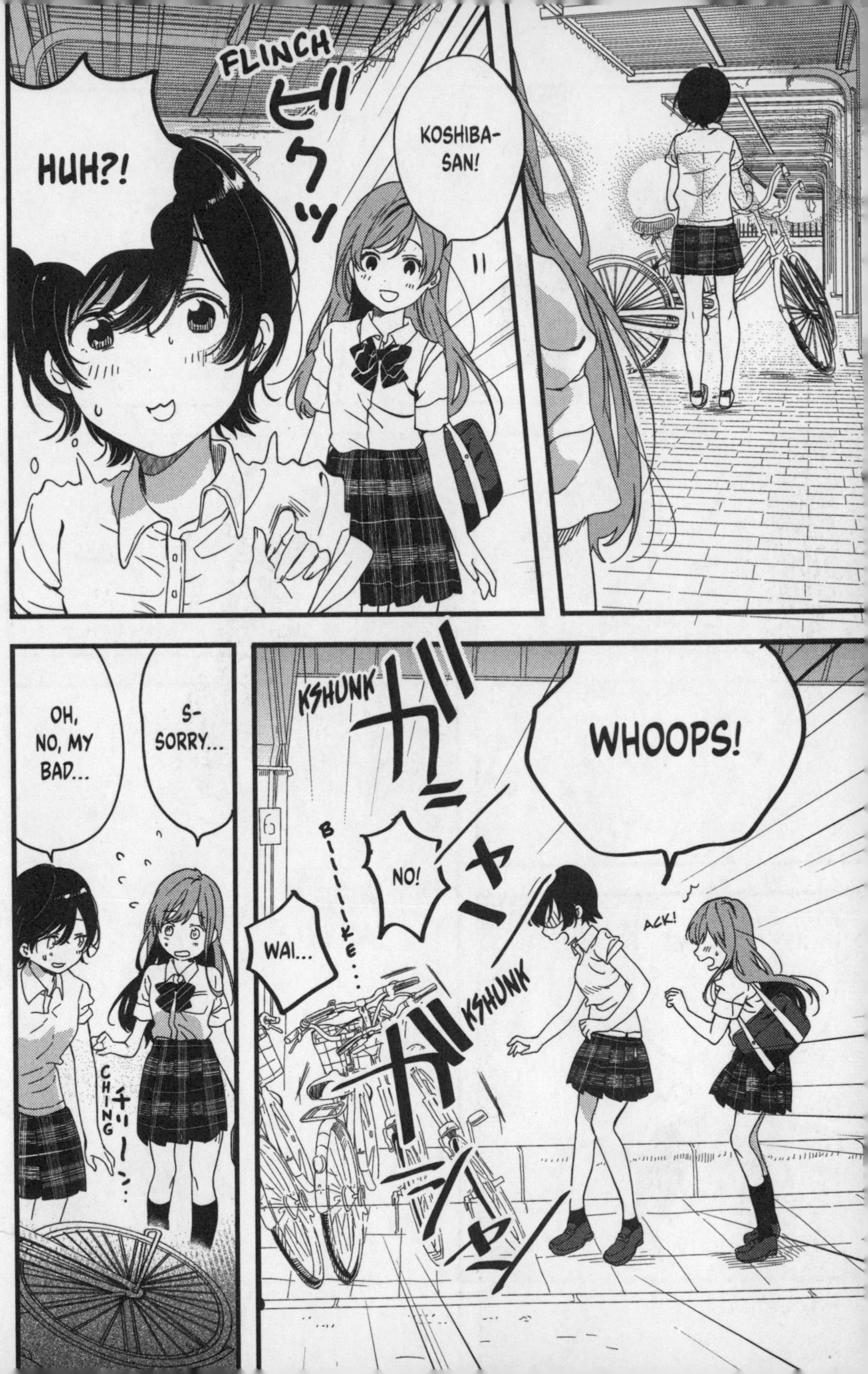
KOSHIBA-SAN!
FLINCH
HUH?!
WHOOPS!
ACK!
KSHUNK
NO!
B-I-I-I-KE...
WAI...
KSHUNK
S-SORRY...
OH, NO, MY BAD...
CHING

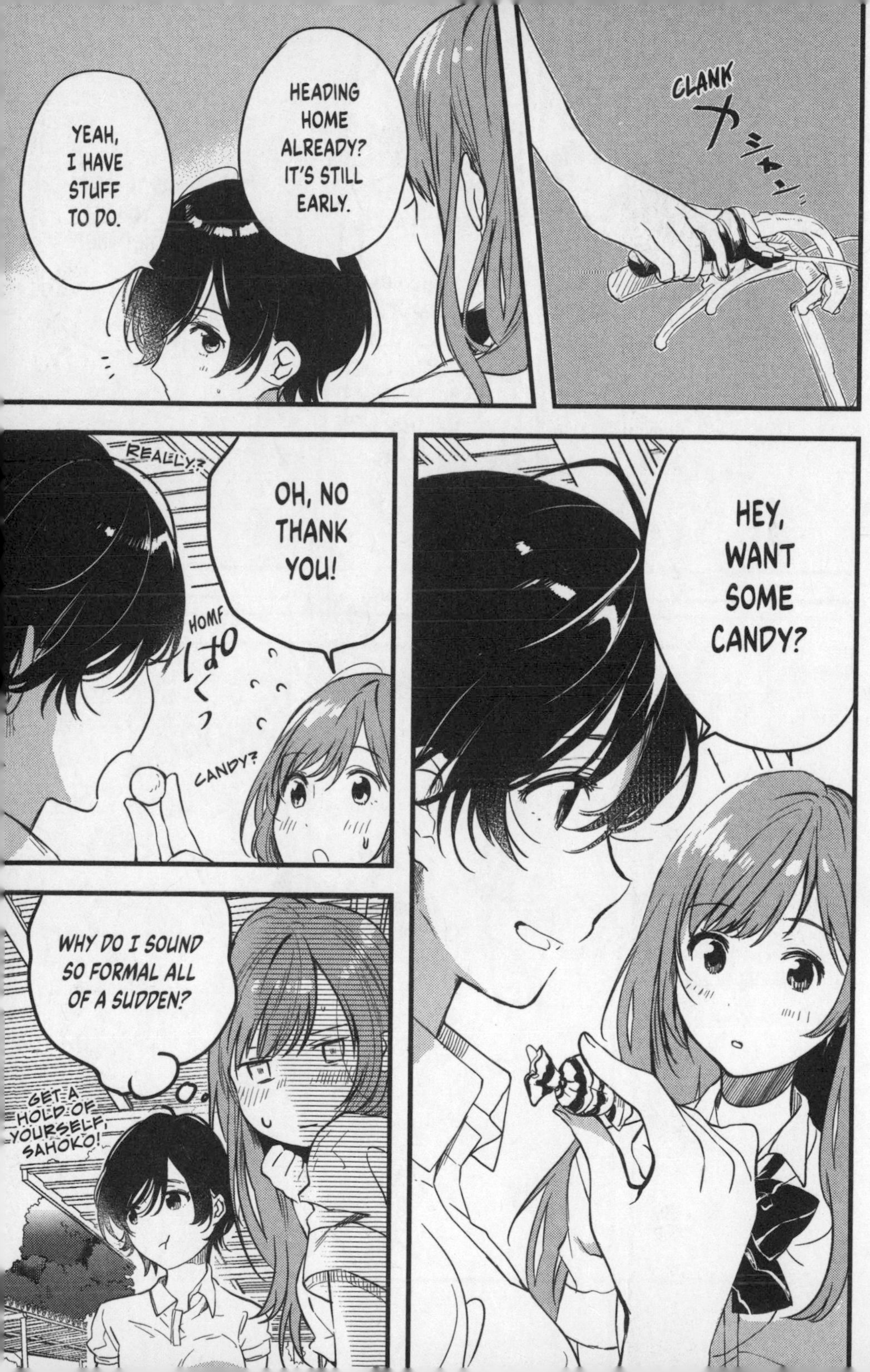
CLANK
HEADING HOME ALREADY? IT'S STILL EARLY.
YEAH, I HAVE STUFF TO DO.
HEY, WANT SOME CANDY?
OH, NO THANK YOU!
REALLY?
HOMF
CANDY?
WHY DO I SOUND SO FORMAL ALL OF A SUDDEN?
GET A HOLD OF YOURSELF, SAHOKO!

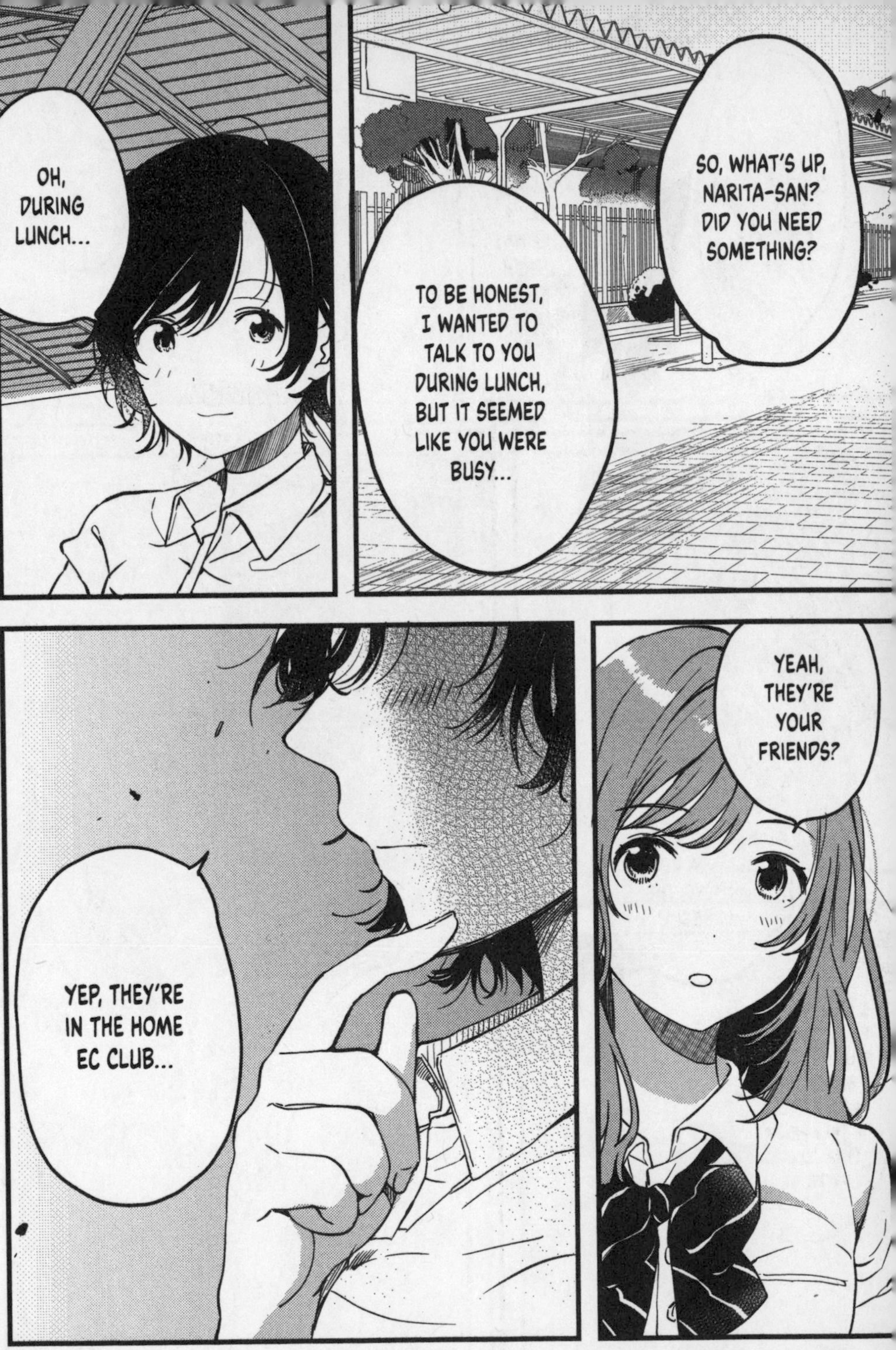
SO, WHAT'S UP, NARITA-SAN? DID YOU NEED SOMETHING?
TO BE HONEST, I WANTED TO TALK TO YOU DURING LUNCH, BUT IT SEEMED LIKE YOU WERE BUSY...
OH, DURING LUNCH...
YEAH, THEY'RE YOUR FRIENDS?
YEP, THEY'RE IN THE HOME EC CLUB...

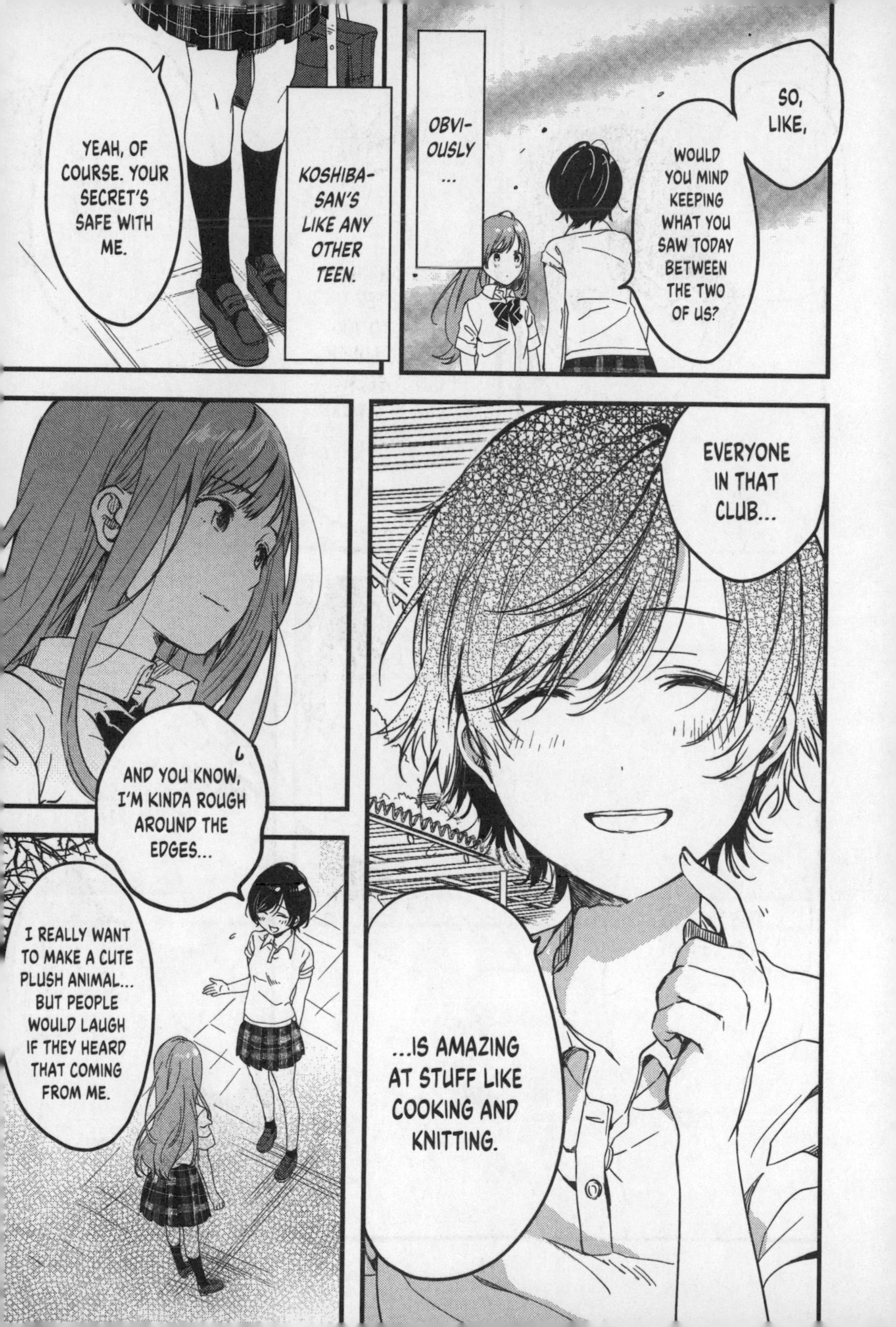
SO, LIKE,
WOULD YOU MIND KEEPING WHAT YOU SAW TODAY BETWEEN THE TWO OF US?
OBVI-OUSLY...
KOSHIBA-SAN'S LIKE ANY OTHER TEEN.
YEAH, OF COURSE. YOUR SECRET'S SAFE WITH ME.
EVERYONE IN THAT CLUB...
...IS AMAZING AT STUFF LIKE COOKING AND KNITTING.
AND YOU KNOW, I'M KINDA ROUGH AROUND THE EDGES...
I REALLY WANT TO MAKE A CUTE PLUSH ANIMAL... BUT PEOPLE WOULD LAUGH IF THEY HEARD THAT COMING FROM ME.

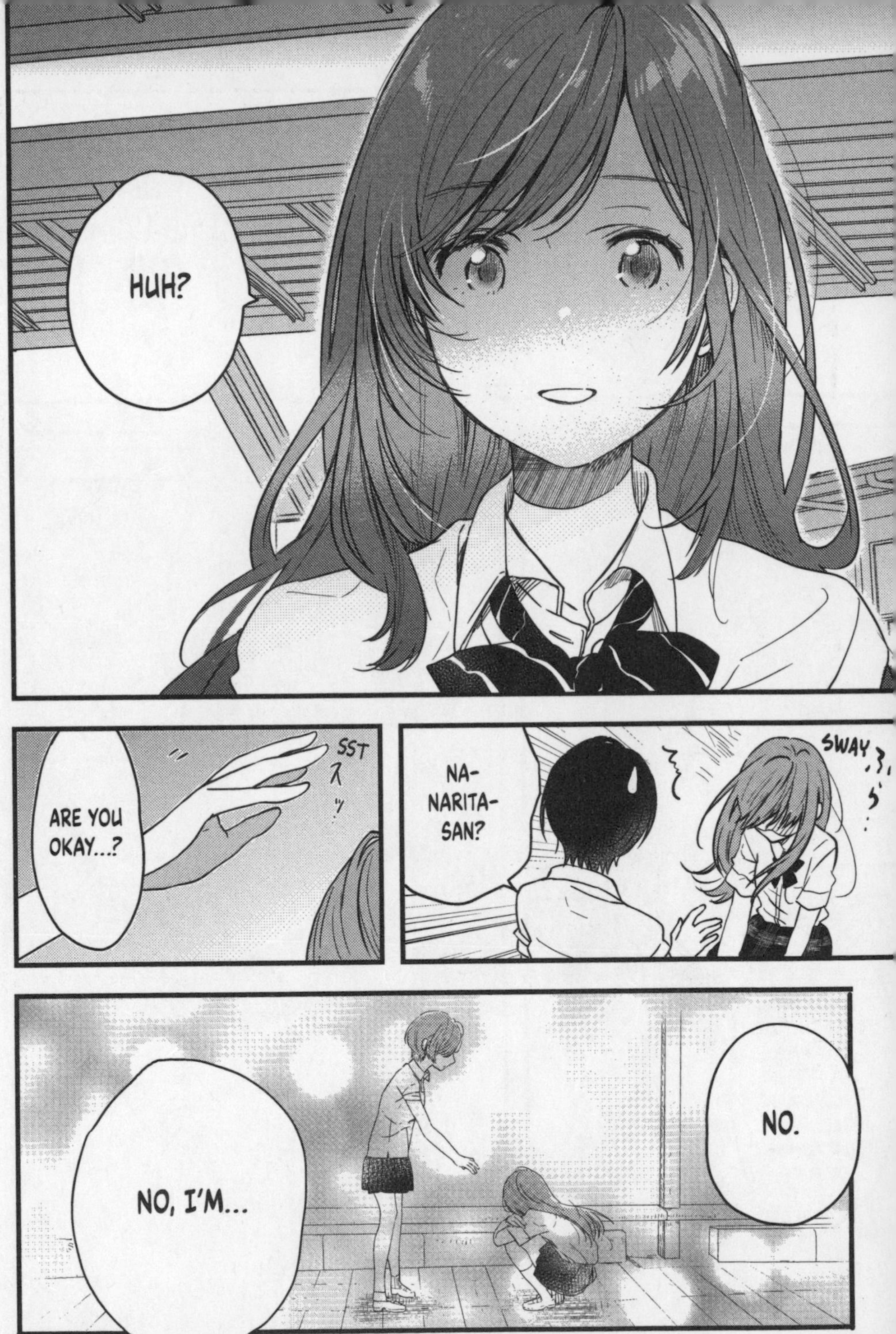
HUH?
SWAY
ふら
NA-NARITA-SAN?
SST
スッ
ARE YOU OKAY...?
NO.
NO, I'M...

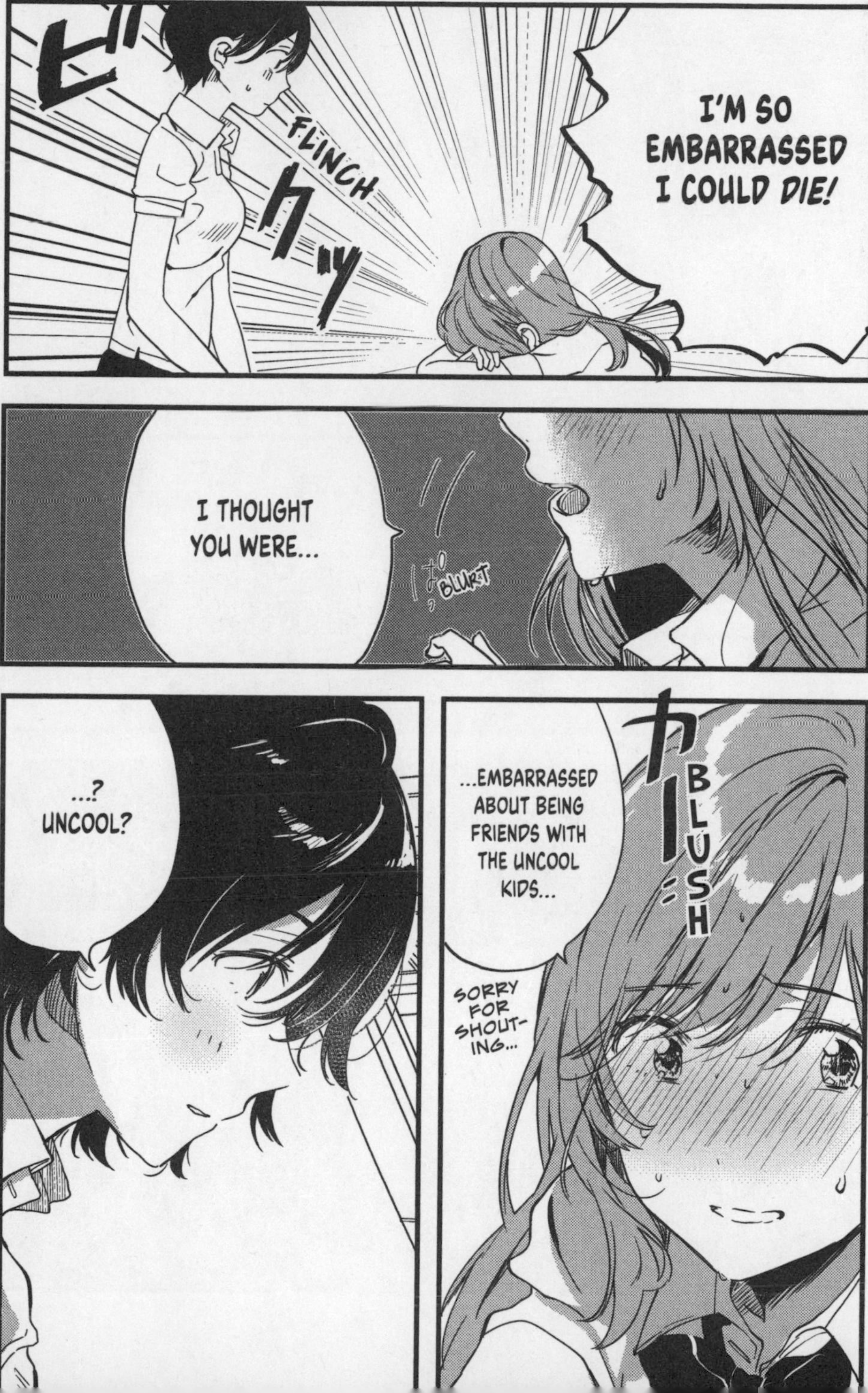
I'M SO EMBARRASSED I COULD DIE!
FLINCH
I THOUGHT YOU WERE...
BLURT
...EMBARRASSED ABOUT BEING FRIENDS WITH THE UNCOOL KIDS...
BLUSH
SORRY FOR SHOUT-ING...
...? UNCOOL?

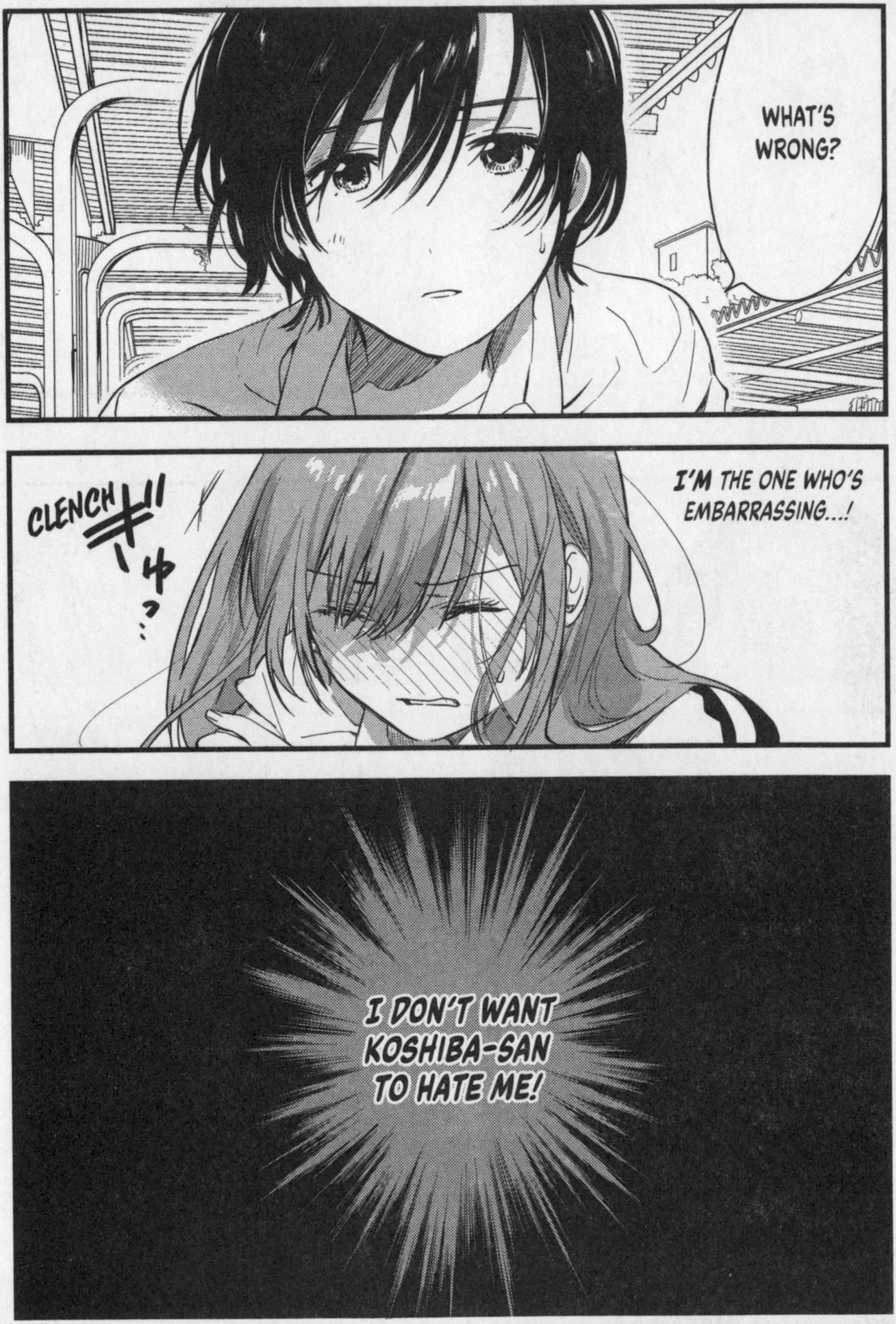
WHAT'S WRONG?
I'M THE ONE WHO'S EMBARRASSING...!
CLENCH
I DON'T WANT KOSHIBA-SAN TO HATE ME!

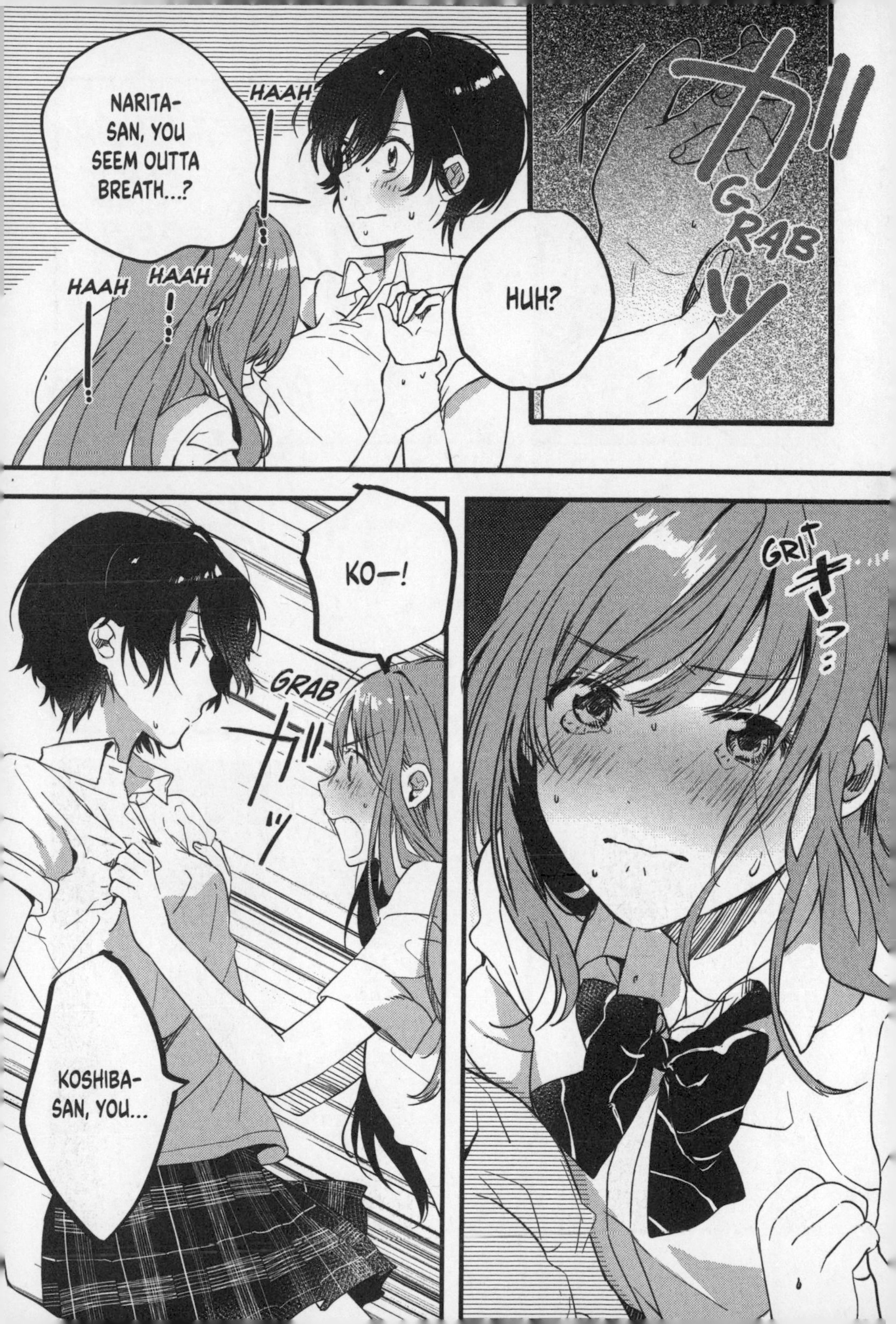
GRAB
HUH?
HAAH
NARITA-SAN, YOU SEEM OUTTA BREATH...?
HAAH
HAAH
GRIT
KO—!
GRAB
KOSHIBA-SAN, YOU...

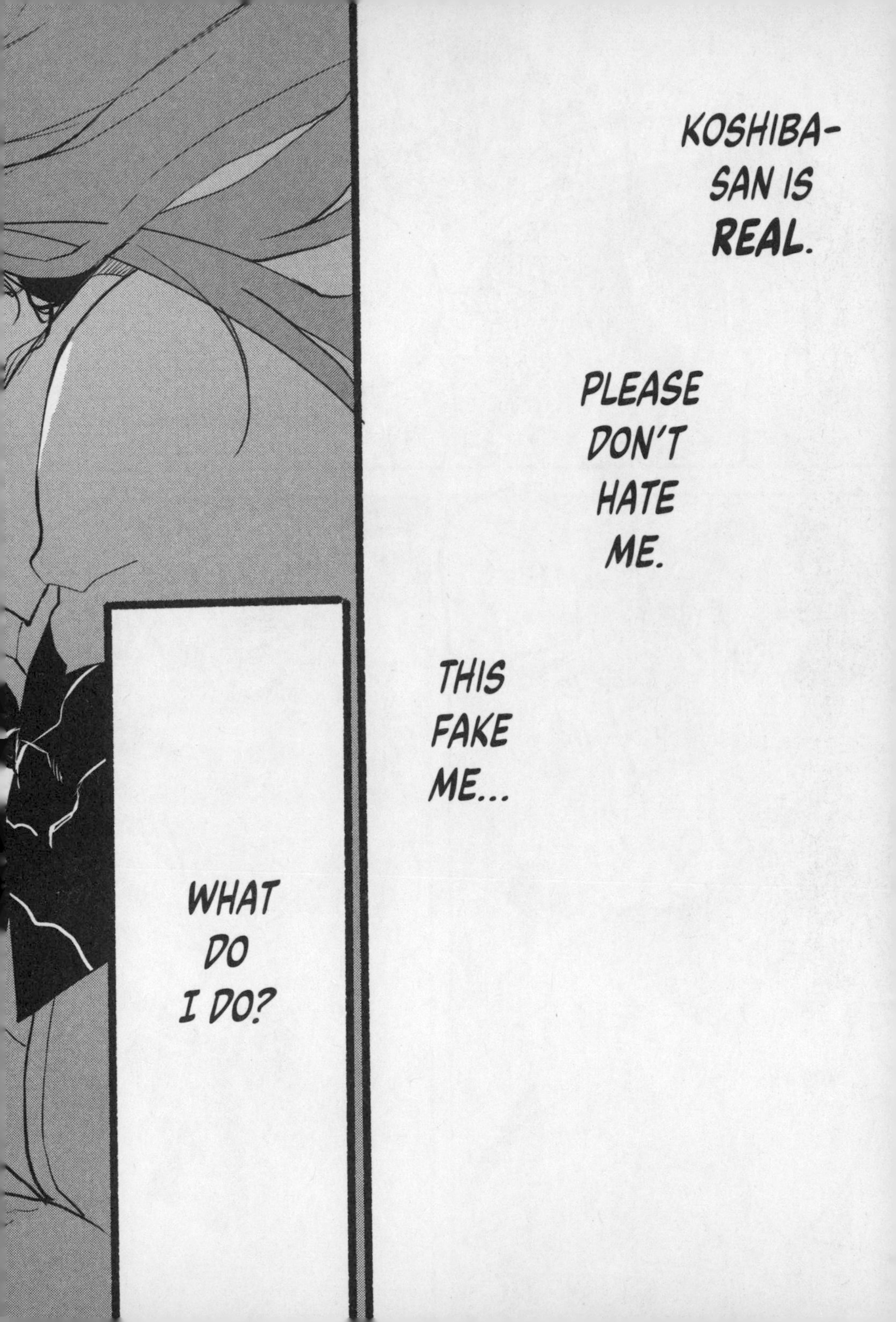
KOSHIBA-SAN IS **REAL**.
PLEASE DON'T HATE ME.
THIS FAKE ME...
WHAT DO I DO?

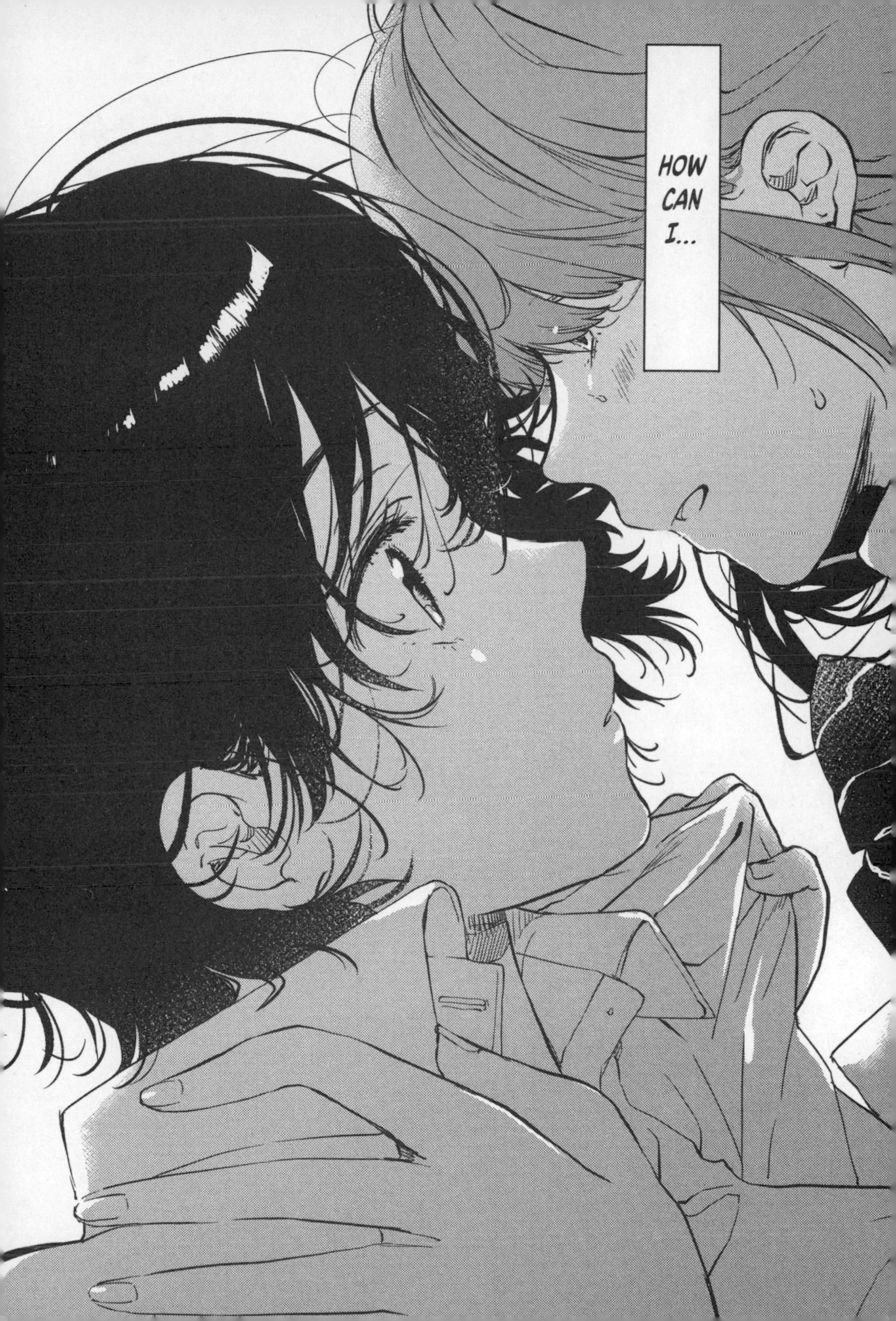
HOW CAN I...

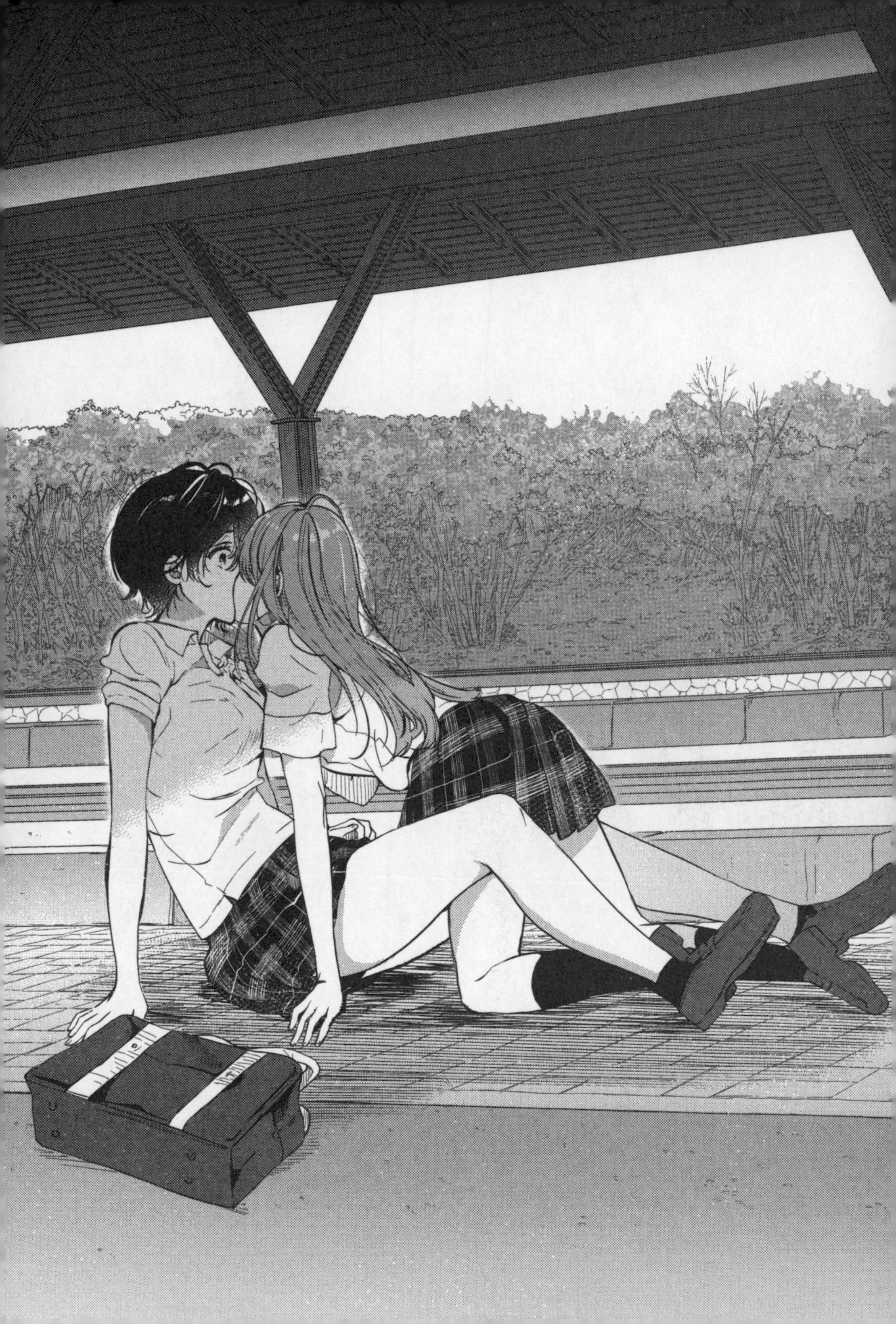

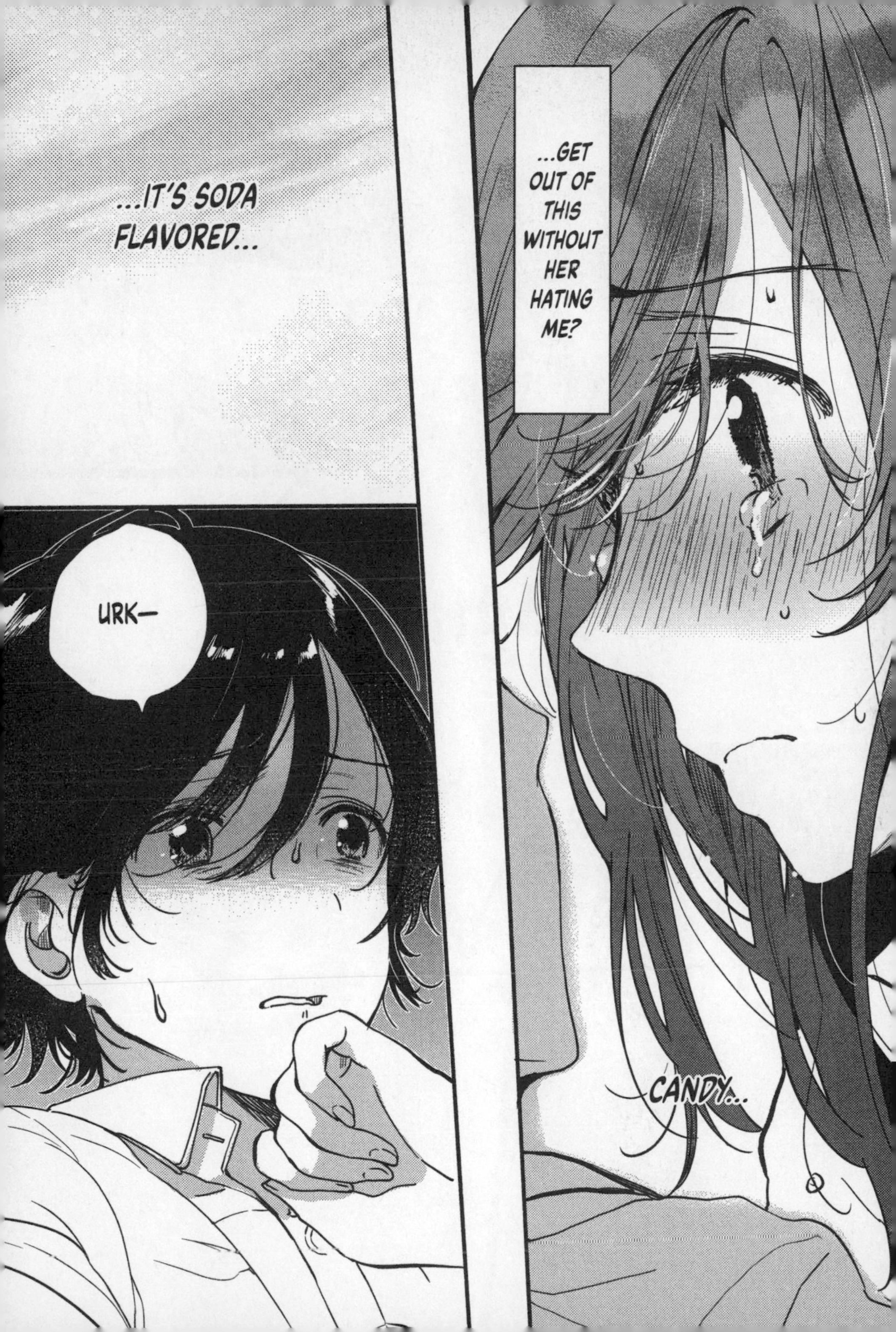
...GET OUT OF THIS WITHOUT HER HATING ME?
CANDY...
...IT'S SODA FLAVORED...
URK—

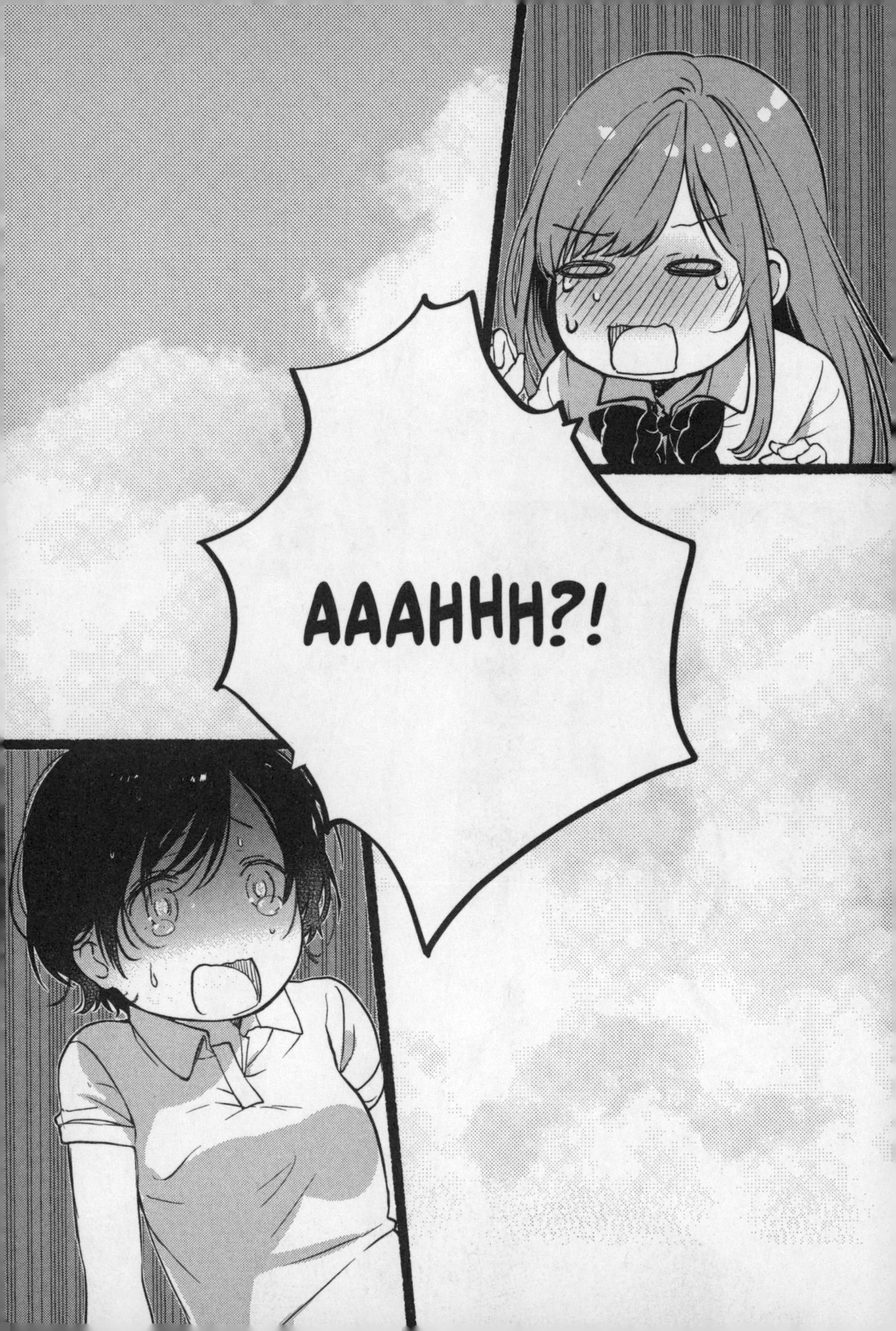
AAAHHH?!

Chapter 2:
No Bother

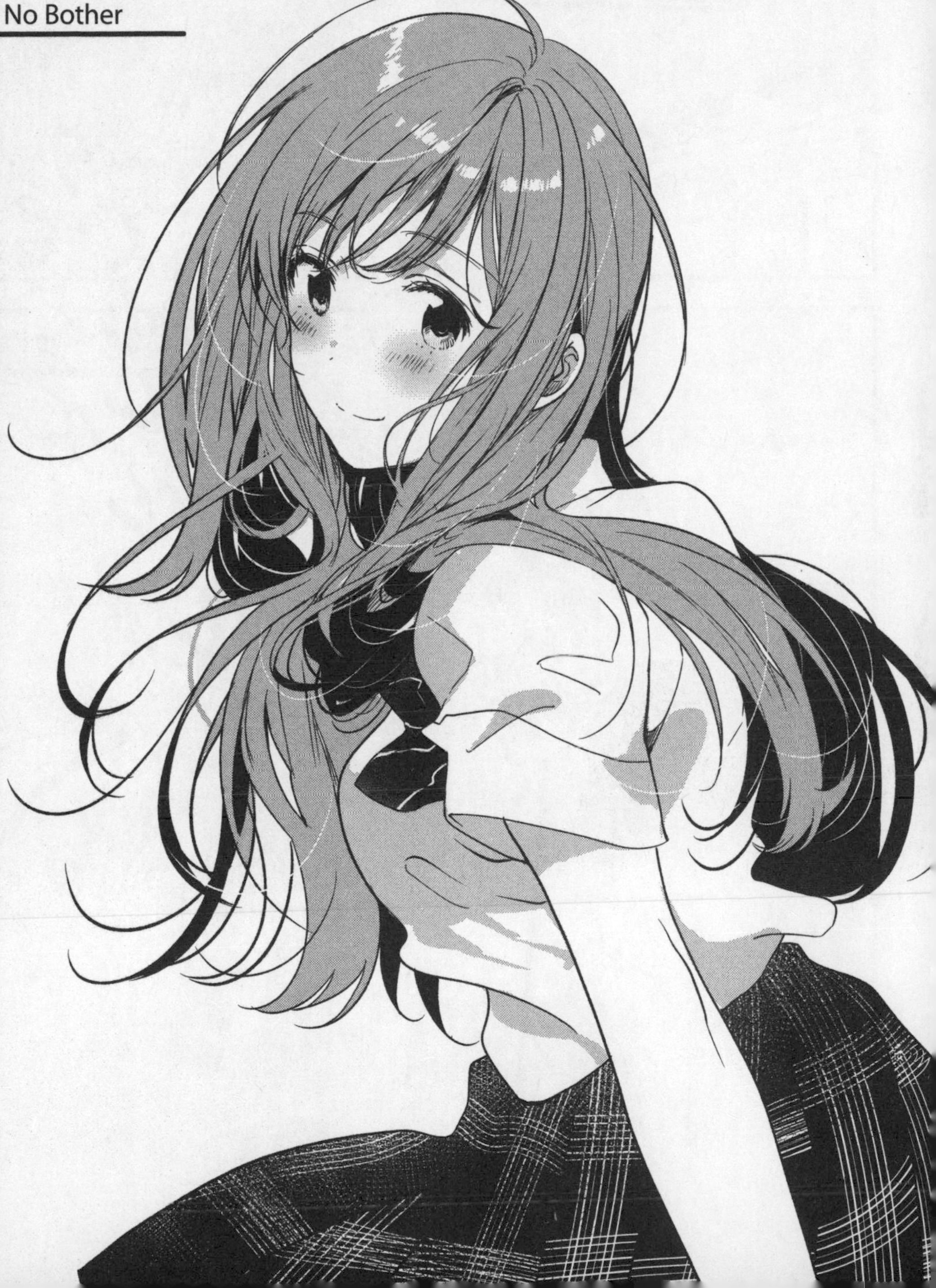

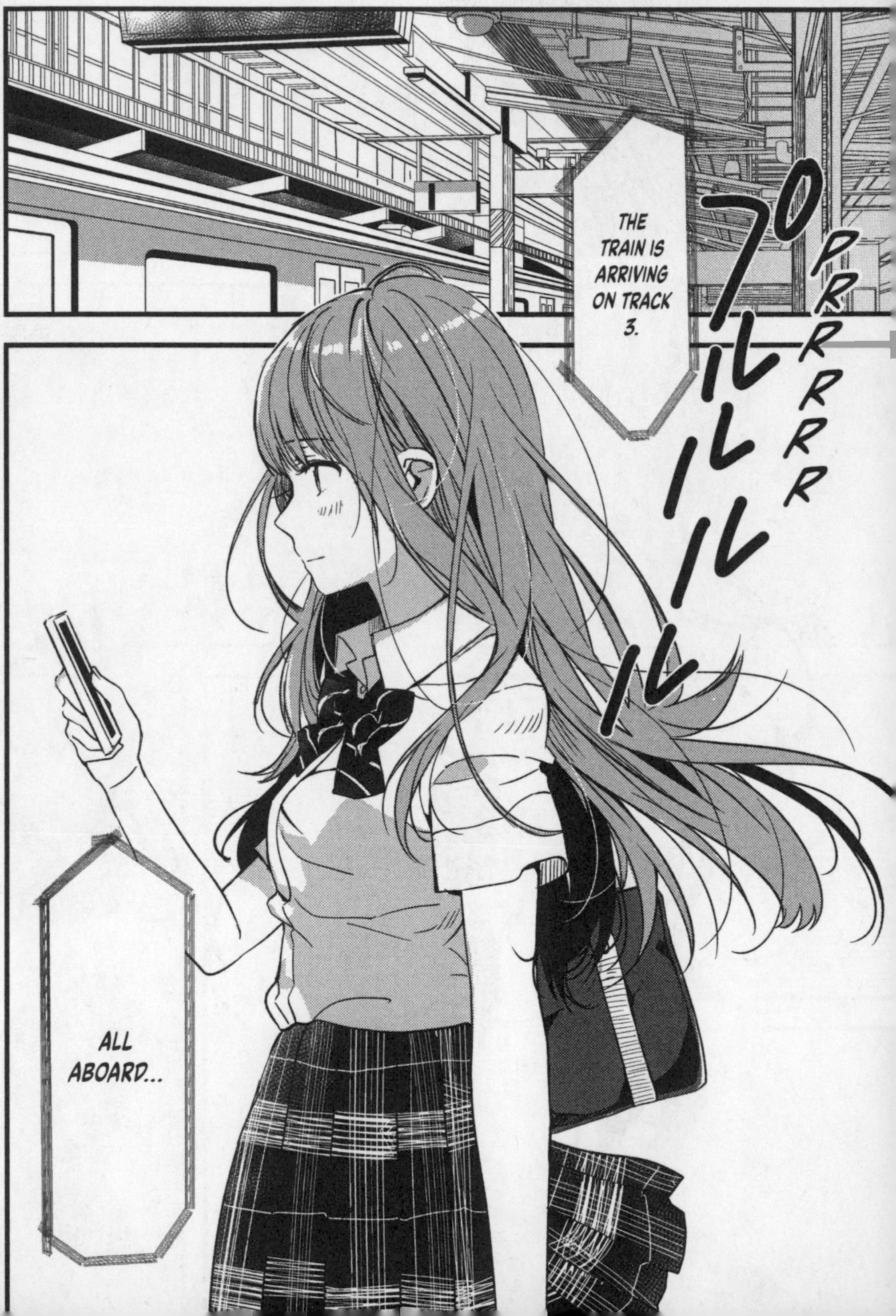
PRRRRRR
THE TRAIN IS ARRIVING ON TRACK 3.
ALL ABOARD...

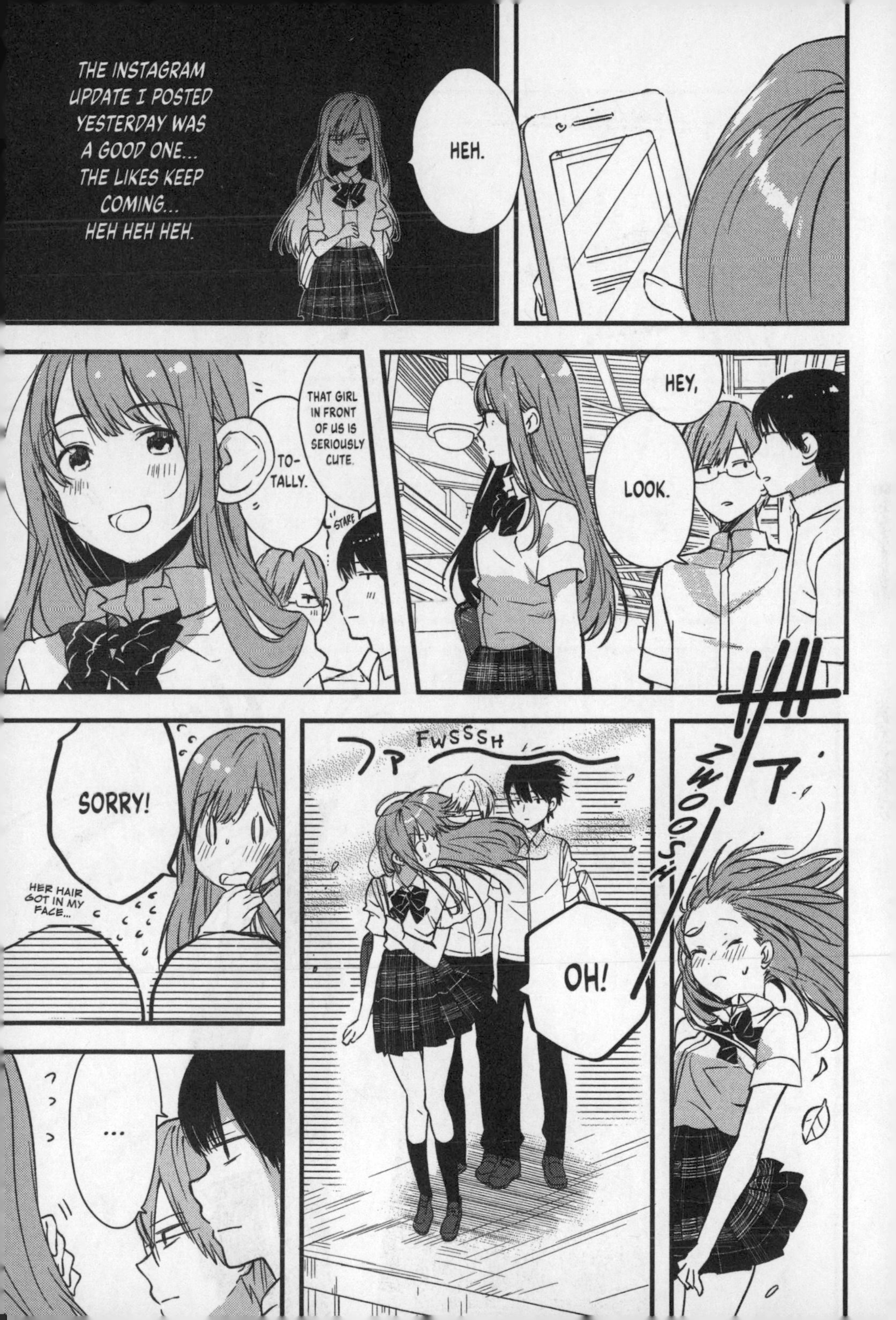
HEH.
THE INSTAGRAM UPDATE I POSTED YESTERDAY WAS A GOOD ONE... THE LIKES KEEP COMING... HEH HEH HEH.
HEY,
LOOK.
THAT GIRL IN FRONT OF US IS SERIOUSLY CUTE.
TO-TALLY.
STARE
ア
ZWOOOSH
ファ
FWSSSH
OH!
SORRY!
HER HAIR GOT IN MY FACE...
...

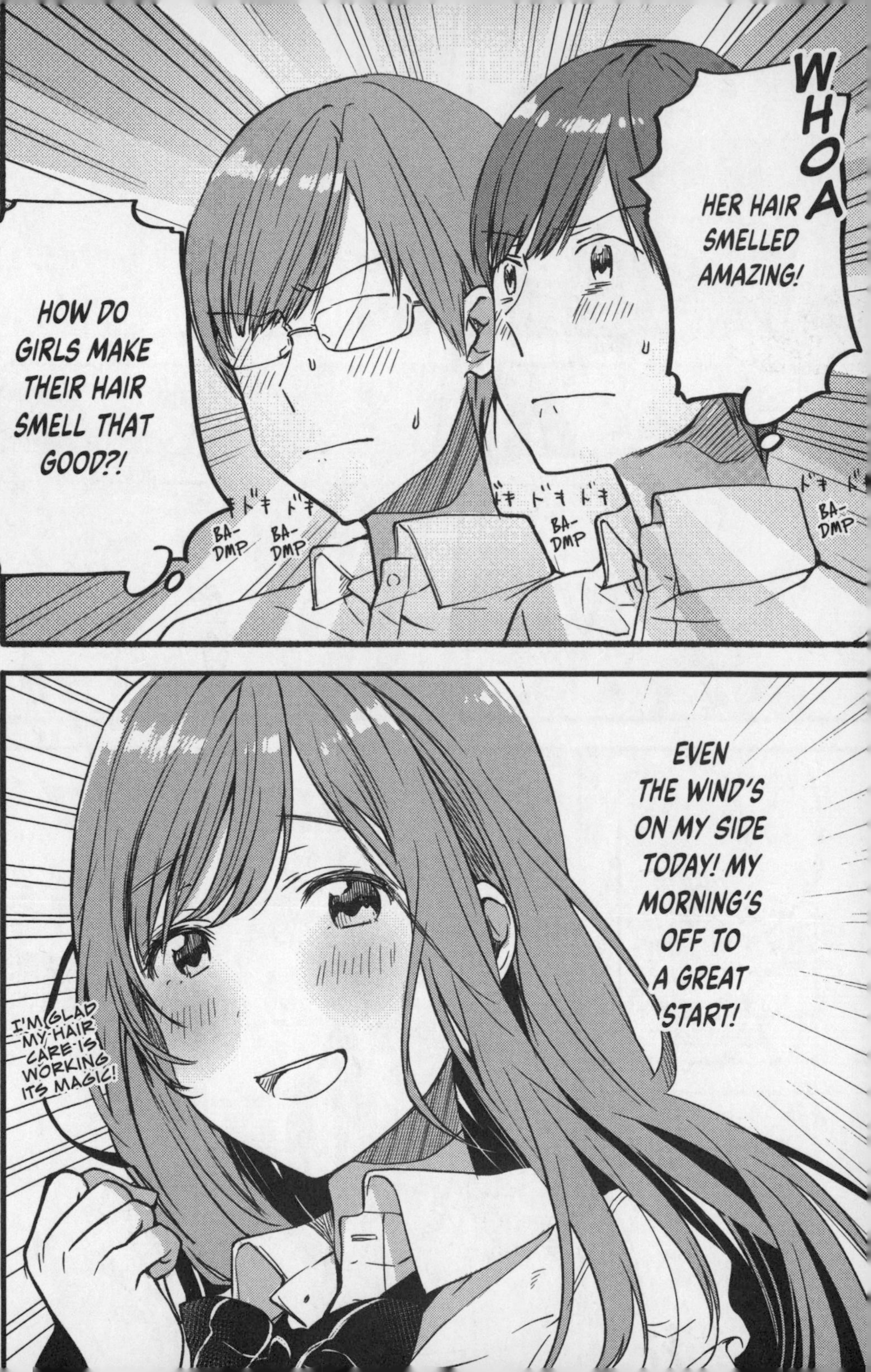
WHOA
HER HAIR SMELLED AMAZING!
ドキ
BA-DMP
ドキドキドキ
BA-DMP
ドキ ドキ
BA-DMP
BA-DMP
HOW DO GIRLS MAKE THEIR HAIR SMELL THAT GOOD?!
EVEN THE WIND'S ON MY SIDE TODAY! MY MORNING'S OFF TO A GREAT START!
I'M GLAD MY HAIR CARE IS WORKING ITS MAGIC!

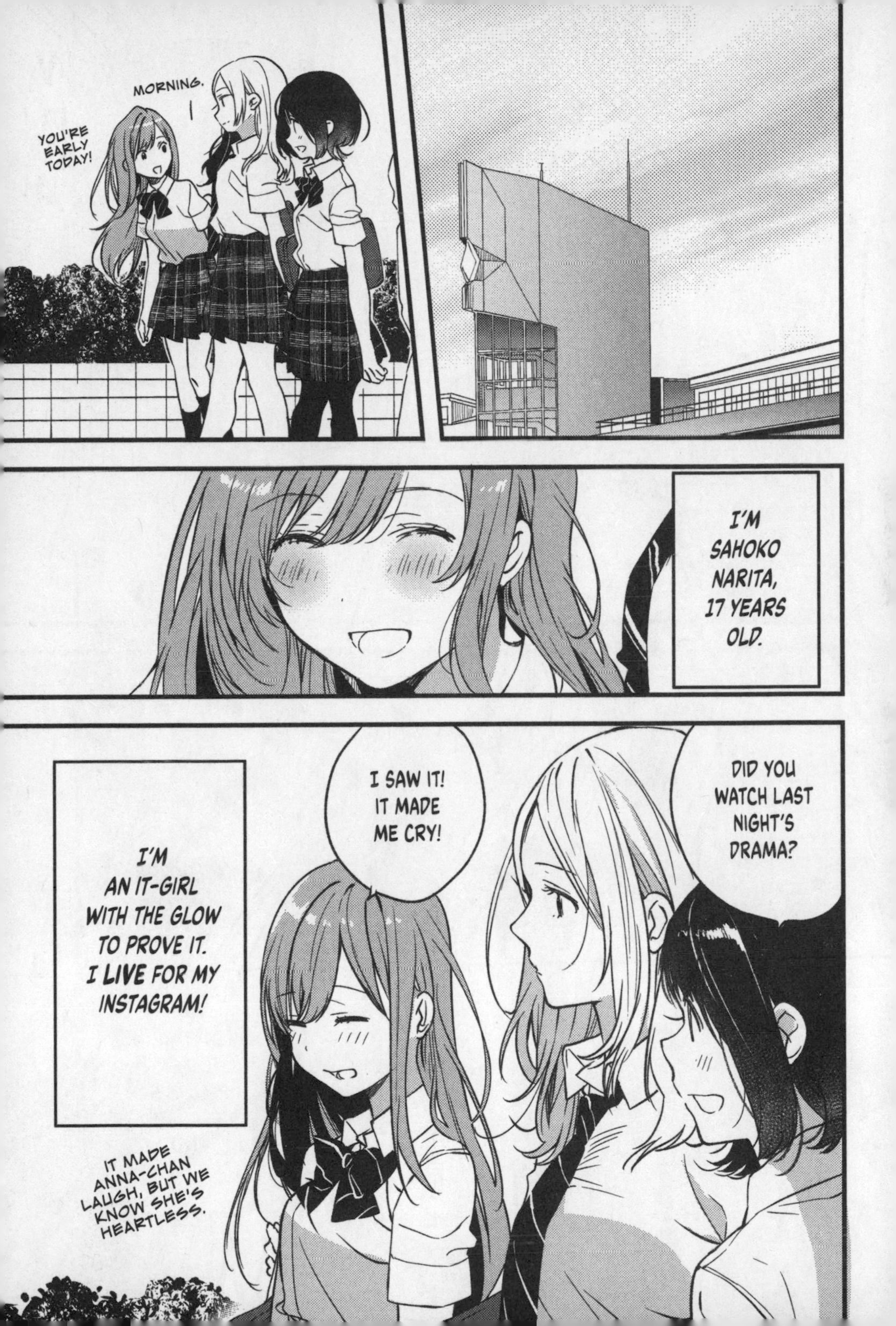
MORNING.
YOU'RE EARLY TODAY!
I'M SAHOKO NARITA, 17 YEARS OLD.
DID YOU WATCH LAST NIGHT'S DRAMA?
I SAW IT! IT MADE ME CRY!
I'M AN IT-GIRL WITH THE GLOW TO PROVE IT. I **LIVE** FOR MY INSTAGRAM!
IT MADE ANNA-CHAN LAUGH, BUT WE KNOW SHE'S HEARTLESS.

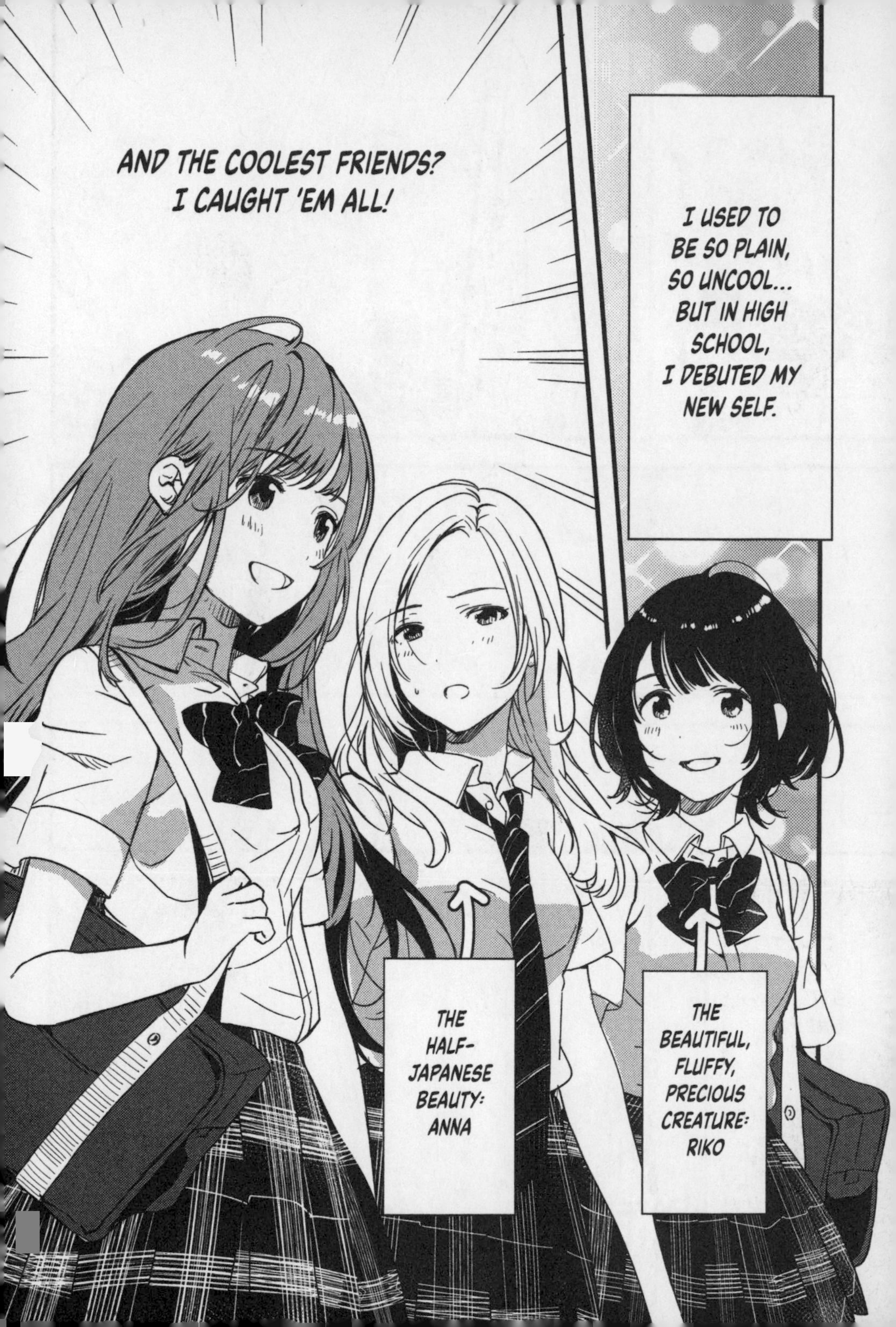
I USED TO BE SO PLAIN, SO UNCOOL... BUT IN HIGH SCHOOL, I DEBUTED MY NEW SELF.
AND THE COOLEST FRIENDS? I CAUGHT 'EM ALL!
THE BEAUTIFUL, FLUFFY, PRECIOUS CREATURE: RIKO
THE HALF-JAPANESE BEAUTY: ANNA

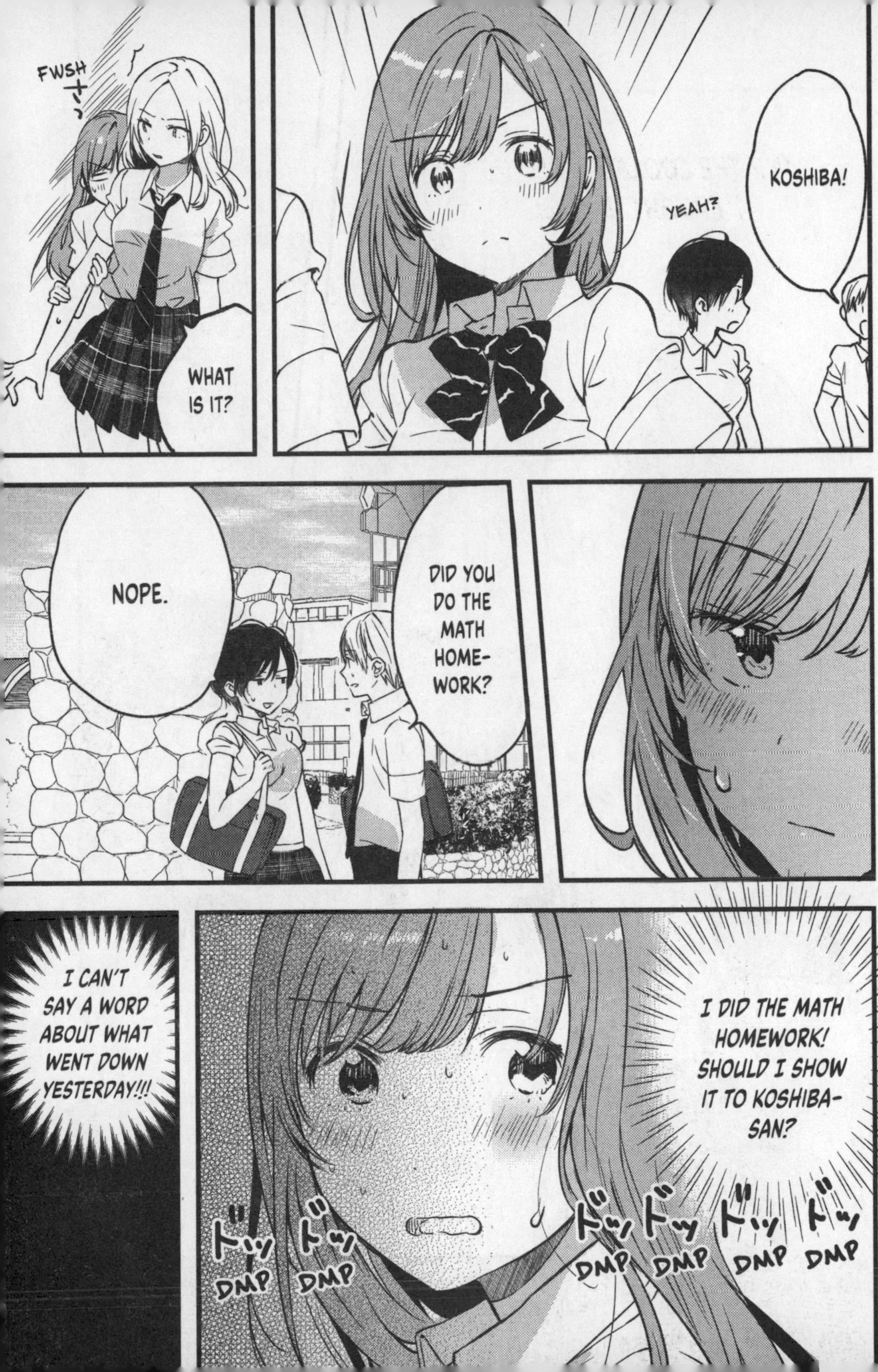
KOSHIBA!
YEAH?
FWSH さっ
WHAT IS IT?
DID YOU DO THE MATH HOMEWORK?
NOPE.
I DID THE MATH HOMEWORK! SHOULD I SHOW IT TO KOSHIBA-SAN?
ドッ DMP ドッ DMP ドッ DMP ドッ DMP
ドッ DMP ドッ DMP
I CAN'T SAY A WORD ABOUT WHAT WENT DOWN YESTERDAY!!!

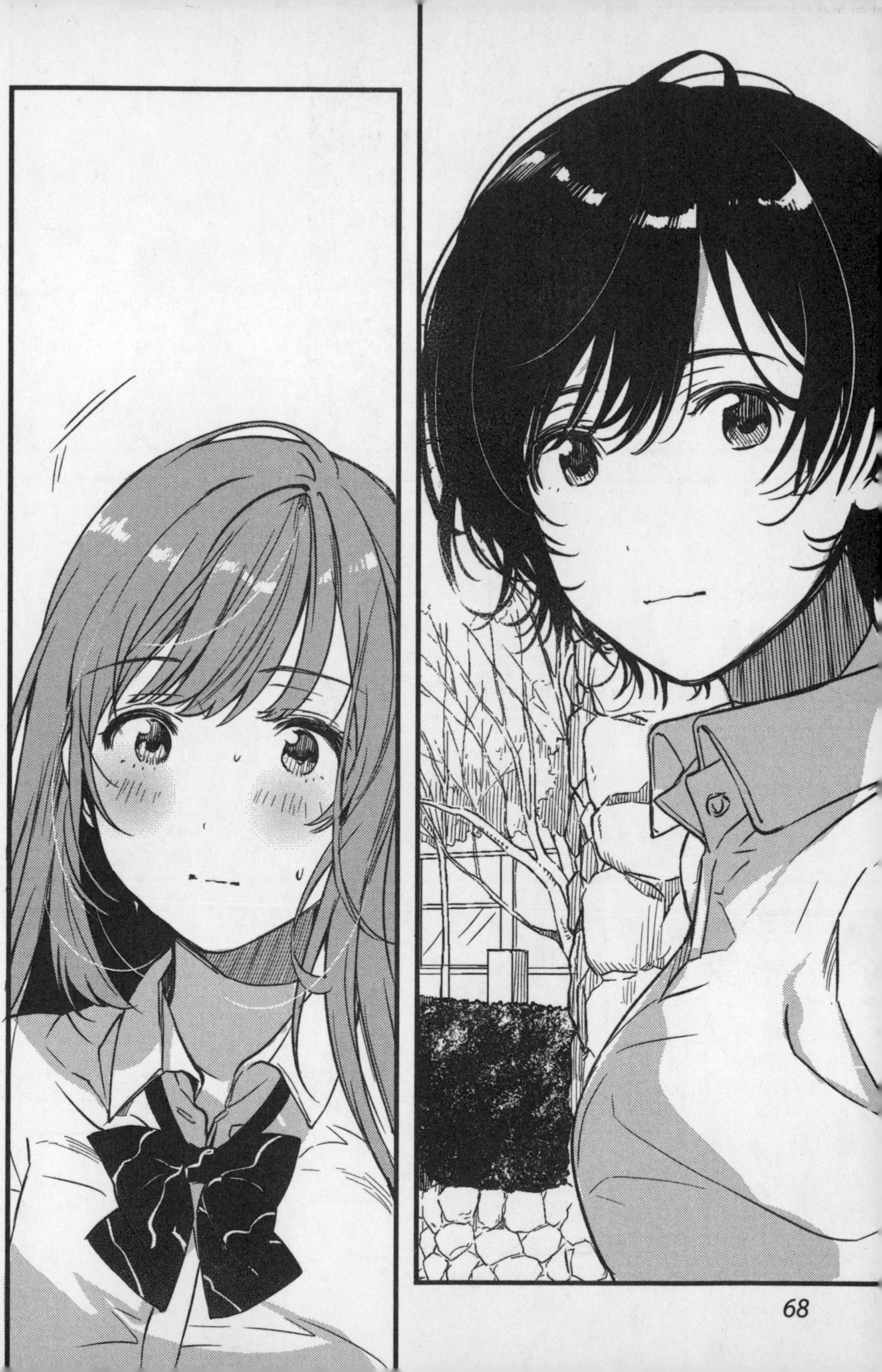

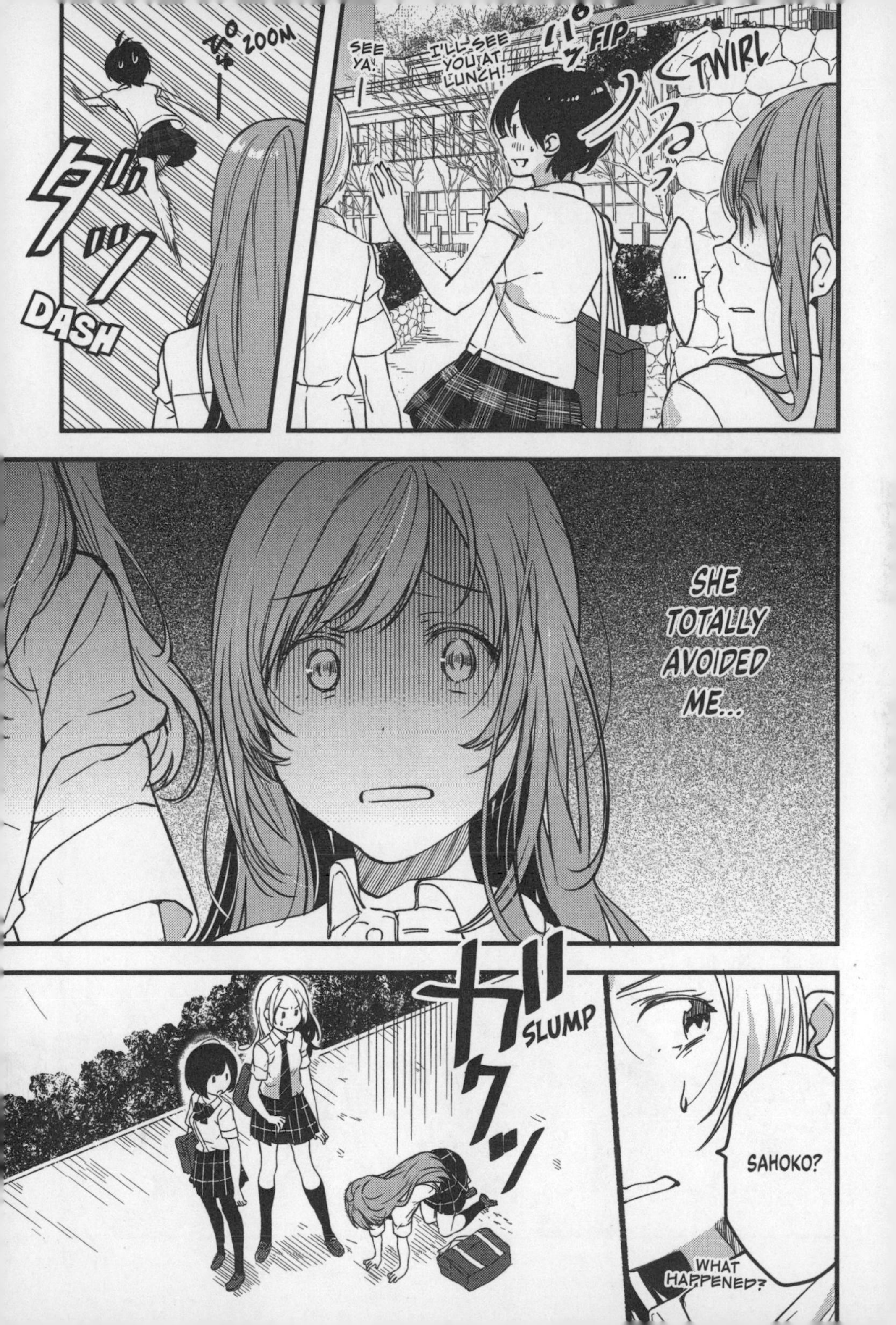
TWIRL
FIP
I'LL SEE YOU AT LUNCH!
SEE YA!
...
ZOOM
DASH
SHE TOTALLY AVOIDED ME...
SAHOKO?
WHAT HAPPENED?
SLUMP

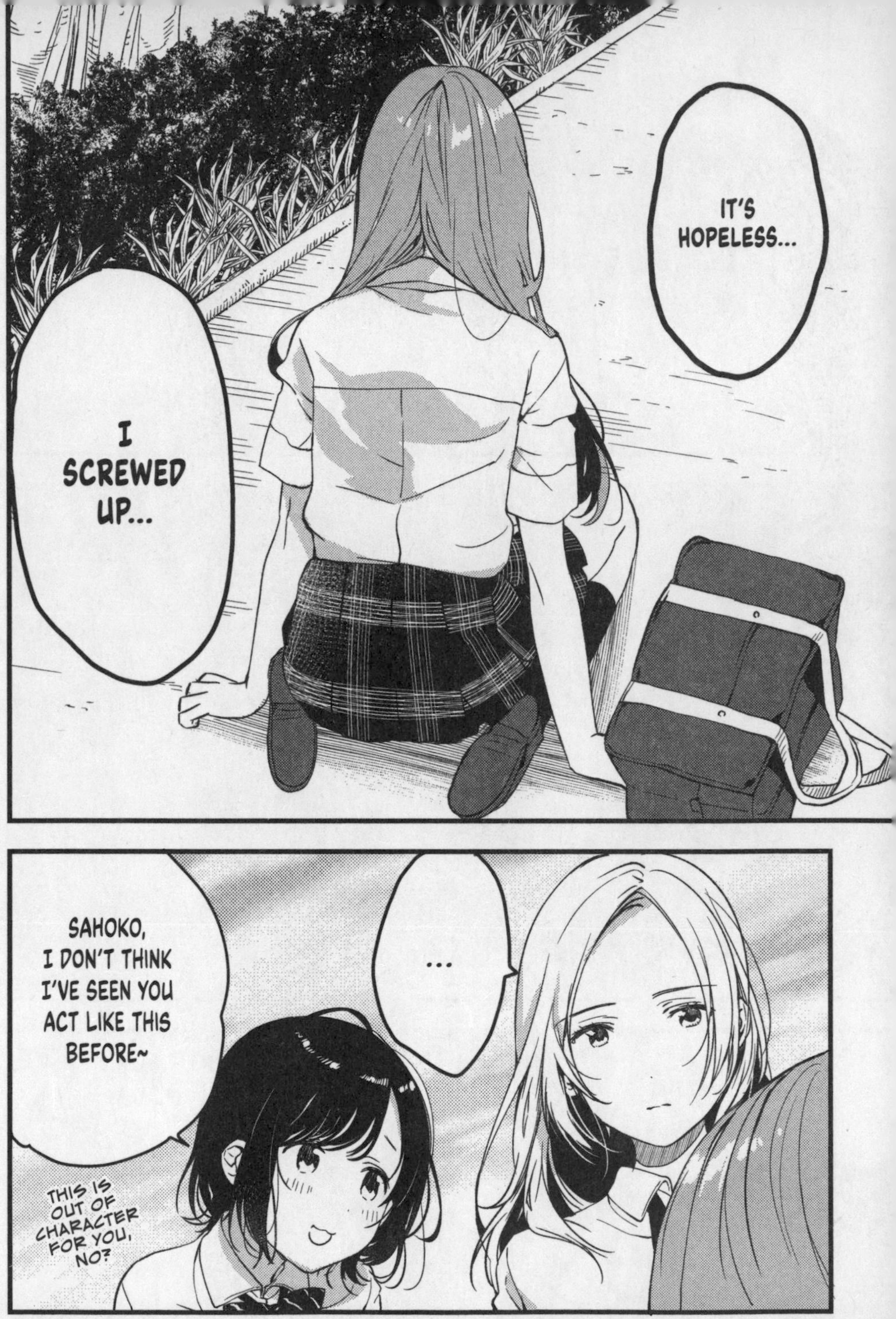
IT'S HOPELESS...
I SCREWED UP...
...
SAHOKO, I DON'T THINK I'VE SEEN YOU ACT LIKE THIS BEFORE~
THIS IS OUT OF CHARACTER FOR YOU, NO?

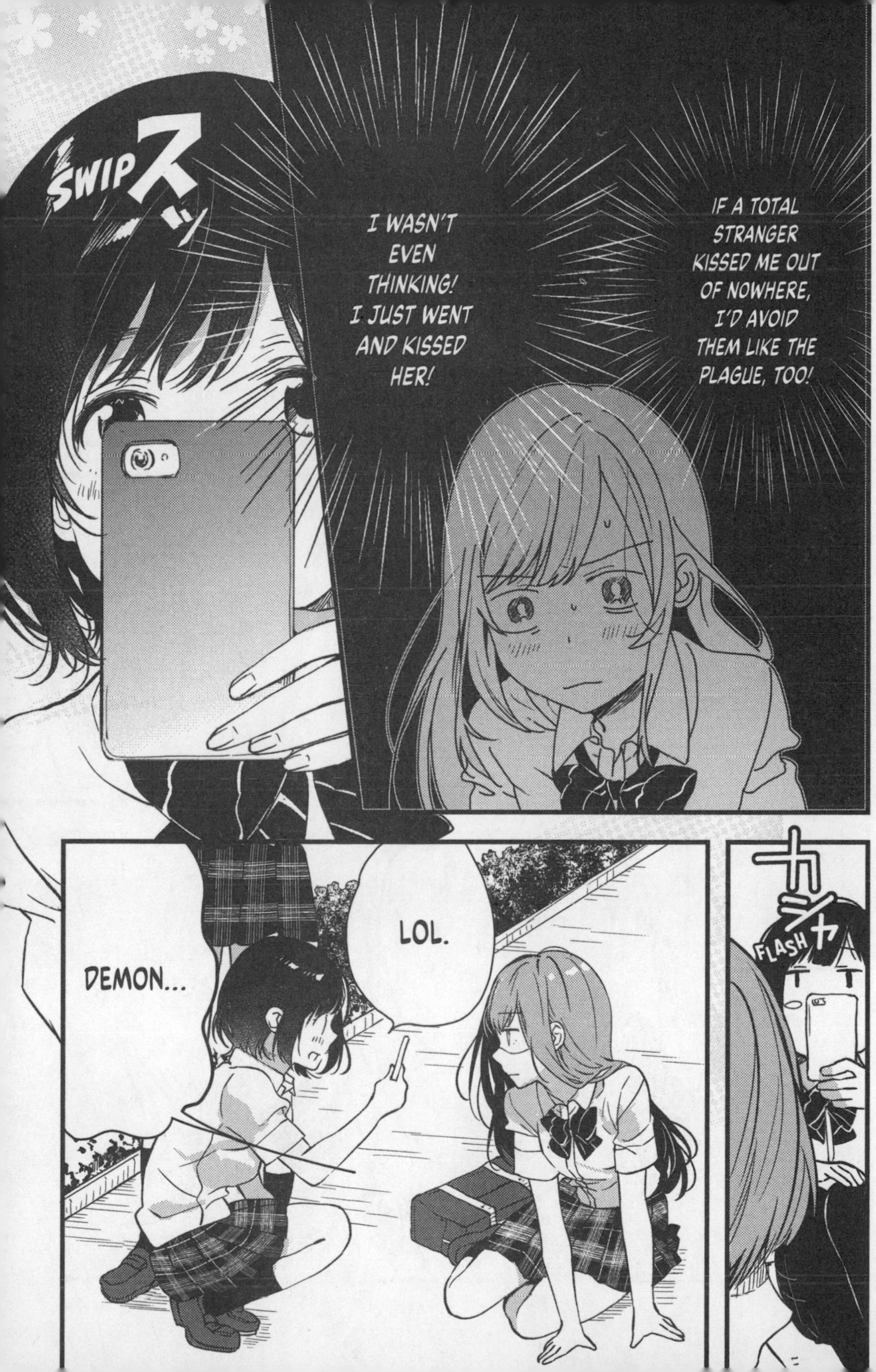
IF A TOTAL STRANGER KISSED ME OUT OF NOWHERE, I'D AVOID THEM LIKE THE PLAGUE, TOO!
I WASN'T EVEN THINKING! I JUST WENT AND KISSED HER!
SWIP
FLASH
LOL.
DEMON...

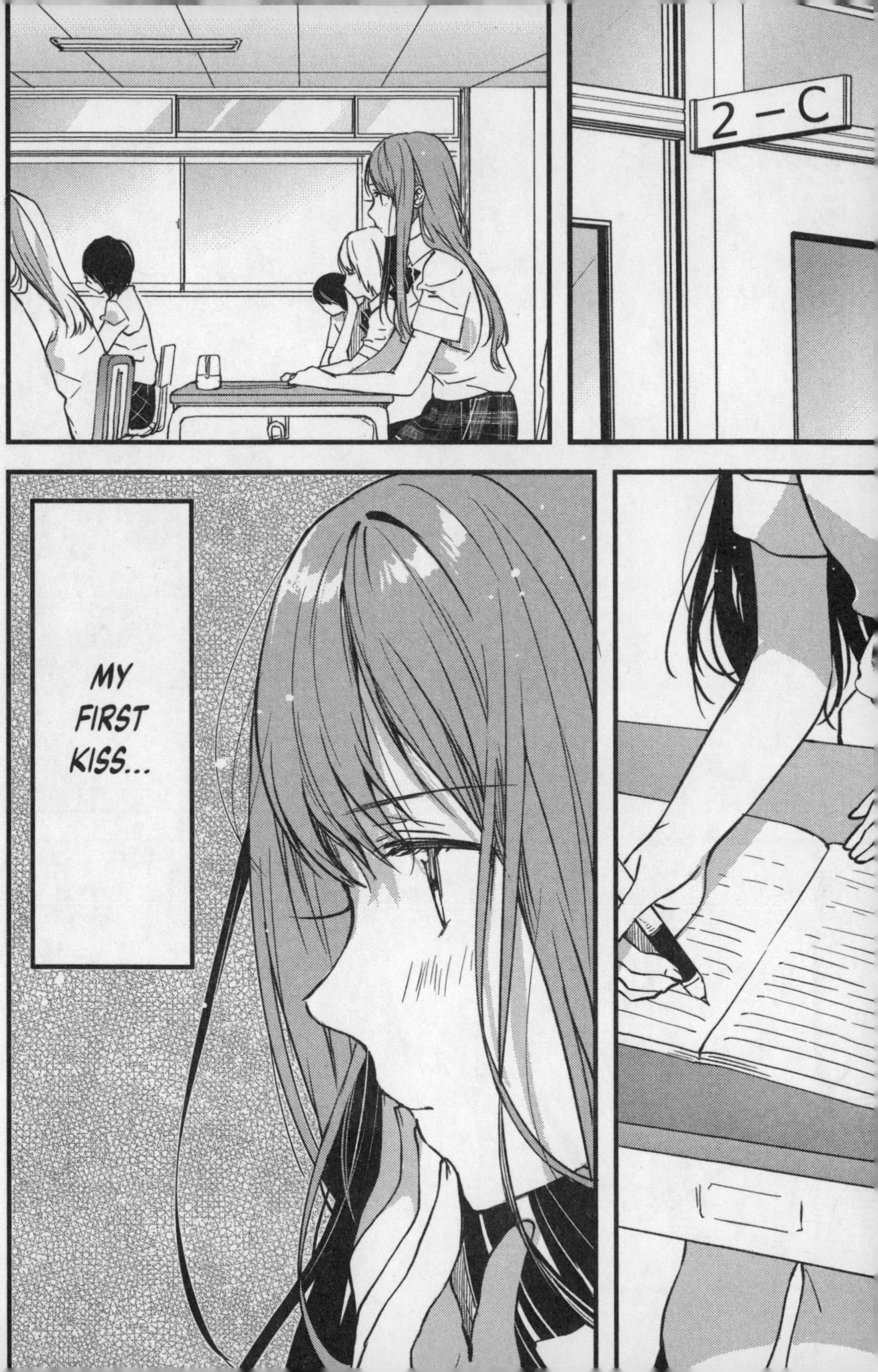
2-C
MY FIRST KISS...

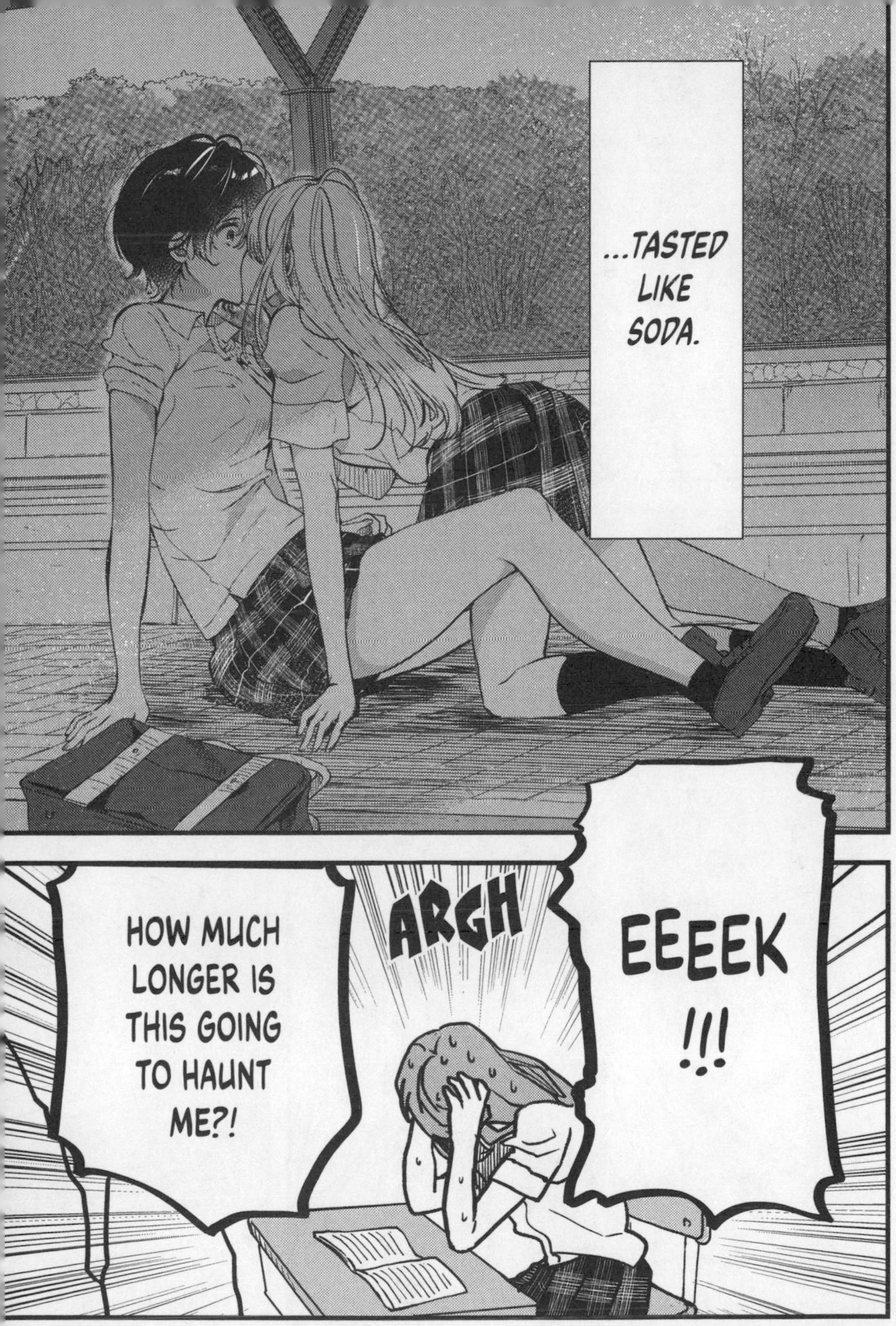
...TASTED LIKE SODA.
EEEEK !!!
ARGH
HOW MUCH LONGER IS THIS GOING TO HAUNT ME?!

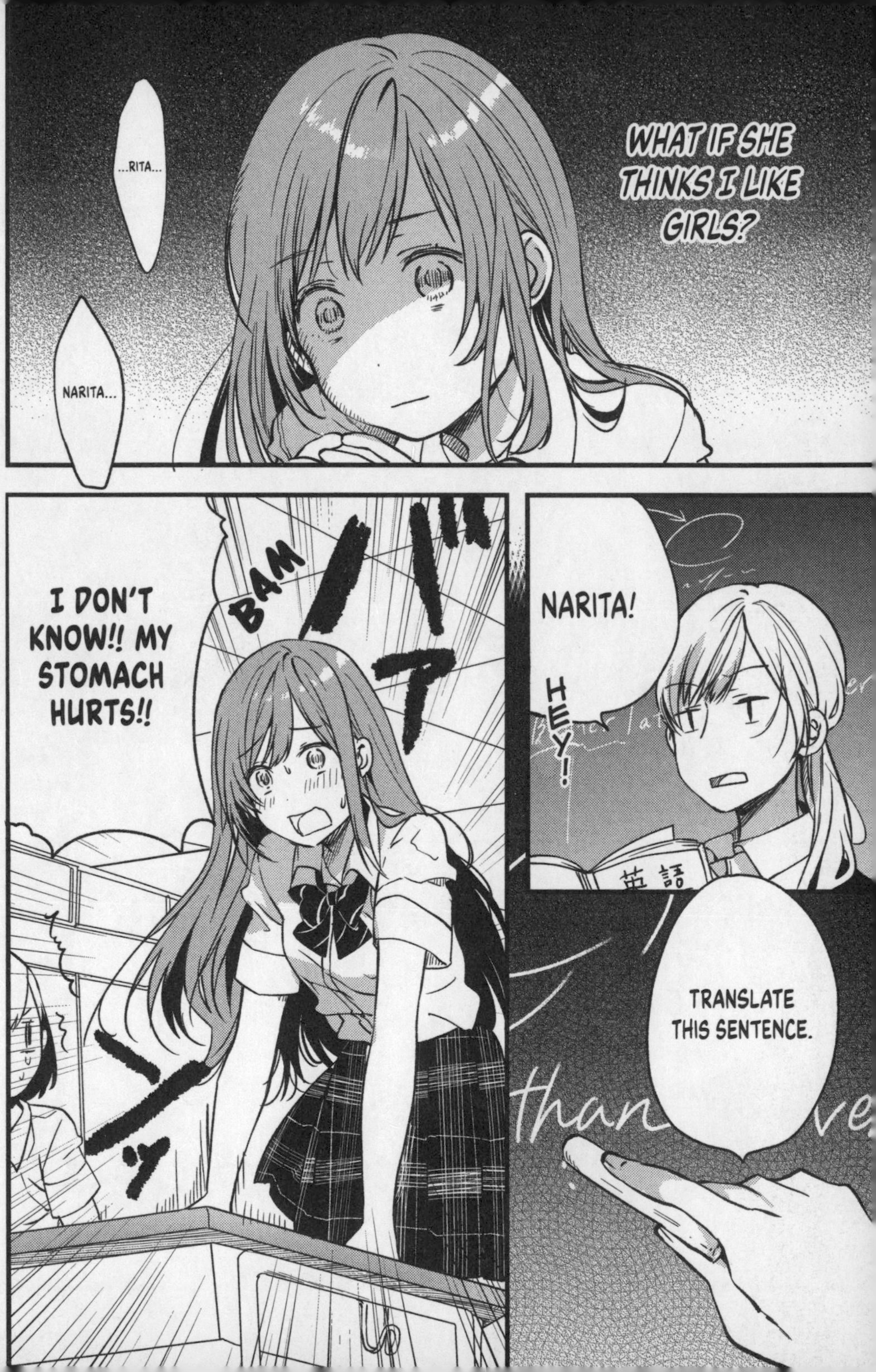
WHAT IF SHE THINKS I LIKE GIRLS?
...RITA...
NARITA...
NARITA!
HEY!
英語
TRANSLATE THIS SENTENCE.
BAM
I DON'T KNOW!! MY STOMACH HURTS!!

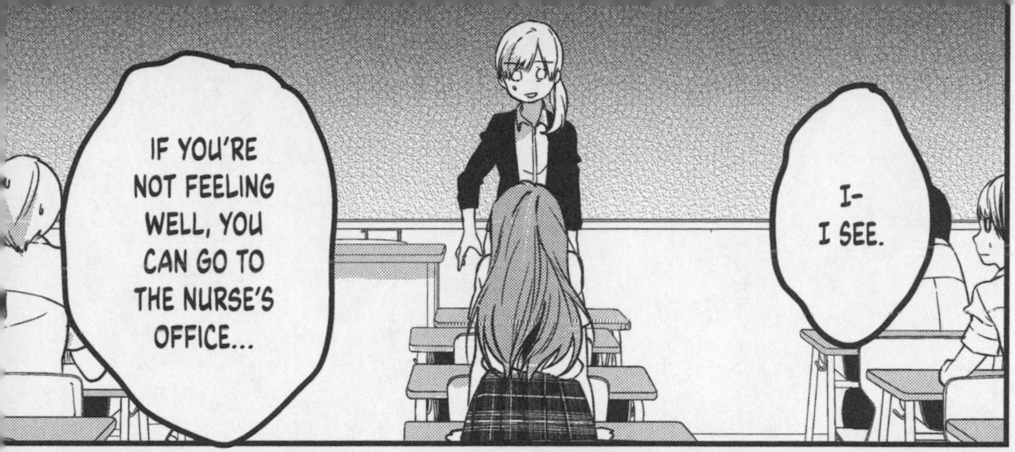
I- I SEE.
IF YOU'RE NOT FEELING WELL, YOU CAN GO TO THE NURSE'S OFFICE...

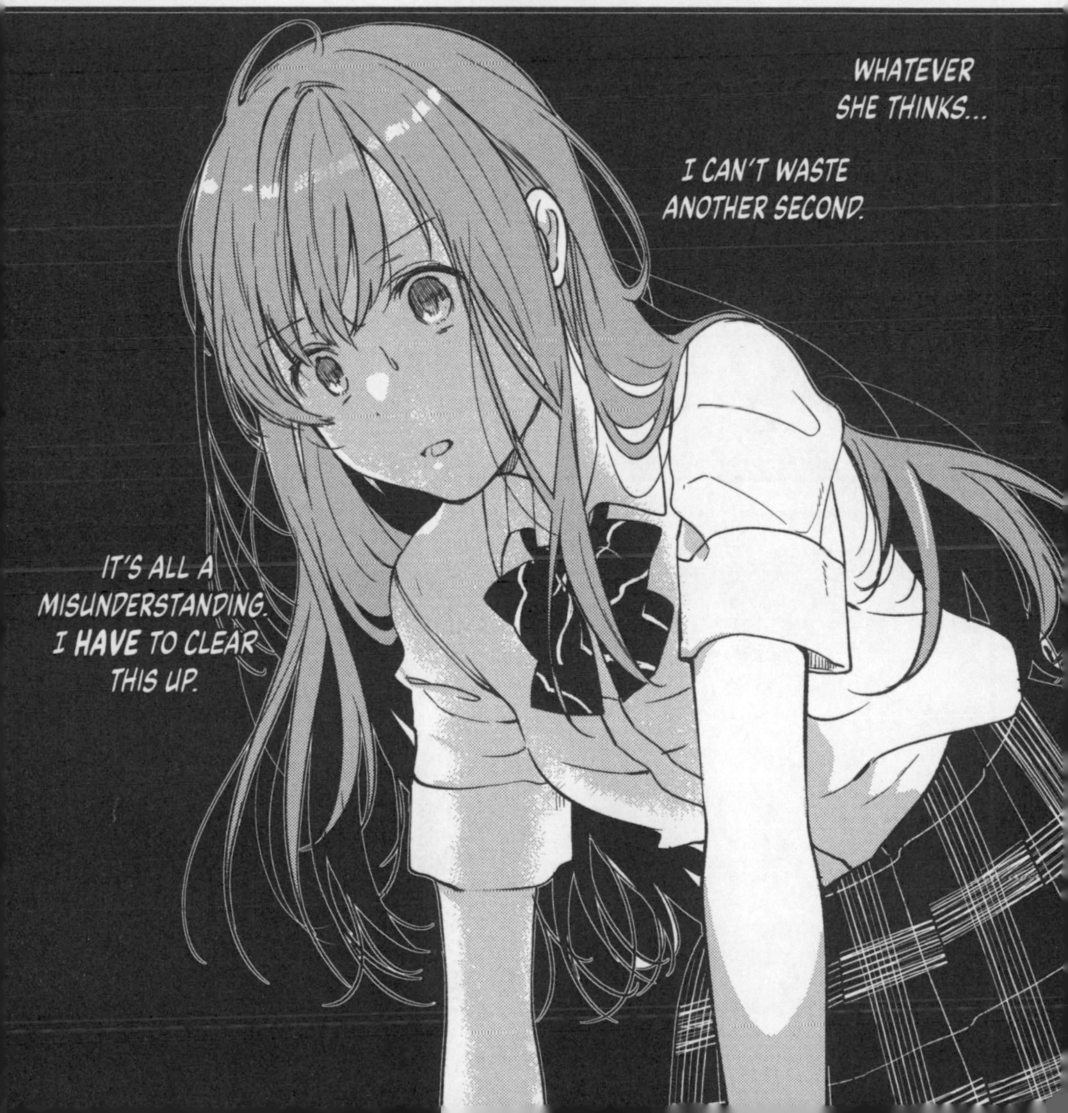
WHATEVER SHE THINKS...
I CAN'T WASTE ANOTHER SECOND.
IT'S ALL A MISUNDERSTANDING. I HAVE TO CLEAR THIS UP.

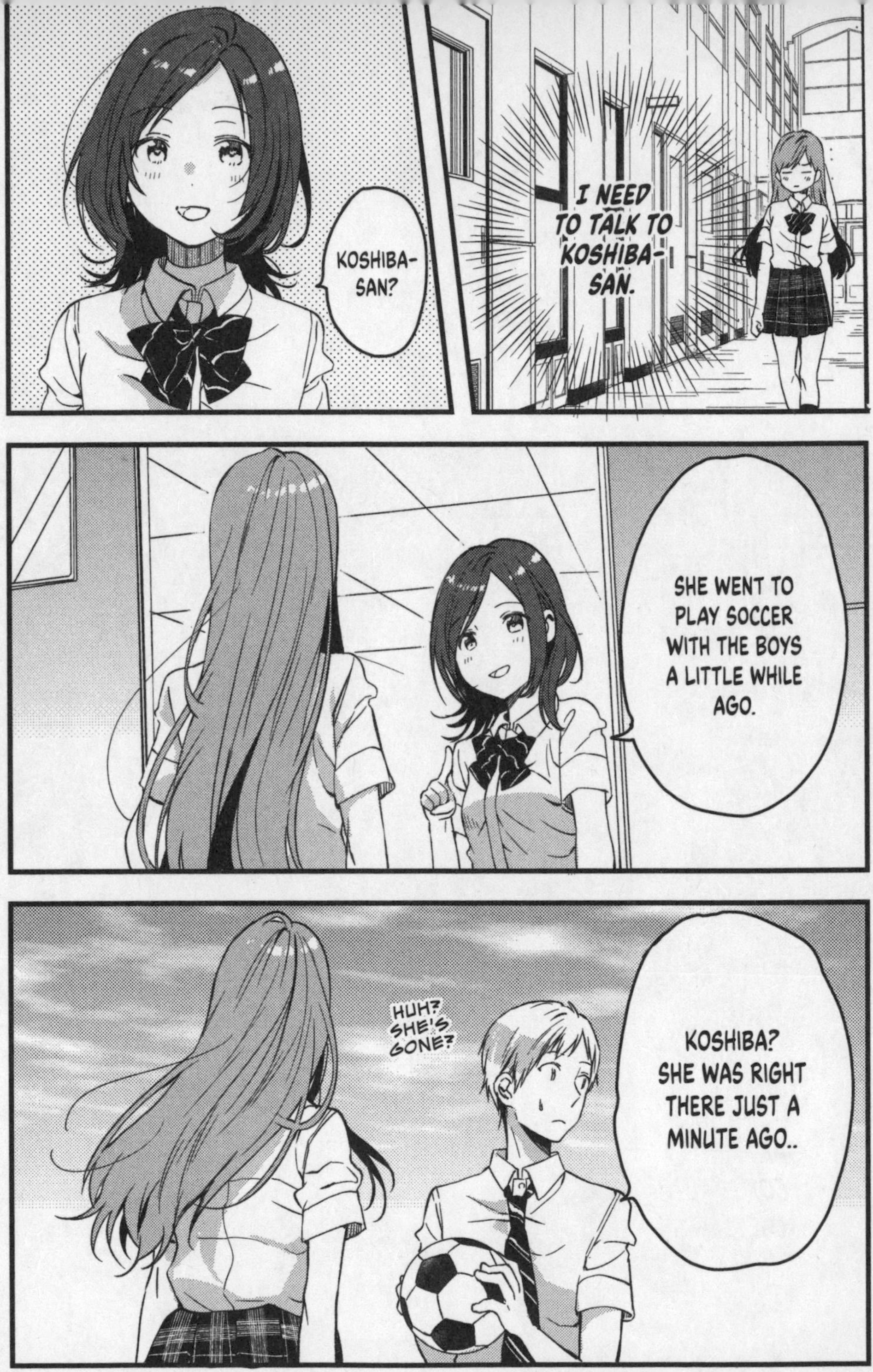
I NEED TO TALK TO KOSHIBA-SAN.
KOSHIBA-SAN?
SHE WENT TO PLAY SOCCER WITH THE BOYS A LITTLE WHILE AGO.
KOSHIBA? SHE WAS RIGHT THERE JUST A MINUTE AGO..
HUH? SHE'S GONE?

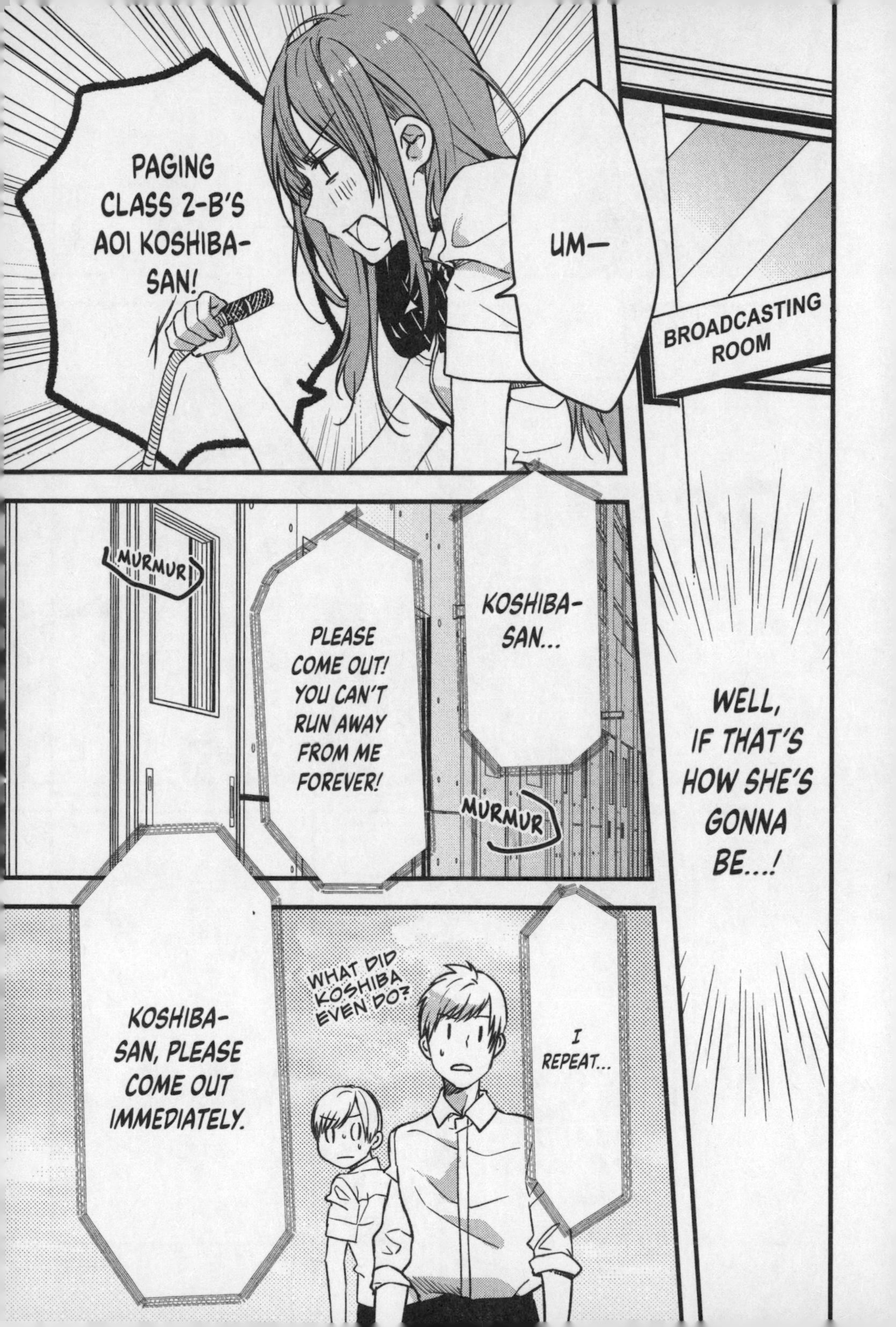
BROADCASTING ROOM
WELL, IF THAT'S HOW SHE'S GONNA BE...!
UM—
PAGING CLASS 2-B'S AOI KOSHIBA-SAN!
KOSHIBA-SAN...
PLEASE COME OUT! YOU CAN'T RUN AWAY FROM ME FOREVER!
MURMUR
MURMUR
I REPEAT...
WHAT DID KOSHIBA EVEN DO?
KOSHIBA-SAN, PLEASE COME OUT IMMEDIATELY.

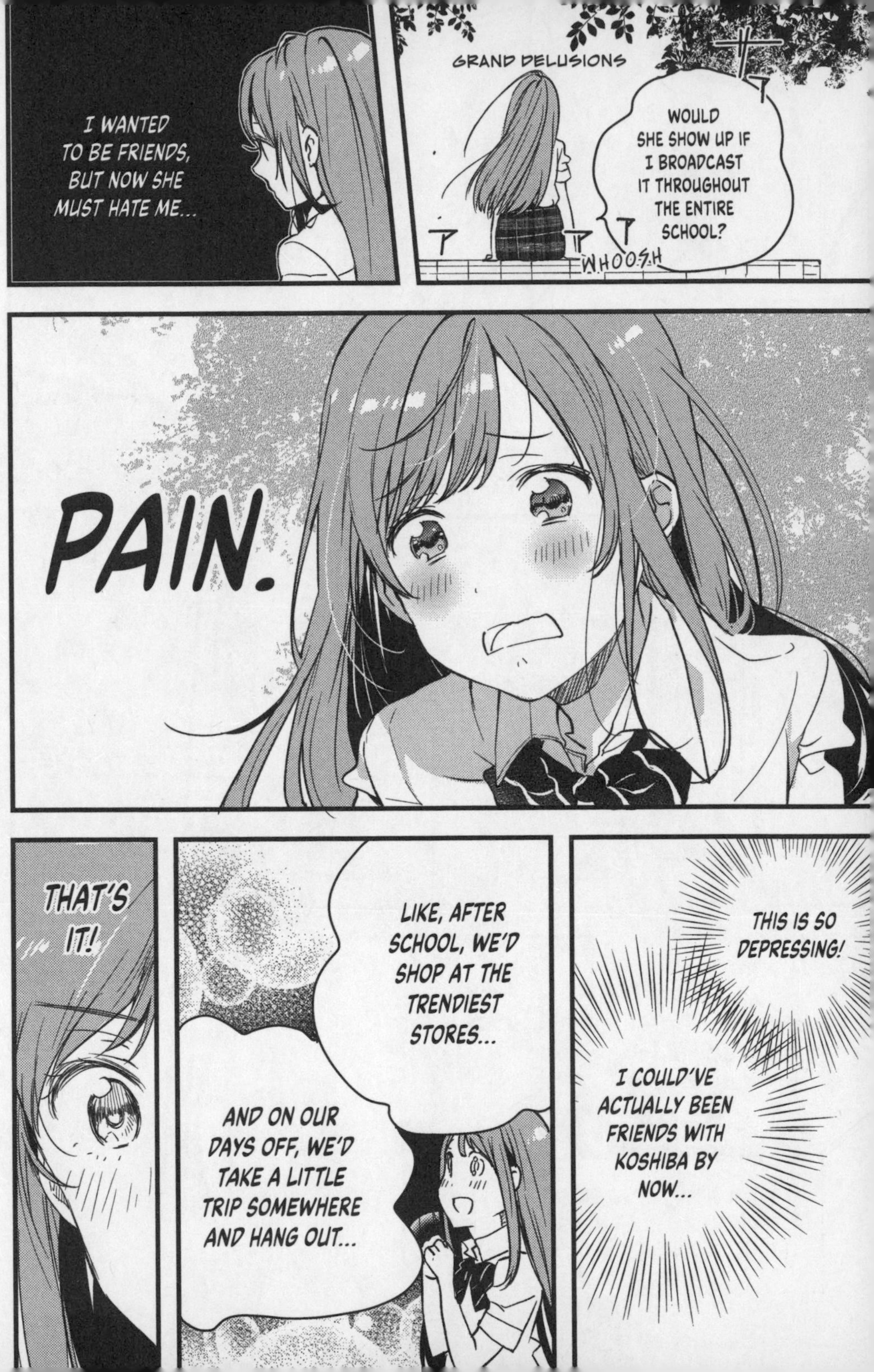
GRAND DELUSIONS
WOULD SHE SHOW UP IF I BROADCAST IT THROUGHOUT THE ENTIRE SCHOOL?
WHOOSH
I WANTED TO BE FRIENDS, BUT NOW SHE MUST HATE ME...
PAIN.
THIS IS SO DEPRESSING!
I COULD'VE ACTUALLY BEEN FRIENDS WITH KOSHIBA BY NOW...
LIKE, AFTER SCHOOL, WE'D SHOP AT THE TRENDIEST STORES...
AND ON OUR DAYS OFF, WE'D TAKE A LITTLE TRIP SOMEWHERE AND HANG OUT...
THAT'S IT!

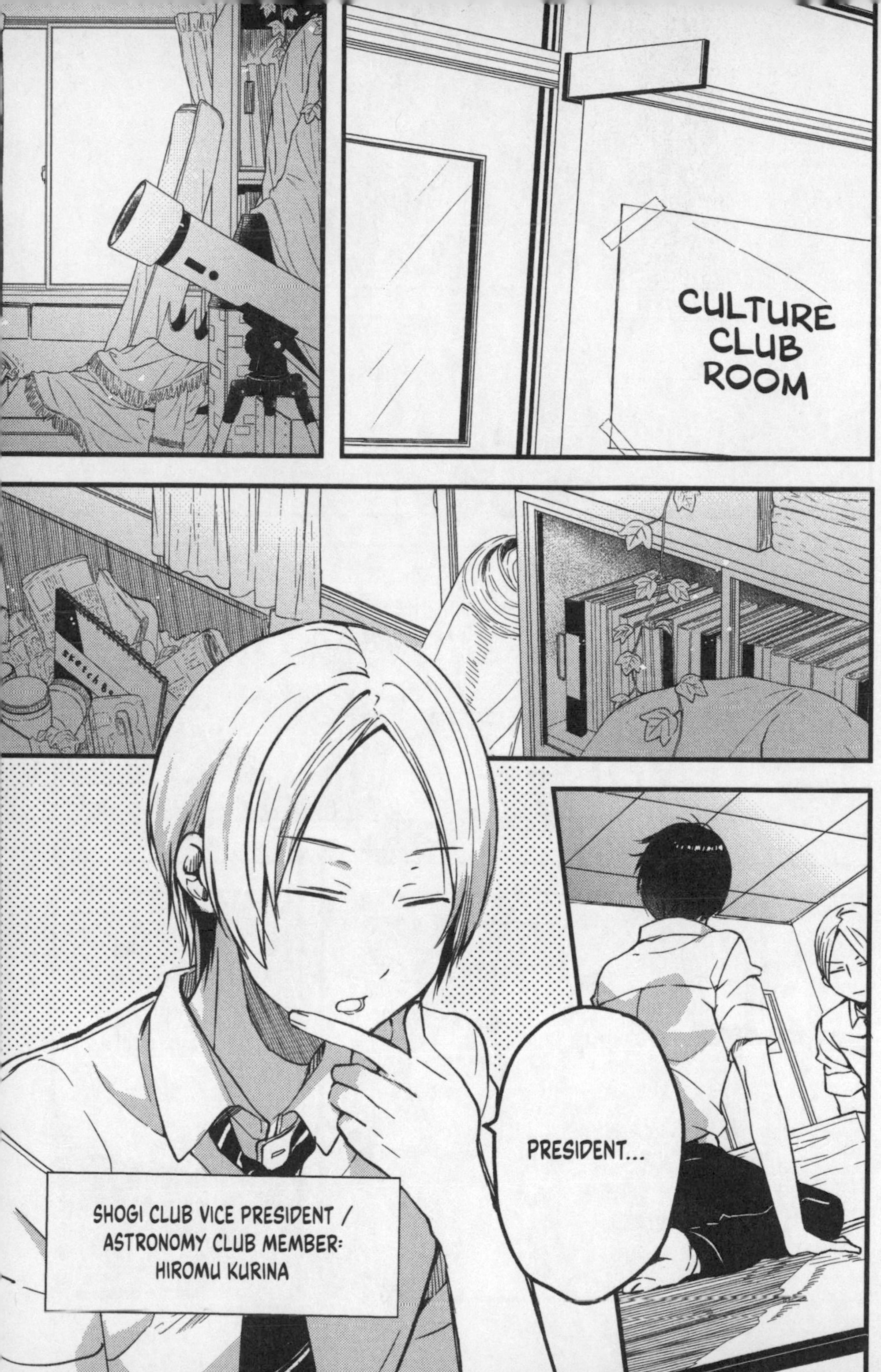
CULTURE CLUB ROOM
PRESIDENT...
SHOGI CLUB VICE PRESIDENT / ASTRONOMY CLUB MEMBER: HIROMU KURINA

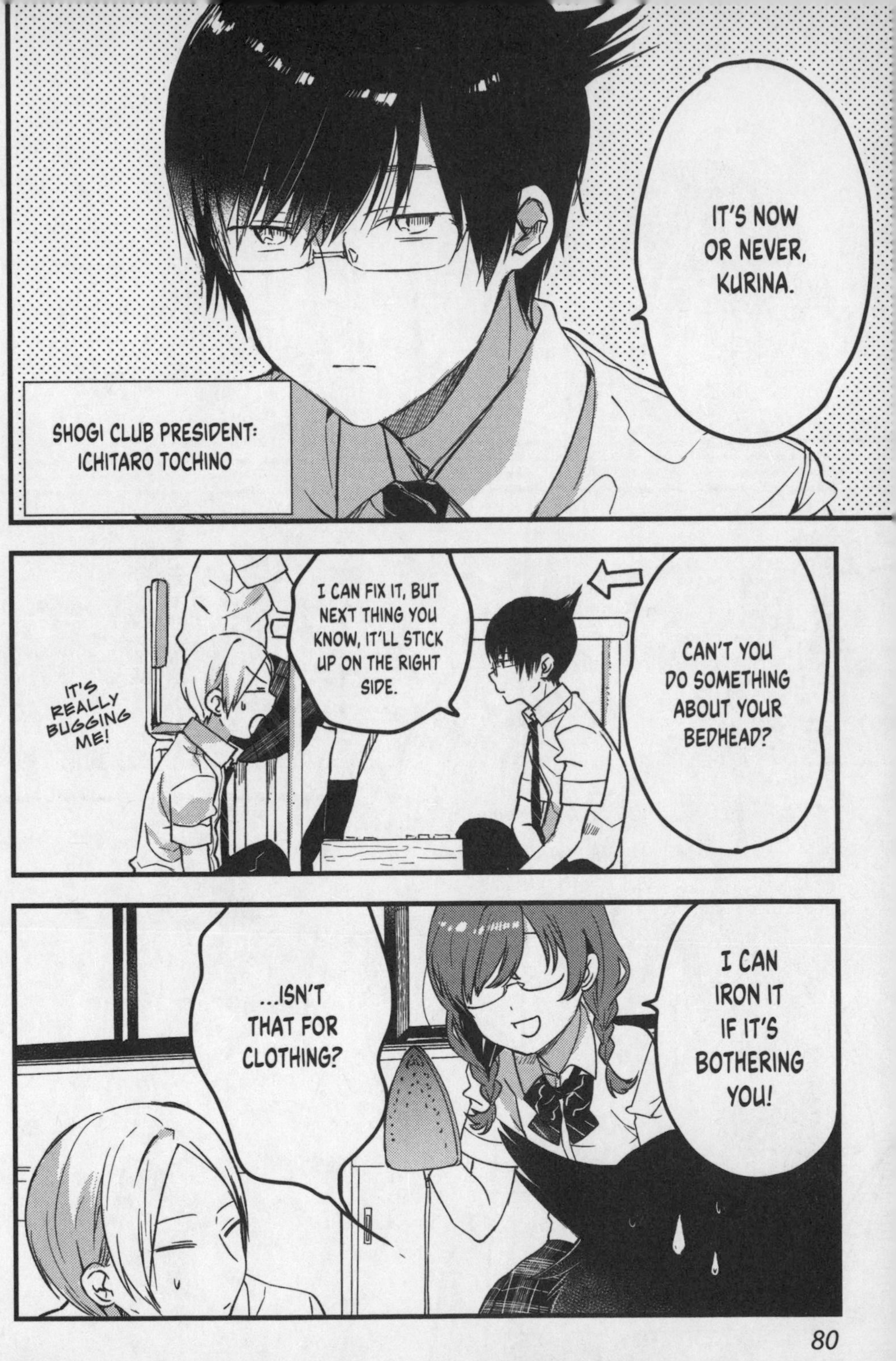
IT'S NOW OR NEVER, KURINA.
SHOGI CLUB PRESIDENT: ICHITARO TOCHINO
CAN'T YOU DO SOMETHING ABOUT YOUR BEDHEAD?
I CAN FIX IT, BUT NEXT THING YOU KNOW, IT'LL STICK UP ON THE RIGHT SIDE.
IT'S REALLY BUGGING ME!
I CAN IRON IT IF IT'S BOTHERING YOU!
...ISN'T THAT FOR CLOTHING?

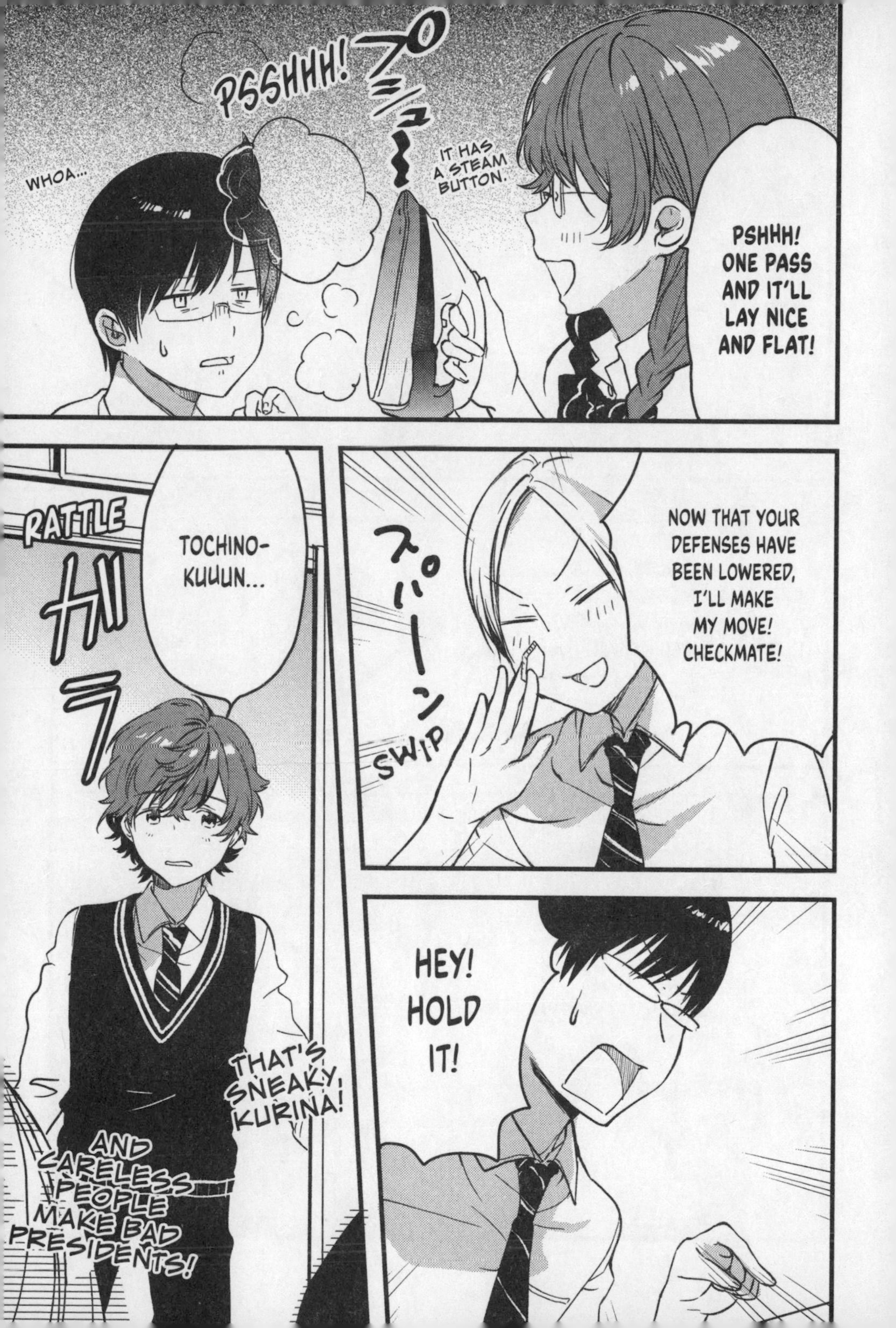
PSHHH! ONE PASS AND IT'LL LAY NICE AND FLAT!
IT HAS A STEAM BUTTON.
PSSHHH!
プシュ〜
WHOA...
NOW THAT YOUR DEFENSES HAVE BEEN LOWERED, I'LL MAKE MY MOVE! CHECKMATE!
スパーン
SWIP
HEY! HOLD IT!
RATTLE
ガラ
TOCHINO-KUUUN...
THAT'S SNEAKY KURINA!
AND CARELESS PEOPLE MAKE BAD PRESIDENTS!

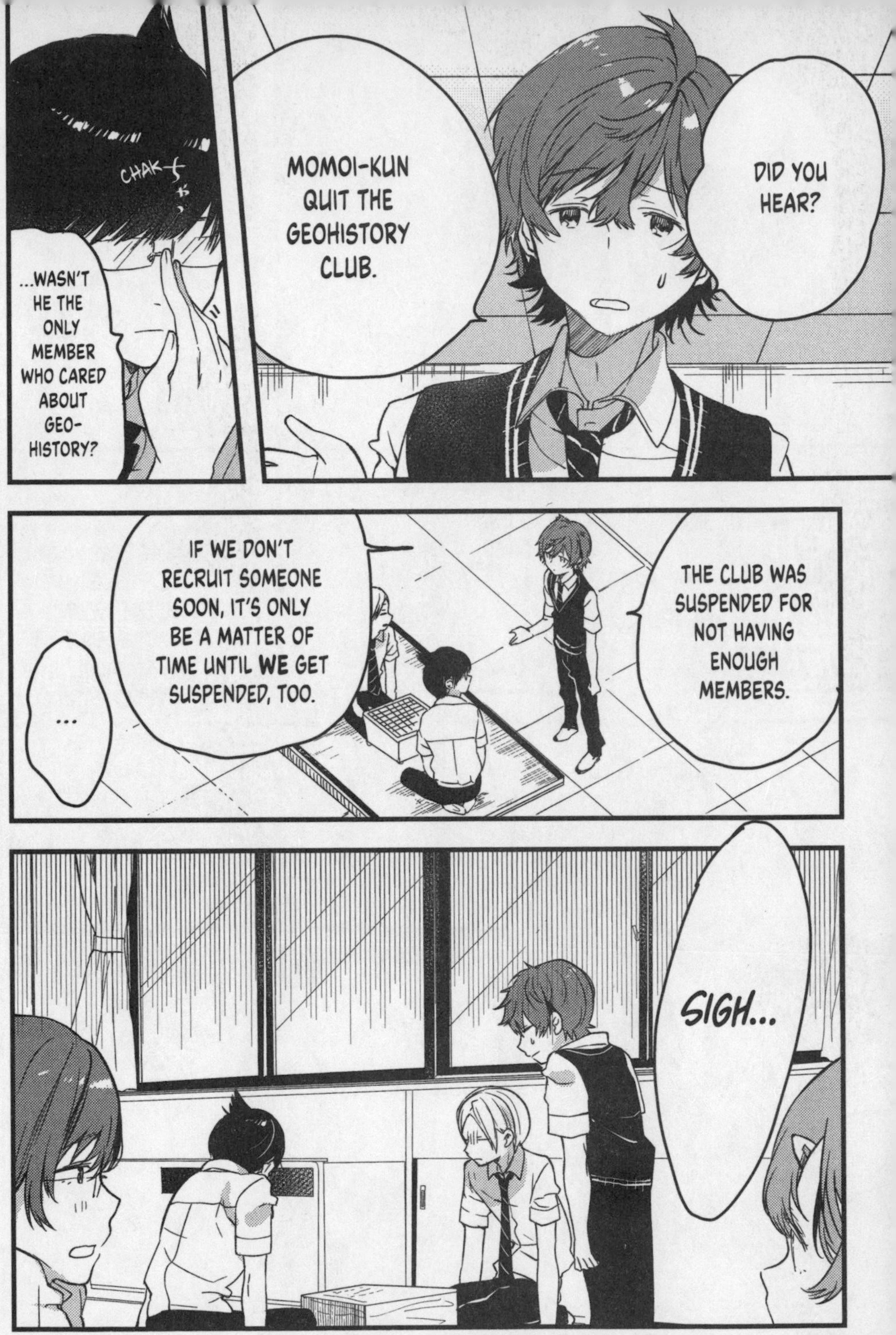
DID YOU HEAR?
MOMOI-KUN QUIT THE GEOHISTORY CLUB.
CHAK
...WASN'T HE THE ONLY MEMBER WHO CARED ABOUT GEO-HISTORY?
THE CLUB WAS SUSPENDED FOR NOT HAVING ENOUGH MEMBERS.
IF WE DON'T RECRUIT SOMEONE SOON, IT'S ONLY BE A MATTER OF TIME UNTIL WE GET SUSPENDED, TOO.
...
SIGH...

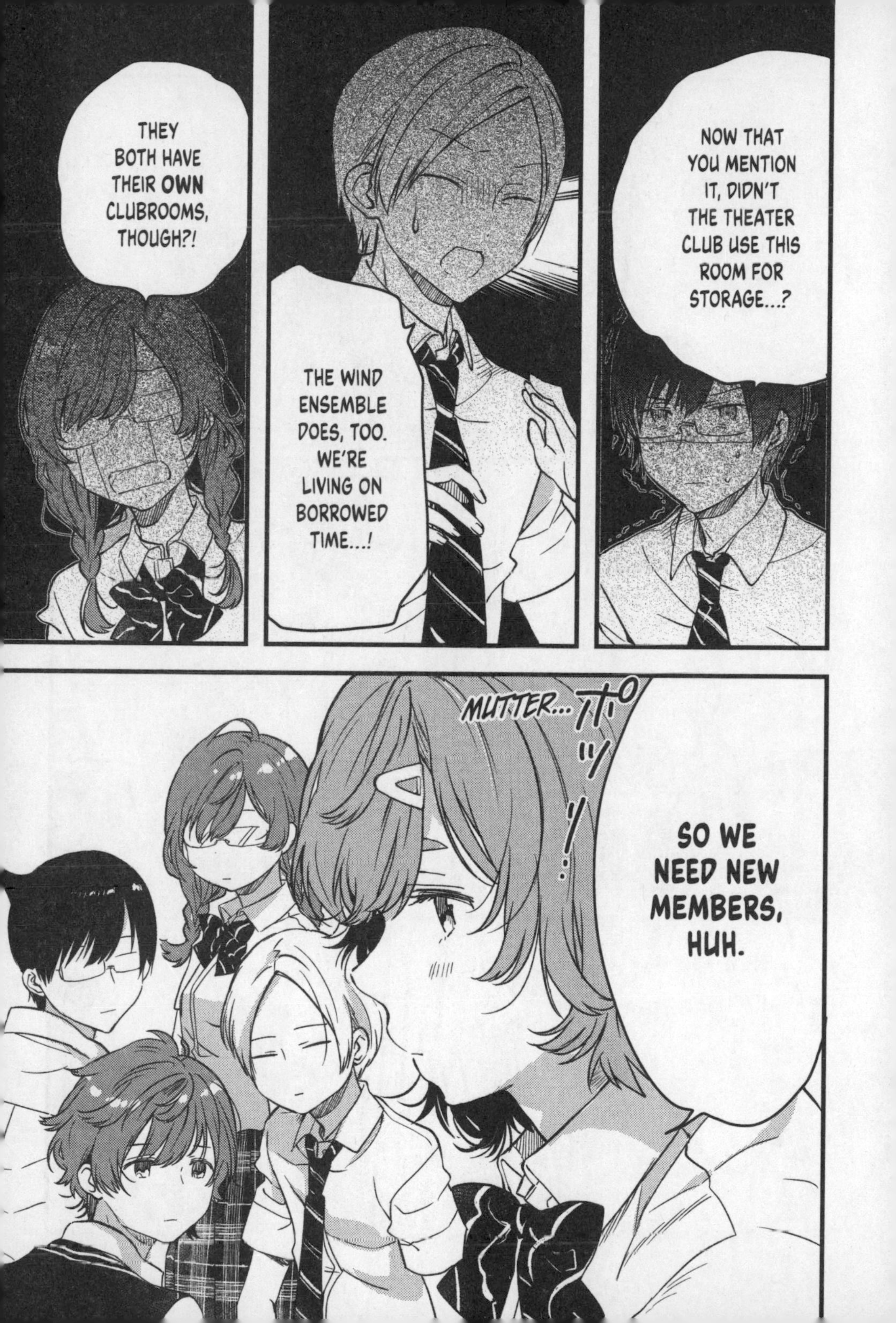
NOW THAT YOU MENTION IT, DIDN'T THE THEATER CLUB USE THIS ROOM FOR STORAGE...?
THE WIND ENSEMBLE DOES, TOO. WE'RE LIVING ON BORROWED TIME...!
THEY BOTH HAVE THEIR OWN CLUBROOMS, THOUGH?!
MUTTER...
SO WE NEED NEW MEMBERS, HUH.

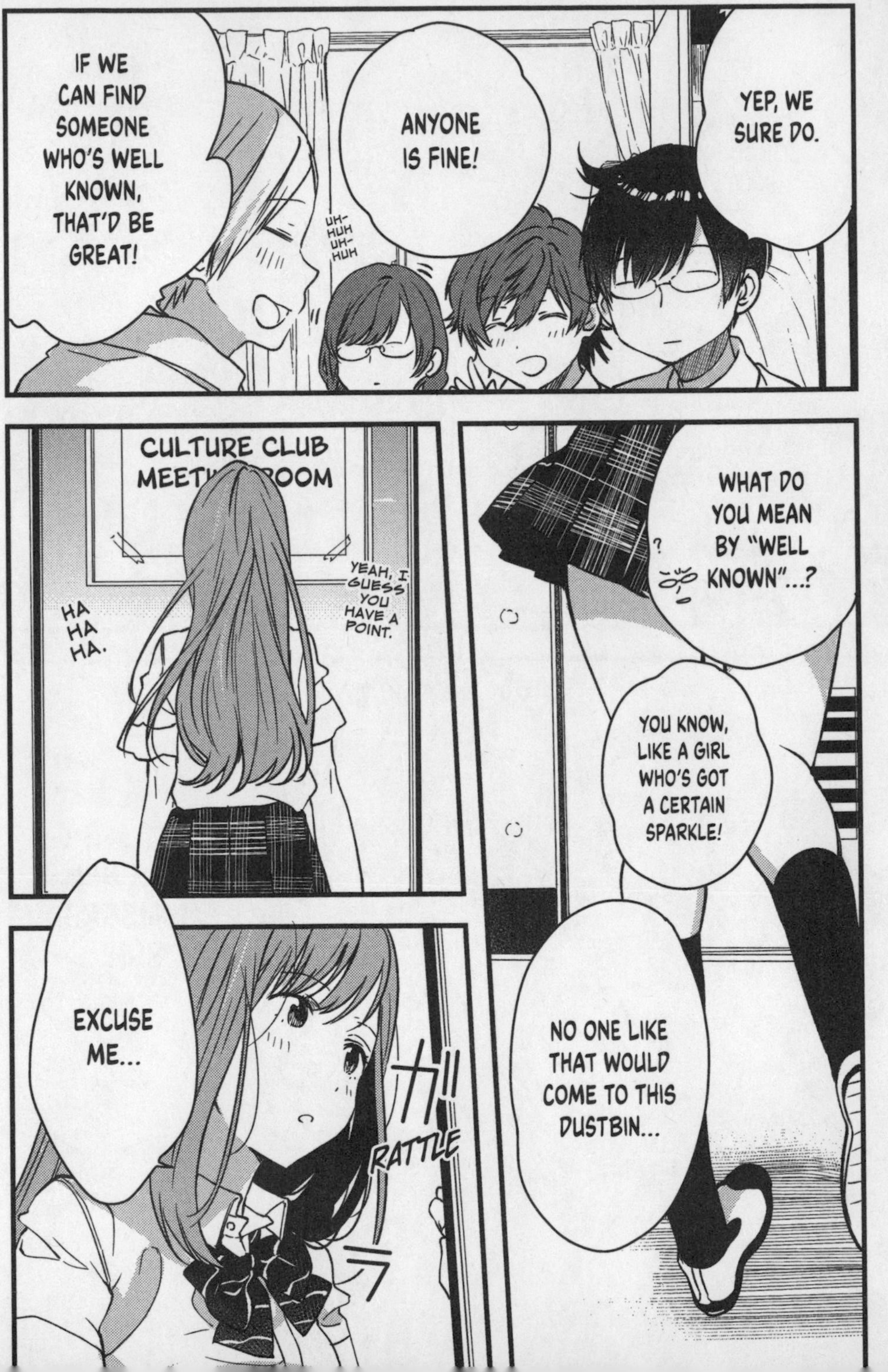
YEP, WE SURE DO.
ANYONE IS FINE!
UH-HUH UH-HUH
IF WE CAN FIND SOMEONE WHO'S WELL KNOWN, THAT'D BE GREAT!
WHAT DO YOU MEAN BY "WELL KNOWN"...?
YOU KNOW, LIKE A GIRL WHO'S GOT A CERTAIN SPARKLE!
NO ONE LIKE THAT WOULD COME TO THIS DUSTBIN...
CULTURE CLUB
MEETI ROOM
YEAH, I GUESS YOU HAVE A POINT.
HA HA HA.
EXCUSE ME...
RATTLE

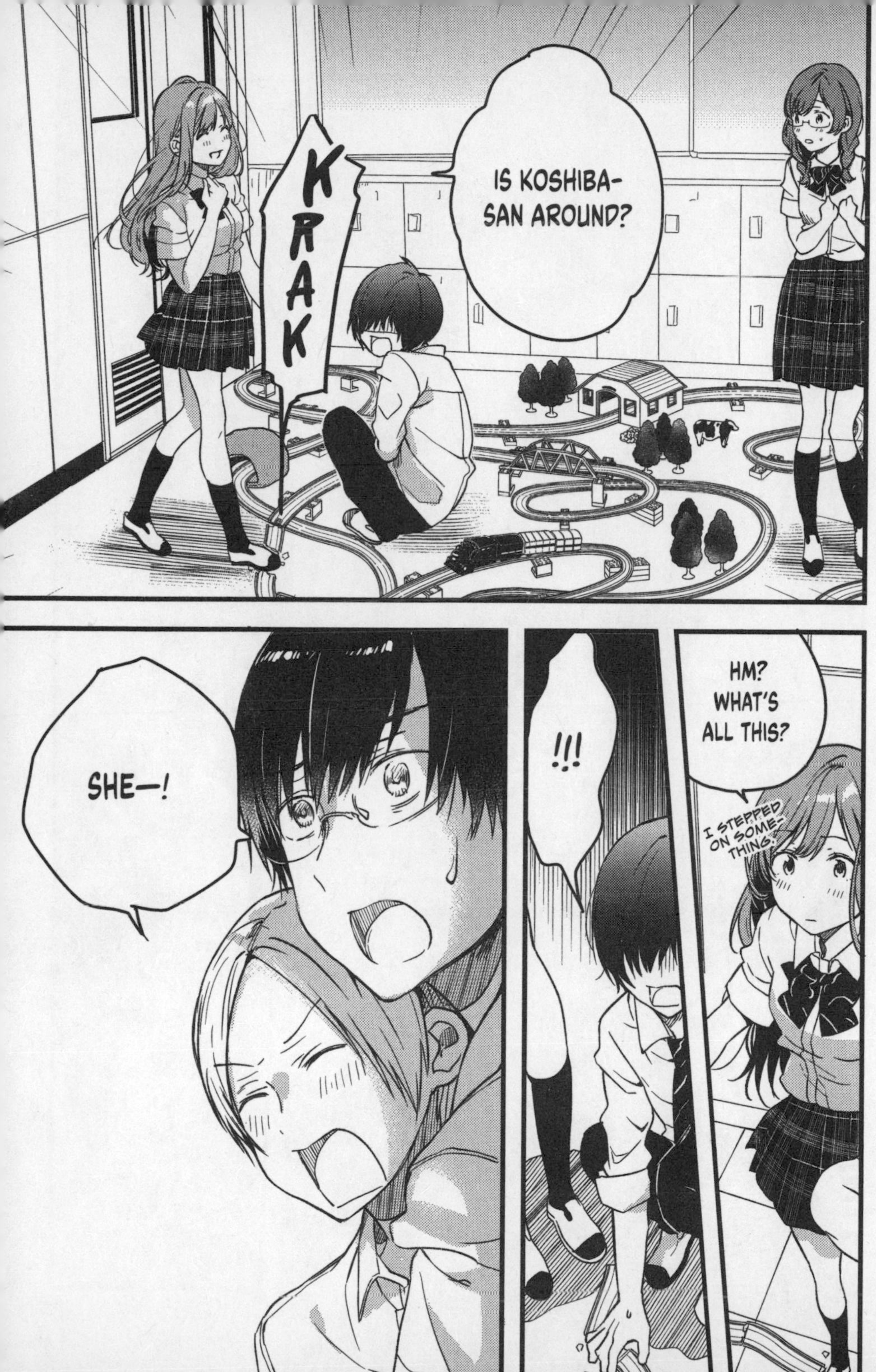
IS KOSHIBA-SAN AROUND?
KRAK
HM? WHAT'S ALL THIS?
I STEPPED ON SOME-THING.
!!!
SHE—!

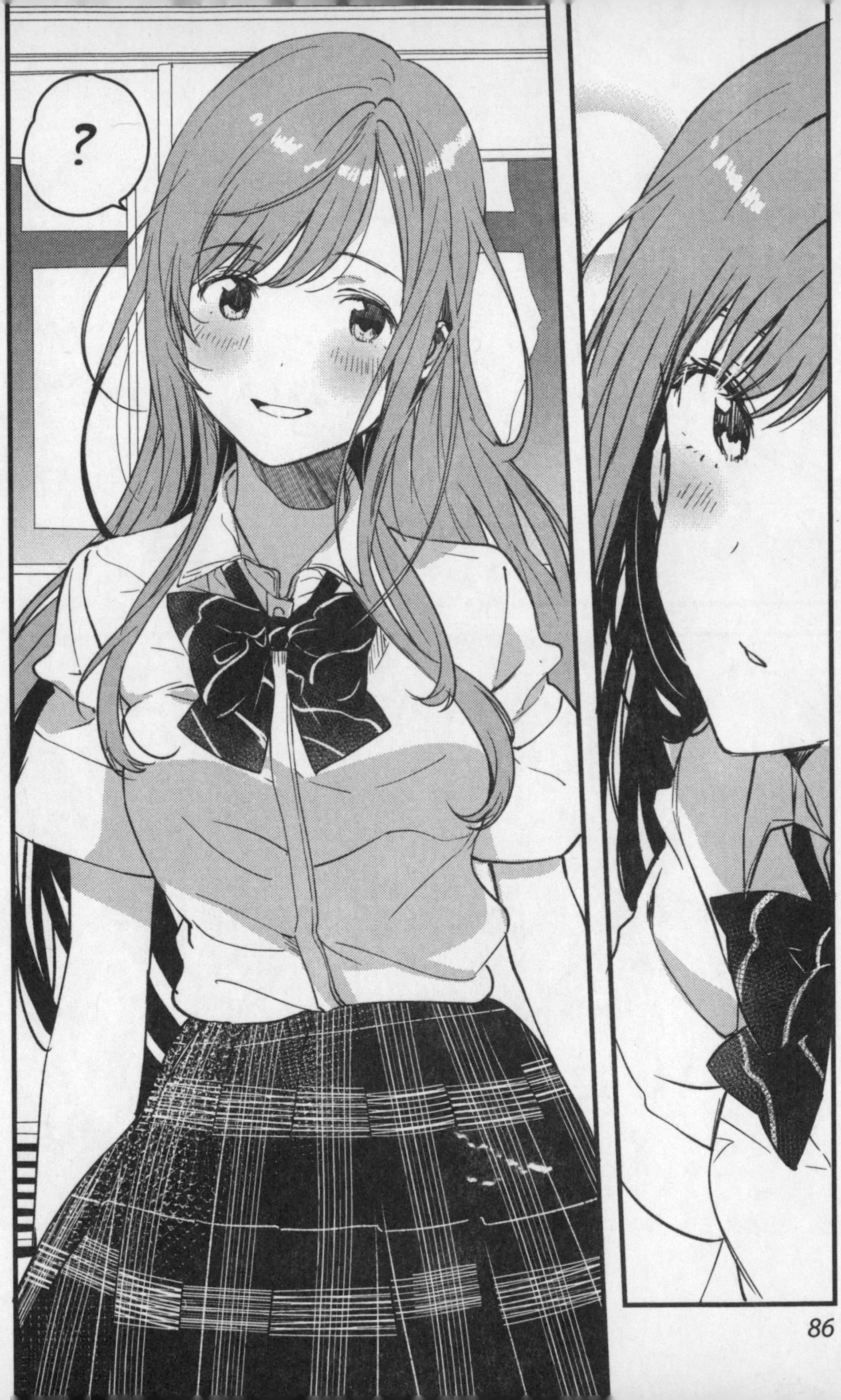
?

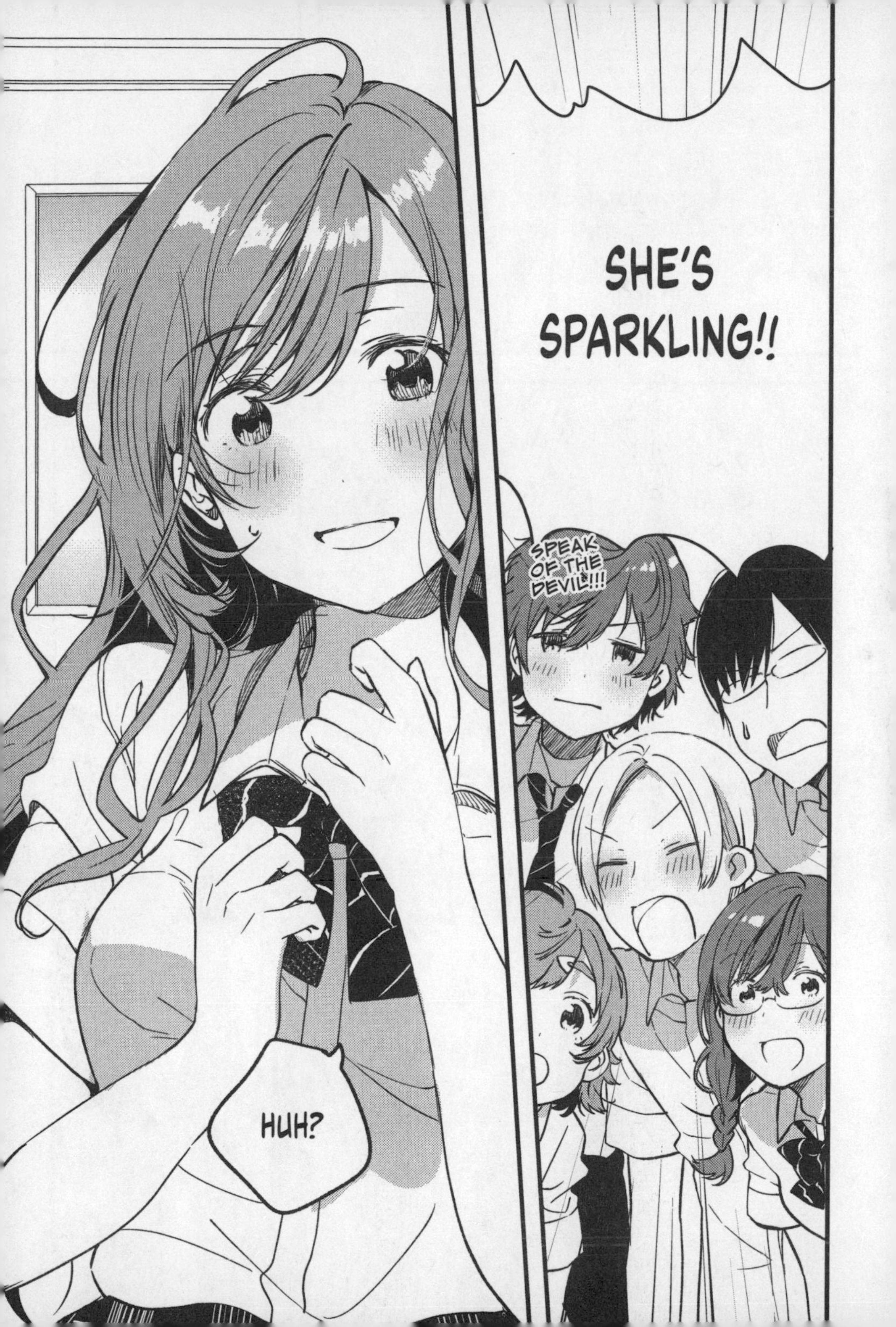
SHE'S SPARKLING!!
SPEAK OF THE DEVIL!!!
HUH?

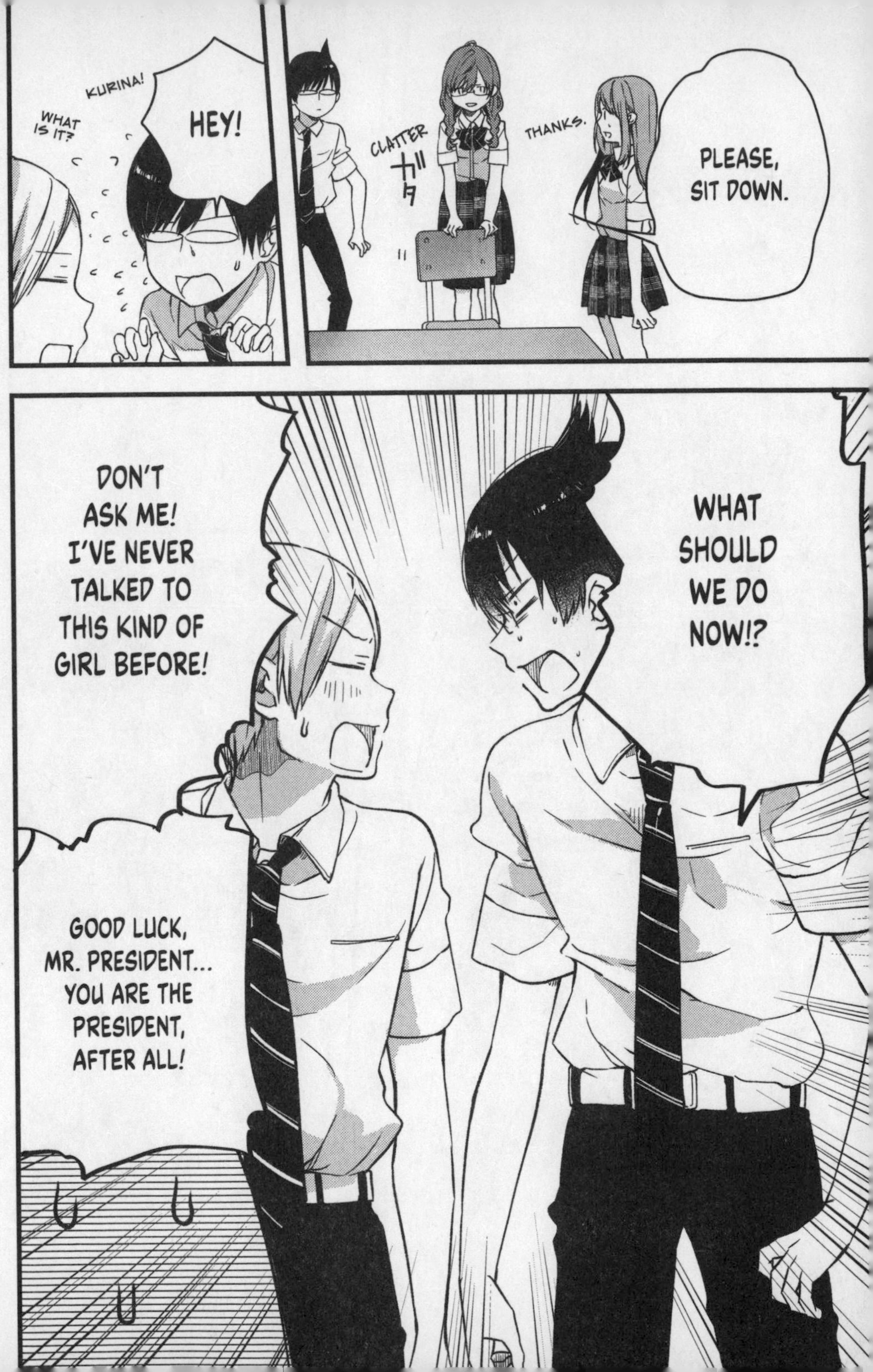
PLEASE, SIT DOWN.
THANKS.
CLATTER
ガタ
HEY!
KURINA!
WHAT IS IT?
WHAT SHOULD WE DO NOW!?
DON'T ASK ME! I'VE NEVER TALKED TO THIS KIND OF GIRL BEFORE!
GOOD LUCK, MR. PRESIDENT... YOU ARE THE PRESIDENT, AFTER ALL!

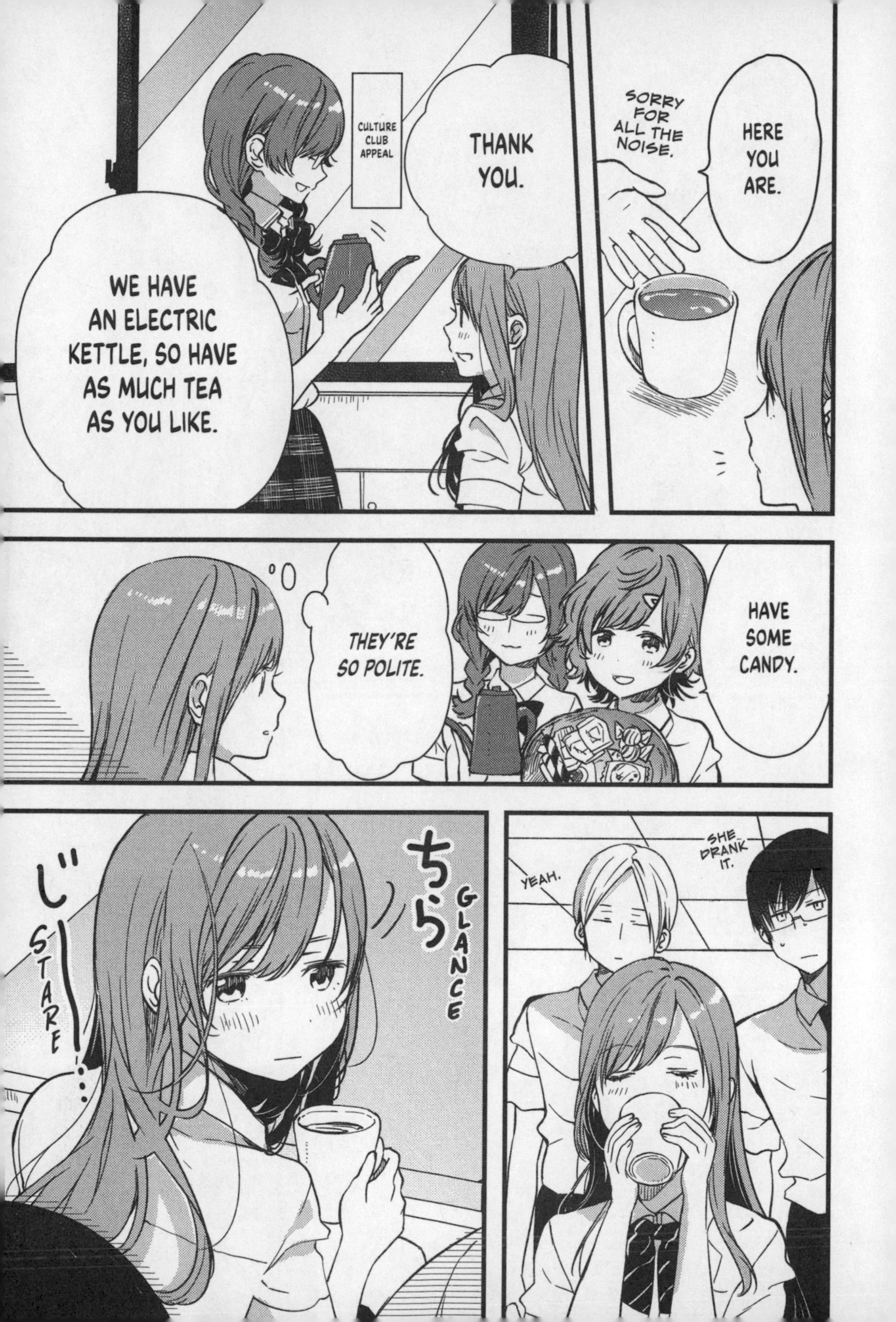
HERE YOU ARE.
SORRY FOR ALL THE NOISE.
THANK YOU.
CULTURE CLUB APPEAL
WE HAVE AN ELECTRIC KETTLE, SO HAVE AS MUCH TEA AS YOU LIKE.
HAVE SOME CANDY.
THEY'RE SO POLITE.
SHE DRANK IT.
YEAH.
ちら GLANCE
じー STARE…

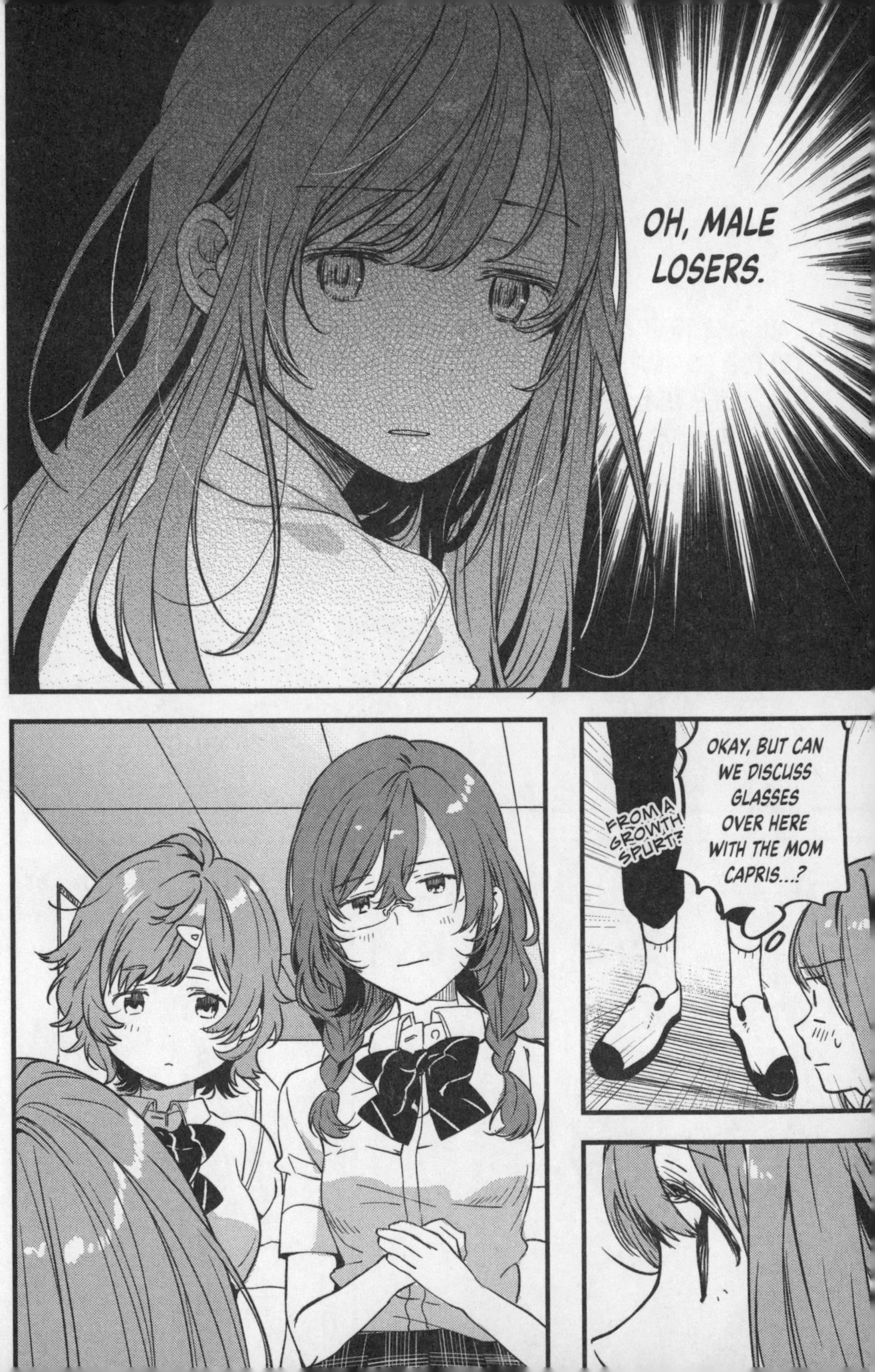
OH, MALE LOSERS.
OKAY, BUT CAN WE DISCUSS GLASSES OVER HERE WITH THE MOM CAPRIS...?
FROM A GROWTH SPURT?

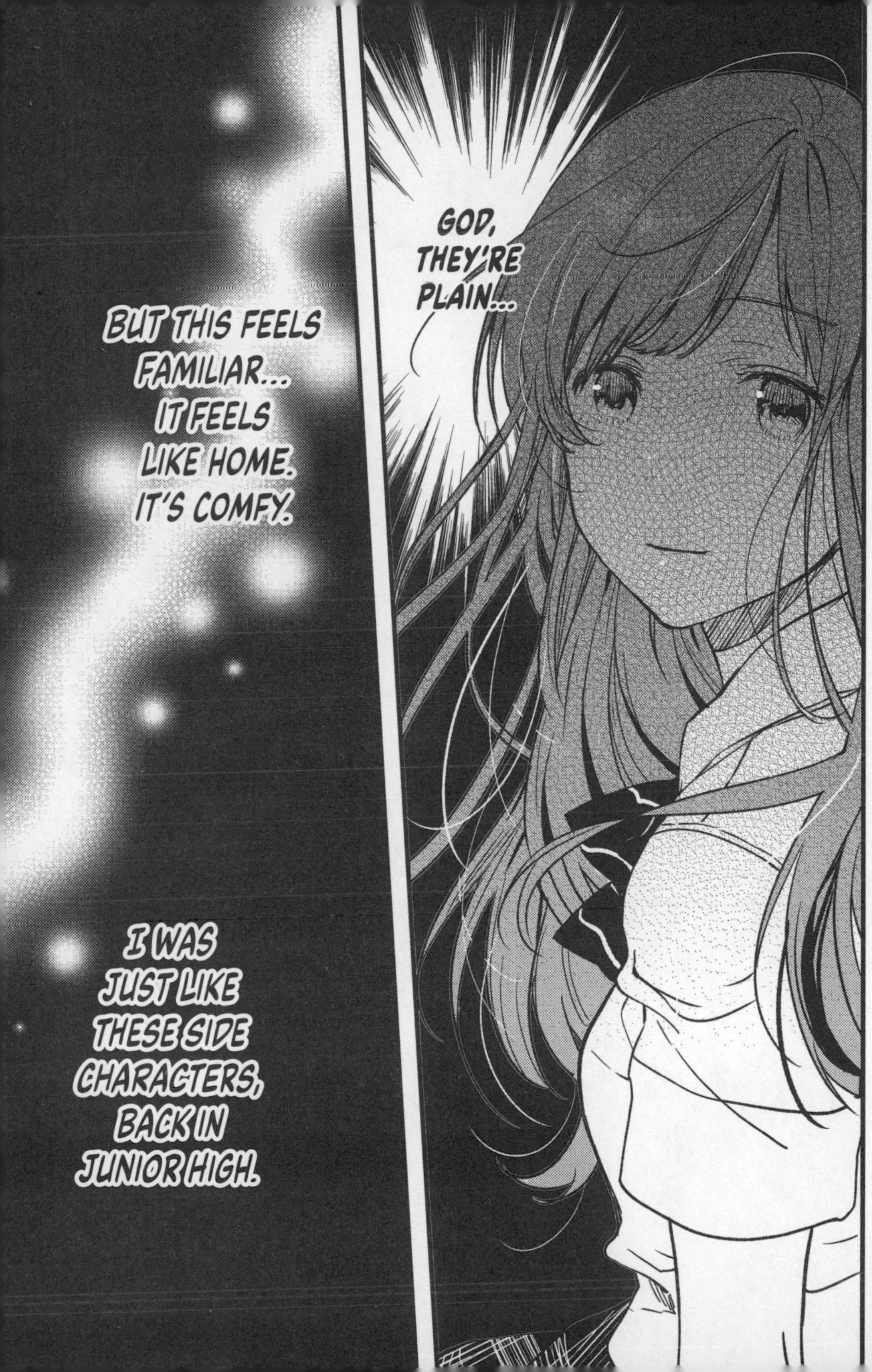
GOD, THEY'RE PLAIN...
BUT THIS FEELS FAMILIAR... IT FEELS LIKE HOME. IT'S COMFY.
I WAS JUST LIKE THESE SIDE CHARACTERS, BACK IN JUNIOR HIGH.

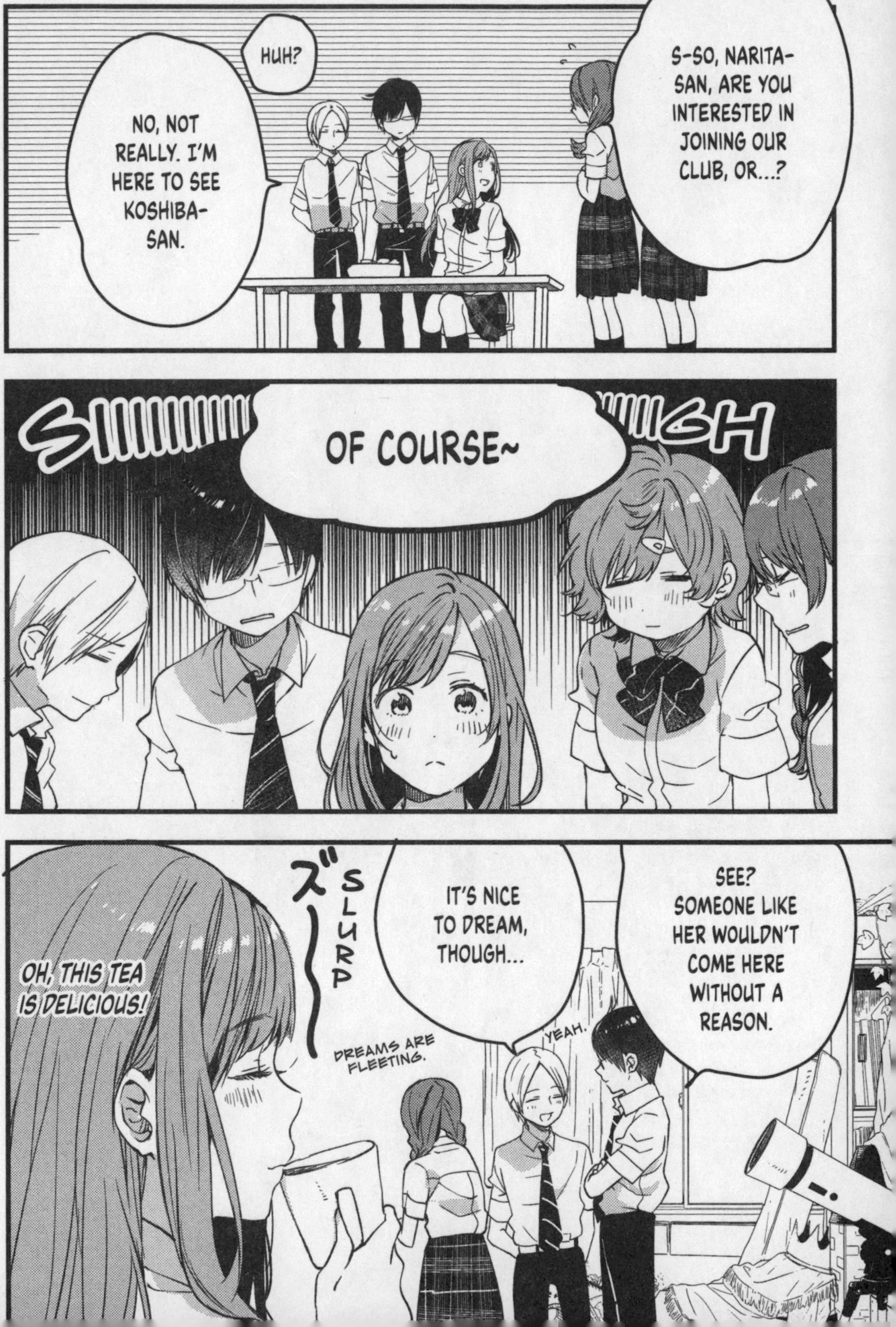
S-SO, NARITA-SAN, ARE YOU INTERESTED IN JOINING OUR CLUB, OR...?
HUH?
NO, NOT REALLY. I'M HERE TO SEE KOSHIBA-SAN.
OF COURSE~
SEE? SOMEONE LIKE HER WOULDN'T COME HERE WITHOUT A REASON.
YEAH.
IT'S NICE TO DREAM, THOUGH...
DREAMS ARE FLEETING.
ズー
SLURP
OH, THIS TEA IS DELICIOUS!

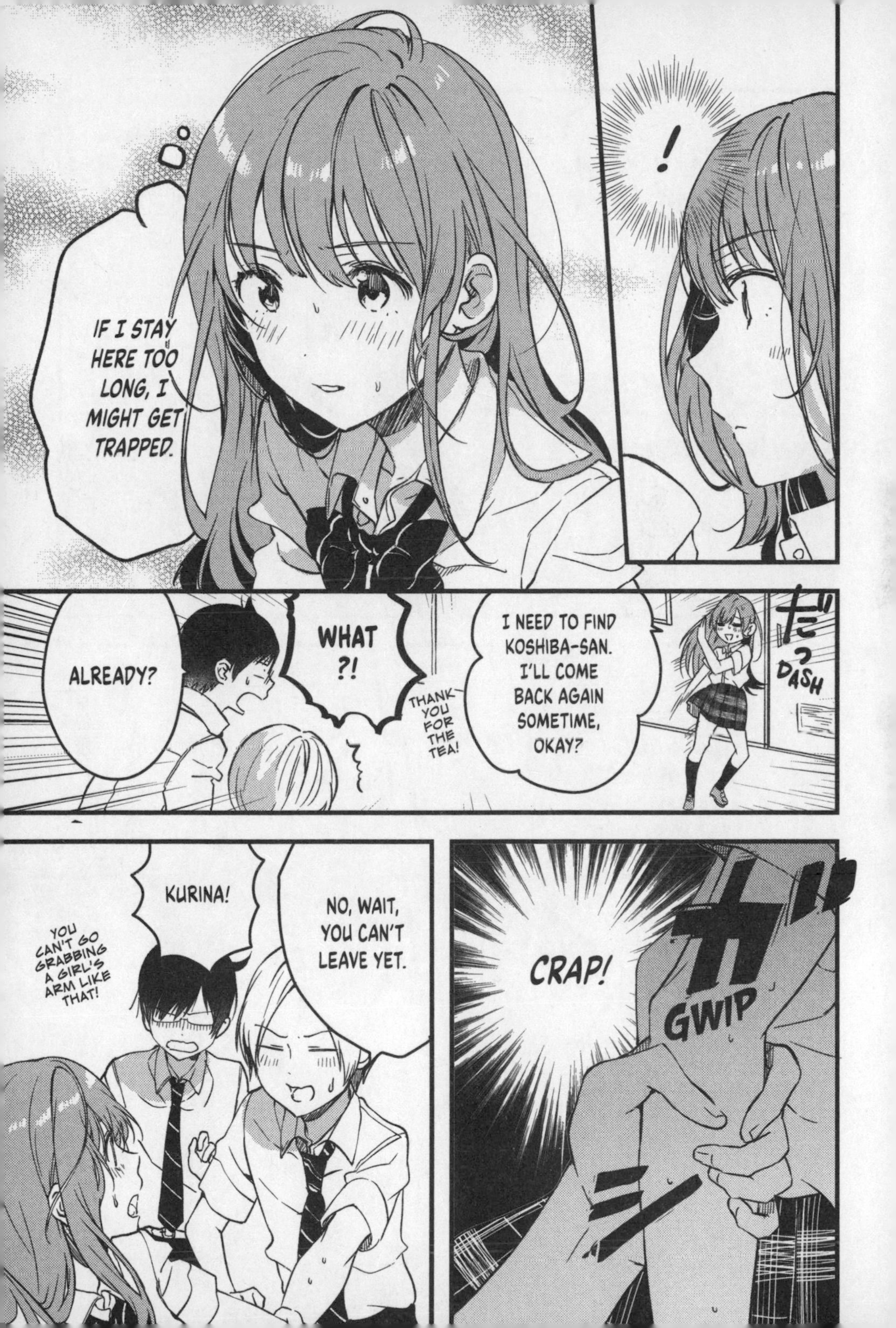
!
IF I STAY HERE TOO LONG, I MIGHT GET TRAPPED.
だっ
DASH
I NEED TO FIND KOSHIBA-SAN. I'LL COME BACK AGAIN SOMETIME, OKAY?
THANK YOU FOR THE TEA!
WHAT ?!
ALREADY?
ガ
GWIP
CRAP!
NO, WAIT, YOU CAN'T LEAVE YET.
KURINA!
YOU CAN'T GO GRABBING A GIRL'S ARM LIKE THAT!

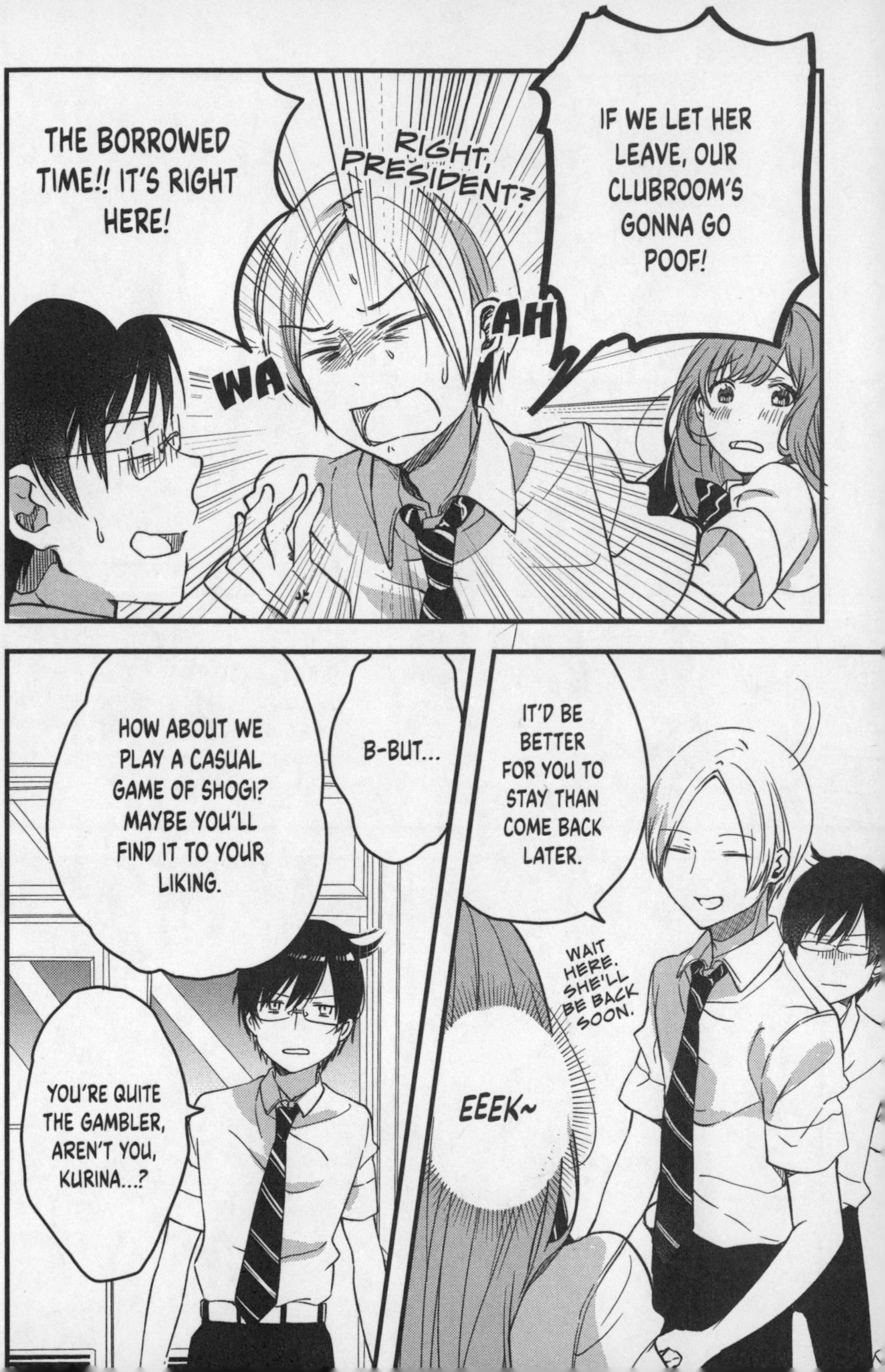
IF WE LET HER LEAVE, OUR CLUBROOM'S GONNA GO POOF!
RIGHT, PRESIDENT?
THE BORROWED TIME!! IT'S RIGHT HERE!
AH
WA
IT'D BE BETTER FOR YOU TO STAY THAN COME BACK LATER.
WAIT HERE. SHE'LL BE BACK SOON.
EEEK~
B-BUT...
HOW ABOUT WE PLAY A CASUAL GAME OF SHOGI? MAYBE YOU'LL FIND IT TO YOUR LIKING.
YOU'RE QUITE THE GAMBLER, AREN'T YOU, KURINA...?

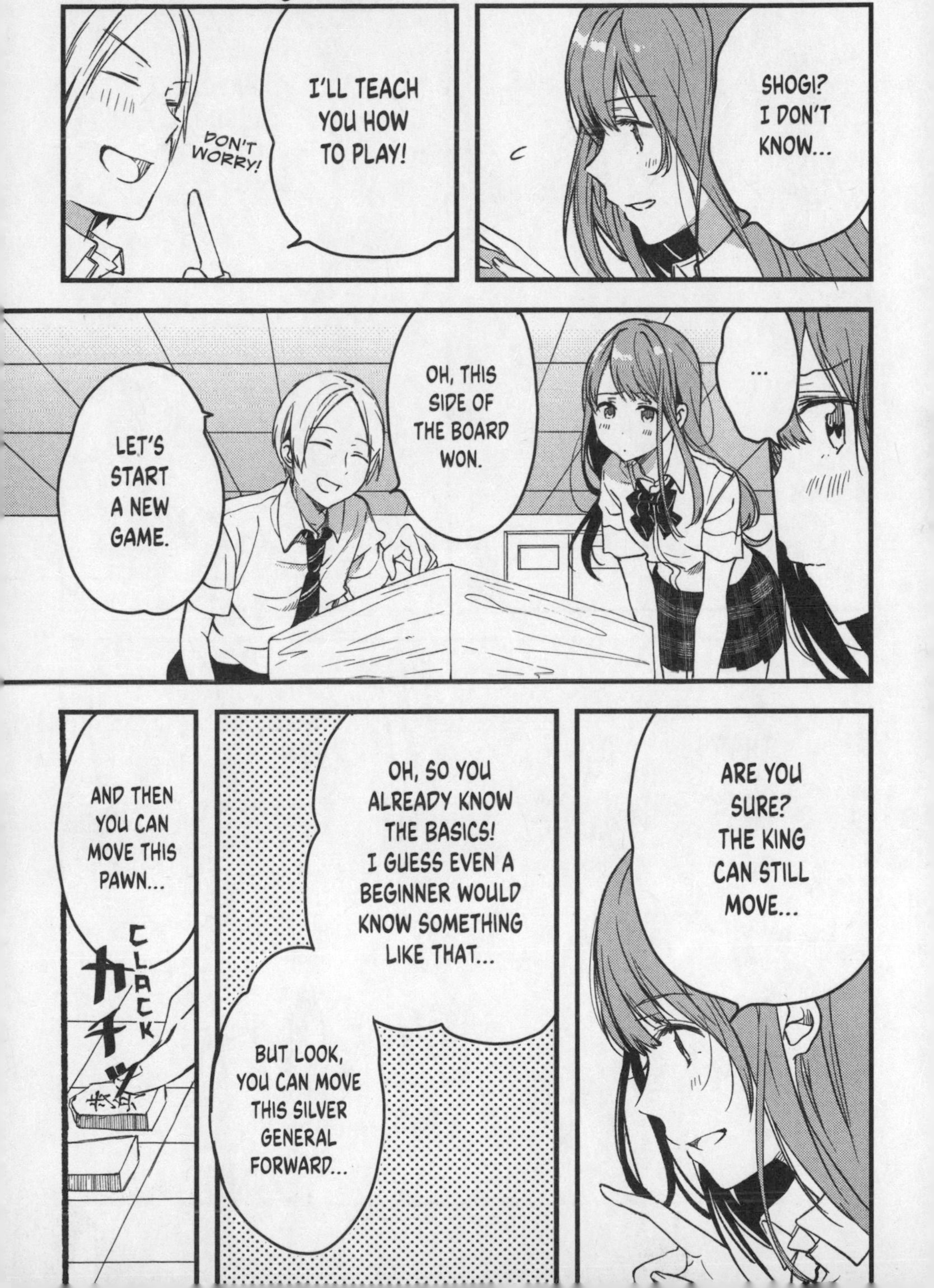
SHOGI? I DON'T KNOW...
I'LL TEACH YOU HOW TO PLAY!
DON'T WORRY!
...
OH, THIS SIDE OF THE BOARD WON.
LET'S START A NEW GAME.
ARE YOU SURE? THE KING CAN STILL MOVE...
OH, SO YOU ALREADY KNOW THE BASICS! I GUESS EVEN A BEGINNER WOULD KNOW SOMETHING LIKE THAT...
BUT LOOK, YOU CAN MOVE THIS SILVER GENERAL FORWARD...
AND THEN YOU CAN MOVE THIS PAWN...
カチッ
CLACK

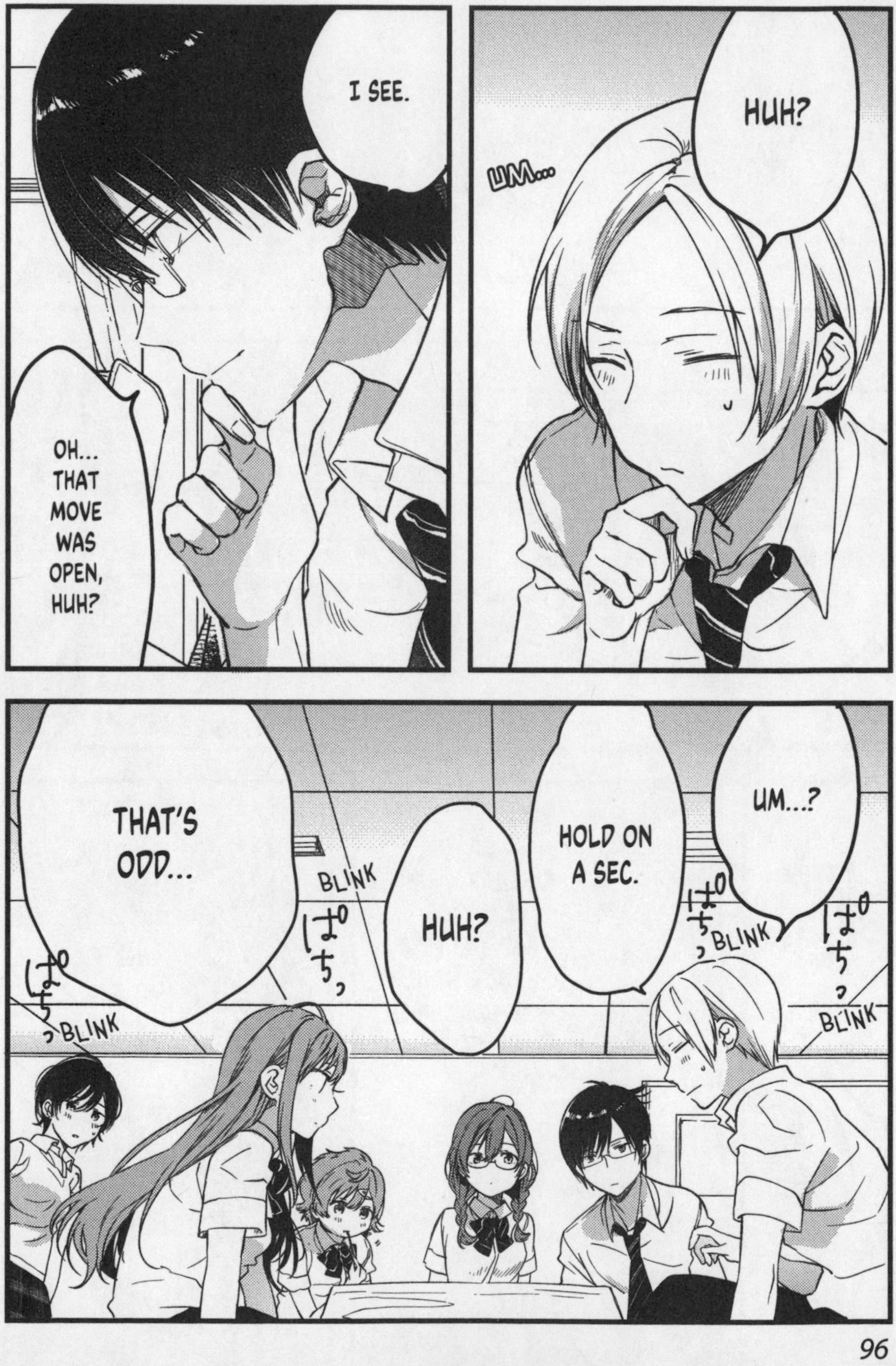
HUH?
UM...
I SEE.
OH... THAT MOVE WAS OPEN, HUH?
UM...?
ぱちっ BLINK
ぱちっ BLINK
HOLD ON A SEC.
HUH?
ぱちっ BLINK
THAT'S ODD...
ぱちっ BLINK

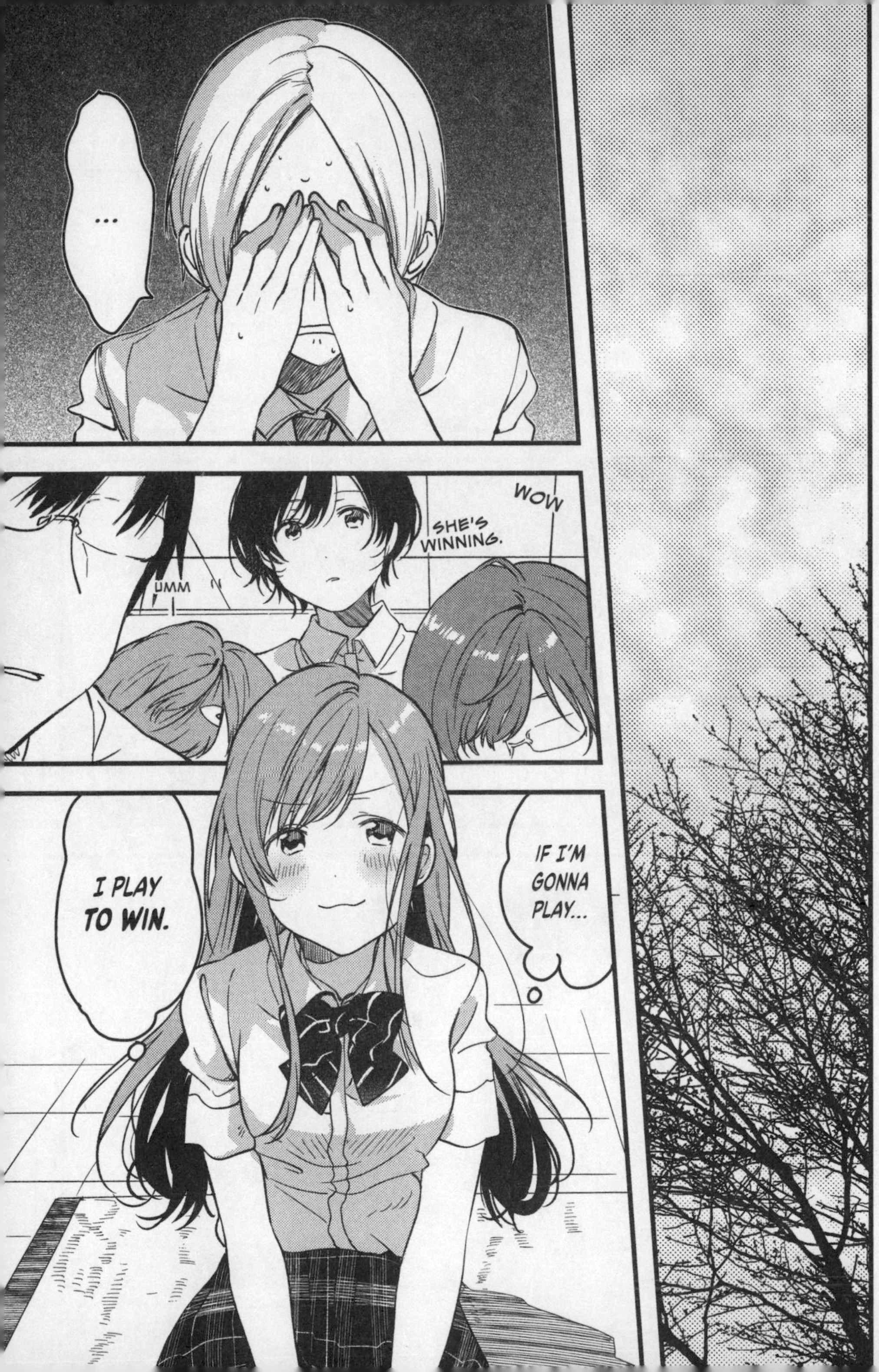
...
WOW
SHE'S WINNING.
UMM
IF I'M GONNA PLAY...
I PLAY TO WIN.

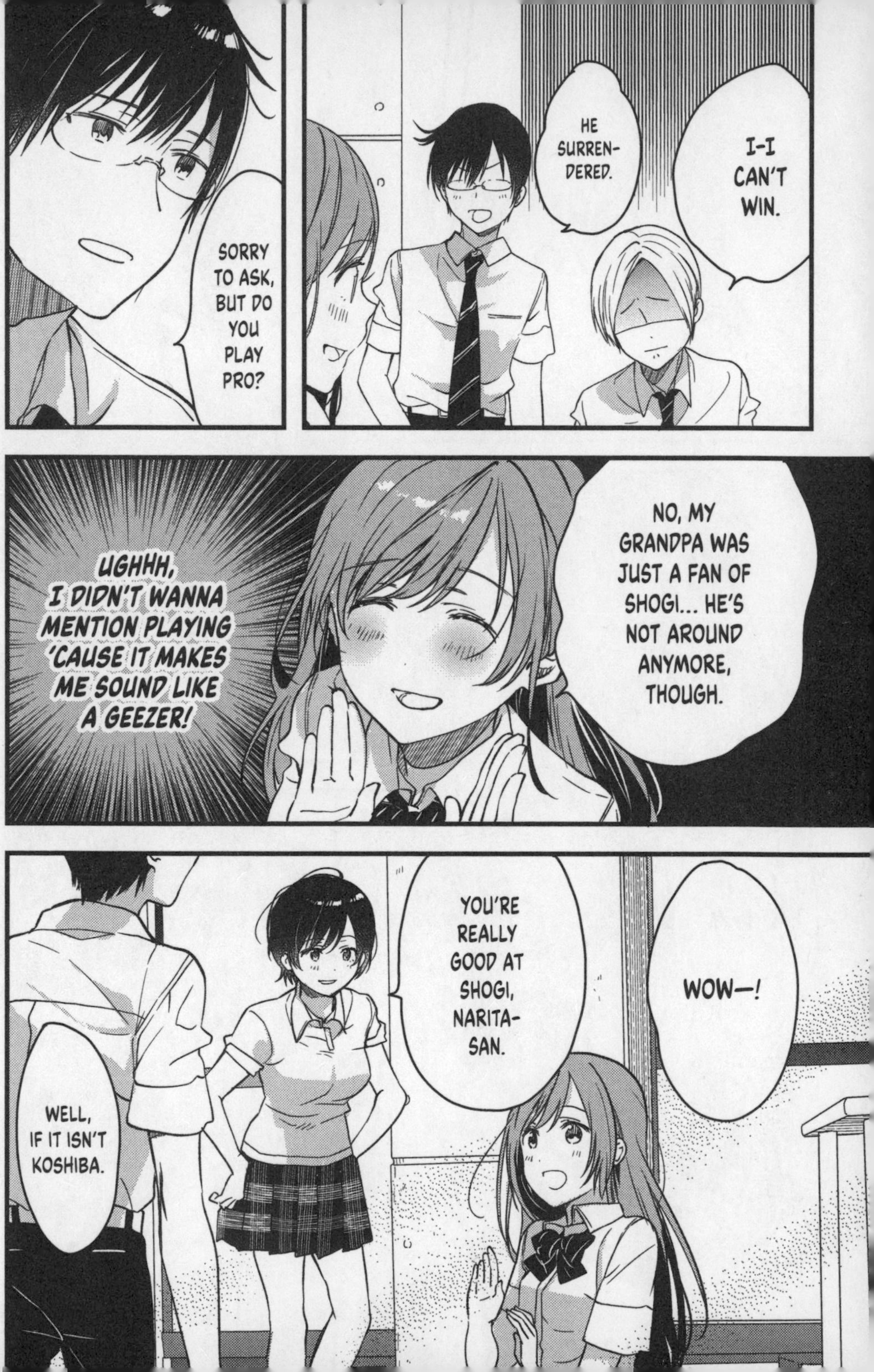
I-I CAN'T WIN.
HE SURREN-DERED.
SORRY TO ASK, BUT DO YOU PLAY PRO?
NO, MY GRANDPA WAS JUST A FAN OF SHOGI... HE'S NOT AROUND ANYMORE, THOUGH.
UGHHH, I DIDN'T WANNA MENTION PLAYING 'CAUSE IT MAKES ME SOUND LIKE A GEEZER!
WOW—!
YOU'RE REALLY GOOD AT SHOGI, NARITA-SAN.
WELL, IF IT ISN'T KOSHIBA.

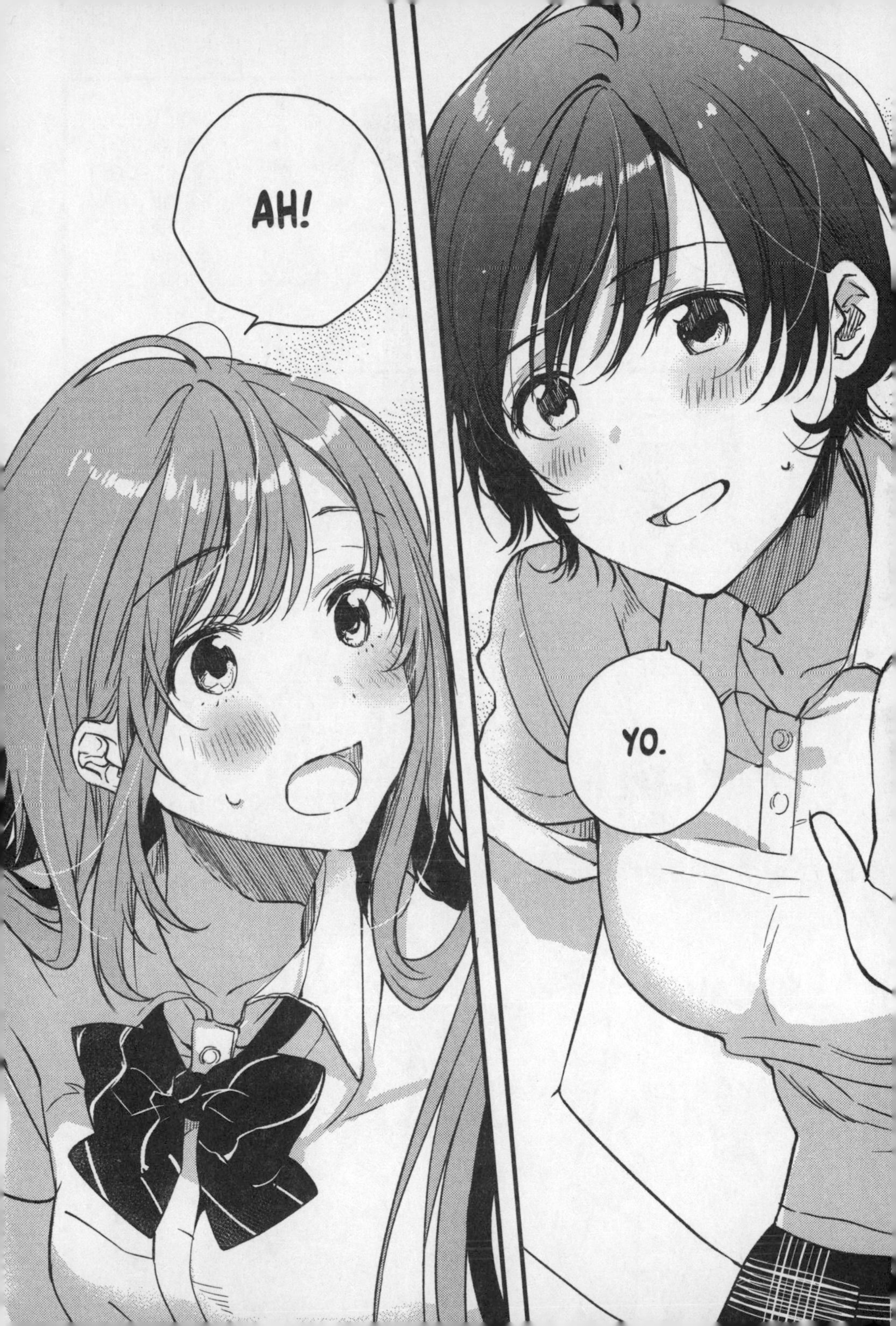
YO.
AH!

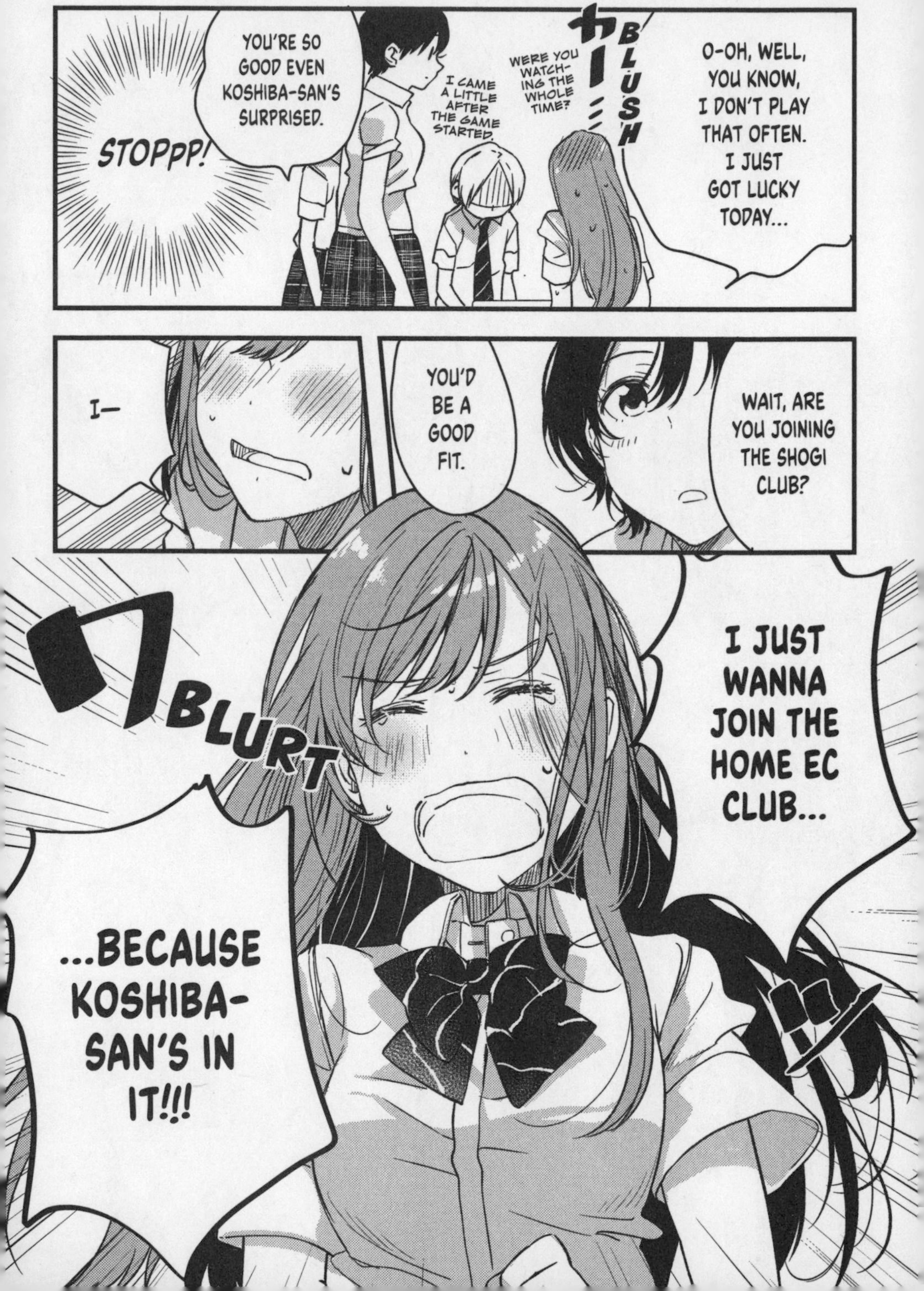
O-OH, WELL, YOU KNOW, I DON'T PLAY THAT OFTEN. I JUST GOT LUCKY TODAY...
BLUSH
WERE YOU WATCHING THE WHOLE TIME?
I CAME A LITTLE AFTER THE GAME STARTED.
YOU'RE SO GOOD EVEN KOSHIBA-SAN'S SURPRISED.
STOPPP!
WAIT, ARE YOU JOINING THE SHOGI CLUB?
YOU'D BE A GOOD FIT.
I—
I JUST WANNA JOIN THE HOME EC CLUB...
BLURT
...BECAUSE KOSHIBA-SAN'S IN IT!!!

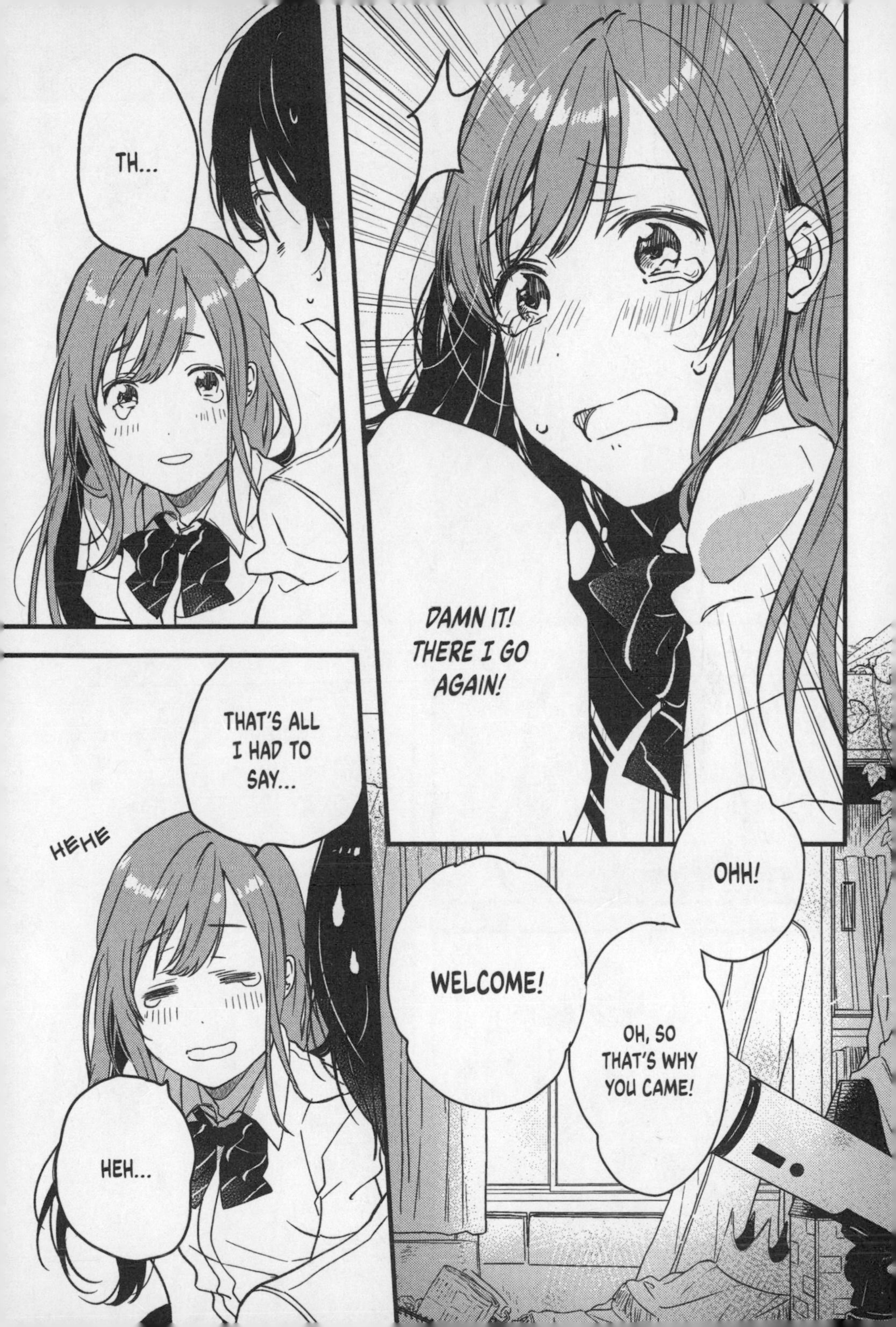
DAMN IT! THERE I GO AGAIN!
TH...
THAT'S ALL I HAD TO SAY...
HEHE
HEH...
OHH!
WELCOME!
OH, SO THAT'S WHY YOU CAME!

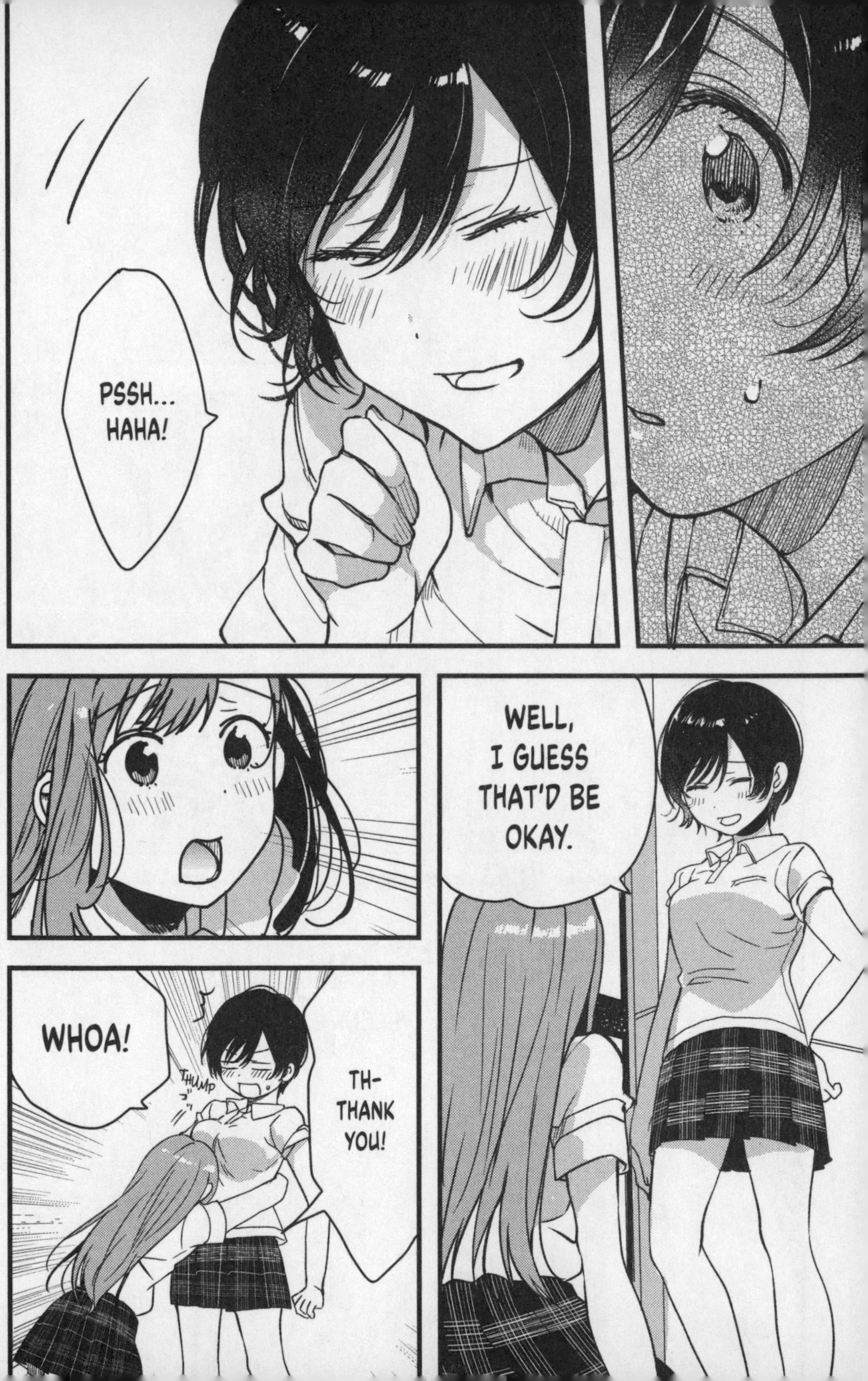
PSSH... HAHA!
WELL, I GUESS THAT'D BE OKAY.
WHOA!
THUMP
TH-THANK YOU!

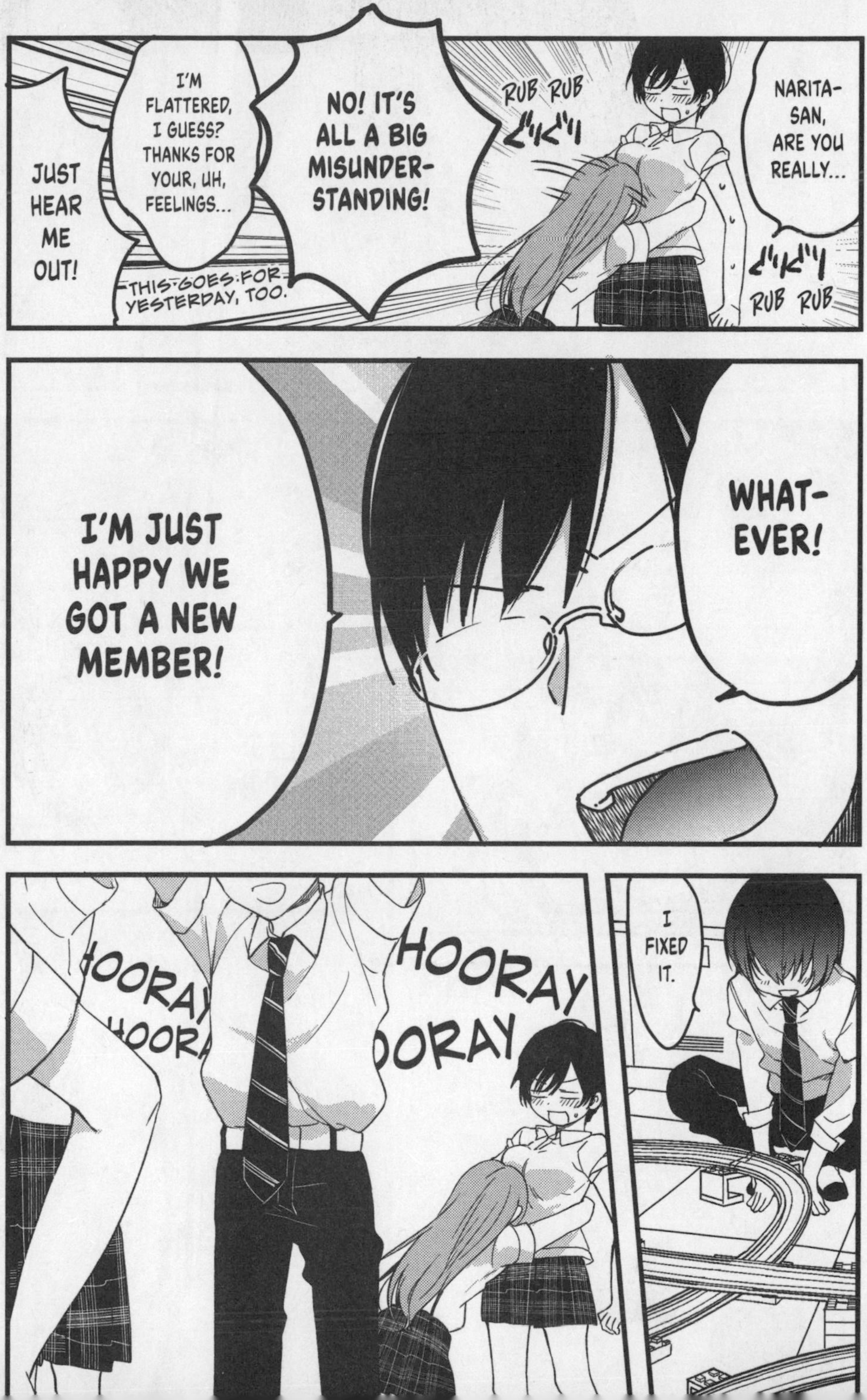
NARITA-SAN, ARE YOU REALLY...
RUB RUB
RUB RUB
NO! IT'S ALL A BIG MISUNDERSTANDING!
I'M FLATTERED, I GUESS? THANKS FOR YOUR, UH, FEELINGS...
THIS GOES FOR YESTERDAY, TOO.
JUST HEAR ME OUT!
WHAT-EVER!
I'M JUST HAPPY WE GOT A NEW MEMBER!
I FIXED IT.
HOORAY
OORAY
OORAY
HOORA

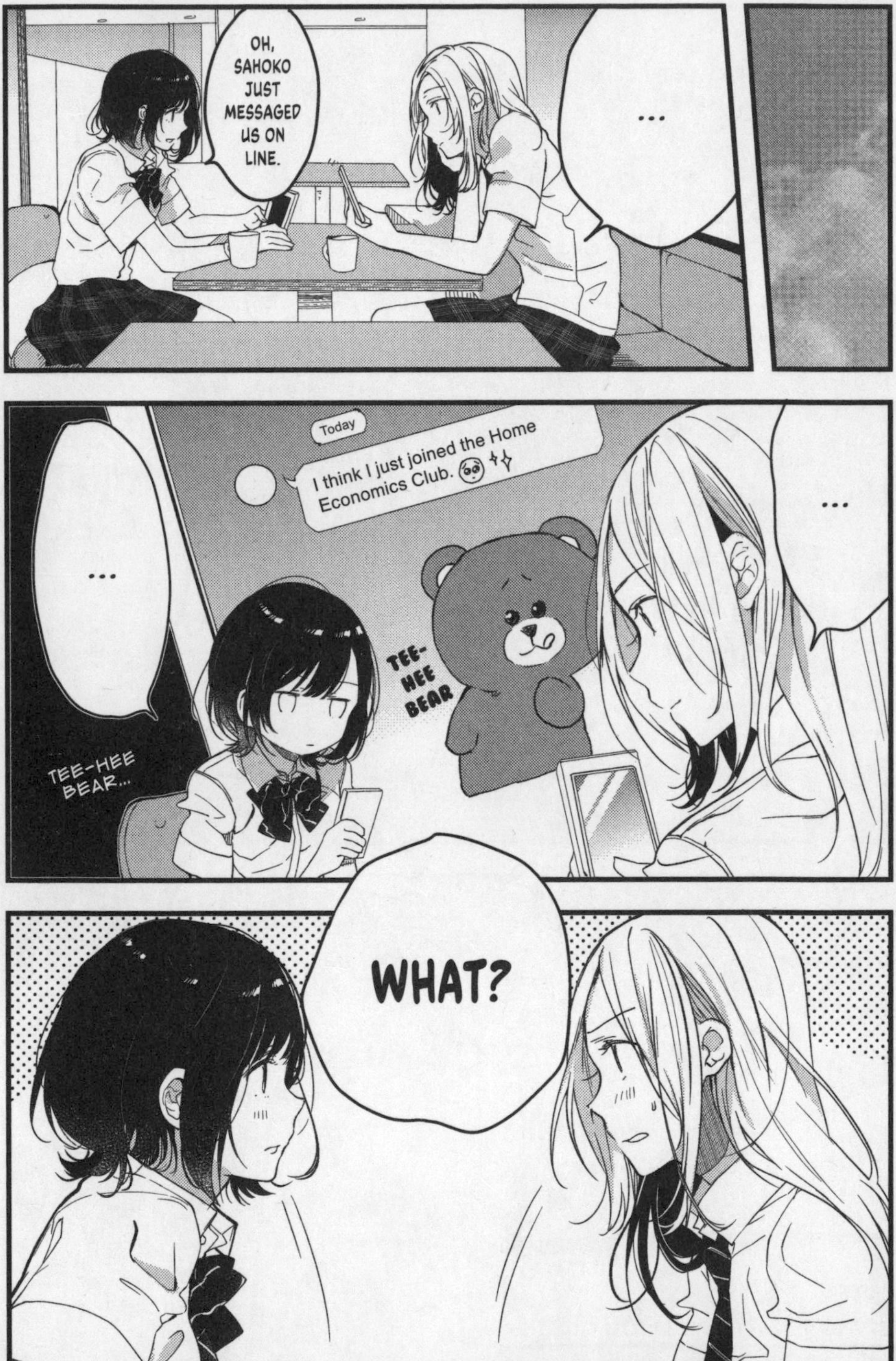
...
OH, SAHOKO JUST MESSAGED US ON LINE.
...
Today
I think I just joined the Home Economics Club.
TEE-HEE BEAR
...
TEE-HEE BEAR...
WHAT?

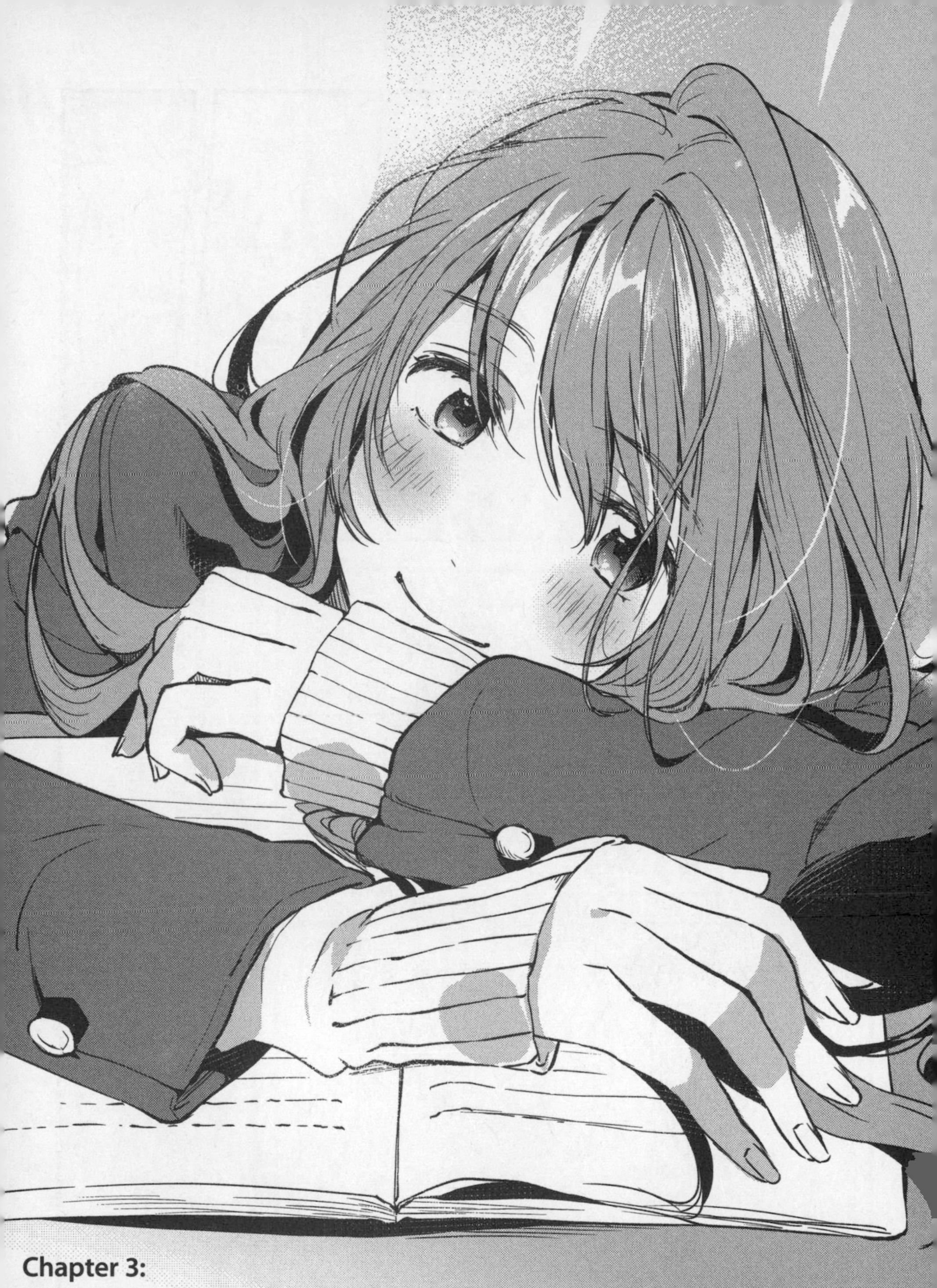

Chapter 3:
I Want to Get to Know You (Part 1)

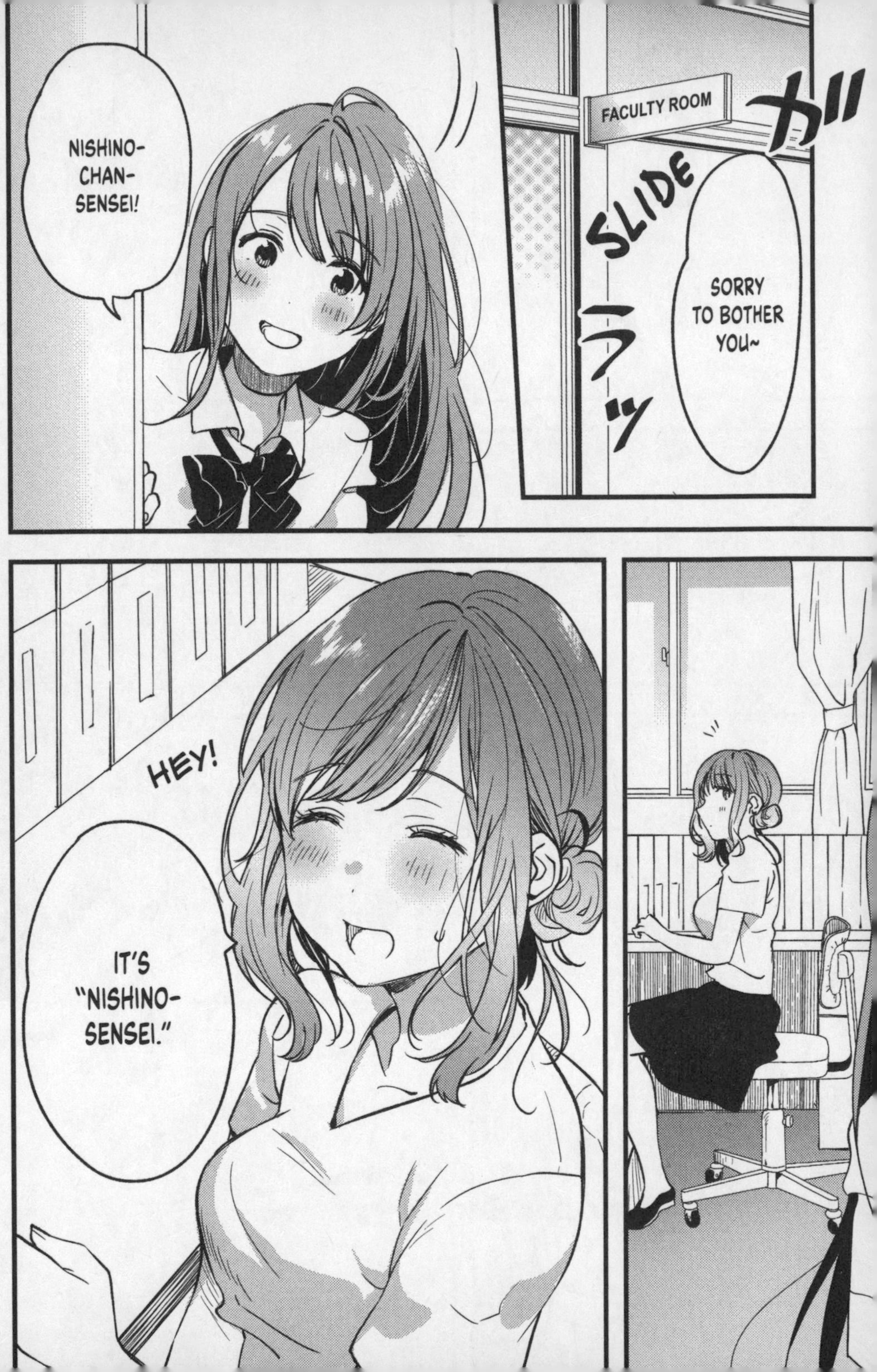
FACULTY ROOM
ガラッ
SLIDE
SORRY TO BOTHER YOU~
NISHINO-CHAN-SENSEI!
HEY!
IT'S "NISHINO-SENSEI."

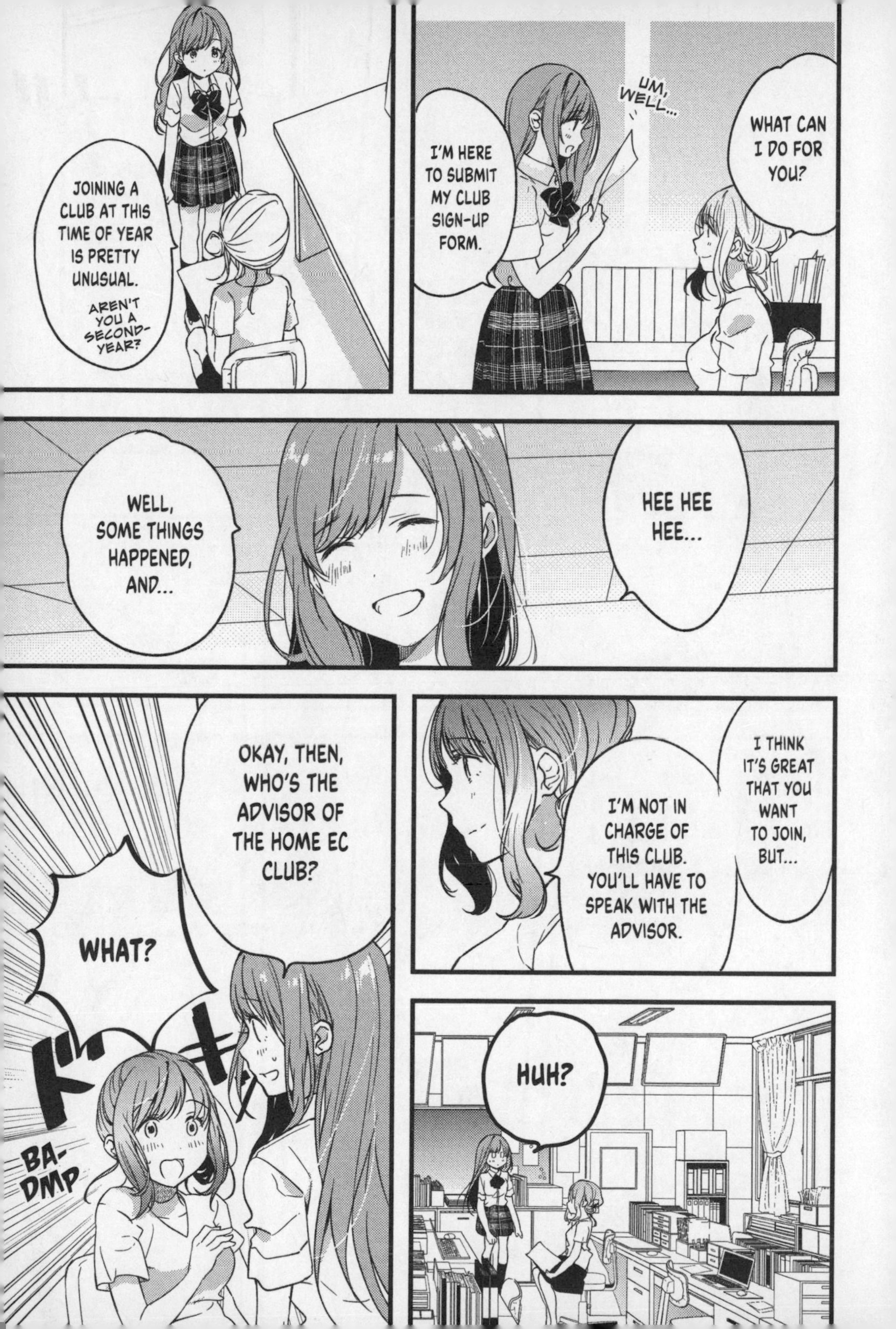
WHAT CAN I DO FOR YOU?
UM, WELL...
I'M HERE TO SUBMIT MY CLUB SIGN-UP FORM.
JOINING A CLUB AT THIS TIME OF YEAR IS PRETTY UNUSUAL.
AREN'T YOU A SECOND-YEAR?
HEE HEE HEE...
WELL, SOME THINGS HAPPENED, AND...
I THINK IT'S GREAT THAT YOU WANT TO JOIN, BUT...
I'M NOT IN CHARGE OF THIS CLUB. YOU'LL HAVE TO SPEAK WITH THE ADVISOR.
HUH?
OKAY, THEN, WHO'S THE ADVISOR OF THE HOME EC CLUB?
WHAT?
BA-DMP

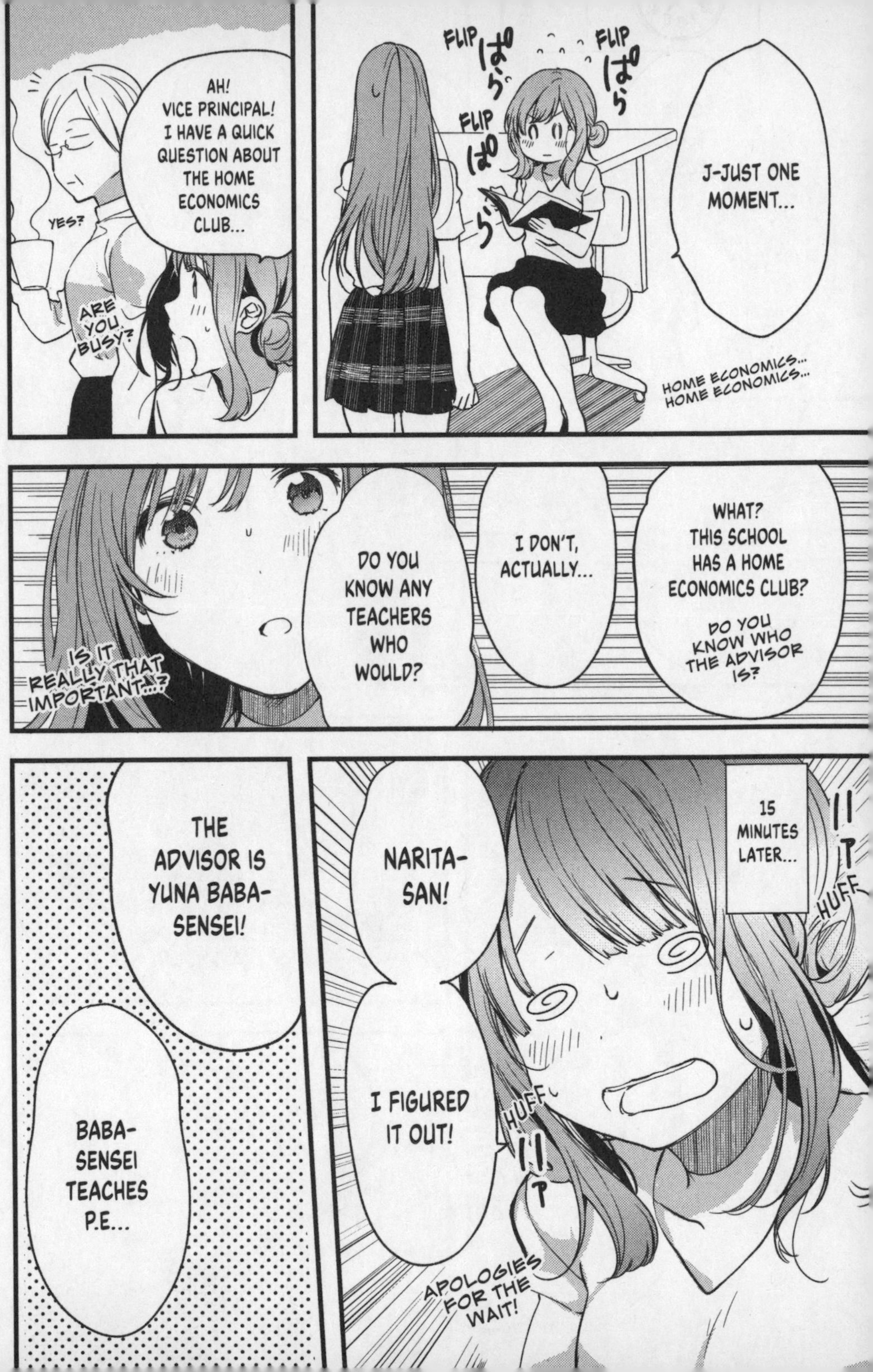
J-JUST ONE MOMENT...
HOME ECONOMICS... HOME ECONOMICS...
FLIP ぱら
FLIP ぱら
FLIP ぱら
AH! VICE PRINCIPAL! I HAVE A QUICK QUESTION ABOUT THE HOME ECONOMICS CLUB...
YES?
ARE YOU BUSY?
WHAT? THIS SCHOOL HAS A HOME ECONOMICS CLUB?
DO YOU KNOW WHO THE ADVISOR IS?
I DON'T, ACTUALLY...
DO YOU KNOW ANY TEACHERS WHO WOULD?
IS IT REALLY THAT IMPORTANT...?
15 MINUTES LATER...
HUFF ハァ
NARITA-SAN!
I FIGURED IT OUT!
HUFF ハァ
APOLOGIES FOR THE WAIT!
THE ADVISOR IS YUNA BABA-SENSEI!
BABA-SENSEI TEACHES P.E...

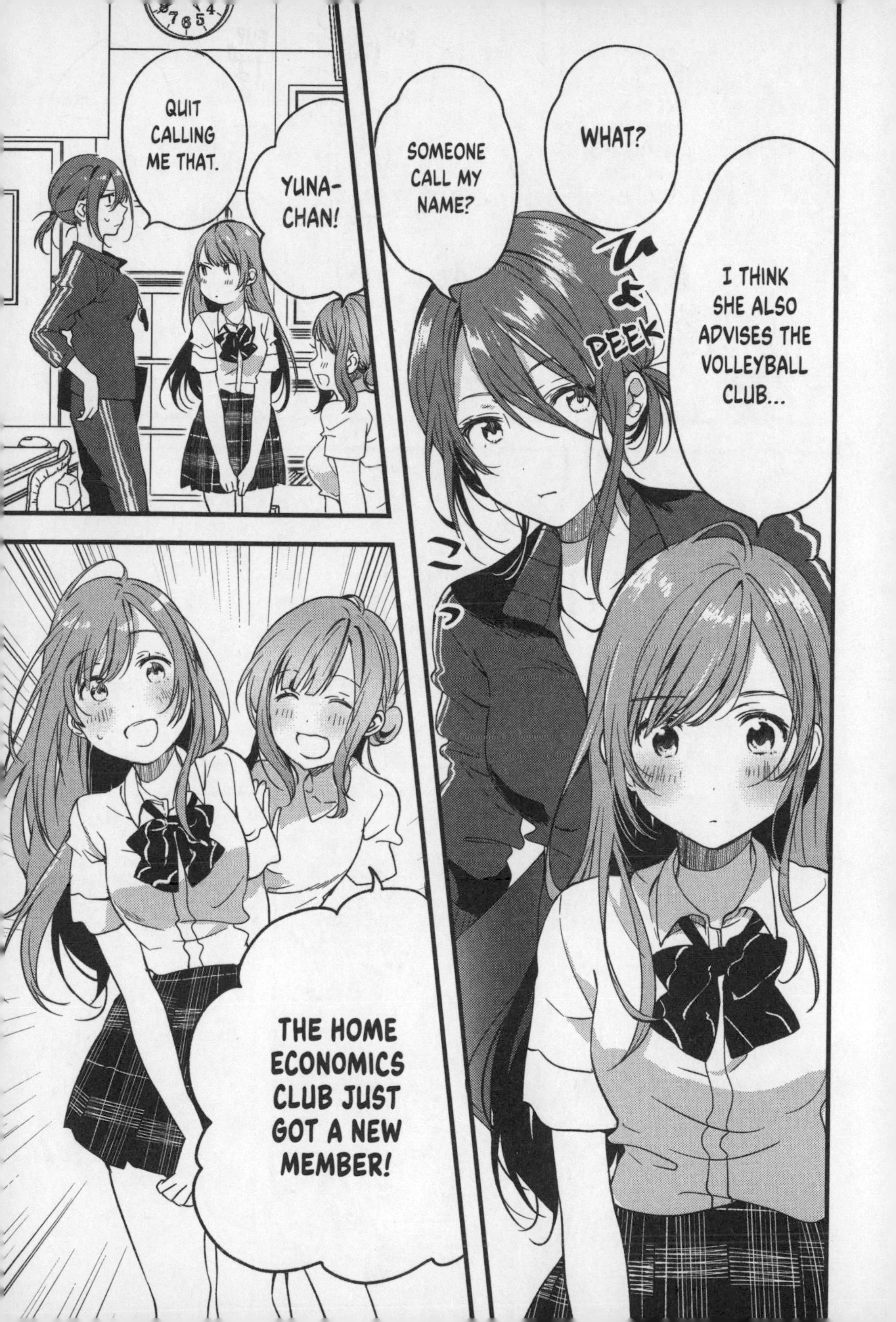
WHAT?
SOMEONE CALL MY NAME?
I THINK SHE ALSO ADVISES THE VOLLEYBALL CLUB...
PEEK
YUNA-CHAN!
QUIT CALLING ME THAT.
THE HOME ECONOMICS CLUB JUST GOT A NEW MEMBER!

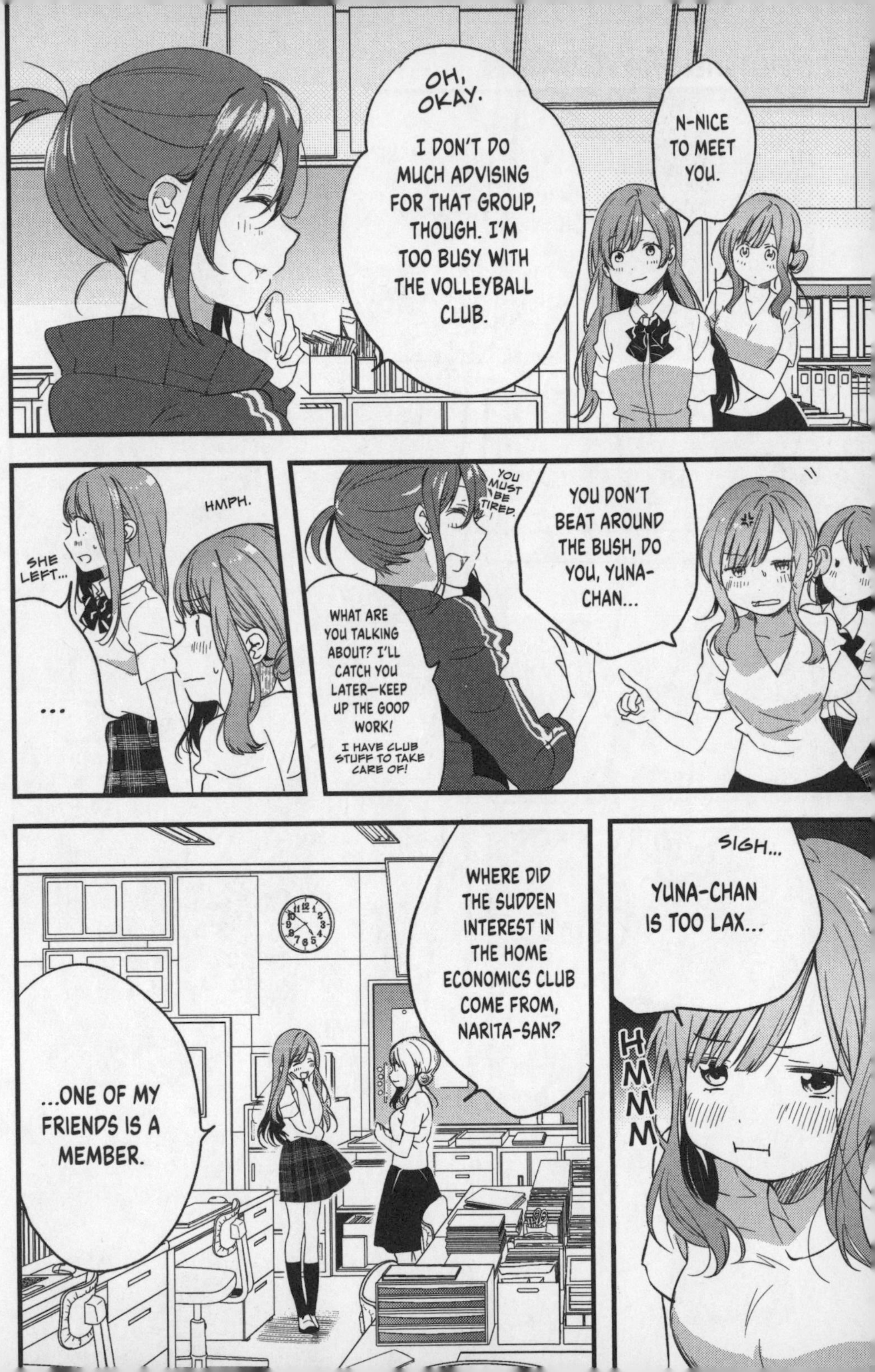
N-NICE TO MEET YOU.
OH, OKAY.
I DON'T DO MUCH ADVISING FOR THAT GROUP, THOUGH. I'M TOO BUSY WITH THE VOLLEYBALL CLUB.
YOU DON'T BEAT AROUND THE BUSH, DO YOU, YUNA-CHAN...
YOU MUST BE TIRED.
WHAT ARE YOU TALKING ABOUT? I'LL CATCH YOU LATER—KEEP UP THE GOOD WORK!
I HAVE CLUB STUFF TO TAKE CARE OF!
HMPH.
SHE LEFT...
...
SIGH...
YUNA-CHAN IS TOO LAX...
HMMM
WHERE DID THE SUDDEN INTEREST IN THE HOME ECONOMICS CLUB COME FROM, NARITA-SAN?
...ONE OF MY FRIENDS IS A MEMBER.

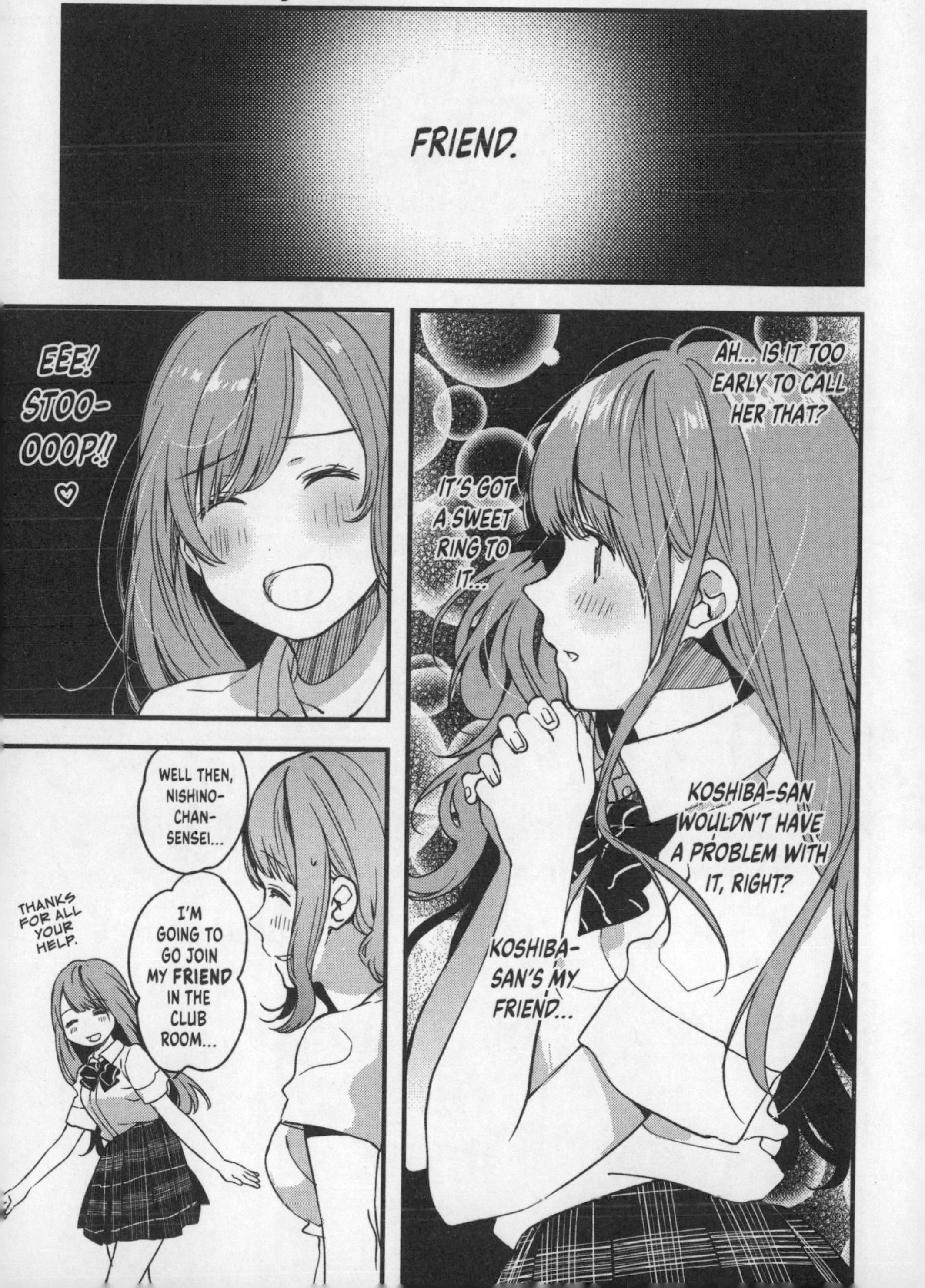
FRIEND.
AH... IS IT TOO EARLY TO CALL HER THAT?
IT'S GOT A SWEET RING TO IT...
KOSHIBA-SAN WOULDN'T HAVE A PROBLEM WITH IT, RIGHT?
KOSHIBA-SAN'S MY FRIEND...
EEE! STOOO-OOOP!! ♡
WELL THEN, NISHINO-CHAN-SENSEI...
I'M GOING TO GO JOIN MY FRIEND IN THE CLUB ROOM...
THANKS FOR ALL YOUR HELP.

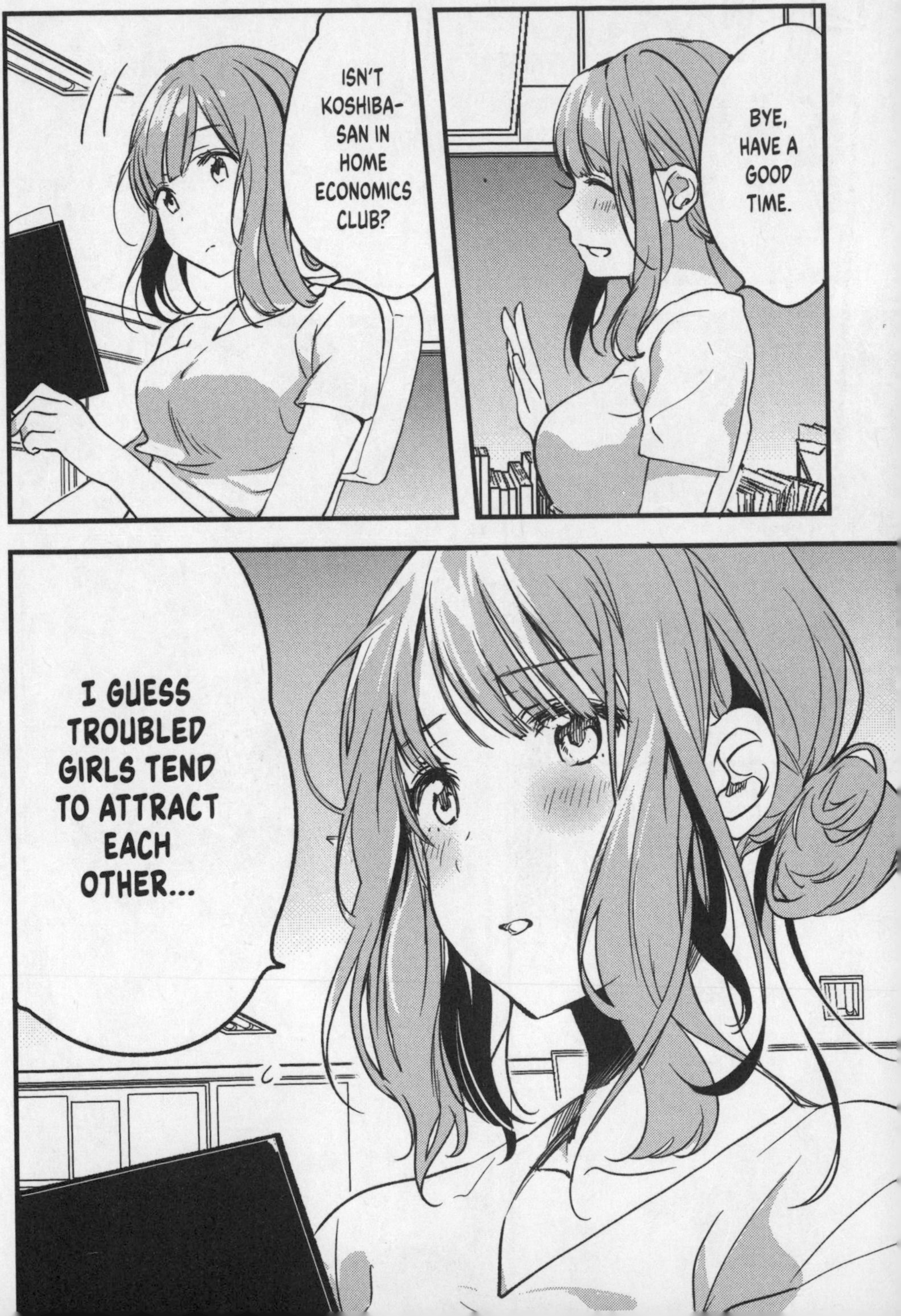
BYE, HAVE A GOOD TIME.
ISN'T KOSHIBA-SAN IN HOME ECONOMICS CLUB?
I GUESS TROUBLED GIRLS TEND TO ATTRACT EACH OTHER...

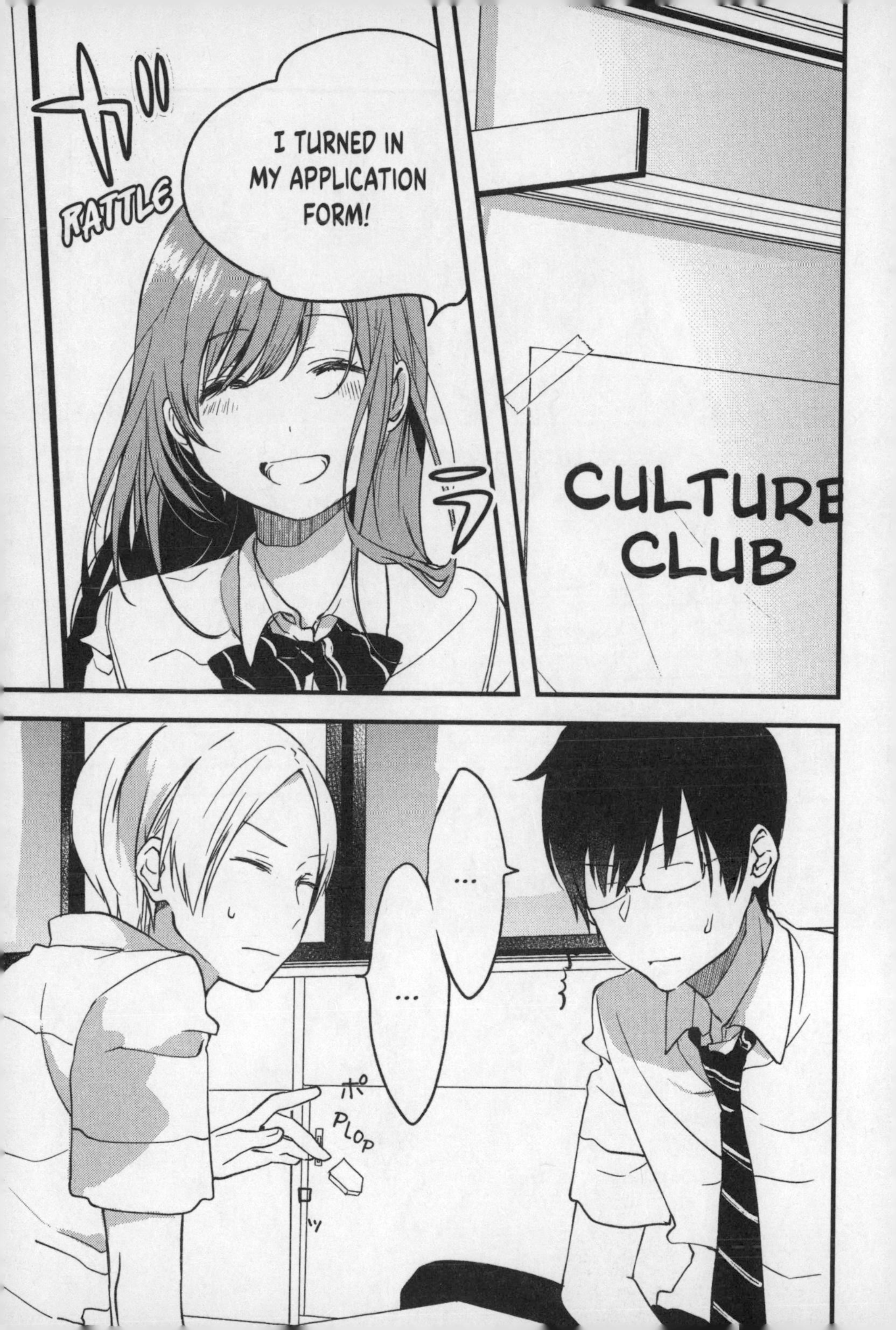
CULTURE CLUB
I TURNED IN MY APPLICATION FORM!
RATTLE
...
...
PLOP

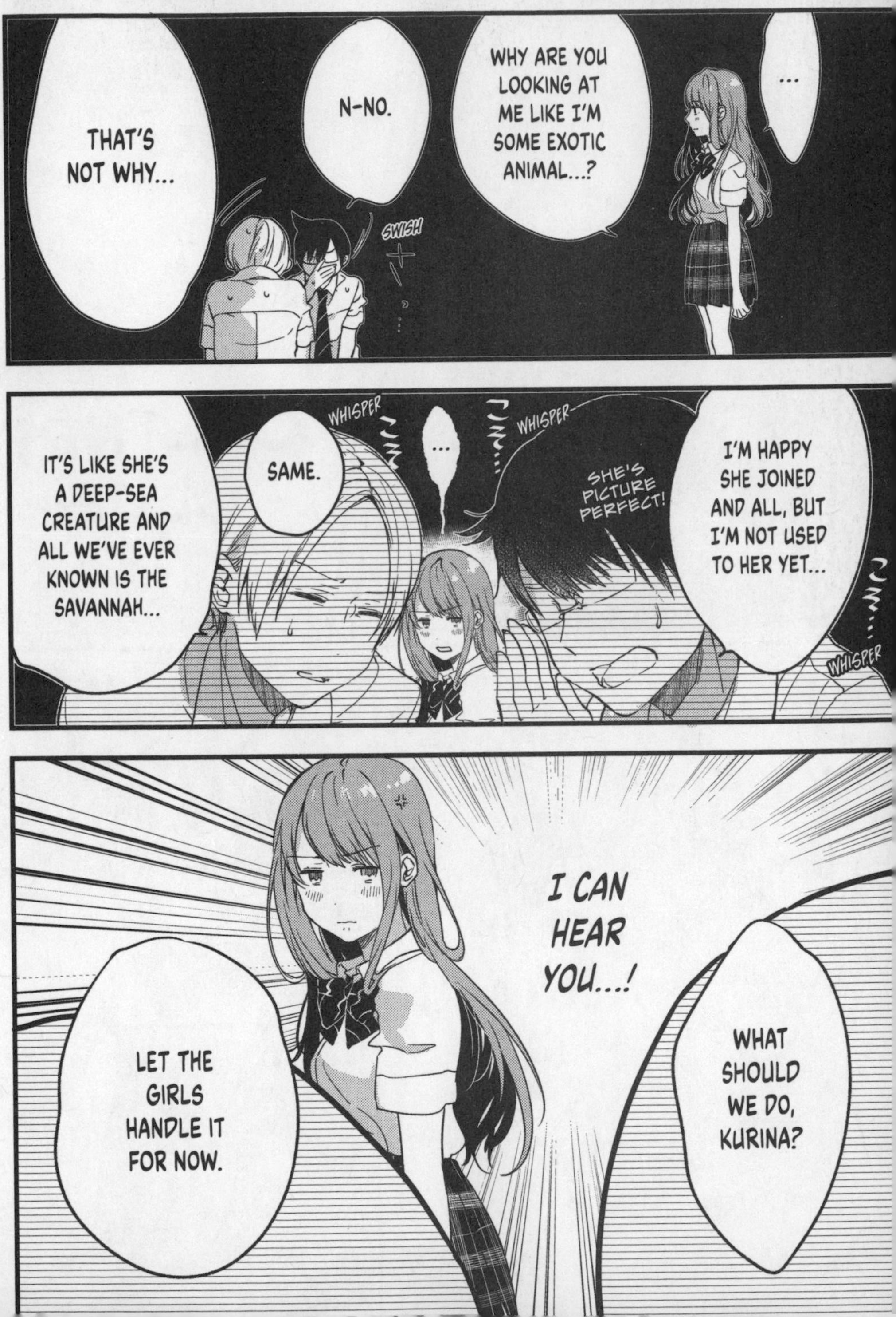
...
WHY ARE YOU LOOKING AT ME LIKE I'M SOME EXOTIC ANIMAL...?
N-NO.
SWISH
THAT'S NOT WHY...
WHISPER
I'M HAPPY SHE JOINED AND ALL, BUT I'M NOT USED TO HER YET...
SHE'S PICTURE PERFECT!
WHISPER
...
WHISPER
SAME.
IT'S LIKE SHE'S A DEEP-SEA CREATURE AND ALL WE'VE EVER KNOWN IS THE SAVANNAH...
WHAT SHOULD WE DO, KURINA?
I CAN HEAR YOU...!
LET THE GIRLS HANDLE IT FOR NOW.

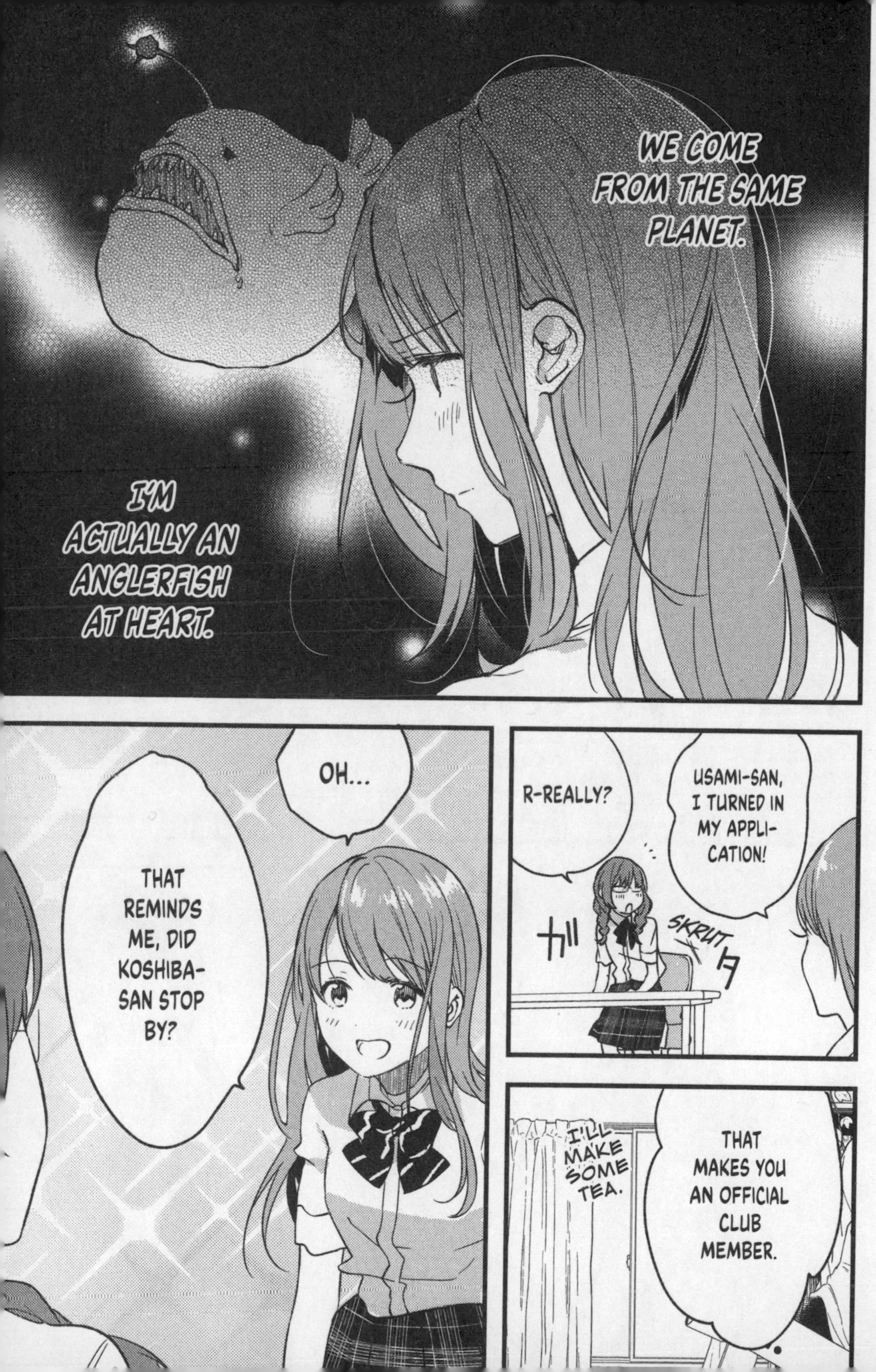
WE COME FROM THE SAME PLANET.
I'M ACTUALLY AN ANGLERFISH AT HEART.
USAMI-SAN, I TURNED IN MY APPLI-CATION!
R-REALLY?
カリ
SKRUT
タ
THAT MAKES YOU AN OFFICIAL CLUB MEMBER.
I'LL MAKE SOME TEA.
OH...
THAT REMINDS ME, DID KOSHIBA-SAN STOP BY?

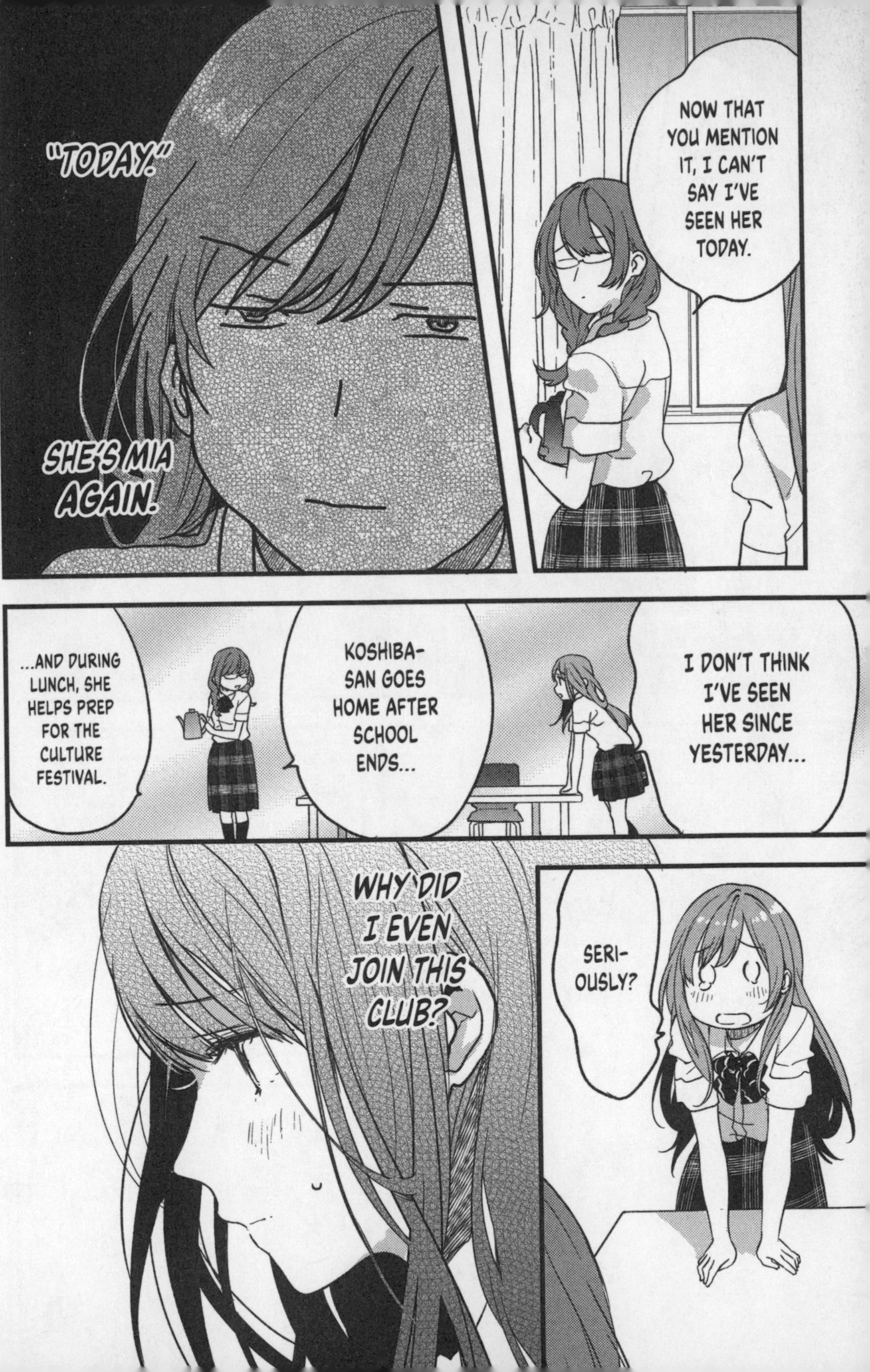
NOW THAT YOU MENTION IT, I CAN'T SAY I'VE SEEN HER TODAY.
"TODAY."
SHE'S MIA AGAIN.
I DON'T THINK I'VE SEEN HER SINCE YESTERDAY...
KOSHIBA-SAN GOES HOME AFTER SCHOOL ENDS...
...AND DURING LUNCH, SHE HELPS PREP FOR THE CULTURE FESTIVAL.
SERI-OUSLY?
WHY DID I EVEN JOIN THIS CLUB?

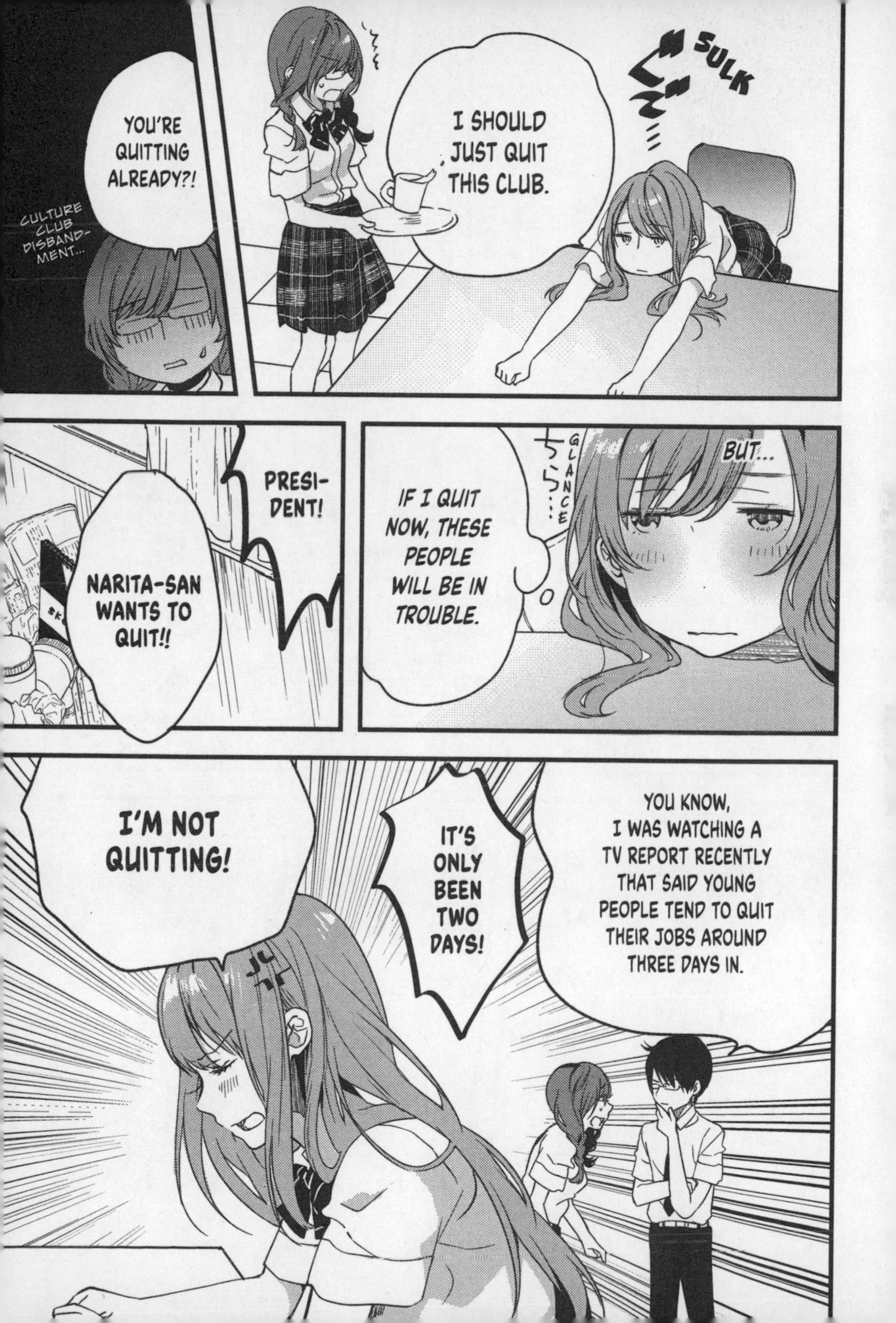
SULK
I SHOULD JUST QUIT THIS CLUB.
YOU'RE QUITTING ALREADY?!
CULTURE CLUB DISBANDMENT...
BUT...
ちら…
GLANCE
IF I QUIT NOW, THESE PEOPLE WILL BE IN TROUBLE.
PRESIDENT!
NARITA-SAN WANTS TO QUIT!!
YOU KNOW, I WAS WATCHING A TV REPORT RECENTLY THAT SAID YOUNG PEOPLE TEND TO QUIT THEIR JOBS AROUND THREE DAYS IN.
IT'S ONLY BEEN TWO DAYS!
I'M NOT QUITTING!

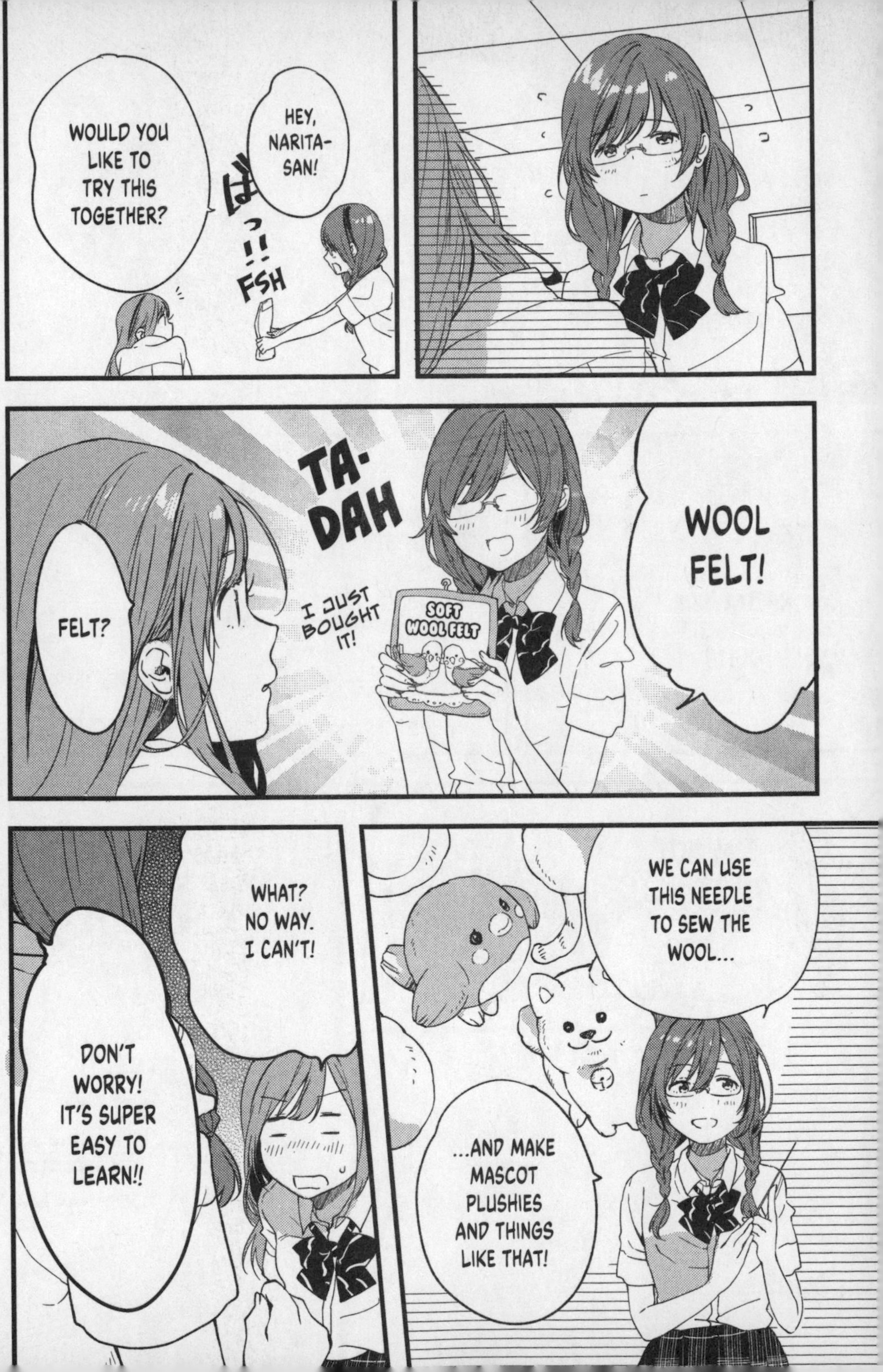
HEY, NARITA-SAN!
はっ!!
FSH
WOULD YOU LIKE TO TRY THIS TOGETHER?
WOOL FELT!
TA-DAH
I JUST BOUGHT IT!
SOFT WOOL FELT
FELT?
WE CAN USE THIS NEEDLE TO SEW THE WOOL...
...AND MAKE MASCOT PLUSHIES AND THINGS LIKE THAT!
WHAT? NO WAY. I CAN'T!
DON'T WORRY! IT'S SUPER EASY TO LEARN!!

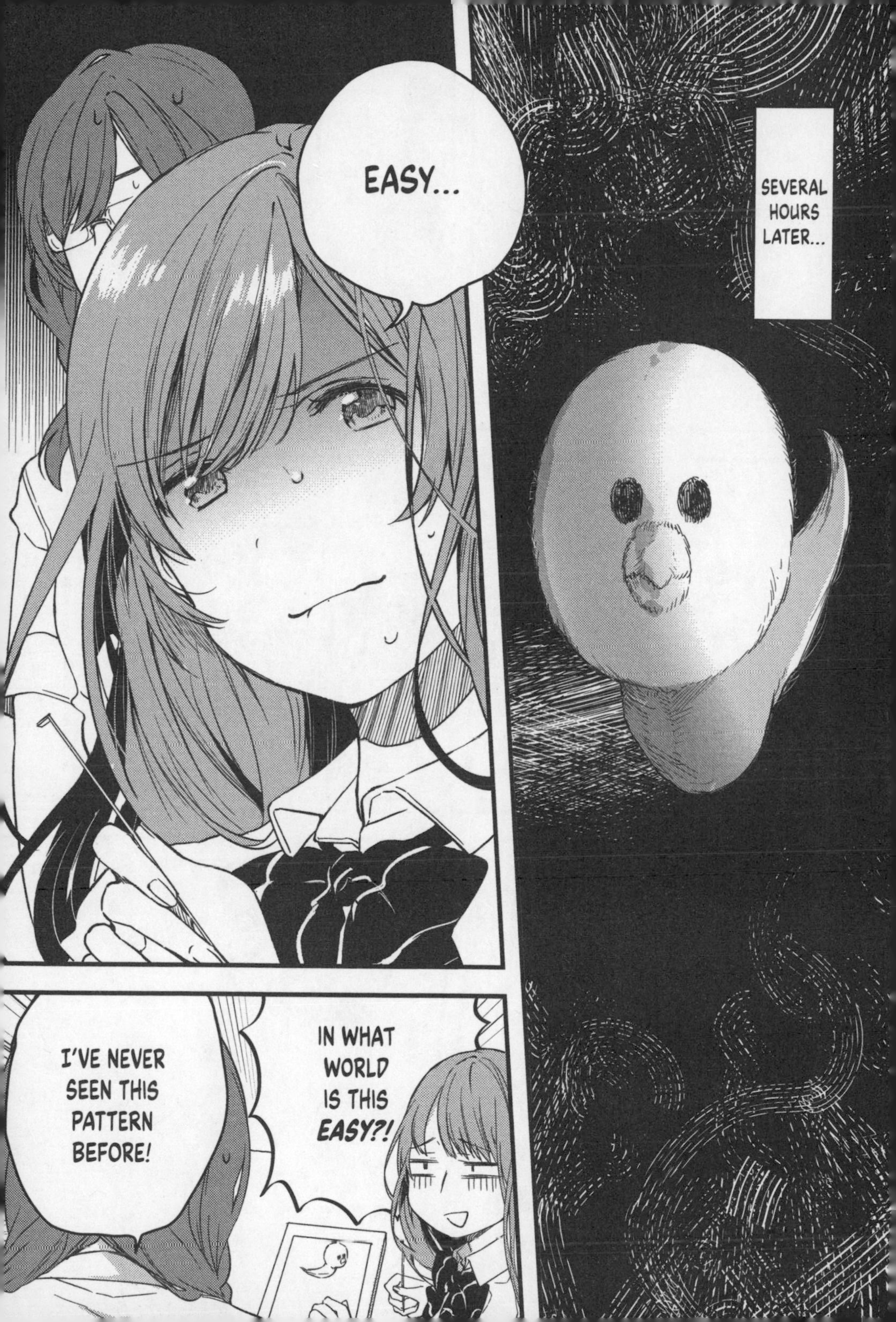
SEVERAL HOURS LATER...
EASY...
IN WHAT WORLD IS THIS *EASY?!*
I'VE NEVER SEEN THIS PATTERN BEFORE!

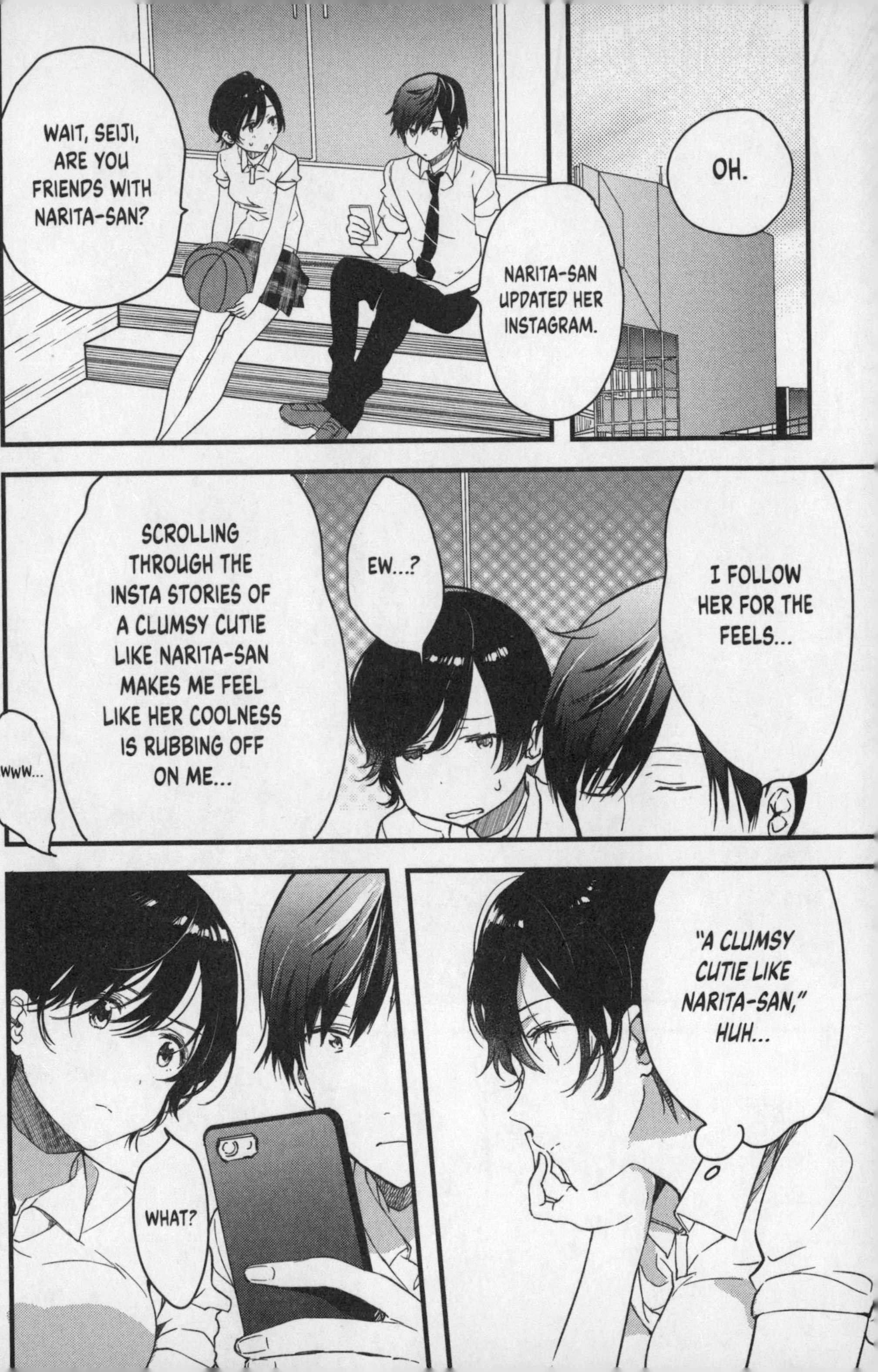
OH.
NARITA-SAN UPDATED HER INSTAGRAM.
WAIT, SEIJI, ARE YOU FRIENDS WITH NARITA-SAN?
I FOLLOW HER FOR THE FEELS...
EW...?
SCROLLING THROUGH THE INSTA STORIES OF A CLUMSY CUTIE LIKE NARITA-SAN MAKES ME FEEL LIKE HER COOLNESS IS RUBBING OFF ON ME...
EWWW...
"A CLUMSY CUTIE LIKE NARITA-SAN," HUH...
WHAT?

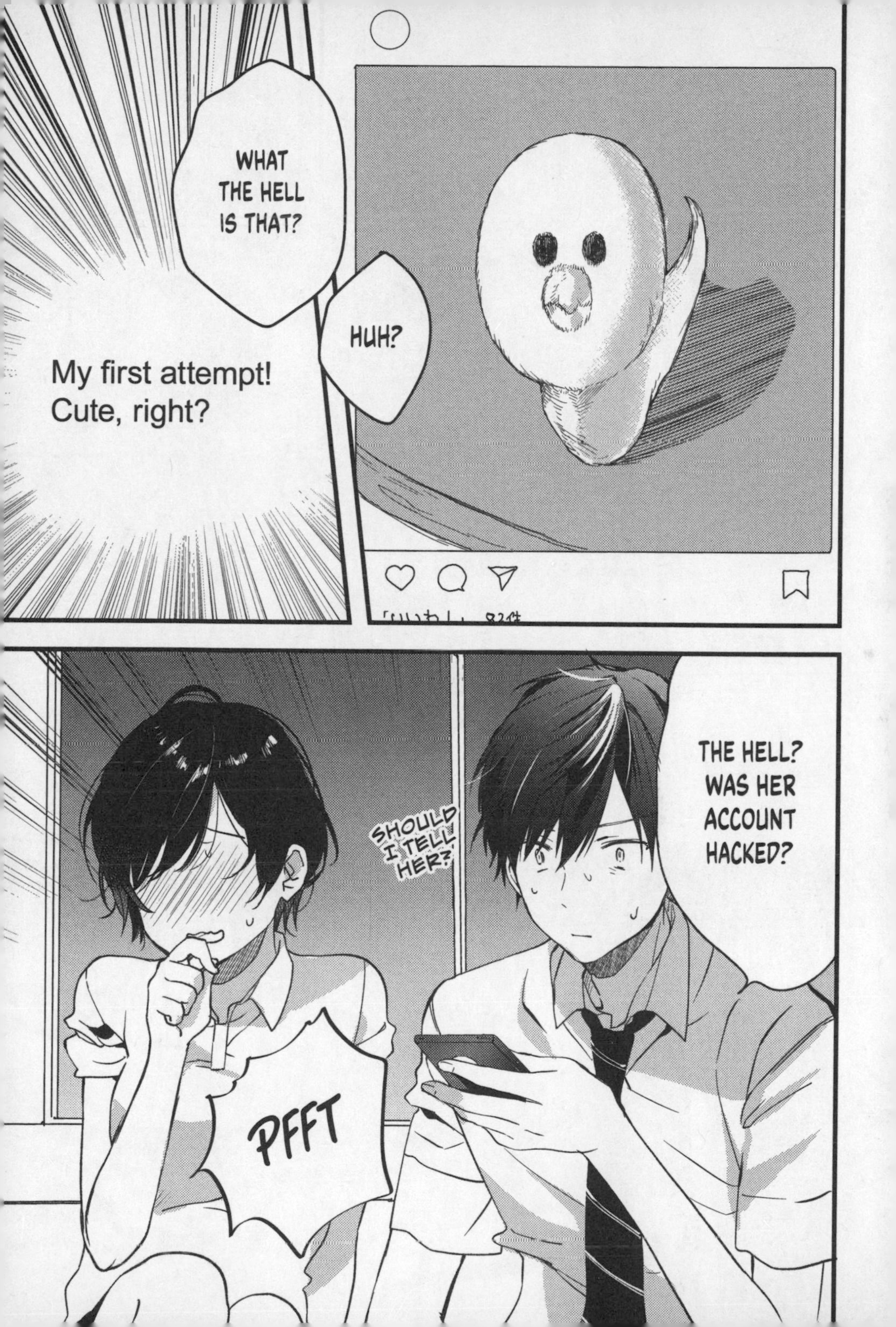
WHAT THE HELL IS THAT?
HUH?
My first attempt! Cute, right?
THE HELL? WAS HER ACCOUNT HACKED?
SHOULD I TELL HER?
PFFT

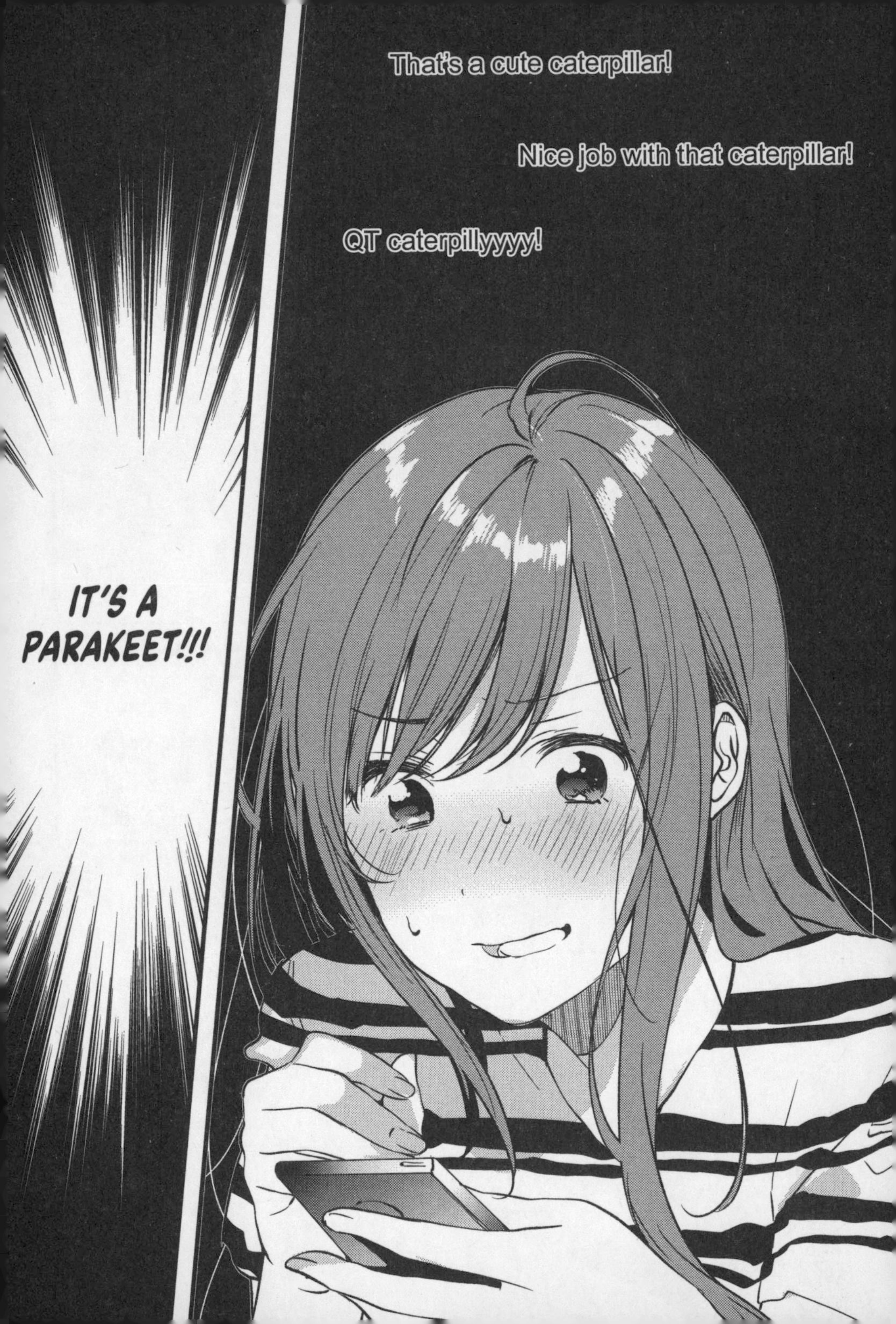
That's a cute caterpillar!
Nice job with that caterpillar!
QT caterpillyyyy!
IT'S A PARAKEET!!!

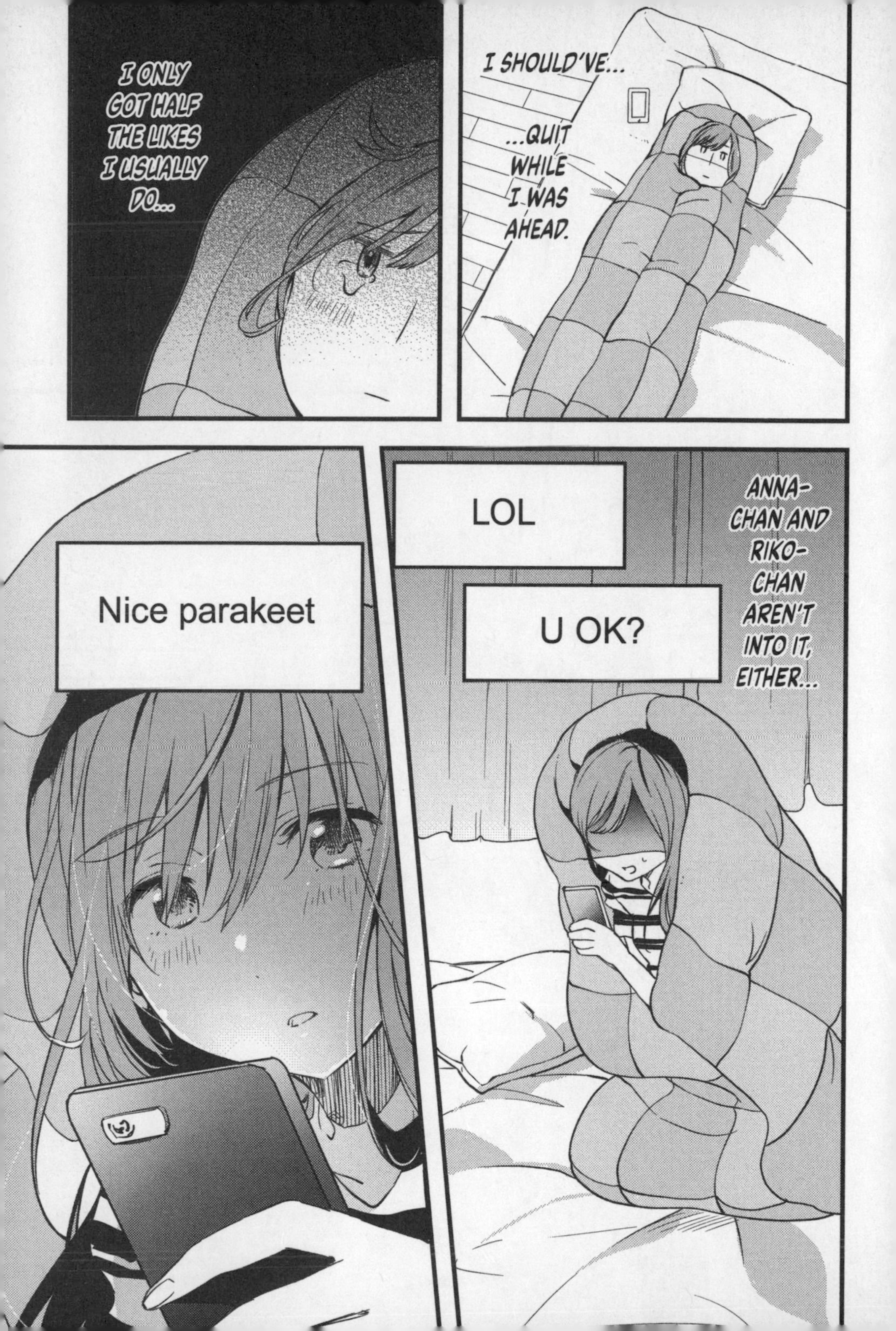
I SHOULD'VE...
...QUIT WHILE I WAS AHEAD.
I ONLY GOT HALF THE LIKES I USUALLY DO...
ANNA-CHAN AND RIKO-CHAN AREN'T INTO IT, EITHER...
LOL
U OK?
Nice parakeet

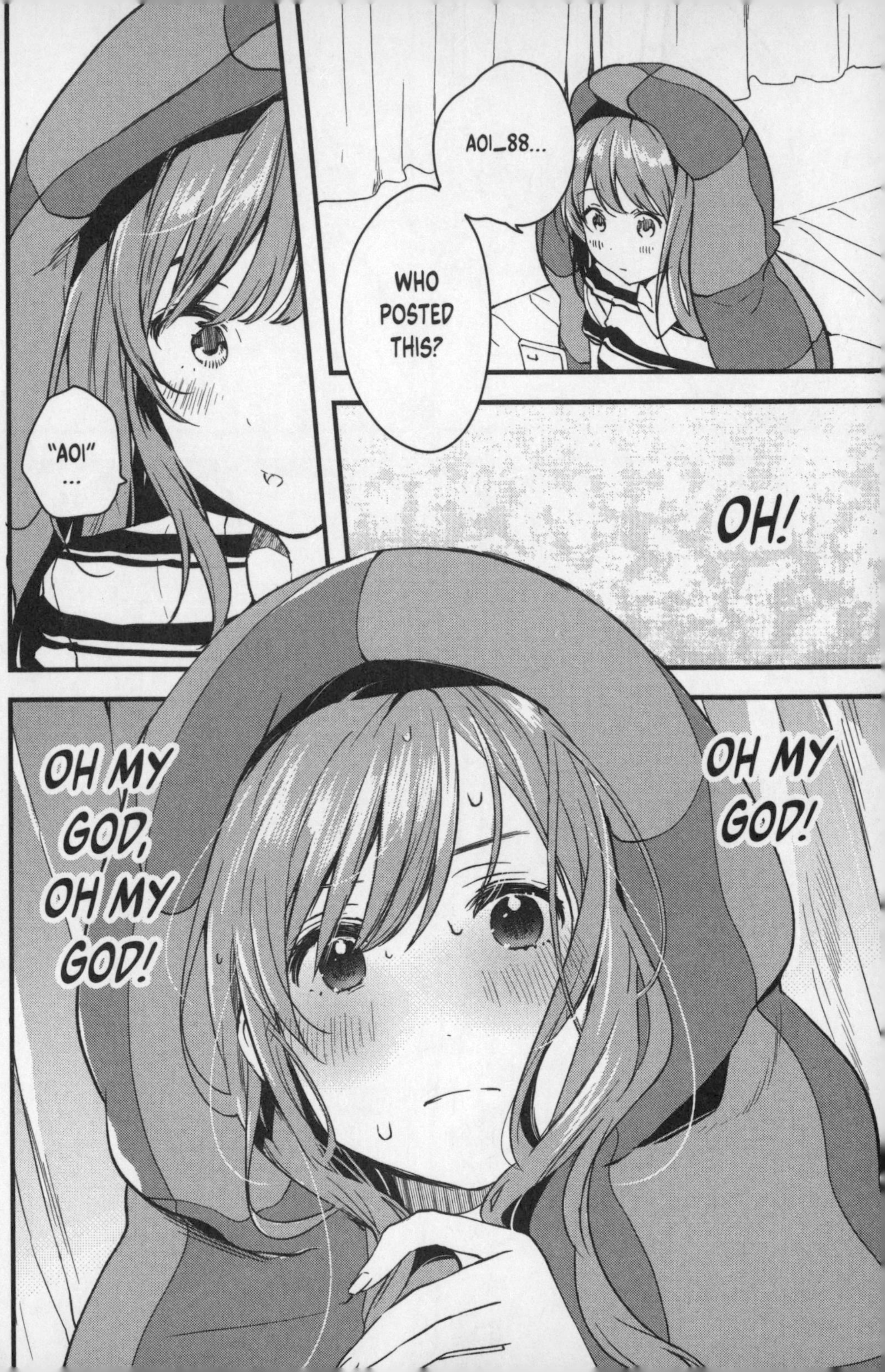
AOI_88...
WHO POSTED THIS?
OH!
"AOI" ...
OH MY GOD!
OH MY GOD, OH MY GOD!

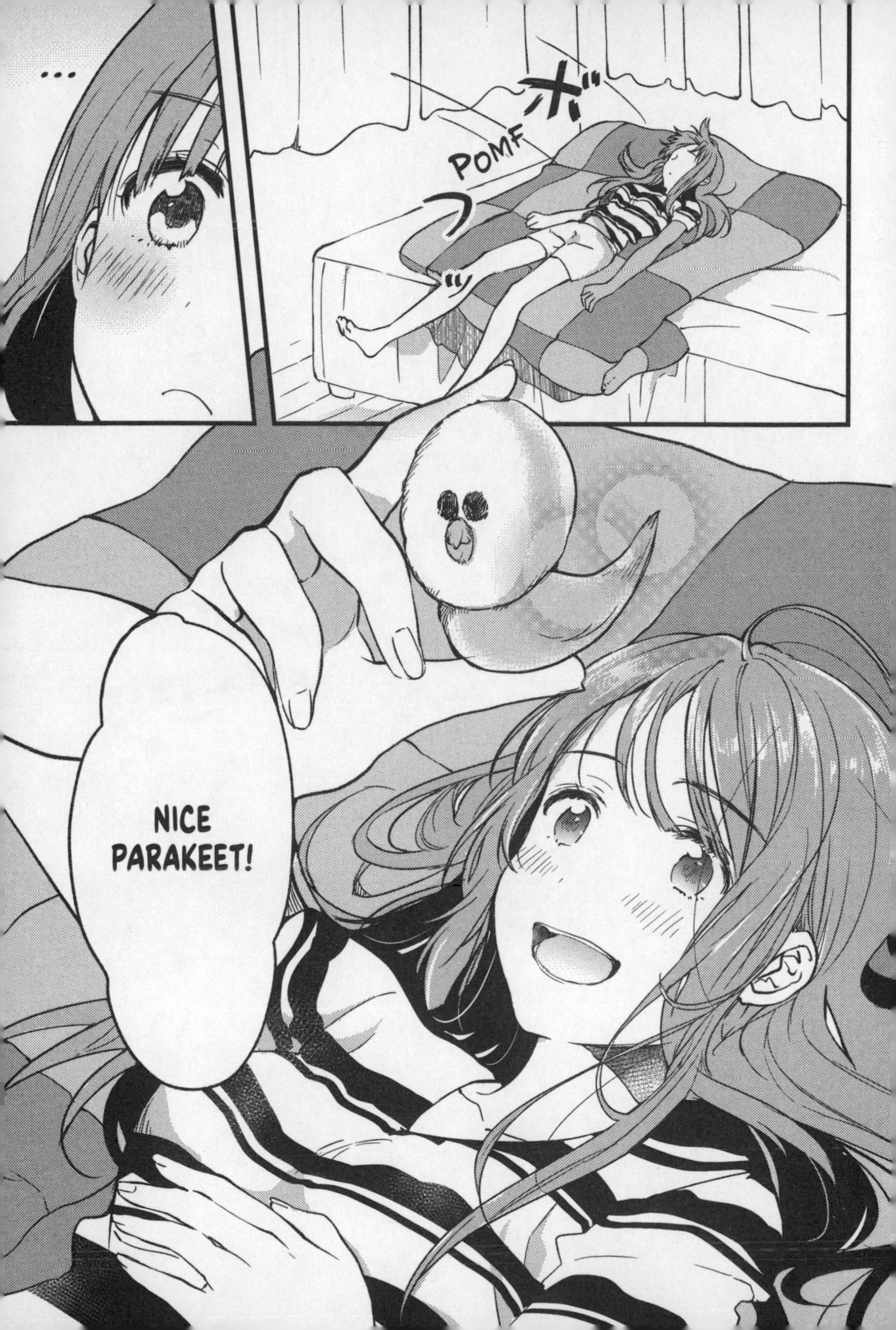
POMF
...
NICE PARAKEET!

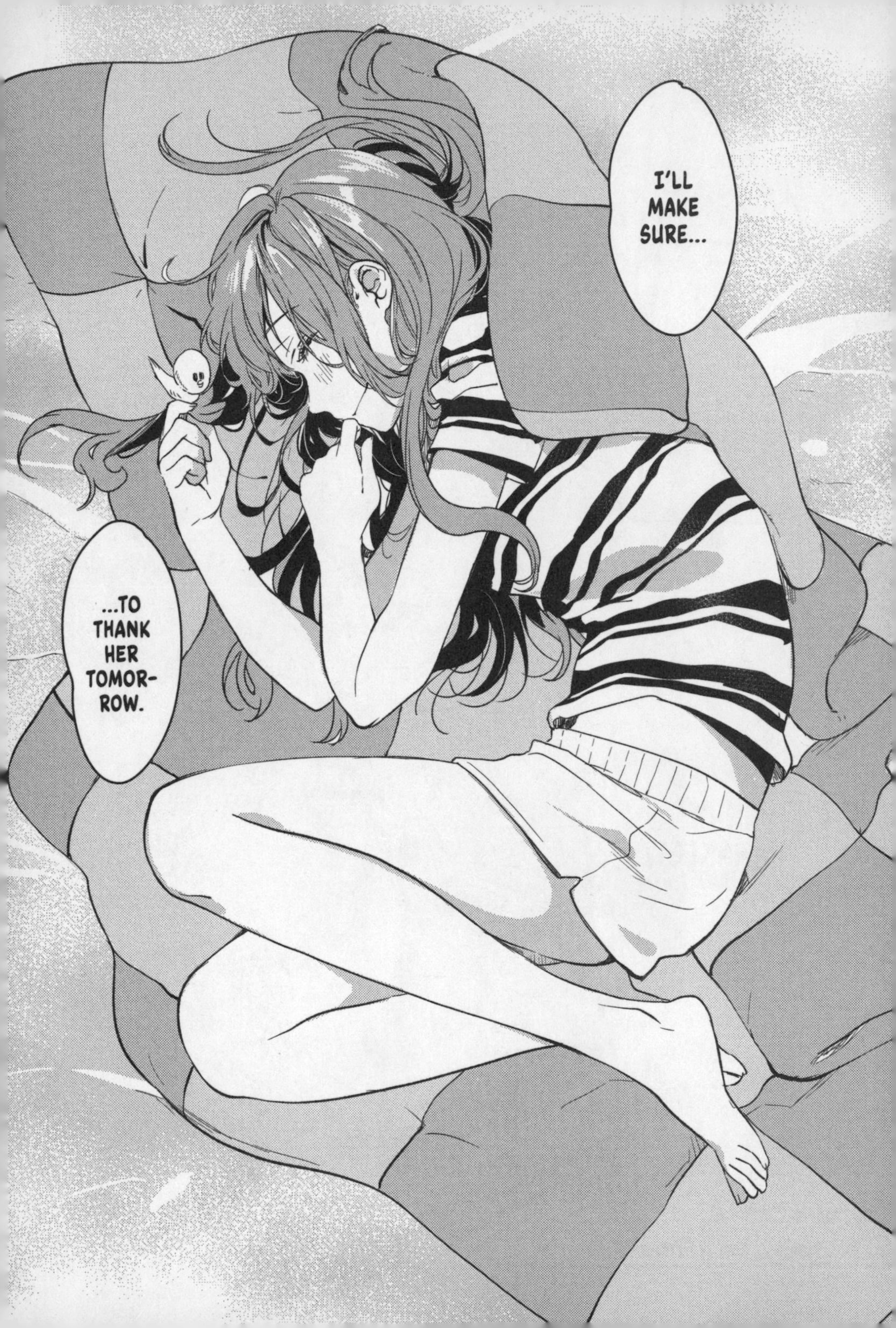
I'LL MAKE SURE...
...TO THANK HER TOMORROW.

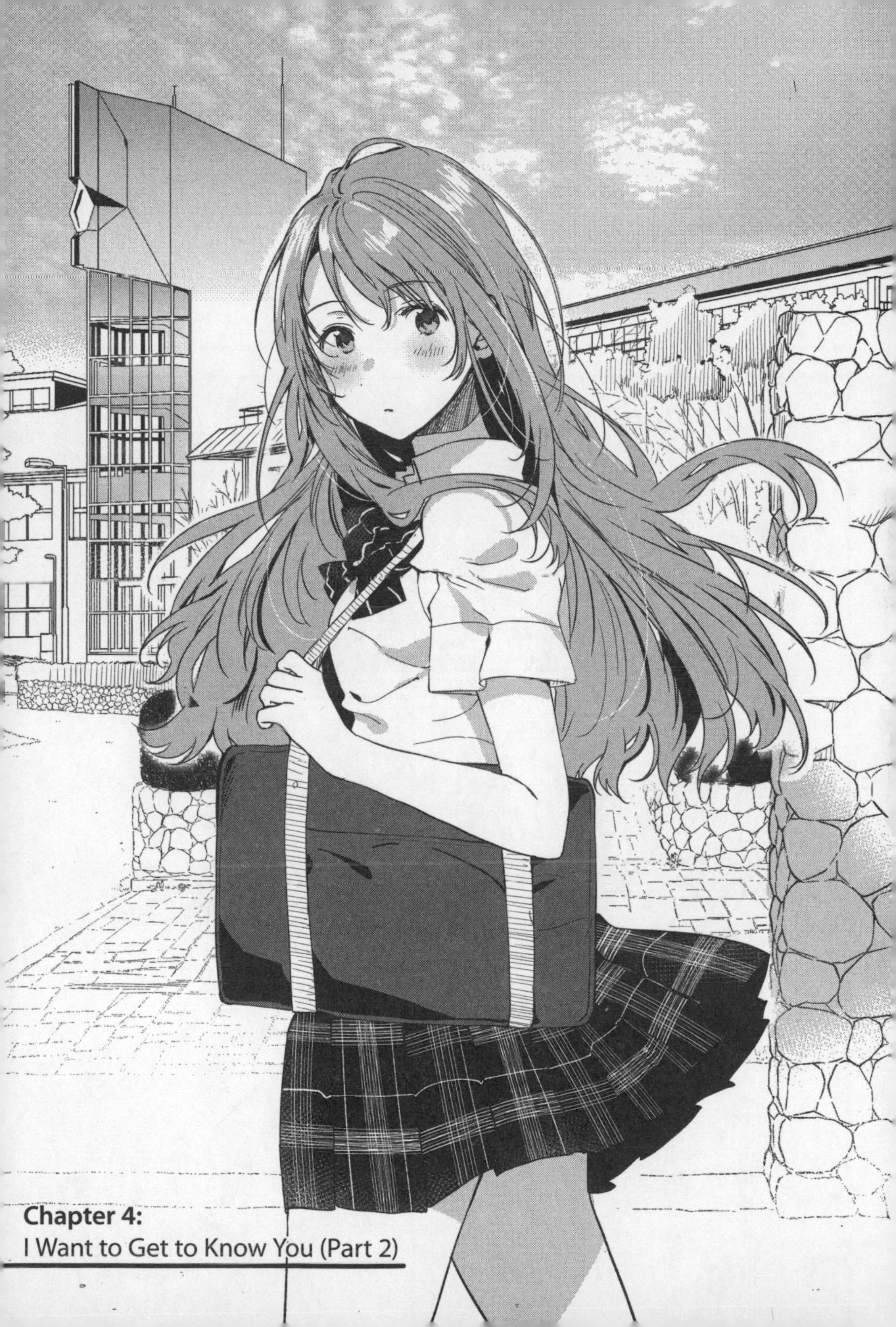

Chapter 4:
I Want to Get to Know You (Part 2)

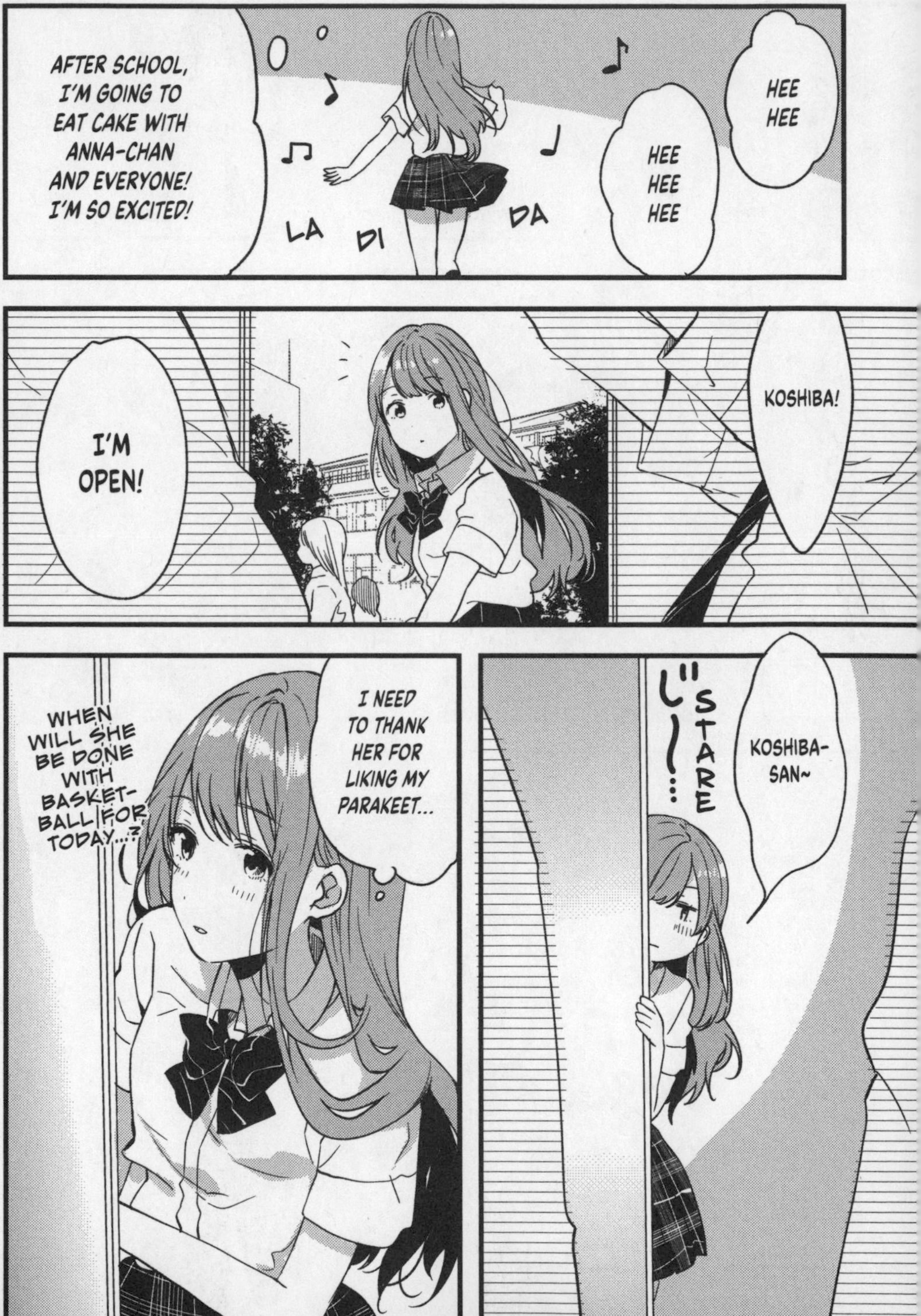

HEE HEE
HEE HEE HEE
AFTER SCHOOL, I'M GOING TO EAT CAKE WITH ANNA-CHAN AND EVERYONE! I'M SO EXCITED!
LA DI DA
KOSHIBA!
I'M OPEN!
KOSHIBA-SAN~
じー…
STARE
I NEED TO THANK HER FOR LIKING MY PARAKEET...
WHEN WILL SHE BE DONE WITH BASKET-BALL FOR TODAY...?

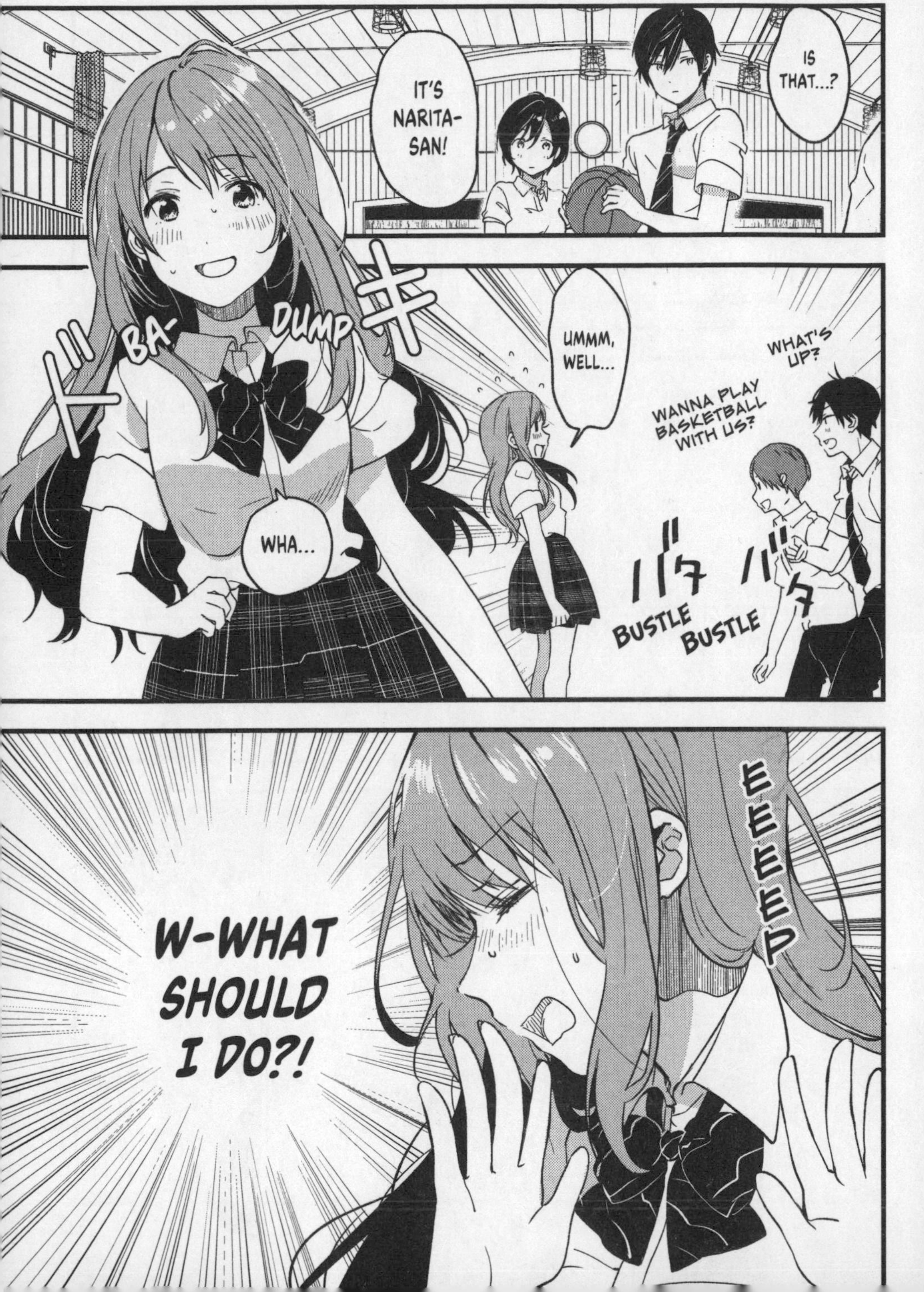
IS THAT...?
IT'S NARITA-SAN!
WHAT'S UP?
WANNA PLAY BASKETBALL WITH US?
バタ バタ
BUSTLE BUSTLE
UMMM, WELL...
BA-DUMP
WHA...
EEEEEP
W-WHAT SHOULD I DO?!

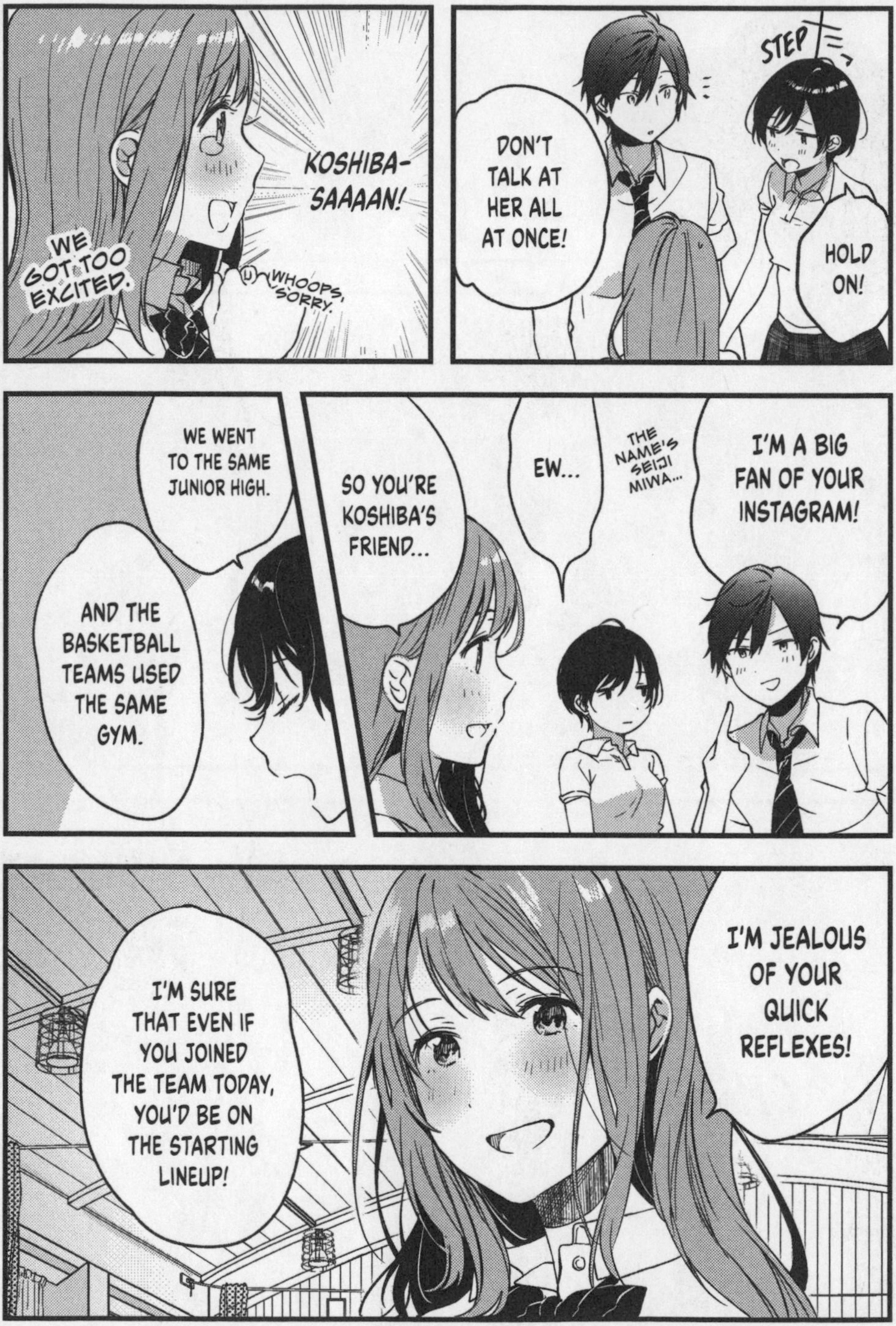
STEP
HOLD ON!
DON'T TALK AT HER ALL AT ONCE!
KOSHIBA-SAAAAN!
WHOOPS, SORRY.
WE GOT TOO EXCITED.
I'M A BIG FAN OF YOUR INSTAGRAM!
THE NAME'S SEIJI MIWA...
EW...
SO YOU'RE KOSHIBA'S FRIEND...
WE WENT TO THE SAME JUNIOR HIGH.
AND THE BASKETBALL TEAMS USED THE SAME GYM.
I'M JEALOUS OF YOUR QUICK REFLEXES!
I'M SURE THAT EVEN IF YOU JOINED THE TEAM TODAY, YOU'D BE ON THE STARTING LINEUP!

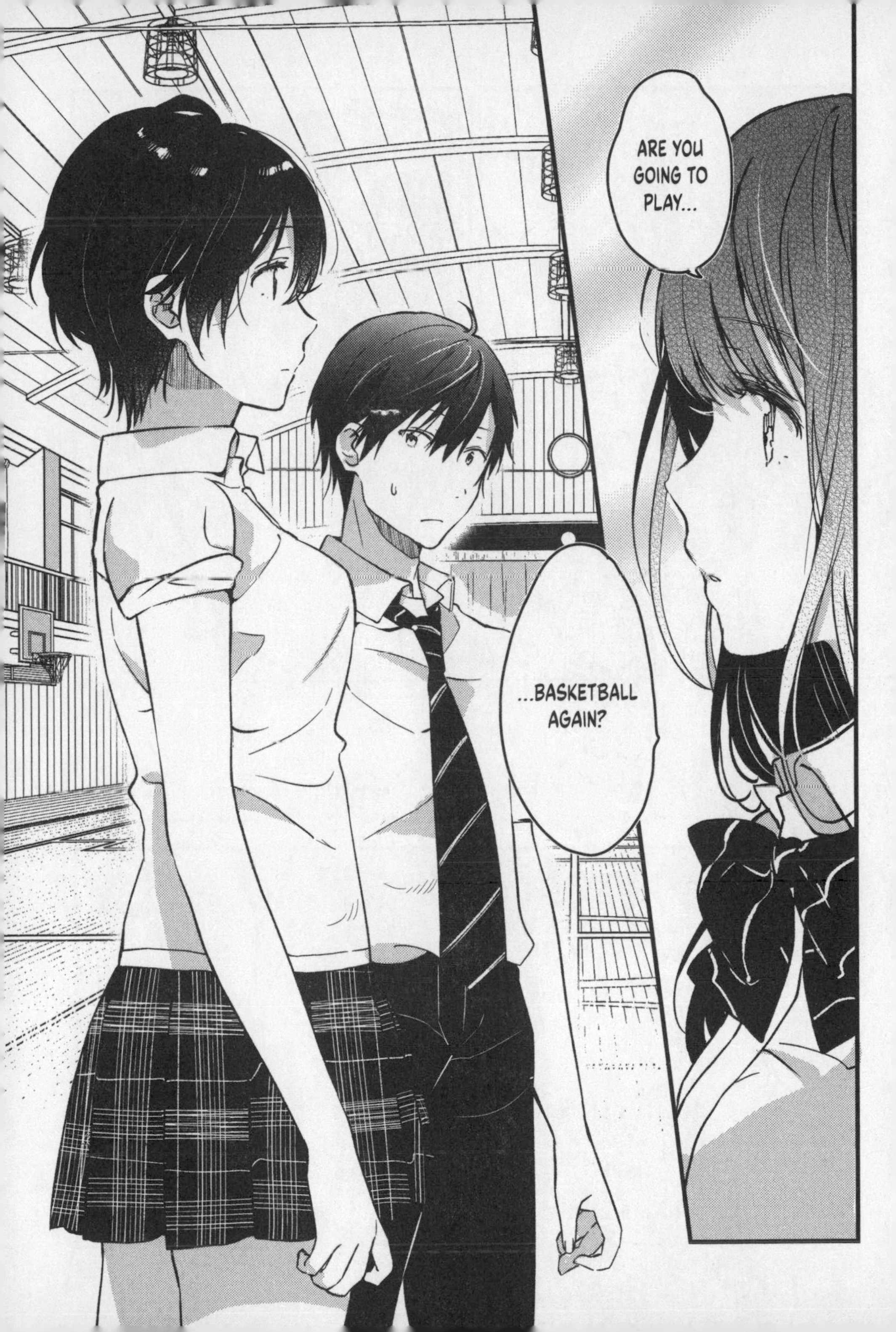
ARE YOU GOING TO PLAY...
...BASKETBALL AGAIN?

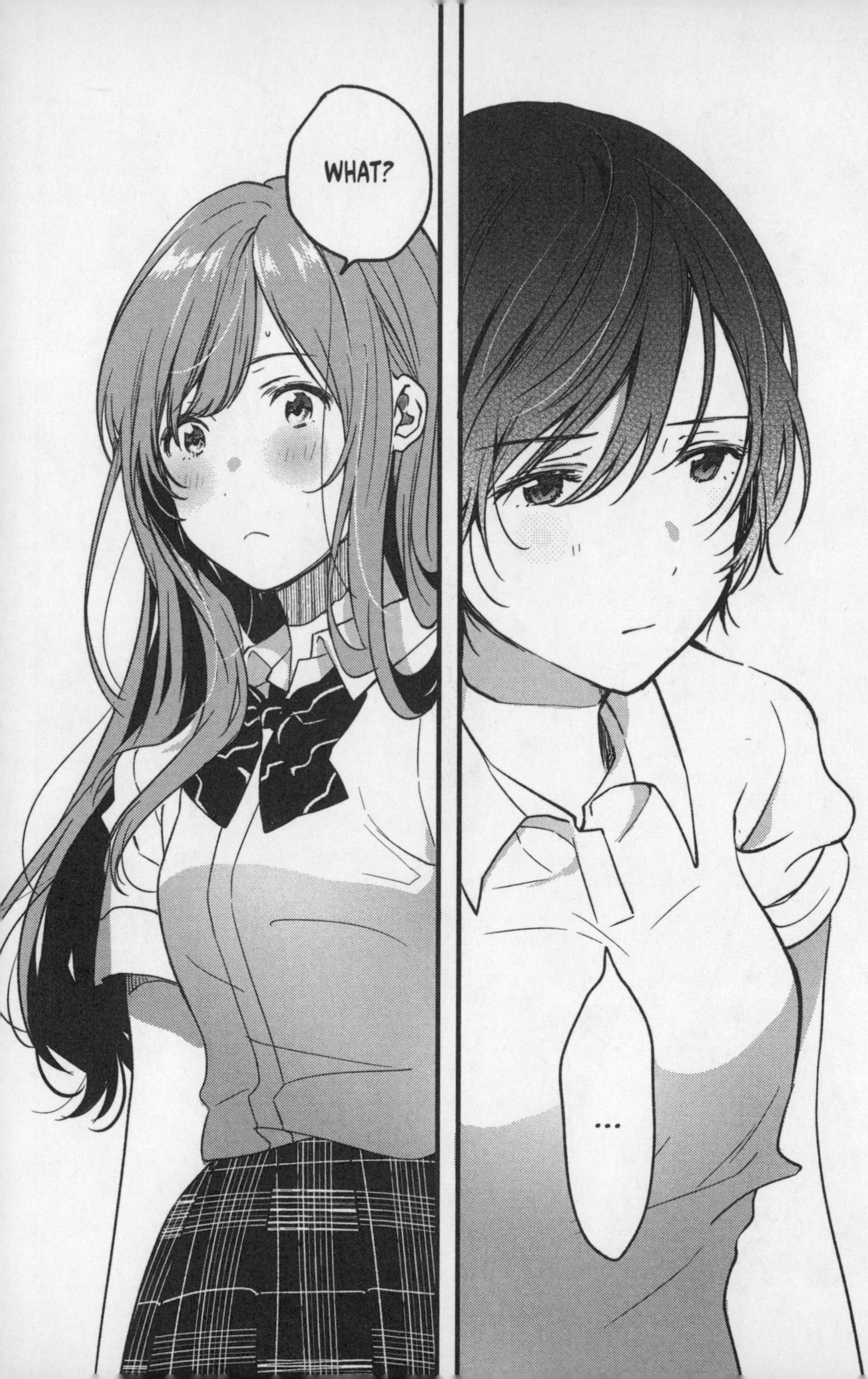
...
WHAT?

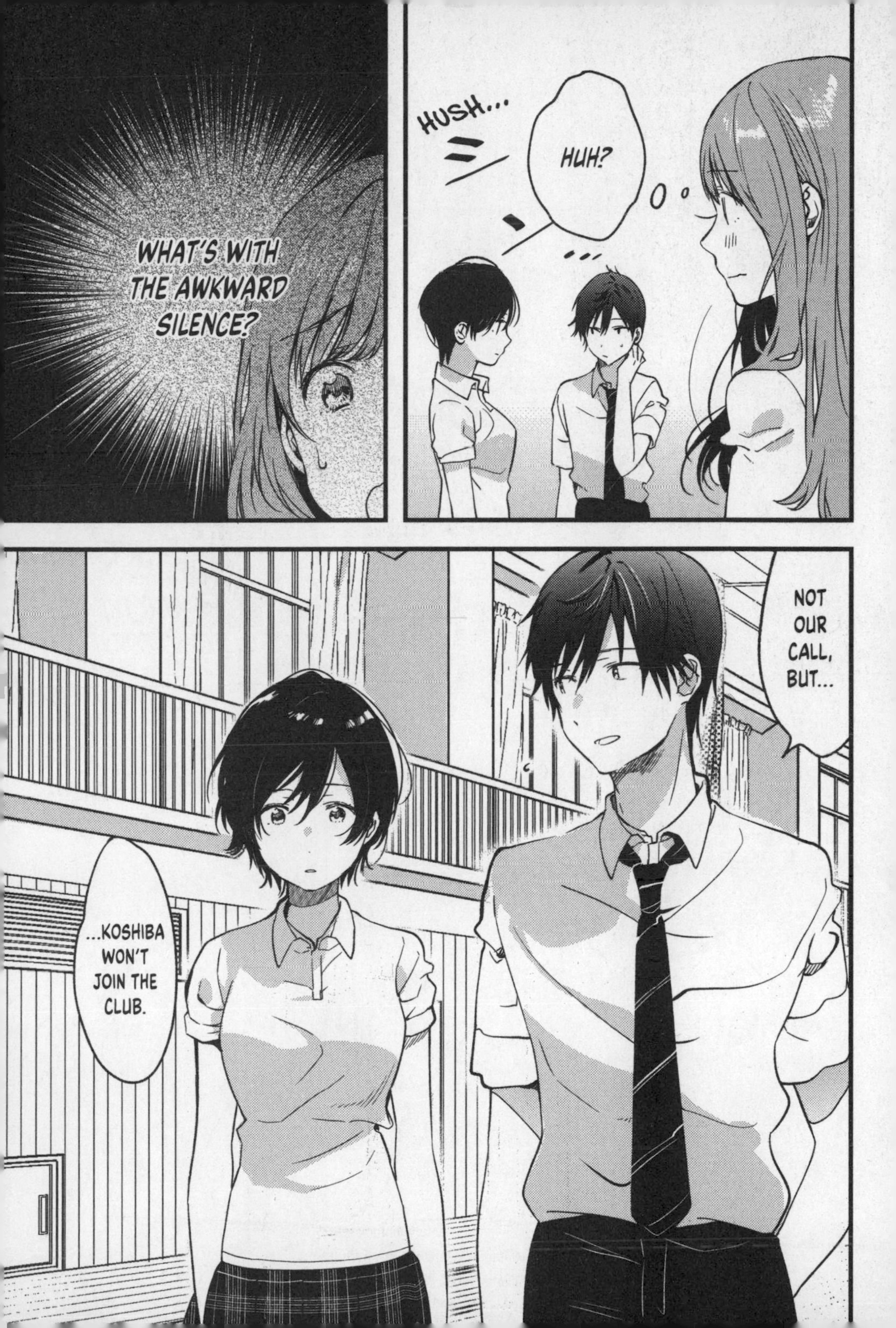
HUSH...
HUH?
...
WHAT'S WITH THE AWKWARD SILENCE?
NOT OUR CALL, BUT...
...KOSHIBA WON'T JOIN THE CLUB.

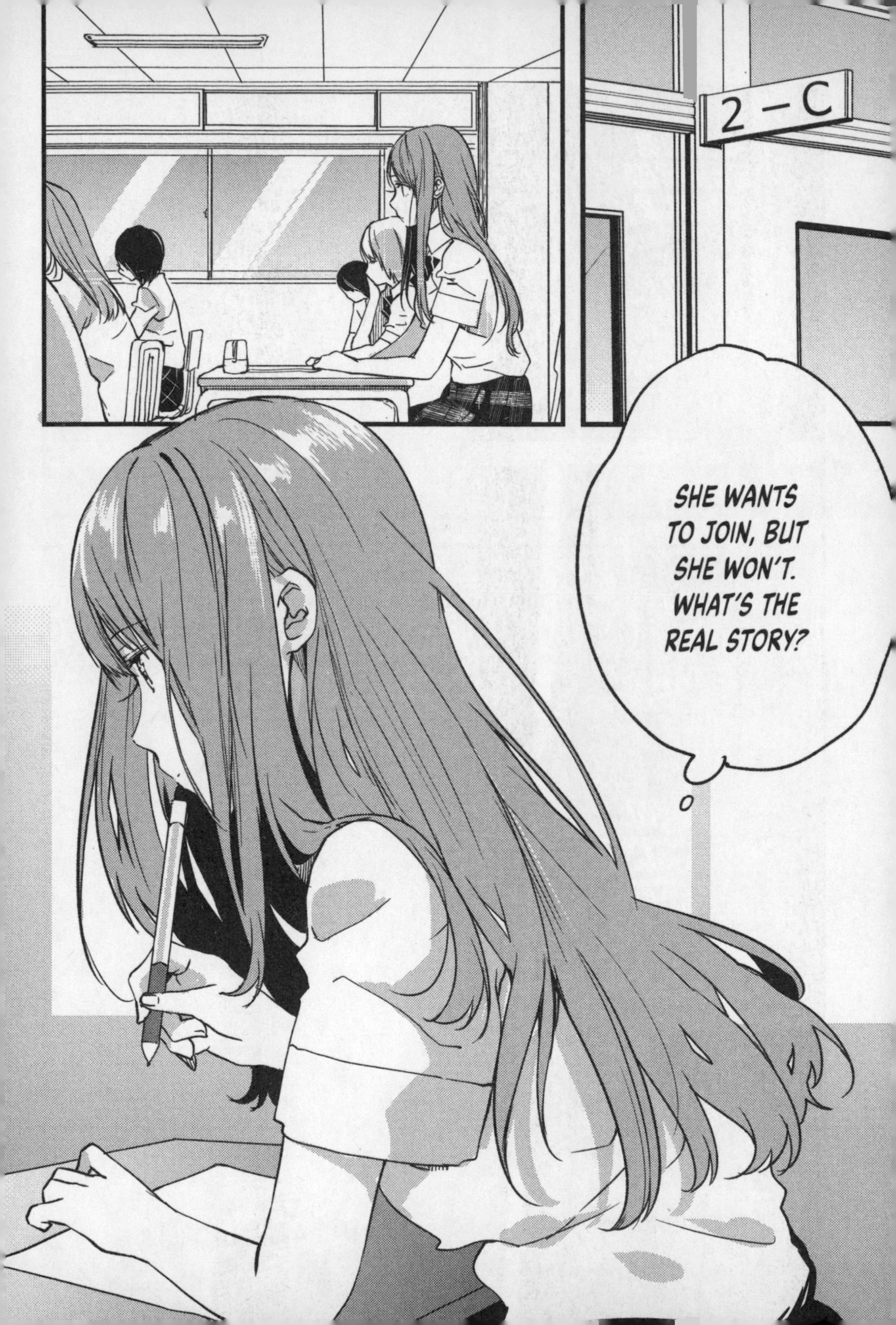
2-C
SHE WANTS TO JOIN, BUT SHE WON'T. WHAT'S THE REAL STORY?

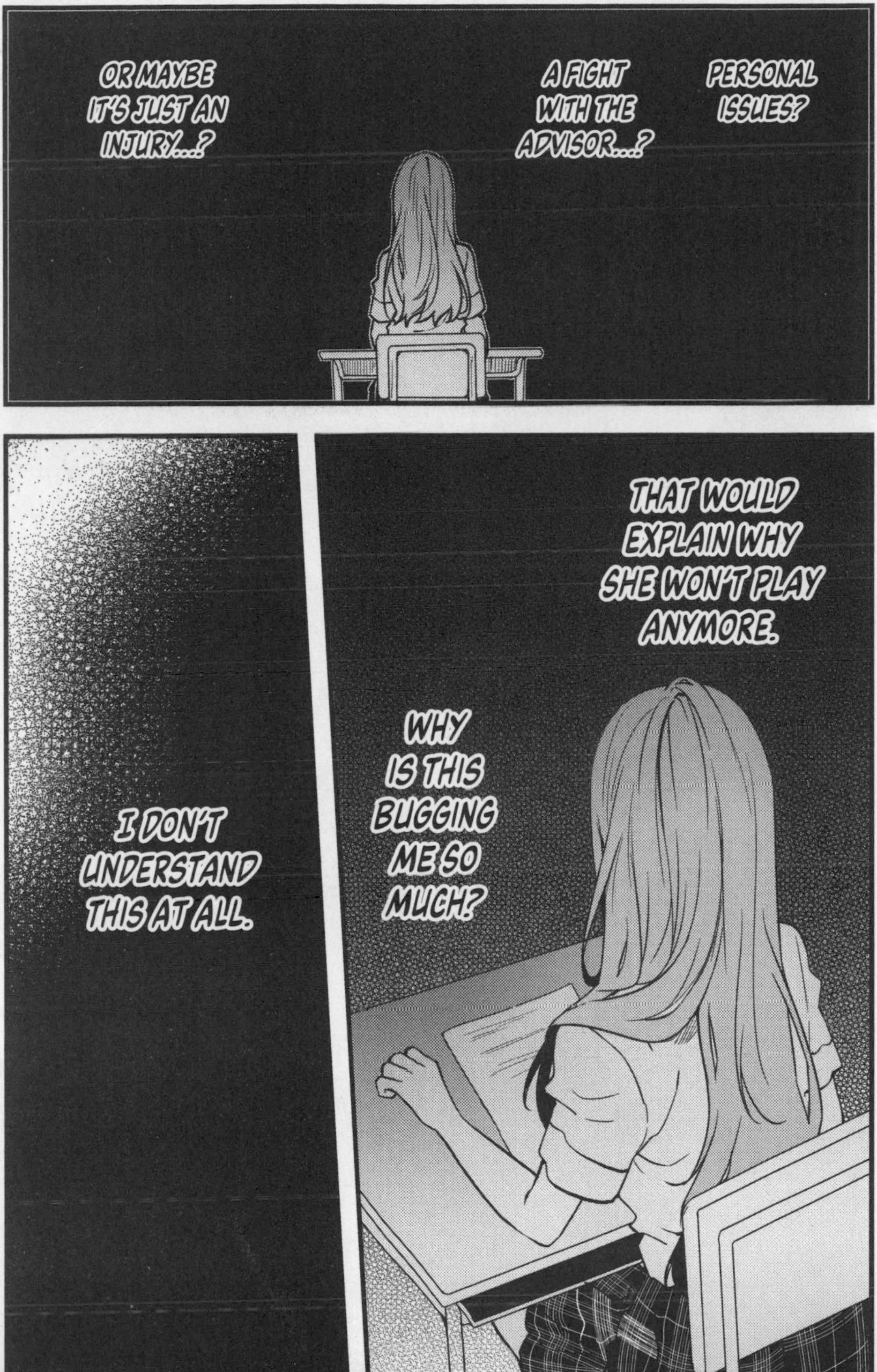
PERSONAL ISSUES?
A FIGHT WITH THE ADVISOR...?
OR MAYBE IT'S JUST AN INJURY...?
THAT WOULD EXPLAIN WHY SHE WON'T PLAY ANYMORE.
WHY IS THIS BUGGING ME SO MUCH?
I DON'T UNDERSTAND THIS AT ALL.

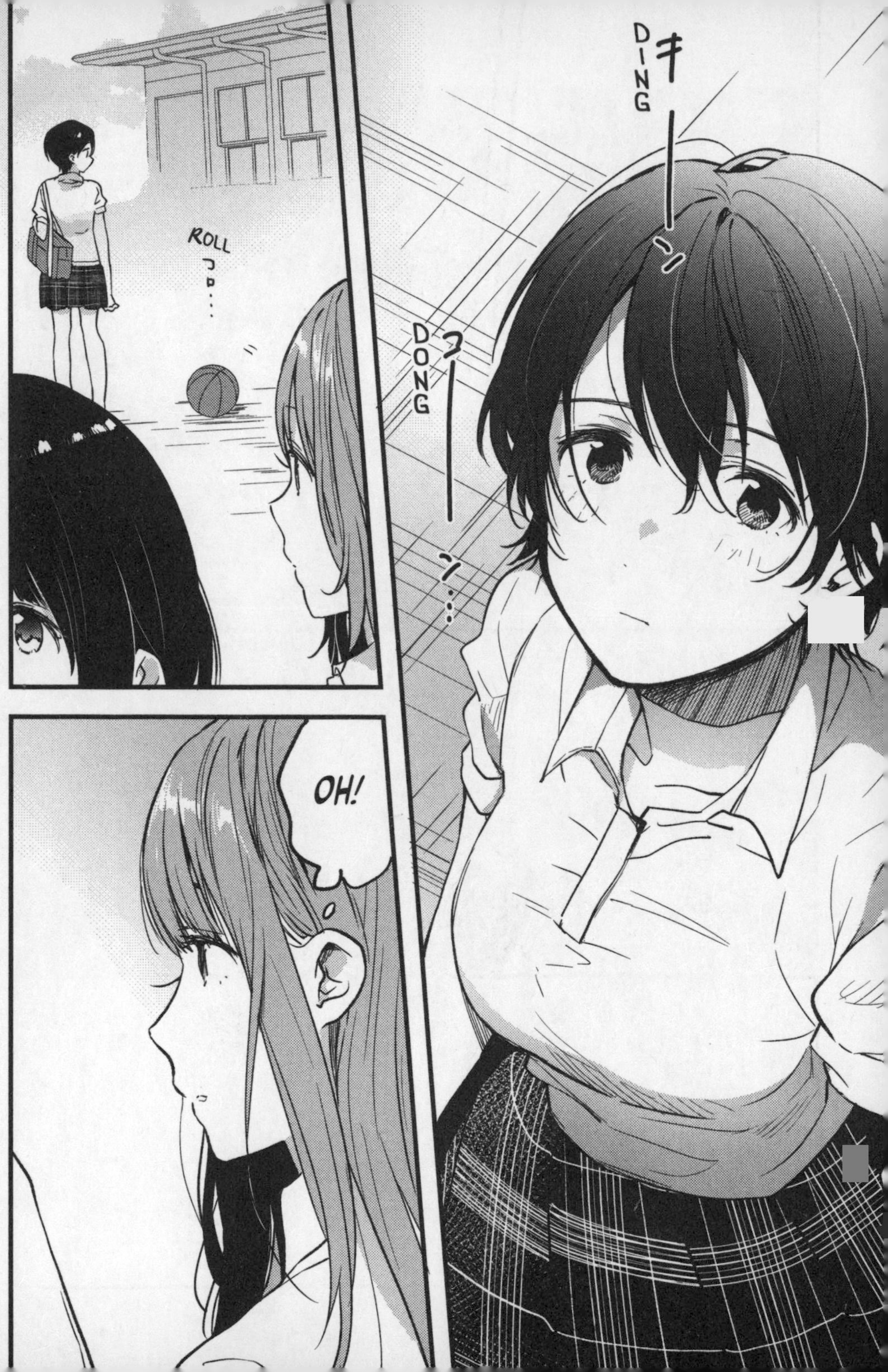
DING
キーン
DONG
コーン…
ROLL
コロ…
OH!

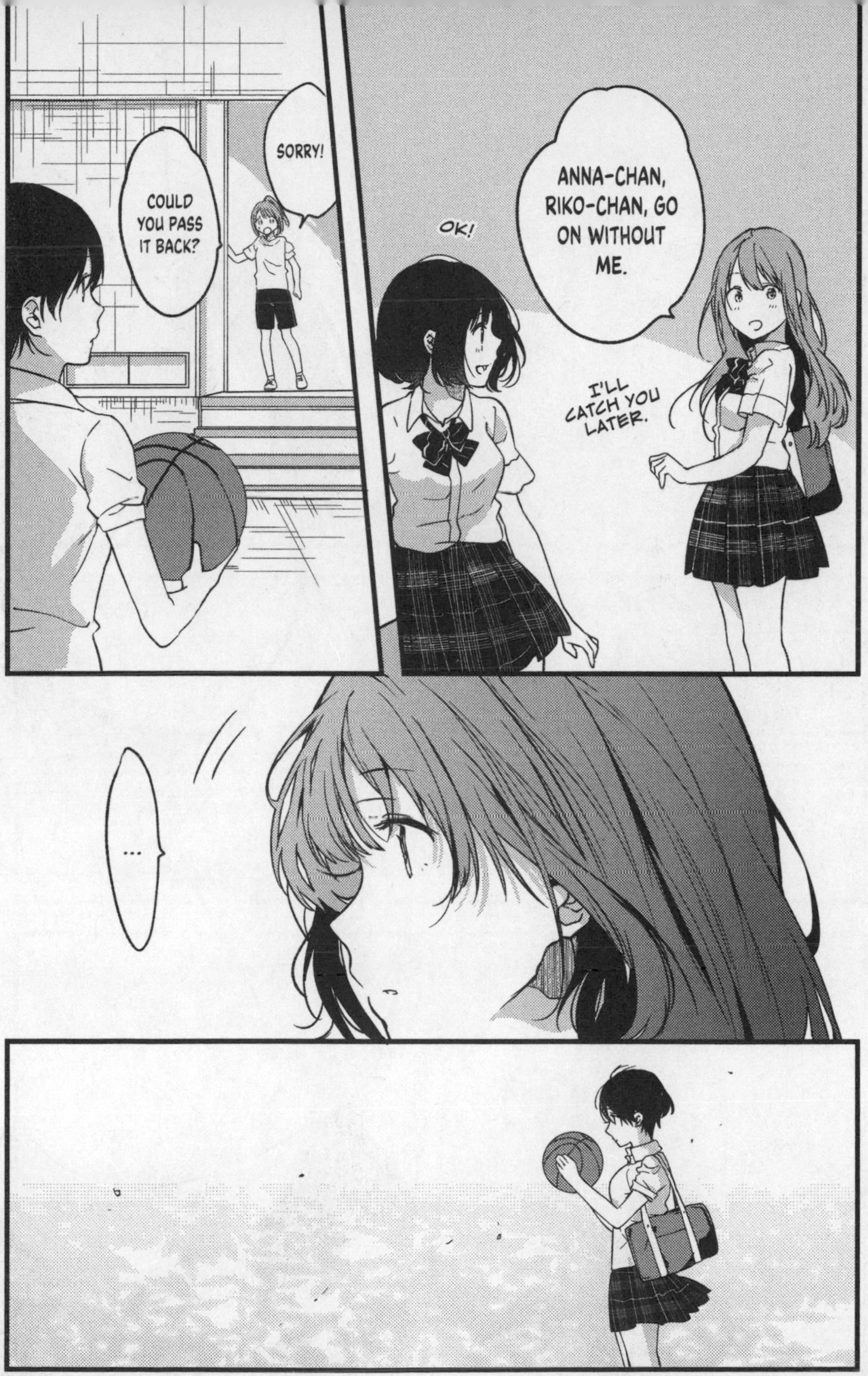
ANNA-CHAN, RIKO-CHAN, GO ON WITHOUT ME.
OK!
I'LL CATCH YOU LATER.
SORRY!
COULD YOU PASS IT BACK?
...

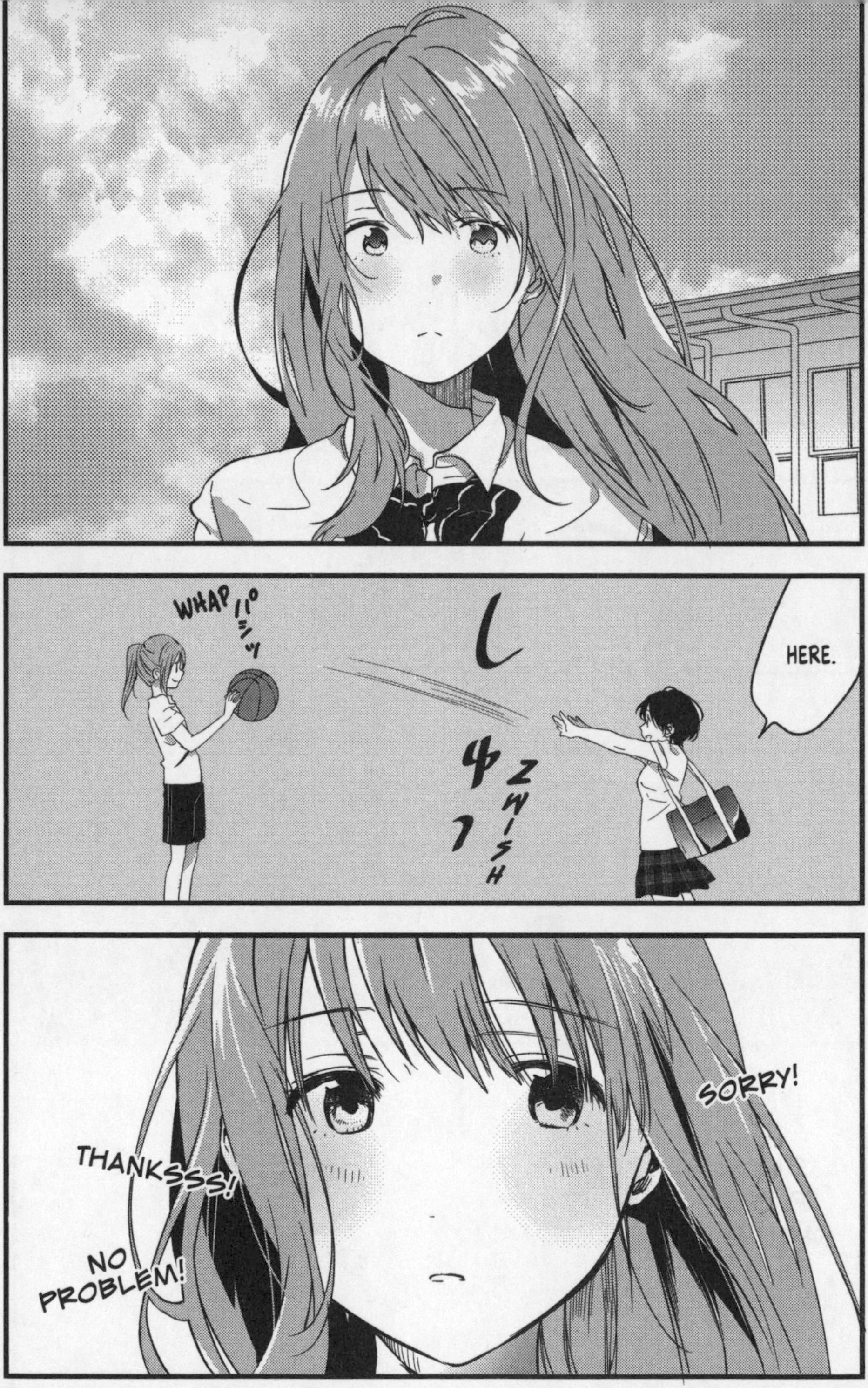
HERE.
ZWISH
WHAP
SORRY!
THANKSSSS!
NO PROBLEM!

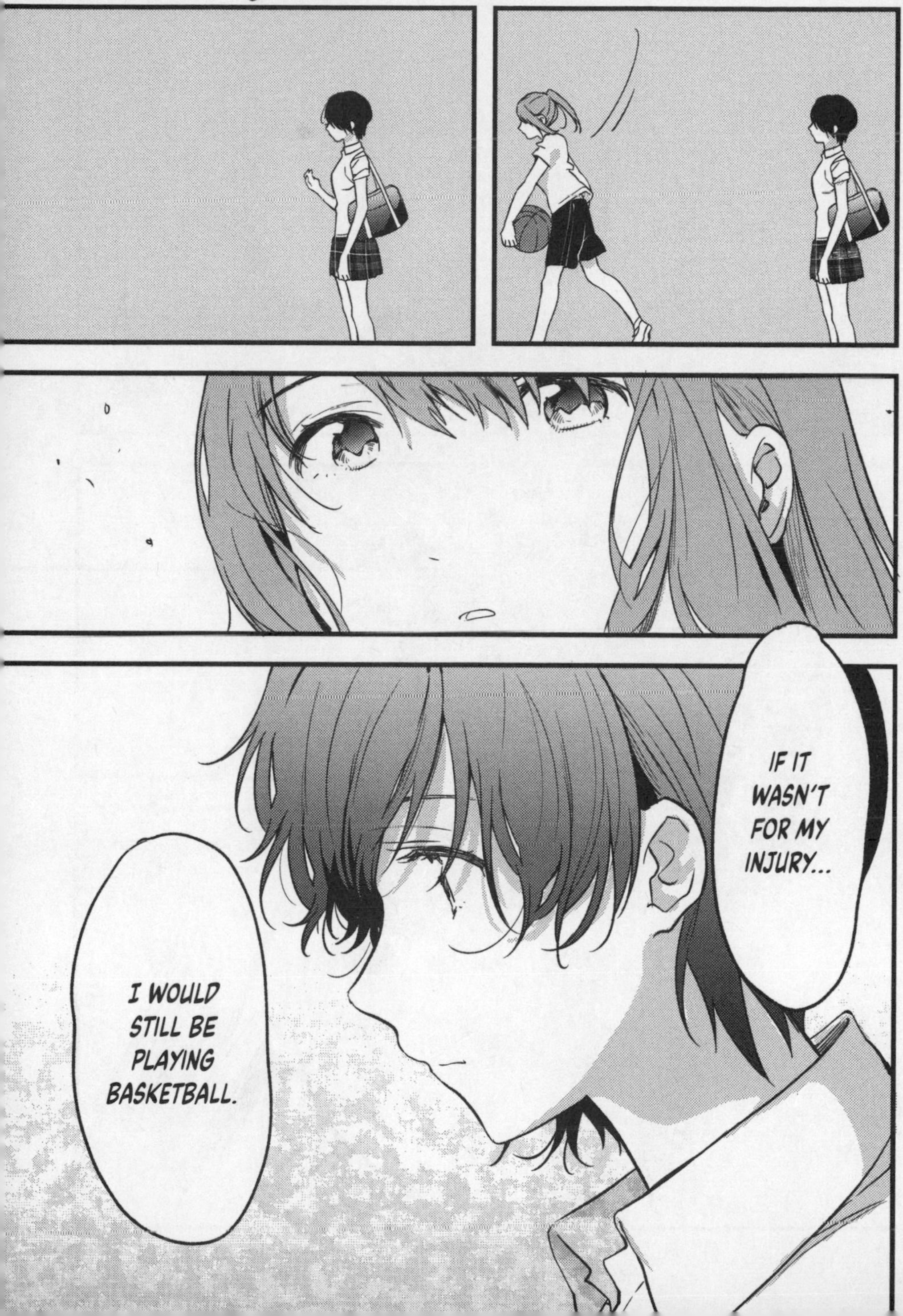
IF IT WASN'T FOR MY INJURY...
I WOULD STILL BE PLAYING BASKETBALL.

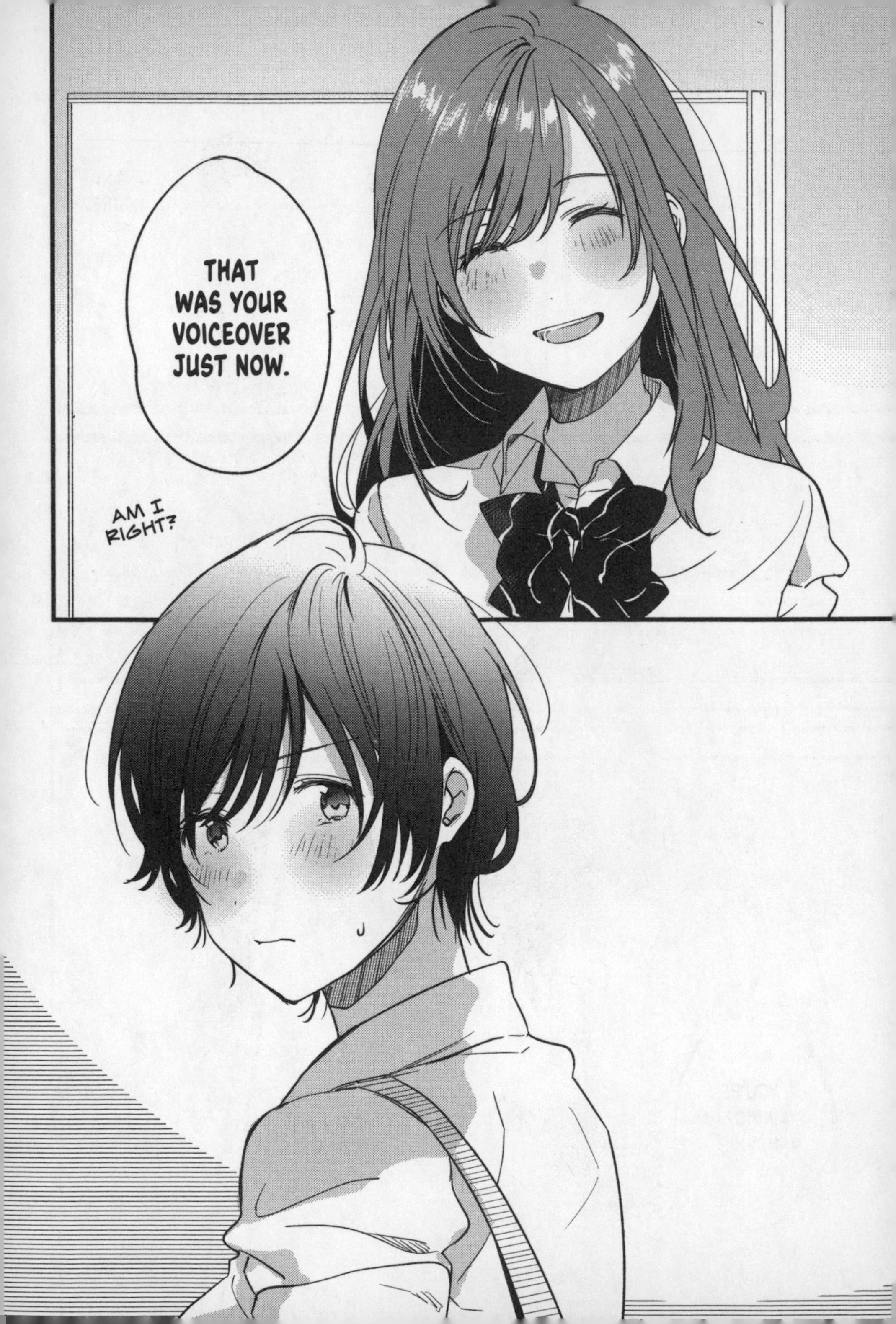
THAT WAS YOUR VOICEOVER JUST NOW.
AM I RIGHT?

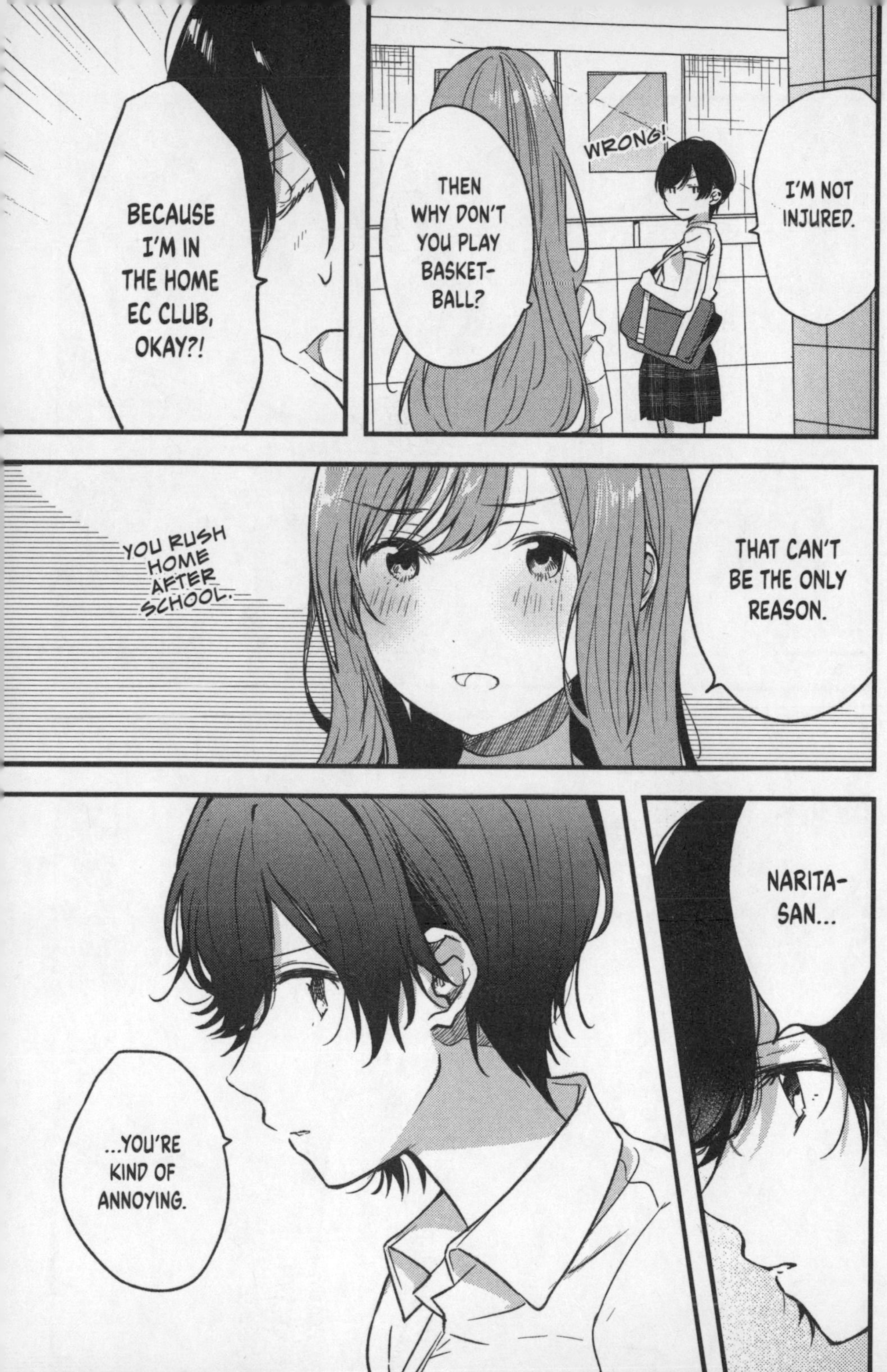
I'M NOT INJURED.
WRONG!
THEN WHY DON'T YOU PLAY BASKET-BALL?
BECAUSE I'M IN THE HOME EC CLUB, OKAY?!
THAT CAN'T BE THE ONLY REASON.
YOU RUSH HOME AFTER SCHOOL.
NARITA-SAN...
...YOU'RE KIND OF ANNOYING.

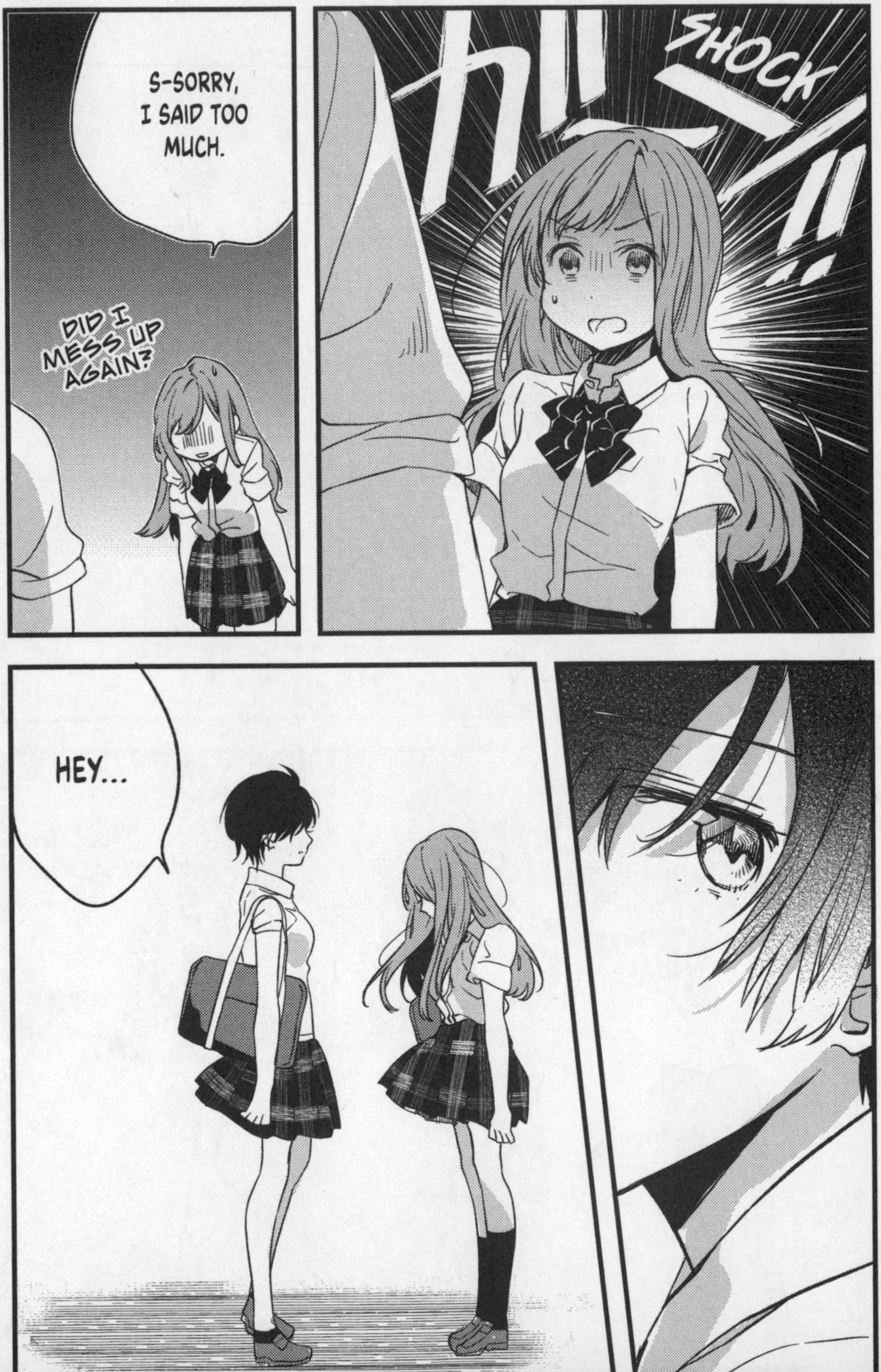
SHOCK
S-SORRY, I SAID TOO MUCH.
DID I MESS UP AGAIN?
HEY...

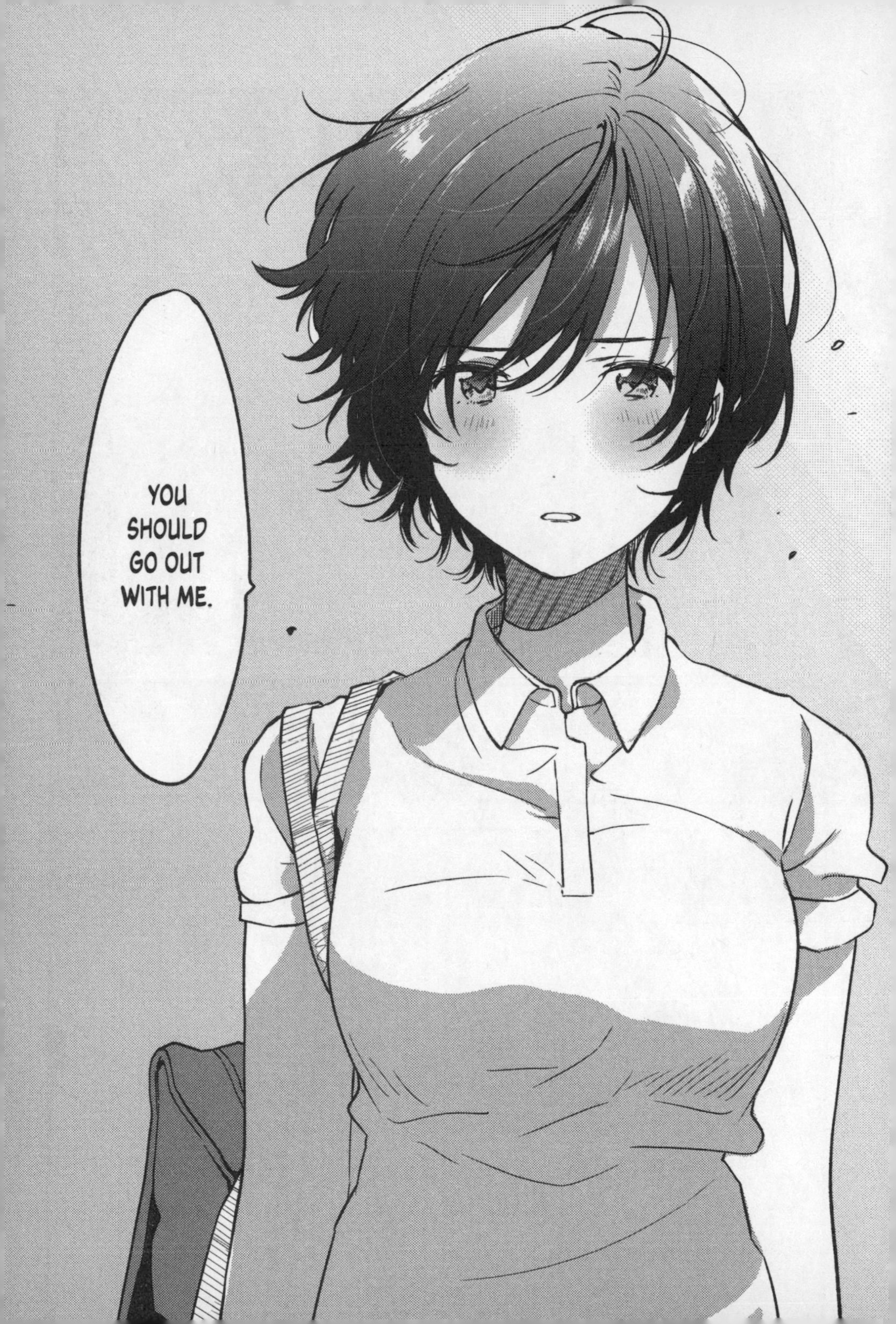
YOU SHOULD GO OUT WITH ME.

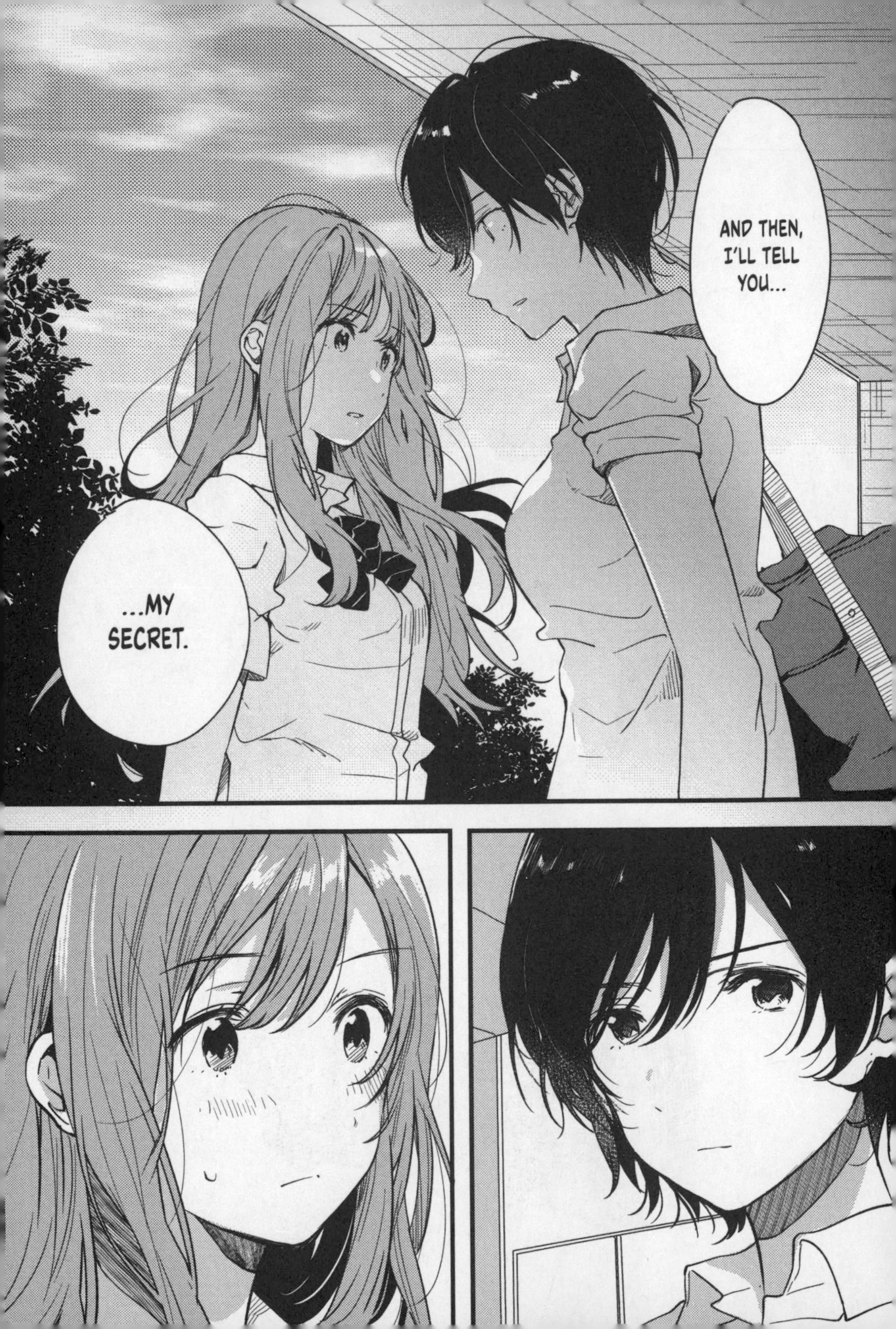
AND THEN, I'LL TELL YOU...
...MY SECRET.

Chapter 5:
The Very Beginning (Part 1)

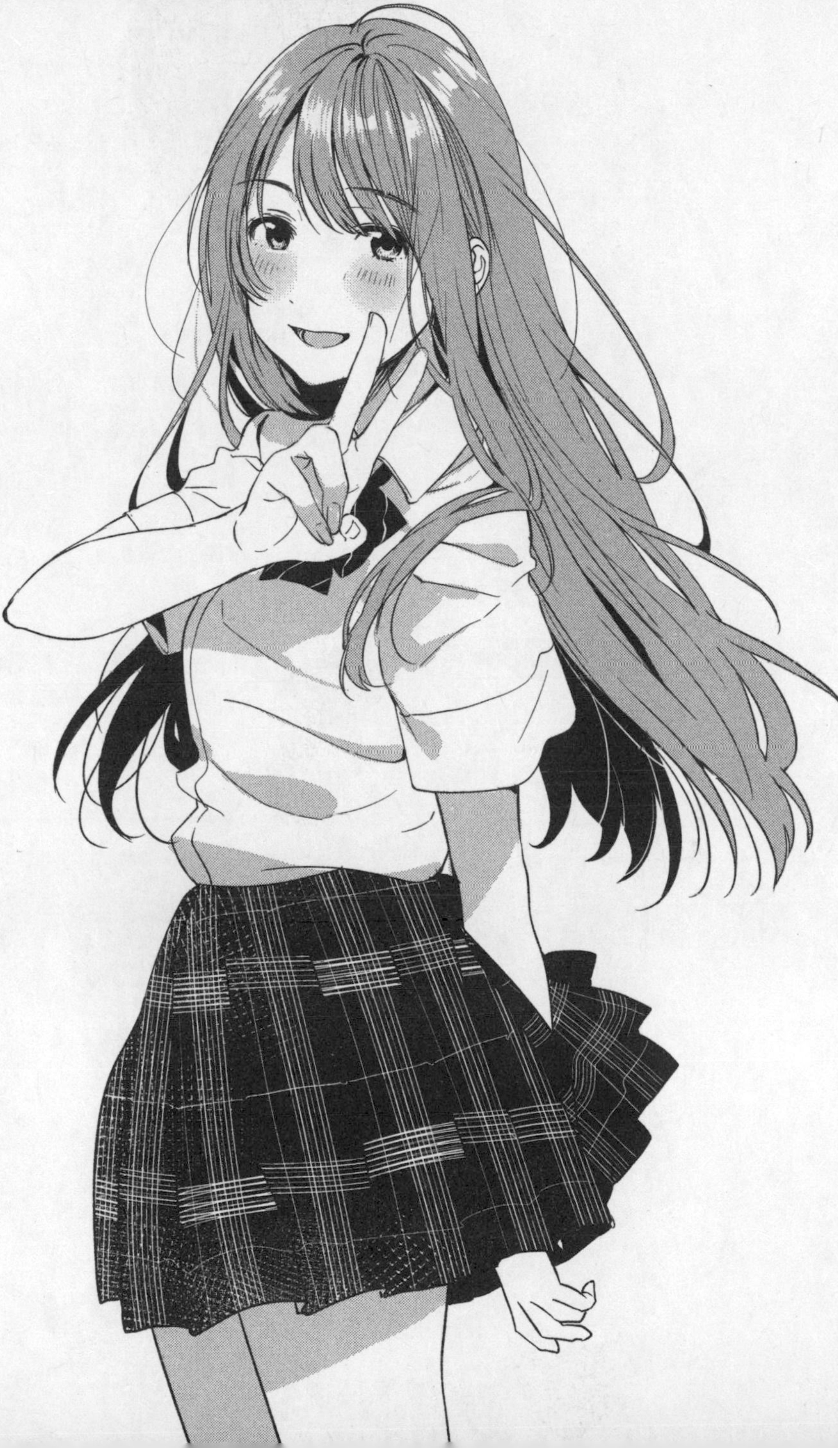

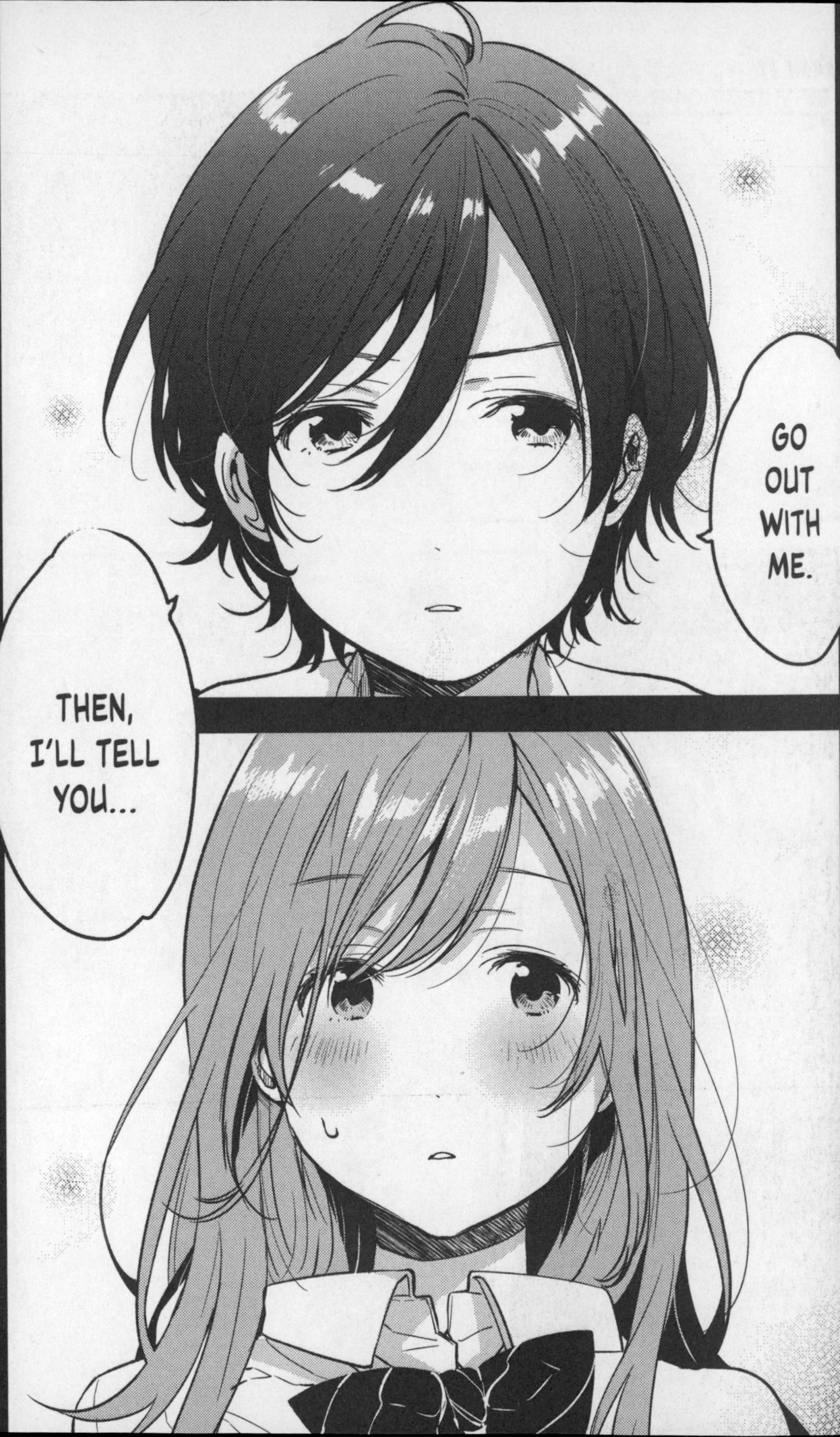
GO OUT WITH ME.
THEN, I'LL TELL YOU...

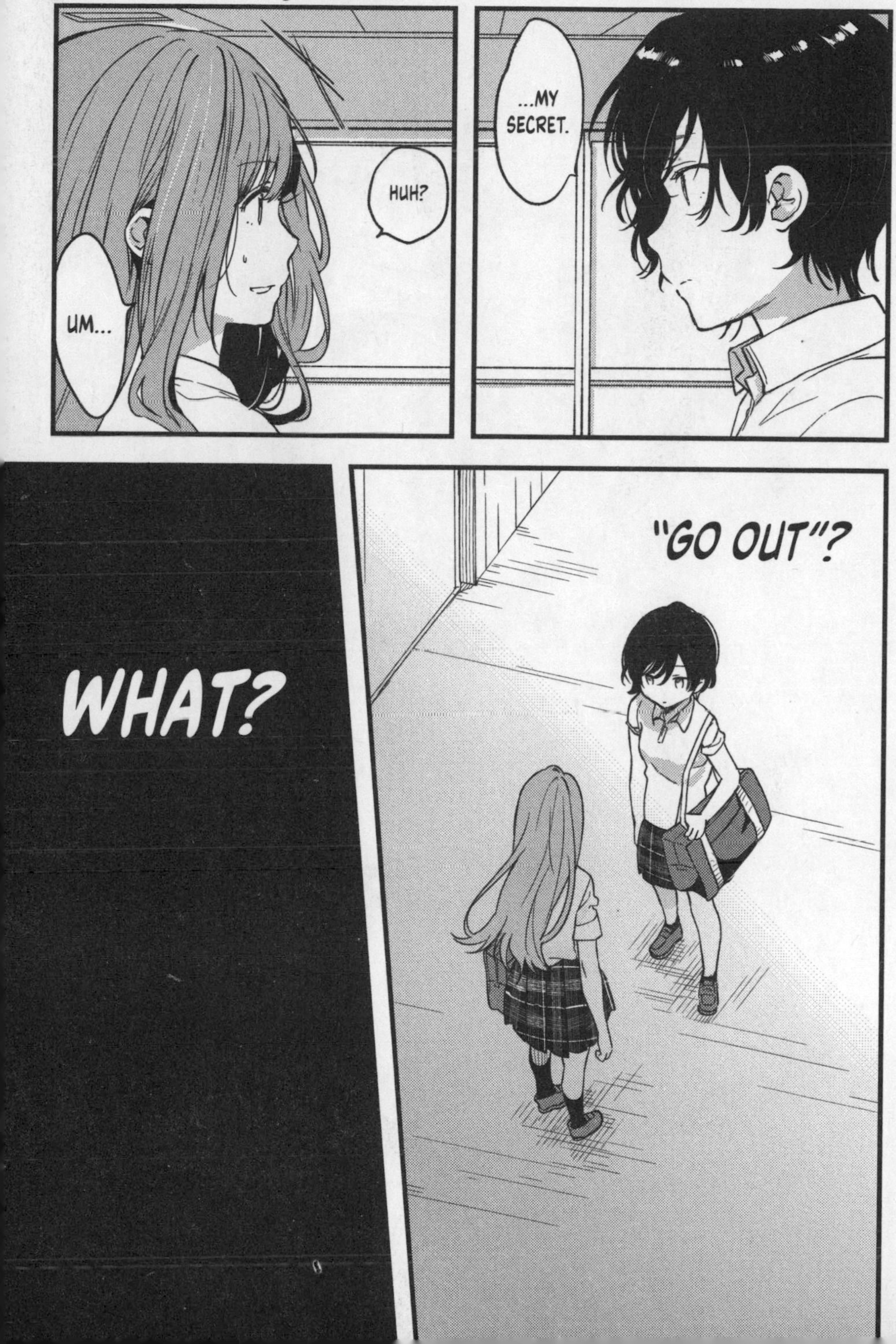
...MY SECRET.
HUH?
UM...
"GO OUT"?
WHAT?

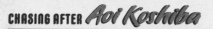

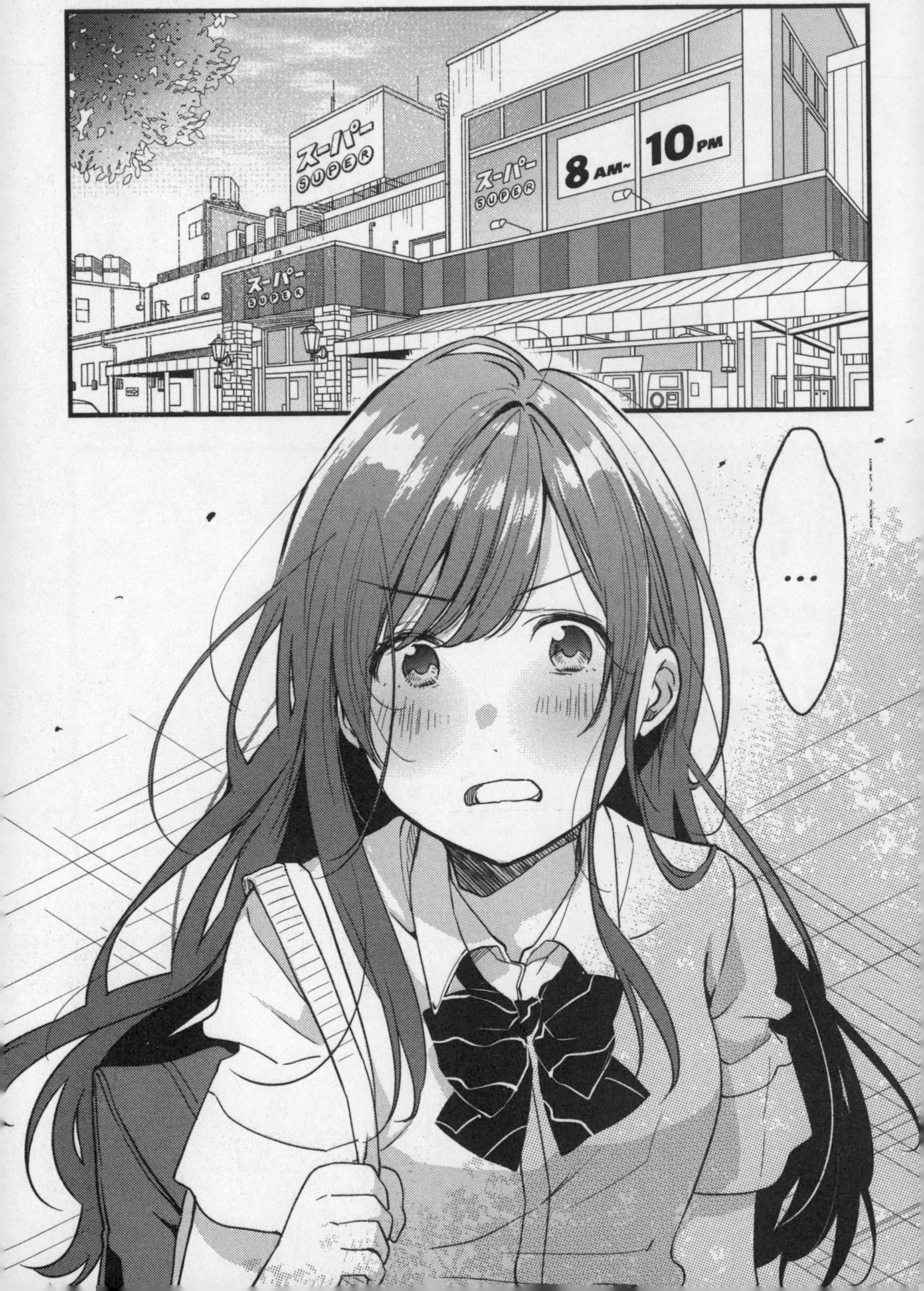
スーパー
SUPER
スーパー
SUPER
8 AM~
10 PM
スーパー
SUPER
...

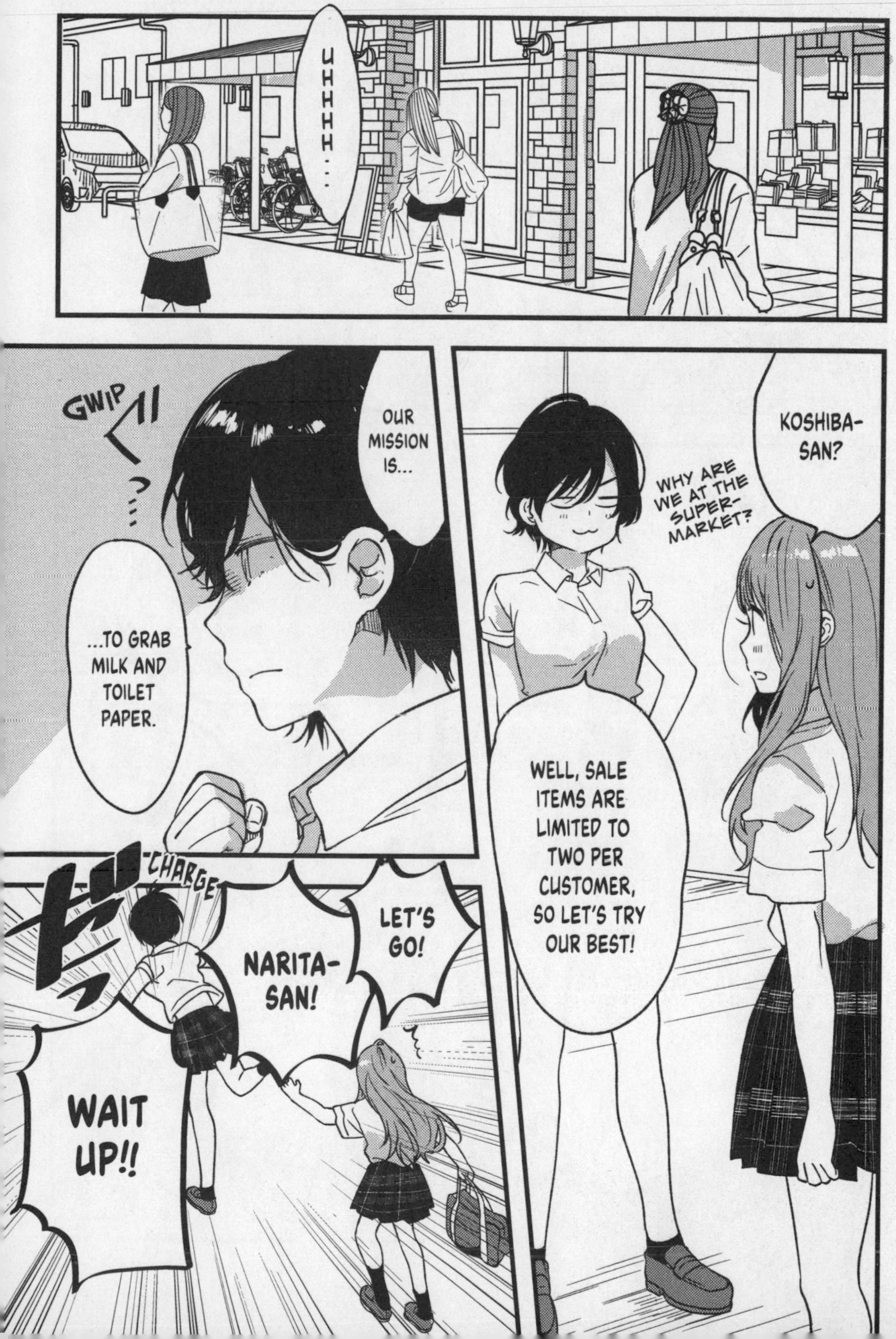
UHHHH...
KOSHIBA-SAN?
WHY ARE WE AT THE SUPER-MARKET?
WELL, SALE ITEMS ARE LIMITED TO TWO PER CUSTOMER, SO LET'S TRY OUR BEST!
OUR MISSION IS...
GWIP
...TO GRAB MILK AND TOILET PAPER.
LET'S GO!
NARITA-SAN!
CHARGE
WAIT UP!!

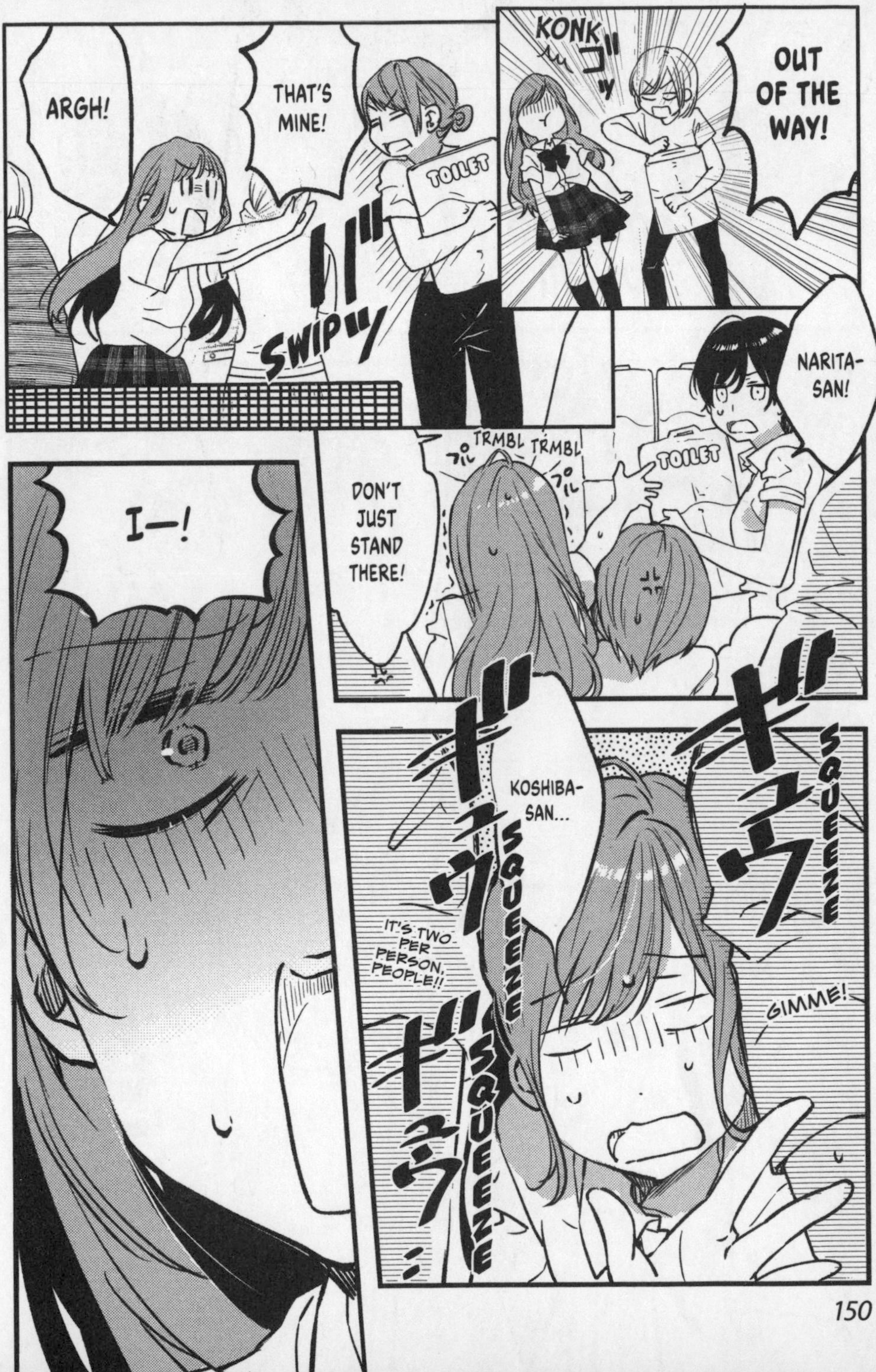
KONK
OUT OF THE WAY!
THAT'S MINE!
ARGH!
SWIP
NARITA-SAN!
TRMBL TRMBL
TOILET
DON'T JUST STAND THERE!
KOSHIBA-SAN...
SQUEEZE
SQUEEZE
SQUEEZE
IT'S TWO PER PERSON, PEOPLE!!
GIMME!
I—!

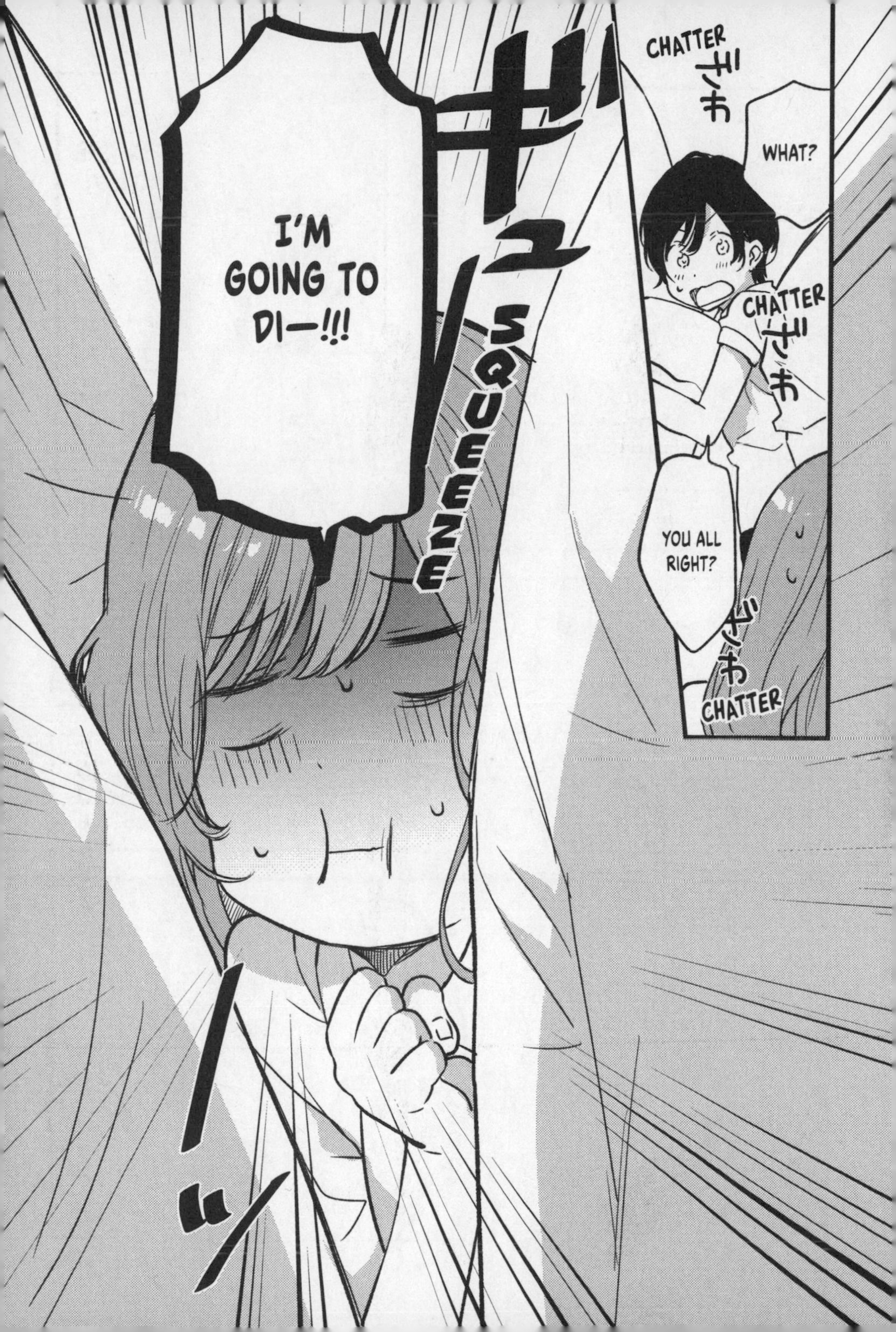
CHATTER
ざわ
WHAT?
CHATTER
ざわ
YOU ALL RIGHT?
ざわ
CHATTER
ギュ
SQUEEZE
I'M GOING TO DI—!!!

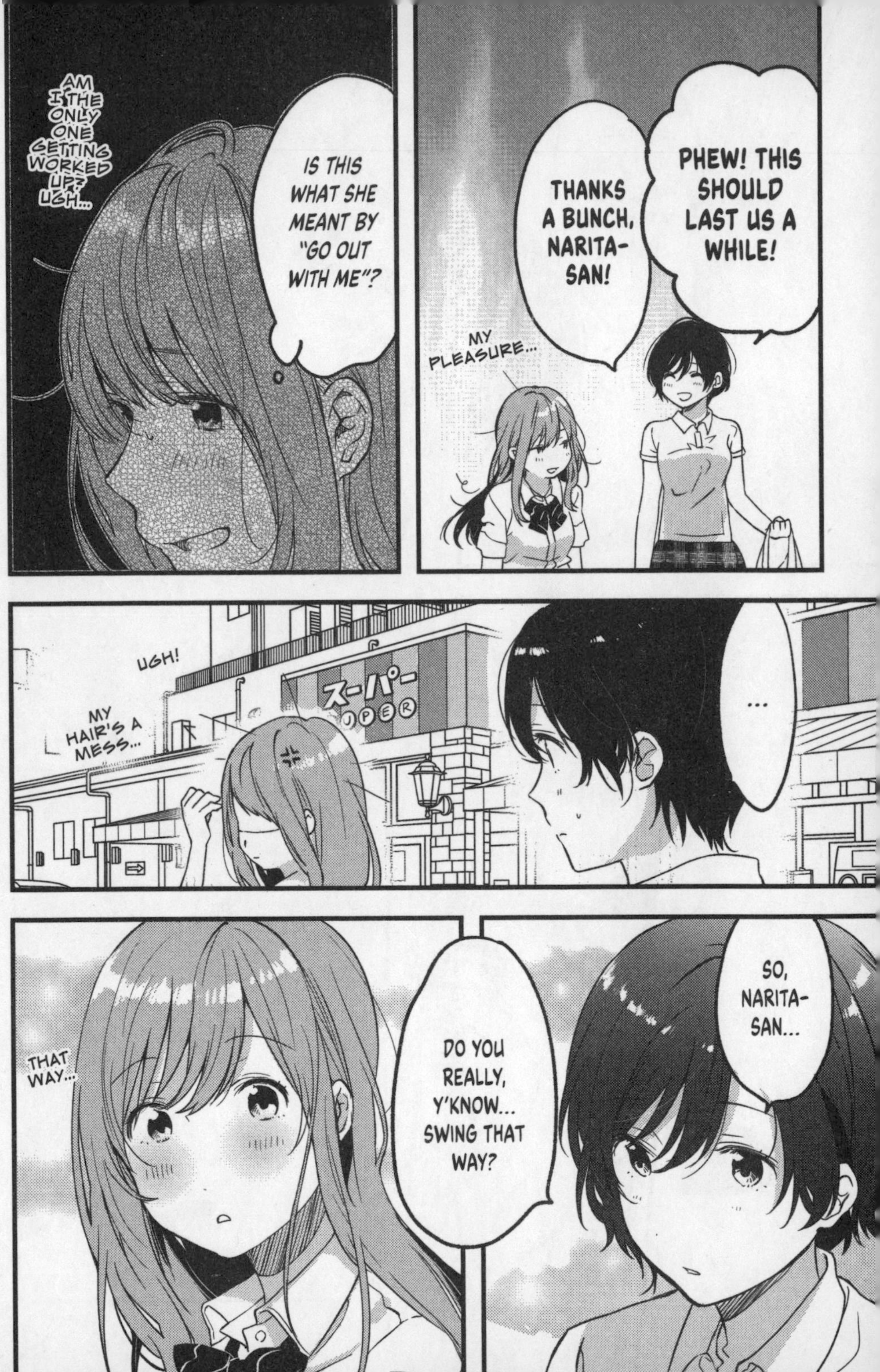
PHEW! THIS SHOULD LAST US A WHILE!
THANKS A BUNCH, NARITA-SAN!
MY PLEASURE...
IS THIS WHAT SHE MEANT BY "GO OUT WITH ME"?
AM I THE ONLY ONE GETTING WORKED UP? UGH...
...
スーパー
UGH!
MY HAIR'S A MESS...
SO, NARITA-SAN...
DO YOU REALLY, Y'KNOW... SWING THAT WAY?
THAT WAY...

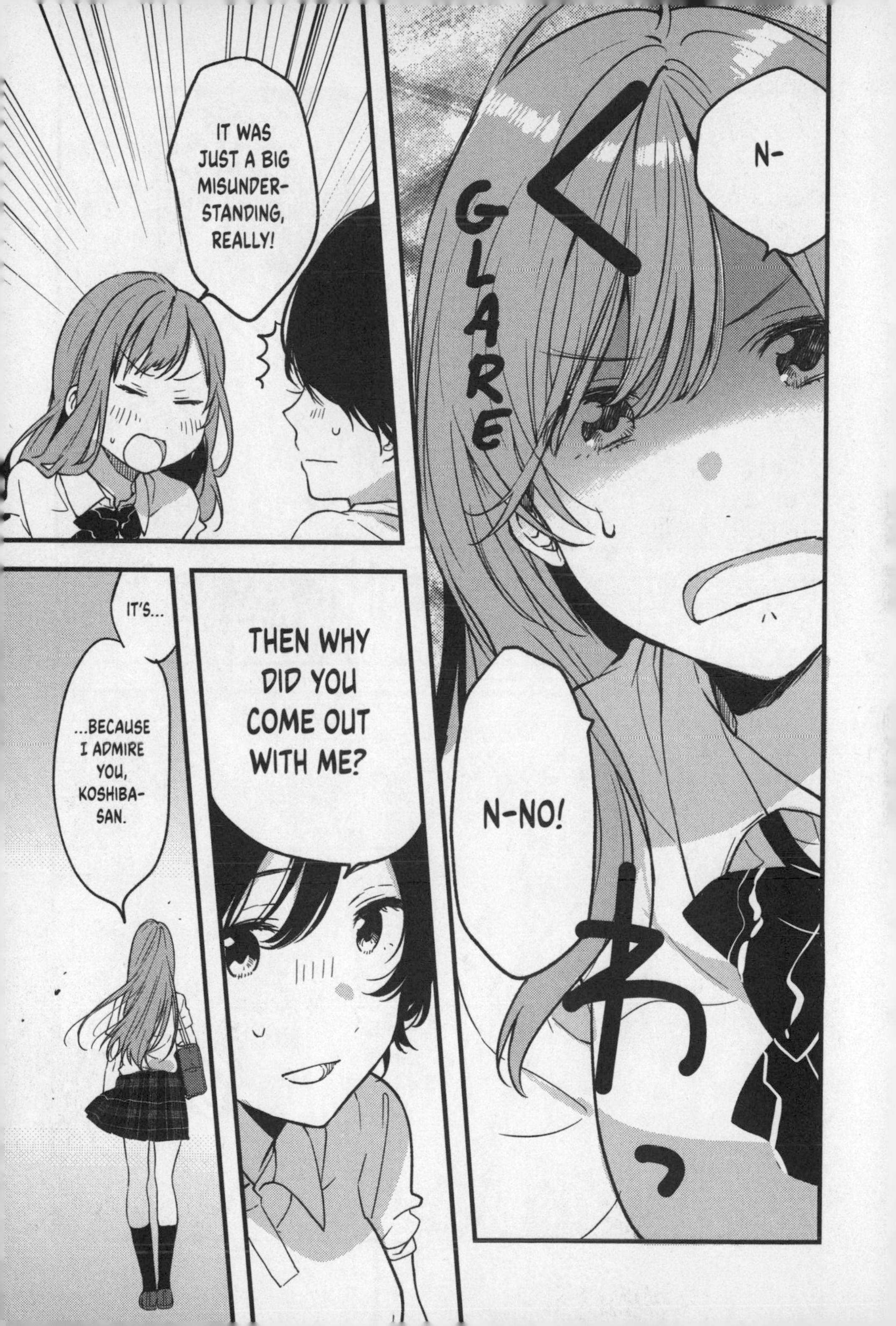
N-
GLARE
N-NO!
わっ
IT WAS JUST A BIG MISUNDER-STANDING, REALLY!
THEN WHY DID YOU COME OUT WITH ME?
IT'S...
...BECAUSE I ADMIRE YOU, KOSHIBA-SAN.

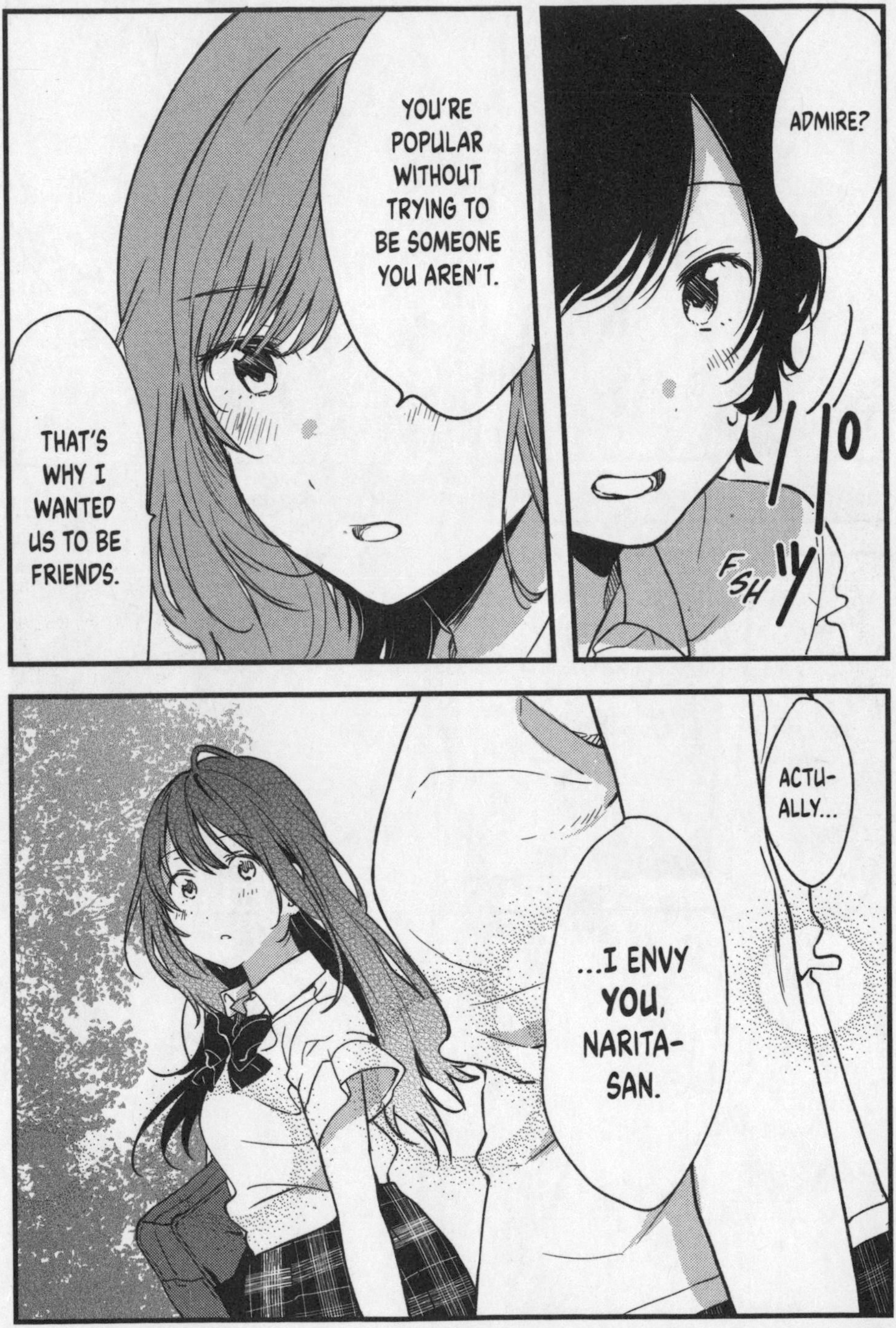
ADMIRE?
FSH
YOU'RE POPULAR WITHOUT TRYING TO BE SOMEONE YOU AREN'T.
THAT'S WHY I WANTED US TO BE FRIENDS.
ACTU-ALLY...
...I ENVY **YOU**, NARITA-SAN.

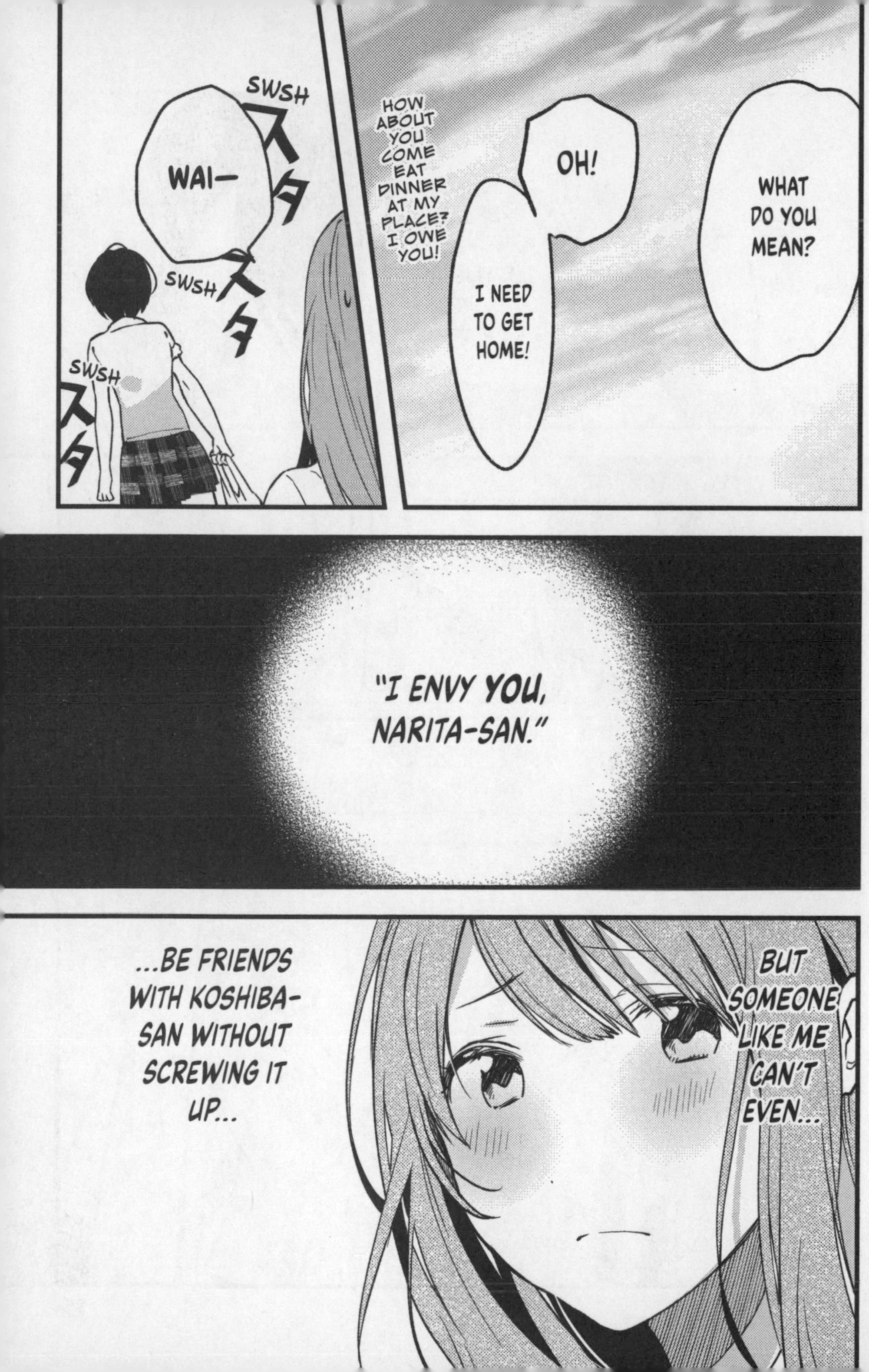
WHAT DO YOU MEAN?
OH!
I NEED TO GET HOME!
HOW ABOUT YOU COME EAT DINNER AT MY PLACE? I OWE YOU!
SWSH
スタ
WAI–
SWSH
スタ
SWSH
スタ
"I ENVY YOU, NARITA-SAN."
BUT SOMEONE LIKE ME CAN'T EVEN...
...BE FRIENDS WITH KOSHIBA-SAN WITHOUT SCREWING IT UP...

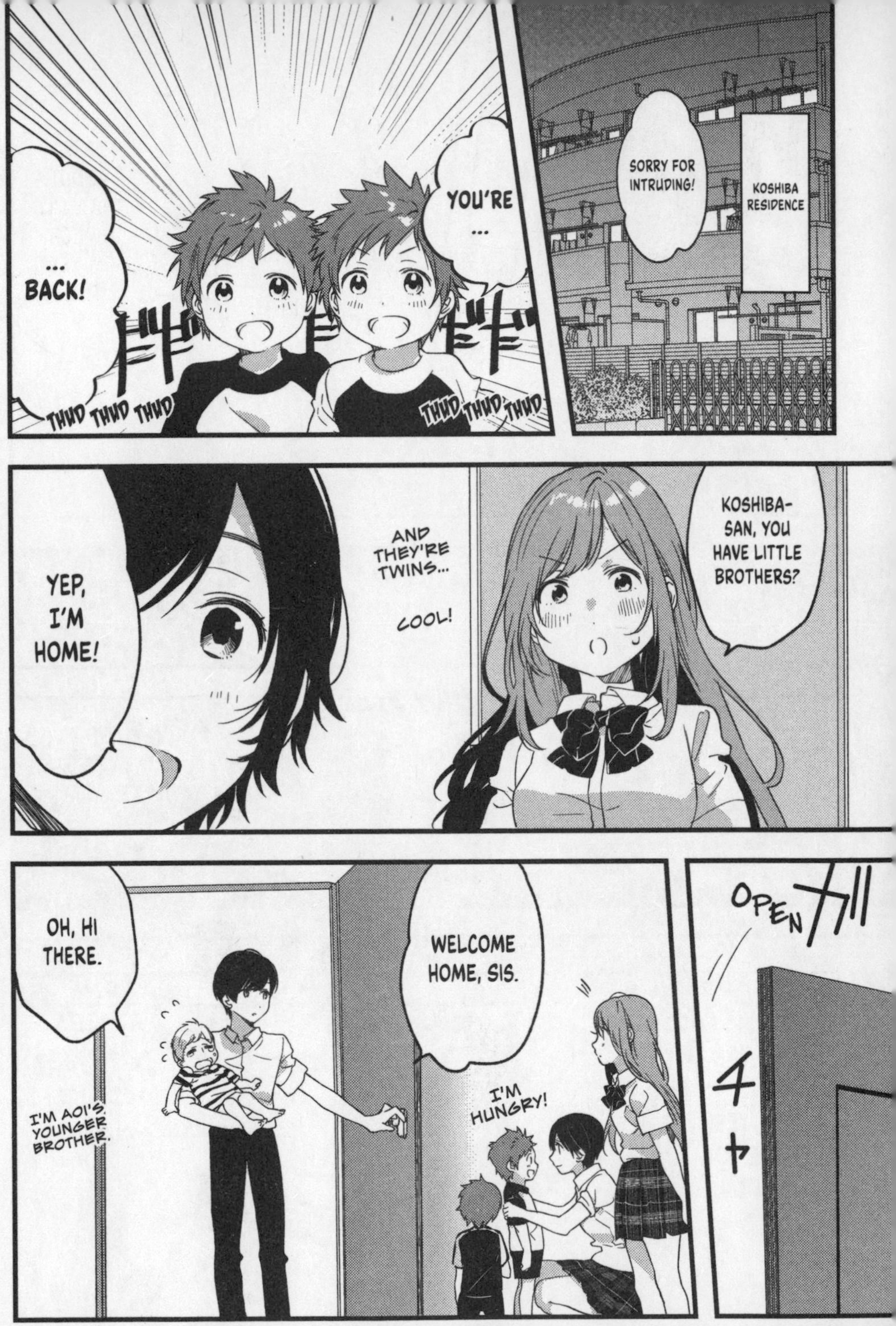
KOSHIBA RESIDENCE
SORRY FOR INTRUDING!
YOU'RE ...
... BACK!
THUD THUD THUD
THUD THUD THUD
KOSHIBA-SAN, YOU HAVE LITTLE BROTHERS?
AND THEY'RE TWINS...
COOL!
YEP, I'M HOME!
OPEN
WELCOME HOME, SIS.
I'M HUNGRY!
OH, HI THERE.
I'M AOI'S YOUNGER BROTHER.

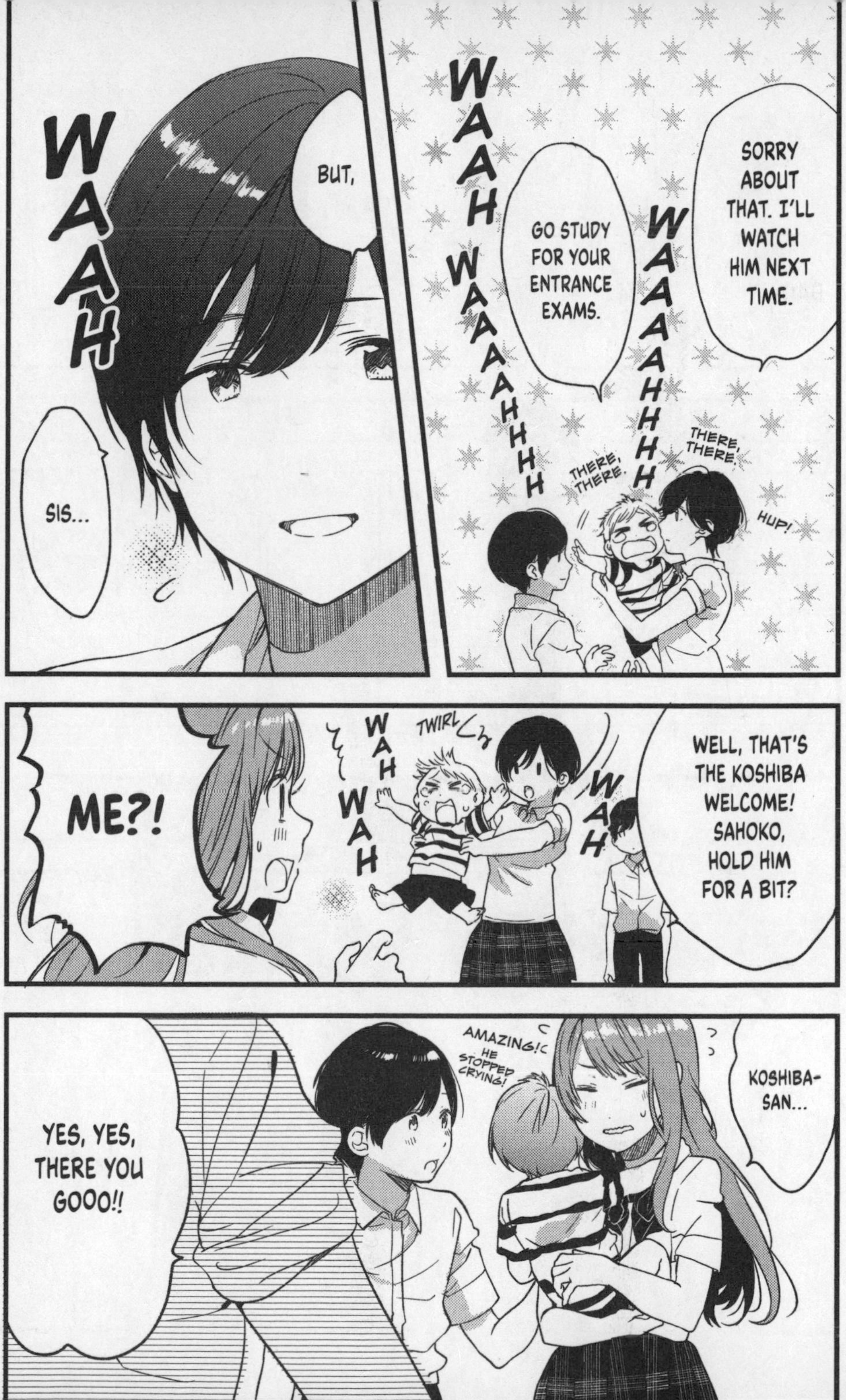
SORRY ABOUT THAT. I'LL WATCH HIM NEXT TIME.
WAAAAAAHHHHH
GO STUDY FOR YOUR ENTRANCE EXAMS.
WAAH WAAAAAHHHHH
THERE, THERE.
HUP!
THERE, THERE.
BUT,
WAAH
SIS...
WELL, THAT'S THE KOSHIBA WELCOME! SAHOKO, HOLD HIM FOR A BIT?
WAH
TWIRL
WAH WAH WAH
ME?!
KOSHIBA-SAN...
AMAZING! HE STOPPED CRYING!
YES, YES, THERE YOU GOOO!!

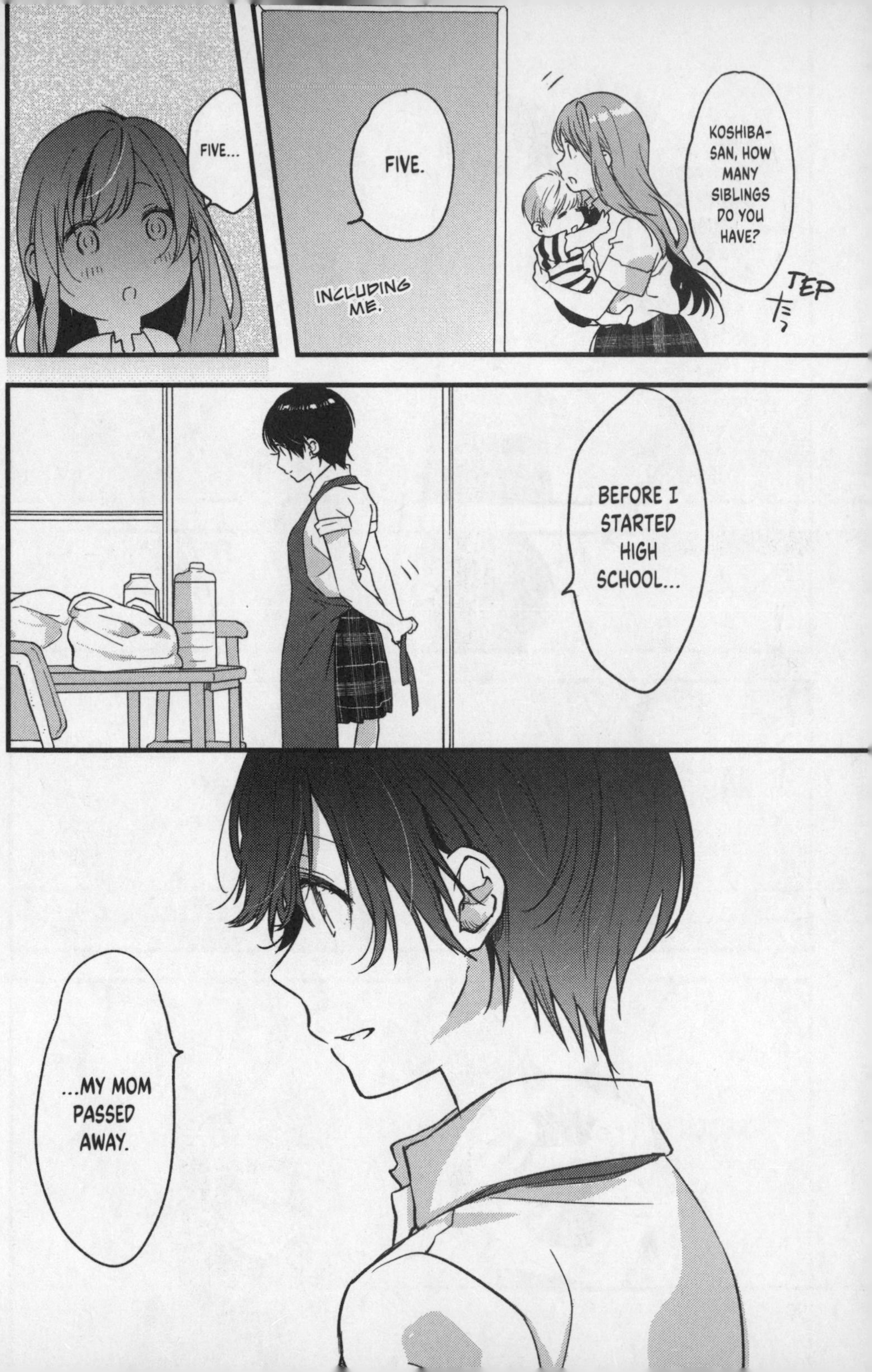
KOSHIBA-SAN, HOW MANY SIBLINGS DO YOU HAVE?
TEP
FIVE.
INCLUDING ME.
FIVE...
BEFORE I STARTED HIGH SCHOOL...
...MY MOM PASSED AWAY.

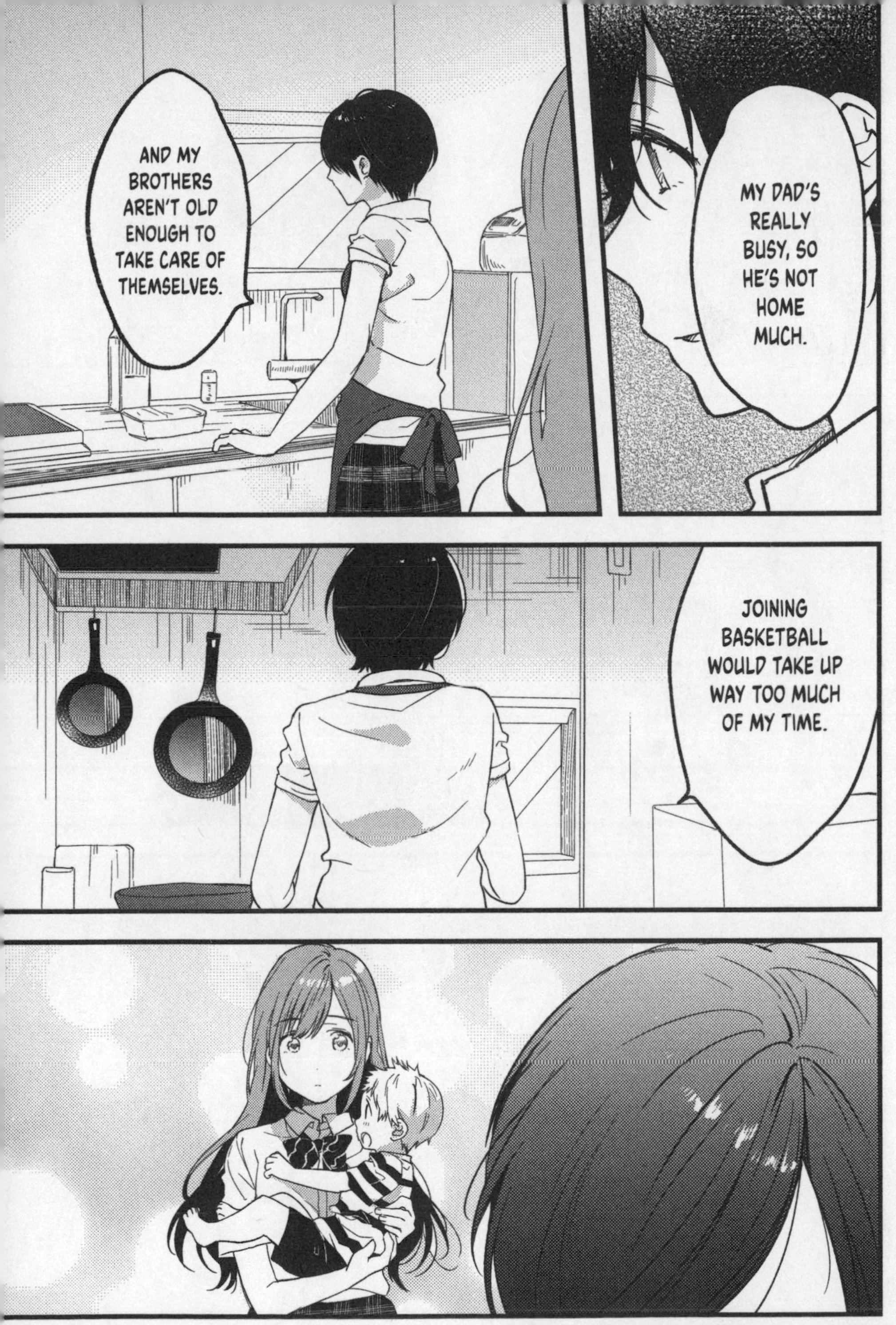
MY DAD'S REALLY BUSY, SO HE'S NOT HOME MUCH.
AND MY BROTHERS AREN'T OLD ENOUGH TO TAKE CARE OF THEMSELVES.
JOINING BASKETBALL WOULD TAKE UP WAY TOO MUCH OF MY TIME.

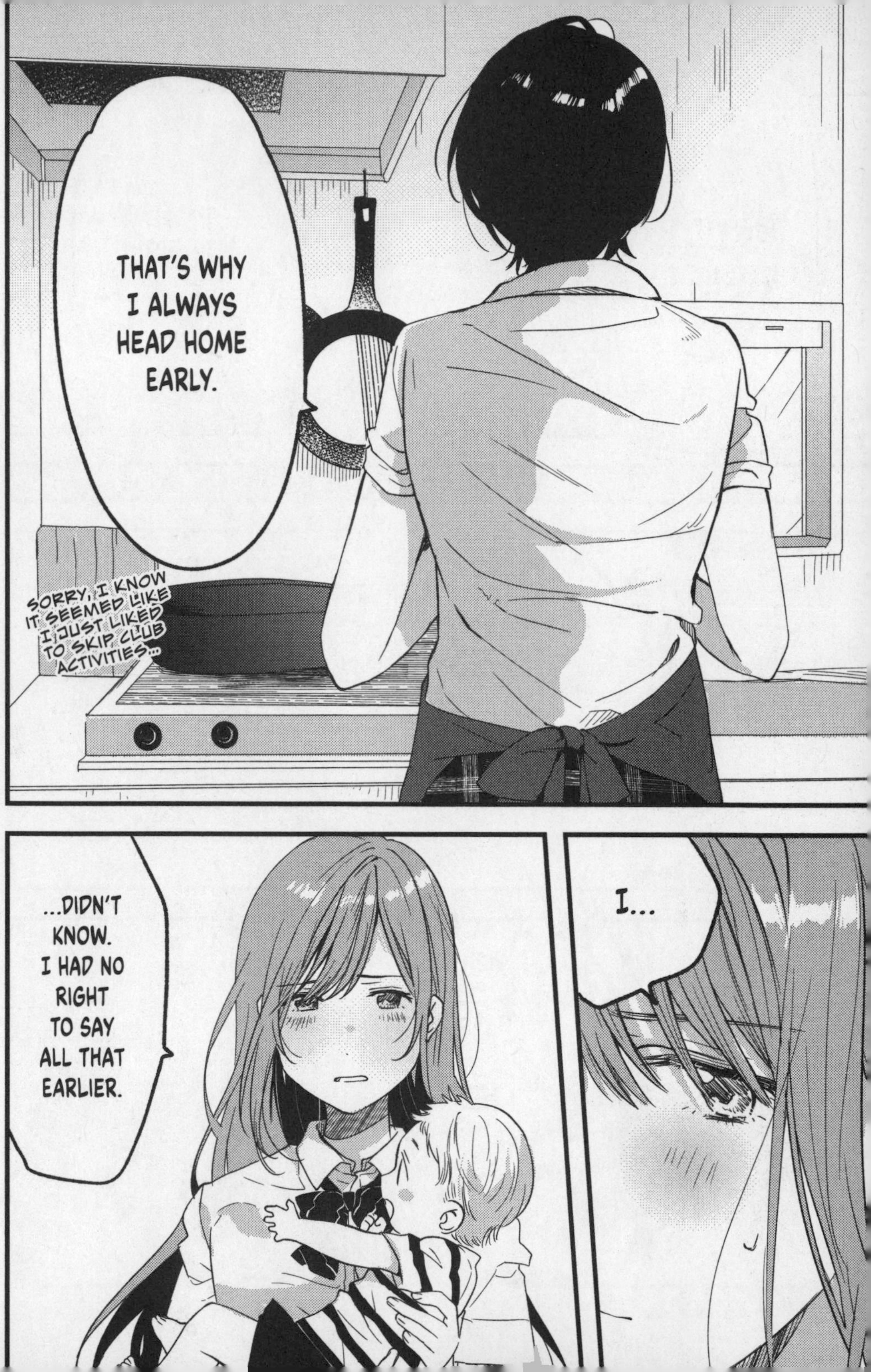
THAT'S WHY I ALWAYS HEAD HOME EARLY.
SORRY, I KNOW IT SEEMED LIKE I JUST LIKED TO SKIP CLUB ACTIVITIES...
I...
...DIDN'T KNOW. I HAD NO RIGHT TO SAY ALL THAT EARLIER.

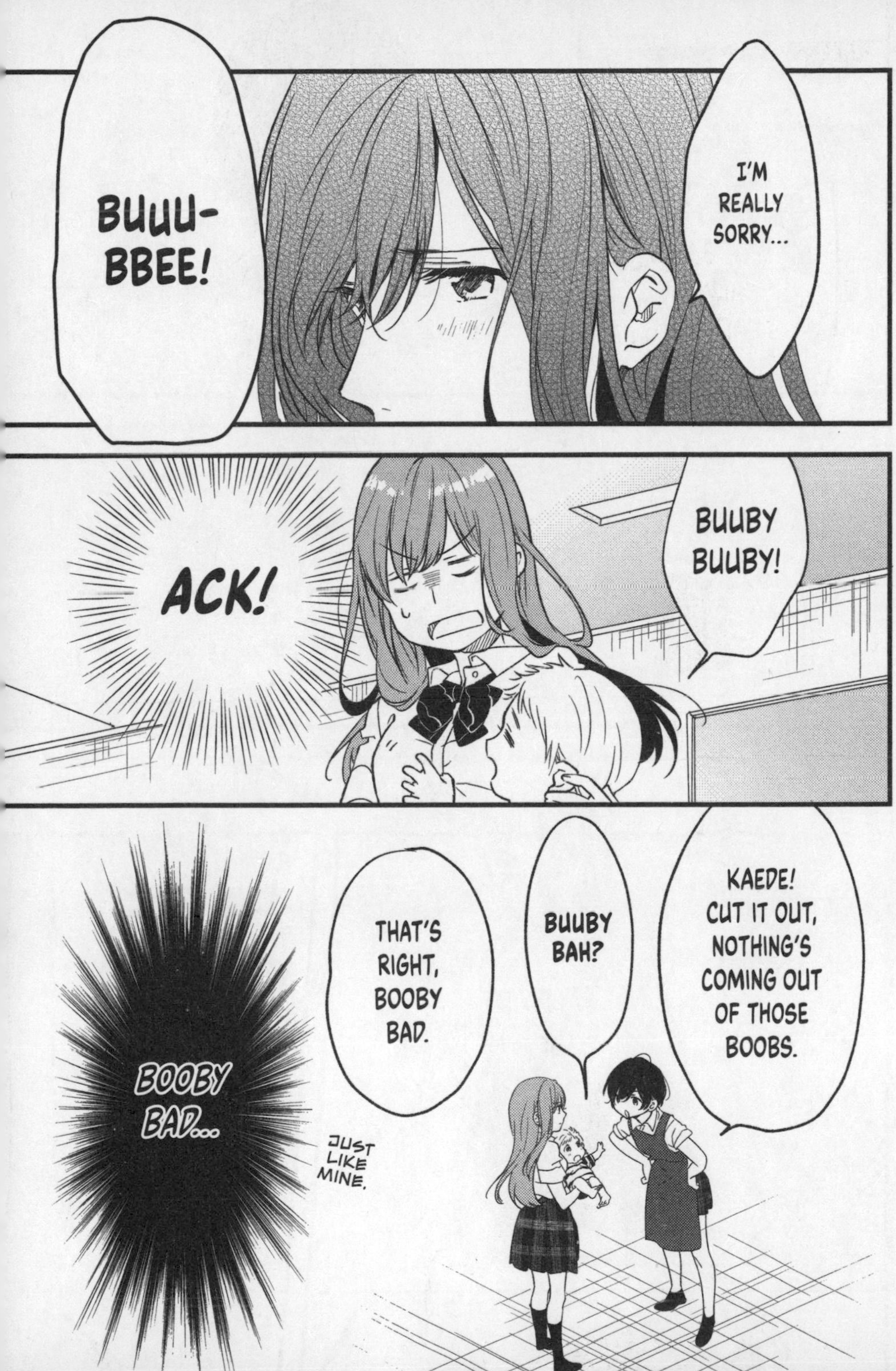
I'M REALLY SORRY...
BUUU-BBEE!
BUUBY BUUBY!
ACK!
KAEDE! CUT IT OUT, NOTHING'S COMING OUT OF THOSE BOOBS.
BUUBY BAH?
THAT'S RIGHT, BOOBY BAD.
BOOBY BAD...
JUST LIKE MINE.

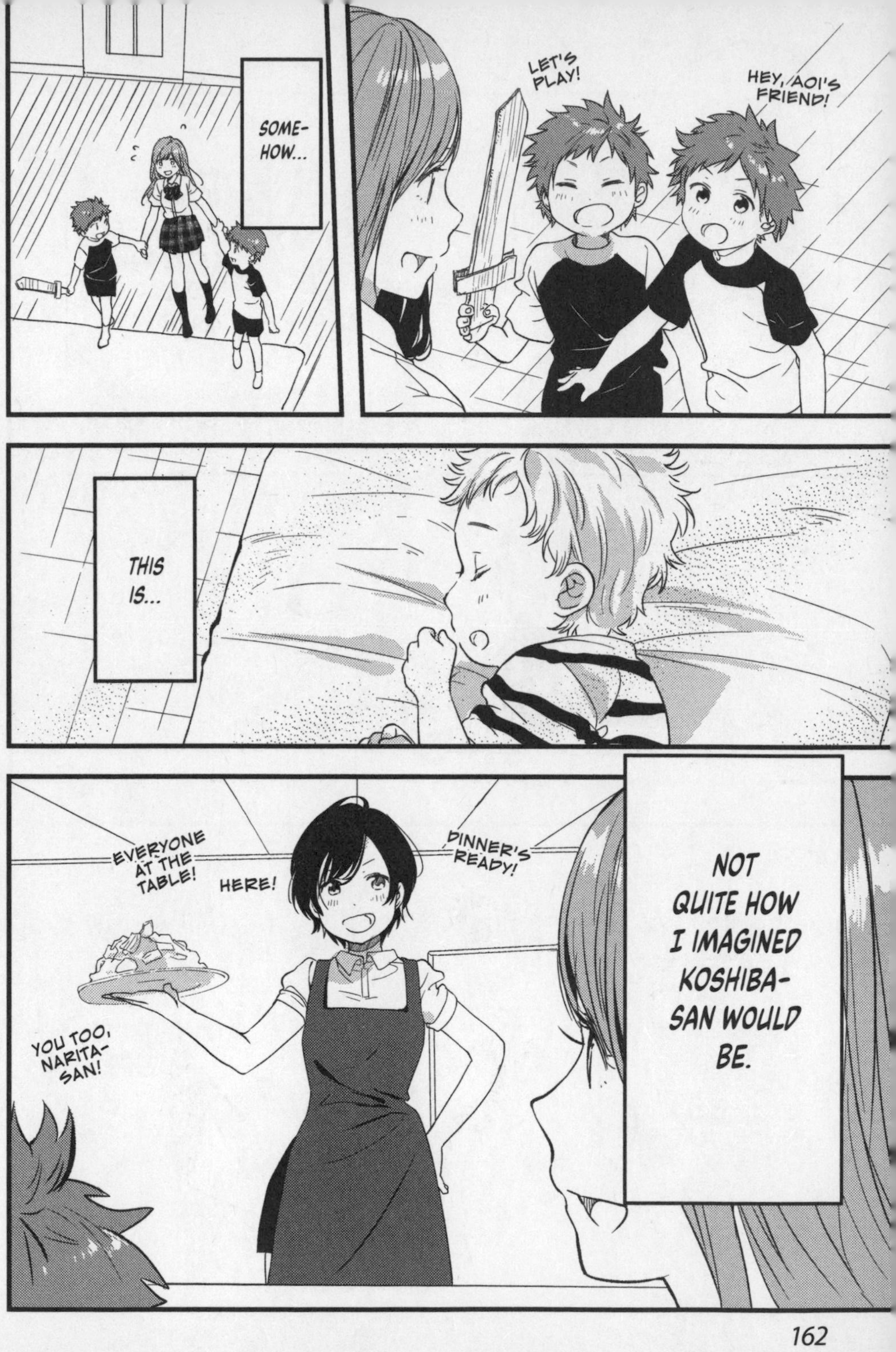
HEY, AOI'S FRIEND!
LET'S PLAY!
SOME-HOW...
THIS IS...
NOT QUITE HOW I IMAGINED KOSHIBA-SAN WOULD BE.
DINNER'S READY!
EVERYONE AT THE TABLE!
HERE!
YOU TOO, NARITA-SAN!

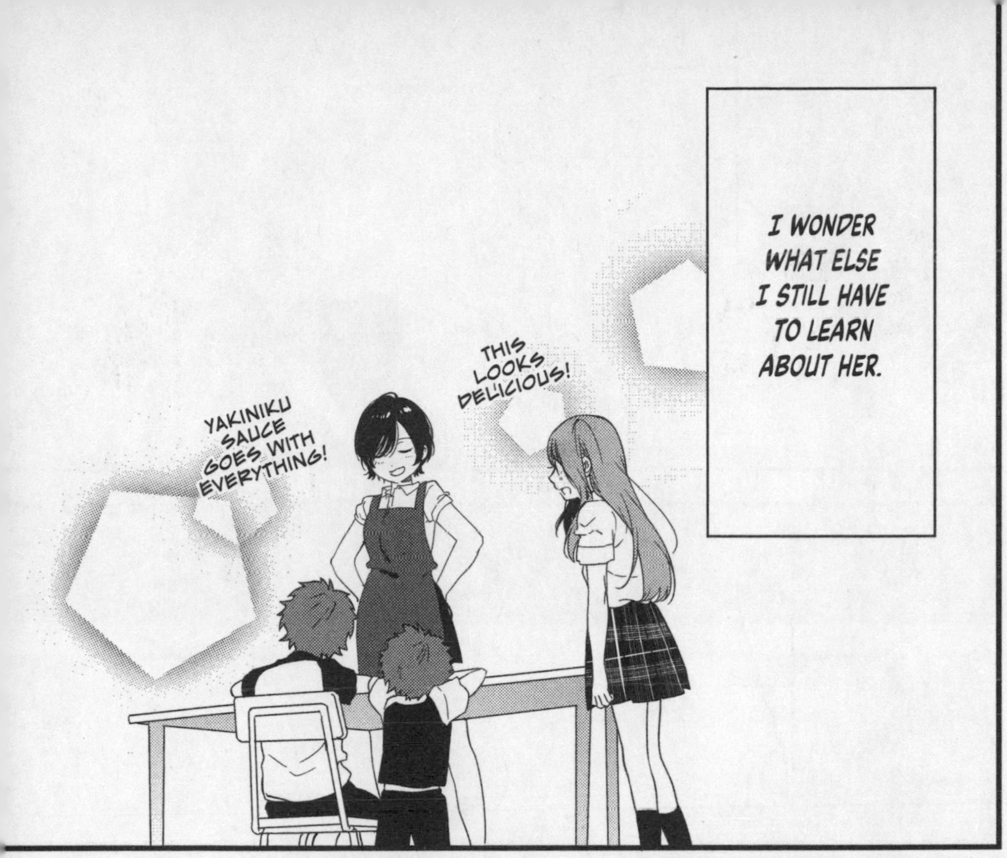
I WONDER WHAT ELSE I STILL HAVE TO LEARN ABOUT HER.
THIS LOOKS DELICIOUS!
YAKINIKU SAUCE GOES WITH EVERYTHING!

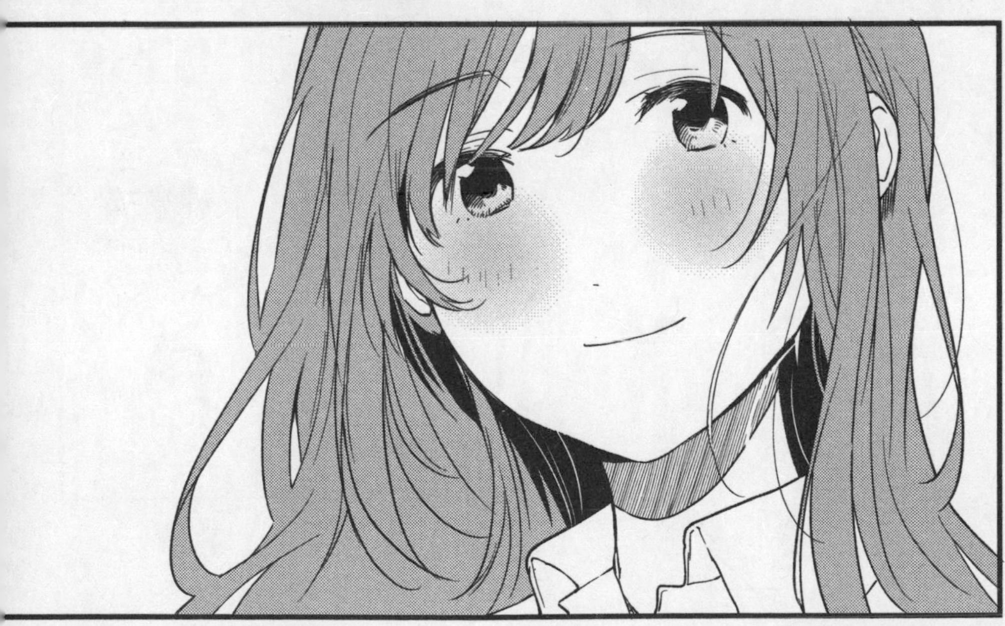

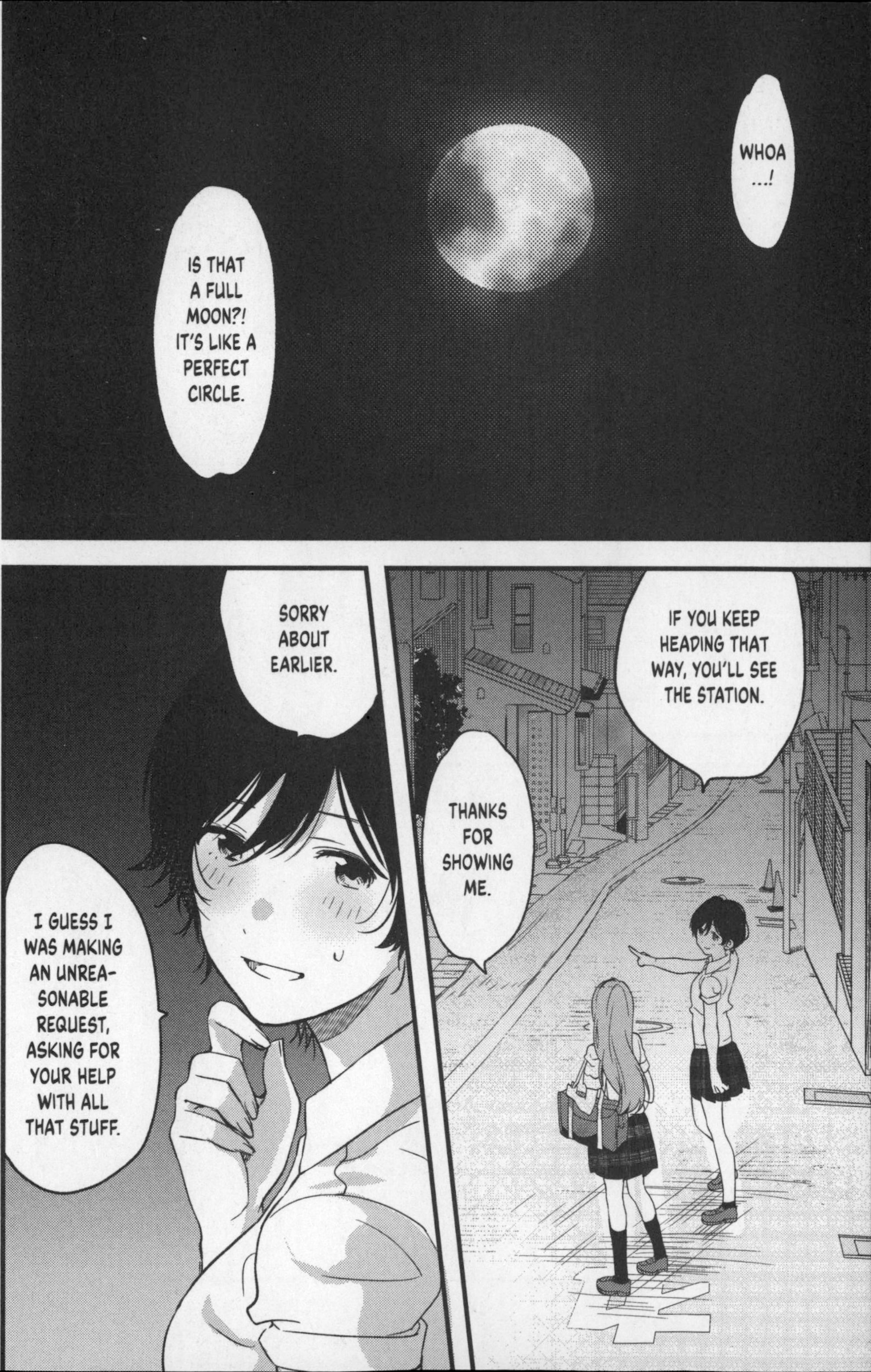
WHOA ...!
IS THAT A FULL MOON?! IT'S LIKE A PERFECT CIRCLE.
IF YOU KEEP HEADING THAT WAY, YOU'LL SEE THE STATION.
THANKS FOR SHOWING ME.
SORRY ABOUT EARLIER.
I GUESS I WAS MAKING AN UNREA-SONABLE REQUEST, ASKING FOR YOUR HELP WITH ALL THAT STUFF.

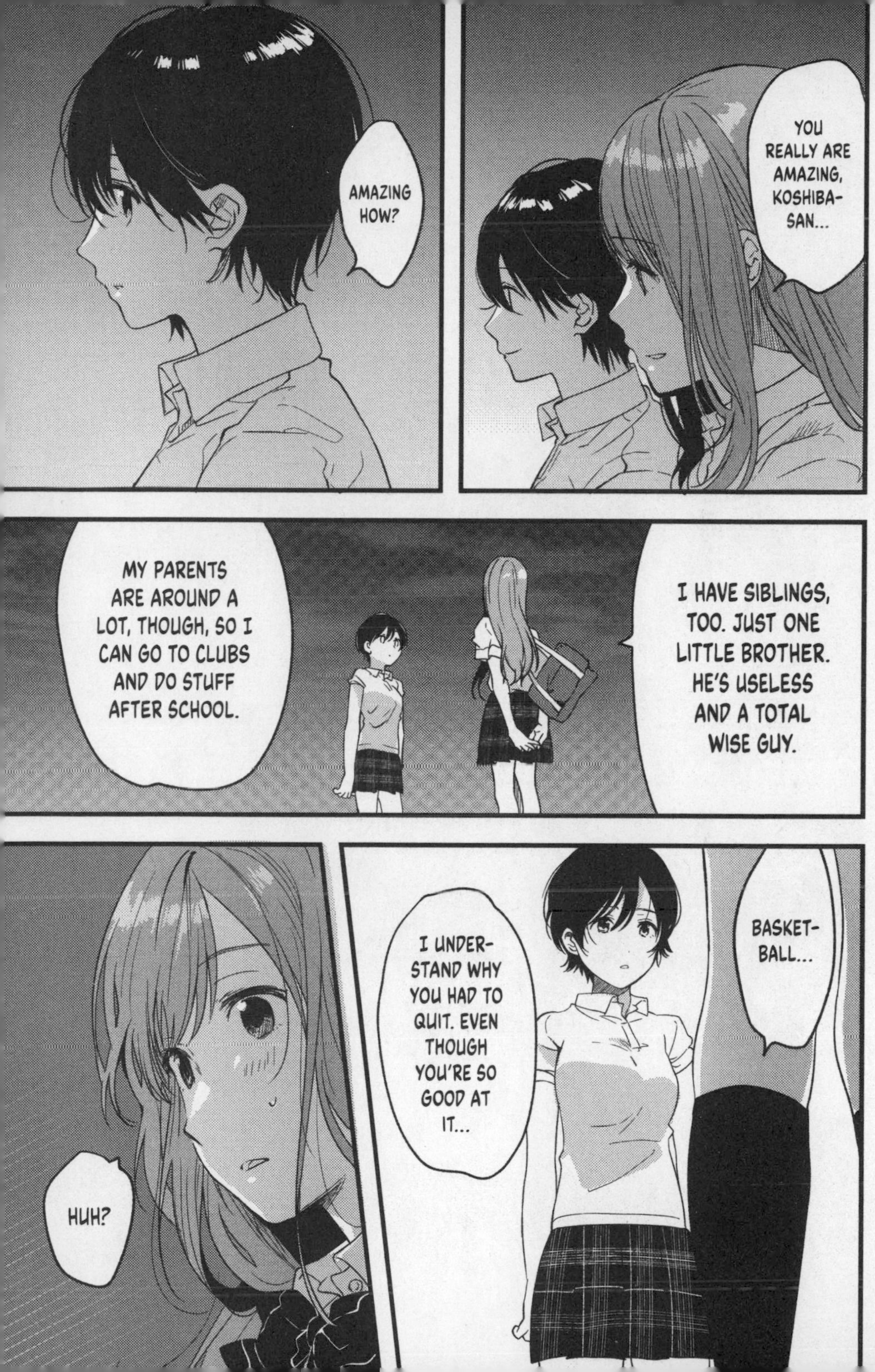
YOU REALLY ARE AMAZING, KOSHIBA-SAN...
AMAZING HOW?
I HAVE SIBLINGS, TOO. JUST ONE LITTLE BROTHER. HE'S USELESS AND A TOTAL WISE GUY.
MY PARENTS ARE AROUND A LOT, THOUGH, SO I CAN GO TO CLUBS AND DO STUFF AFTER SCHOOL.
BASKET-BALL...
I UNDER-STAND WHY YOU HAD TO QUIT. EVEN THOUGH YOU'RE SO GOOD AT IT...
HUH?

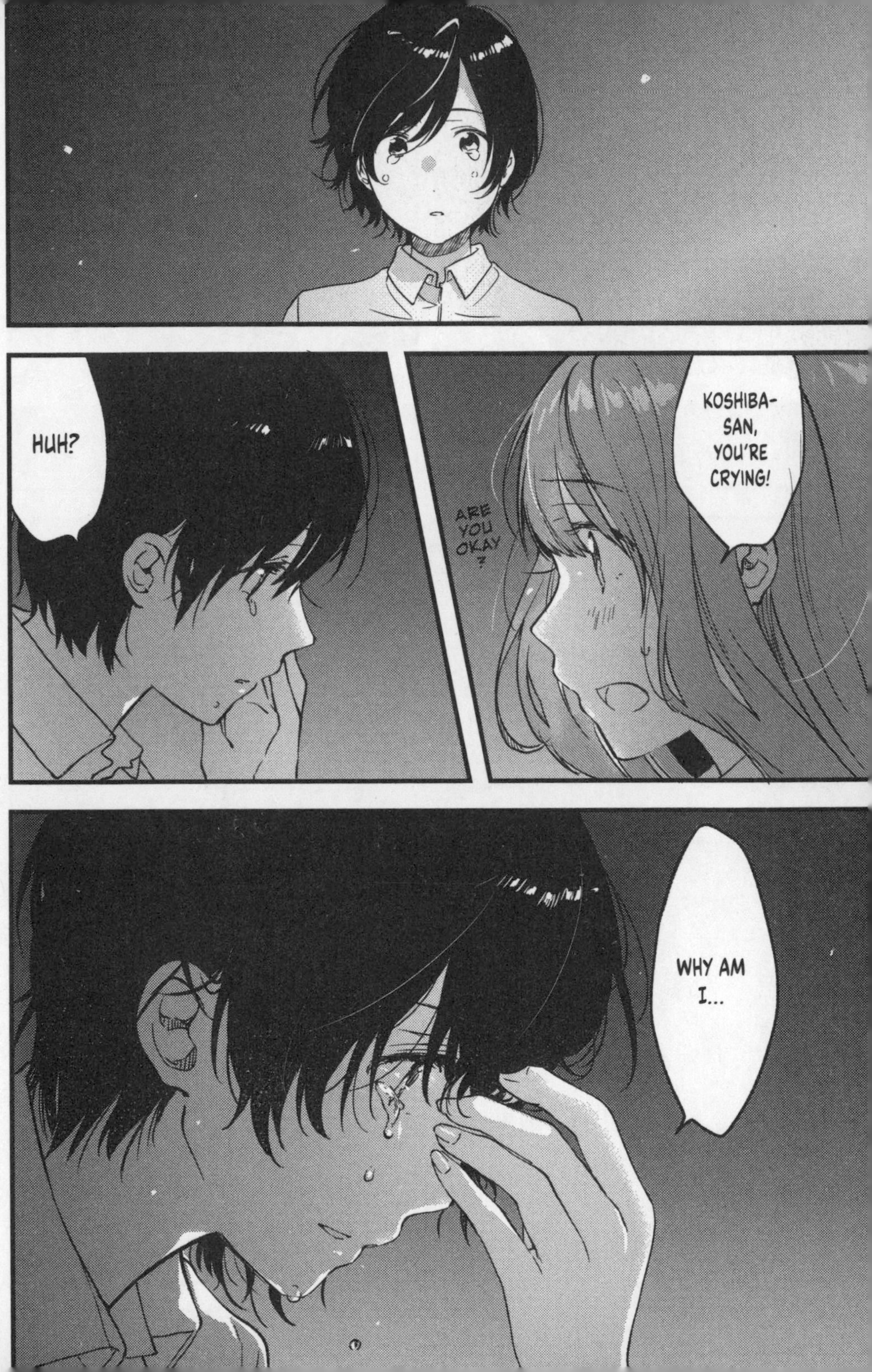
KOSHIBA-SAN, YOU'RE CRYING!
ARE YOU OKAY?
HUH?
WHY AM I...

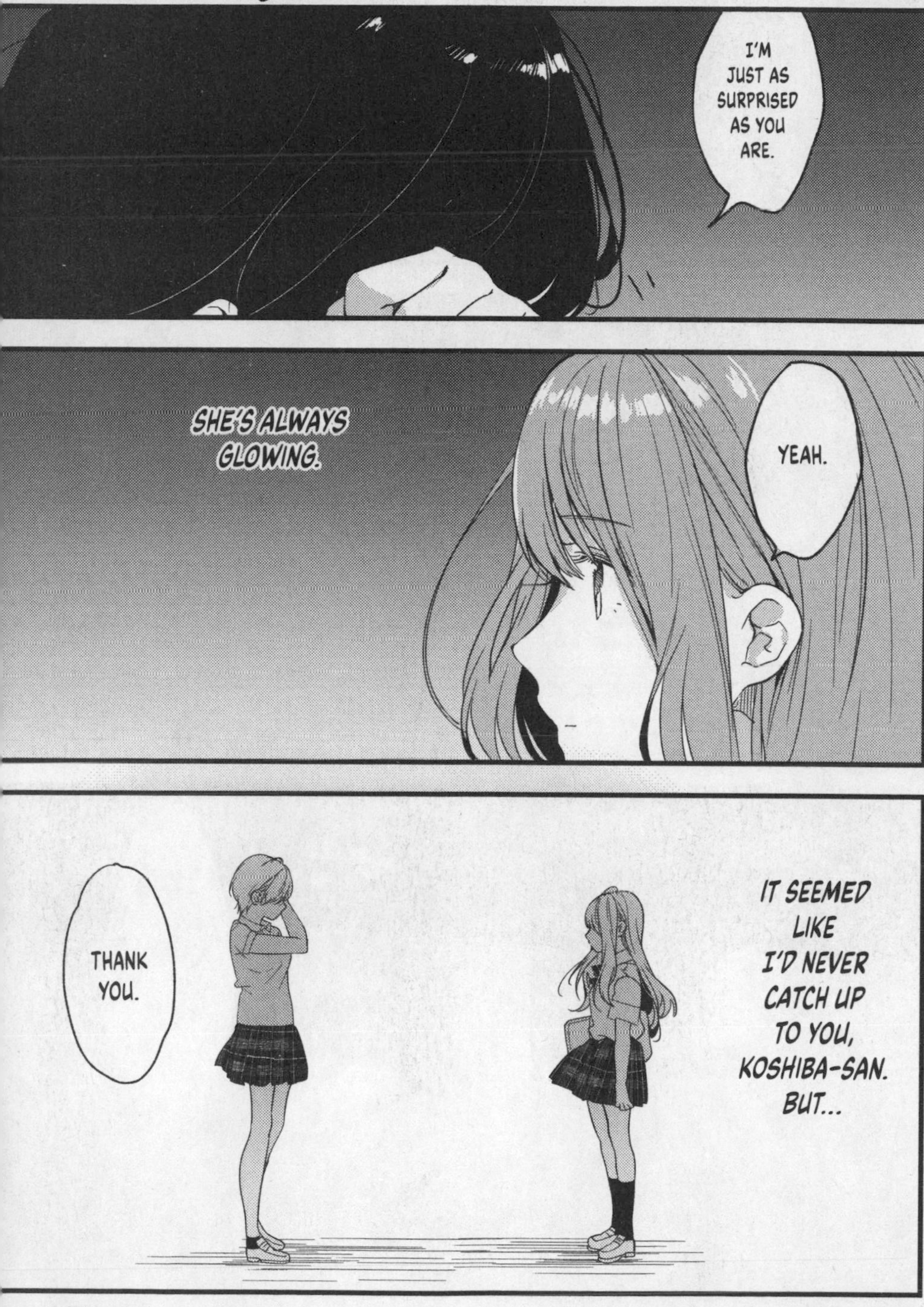
I'M JUST AS SURPRISED AS YOU ARE.
YEAH.
SHE'S ALWAYS GLOWING.
IT SEEMED LIKE I'D NEVER CATCH UP TO YOU, KOSHIBA-SAN. BUT...
THANK YOU.

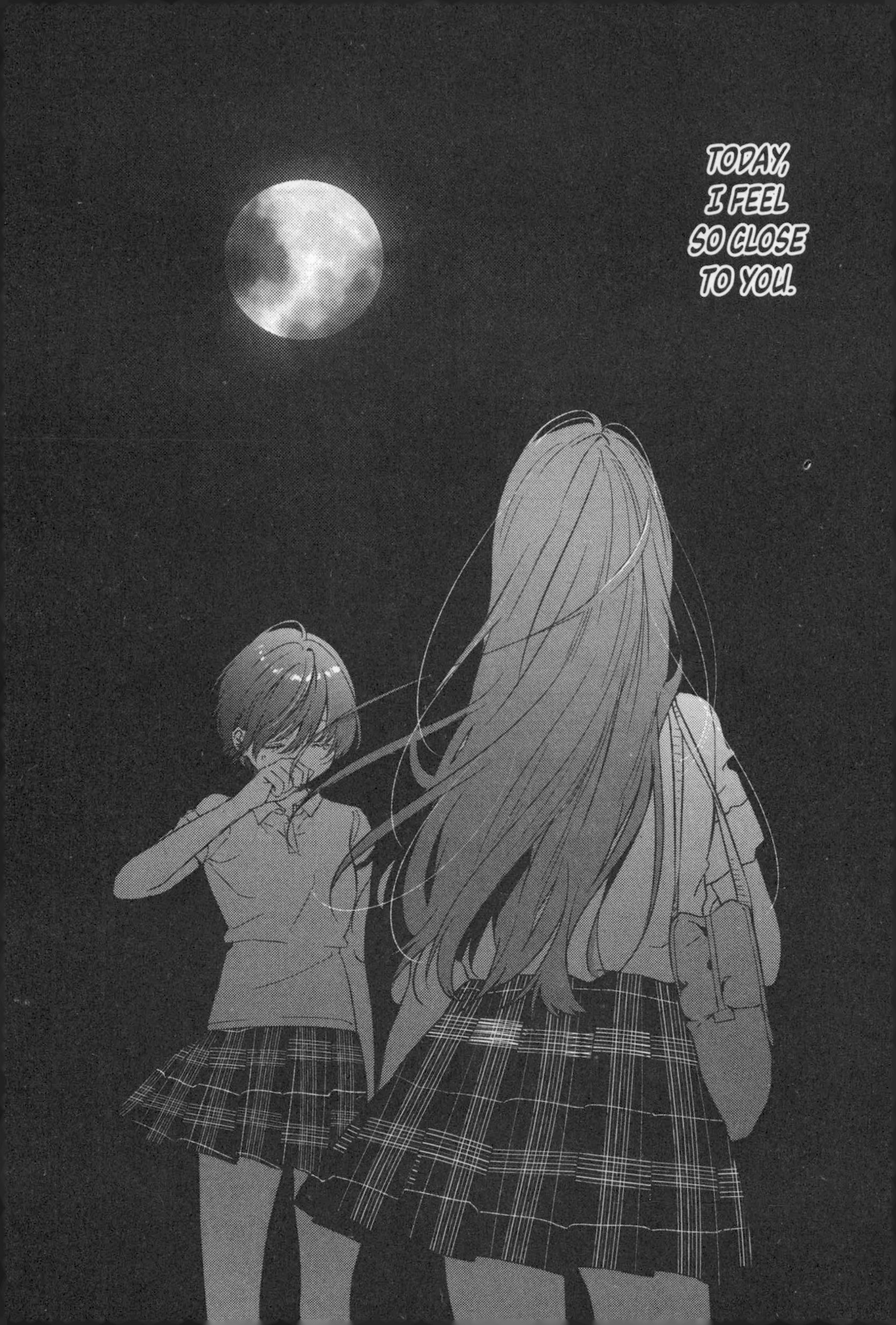
TODAY, I FEEL SO CLOSE TO YOU.

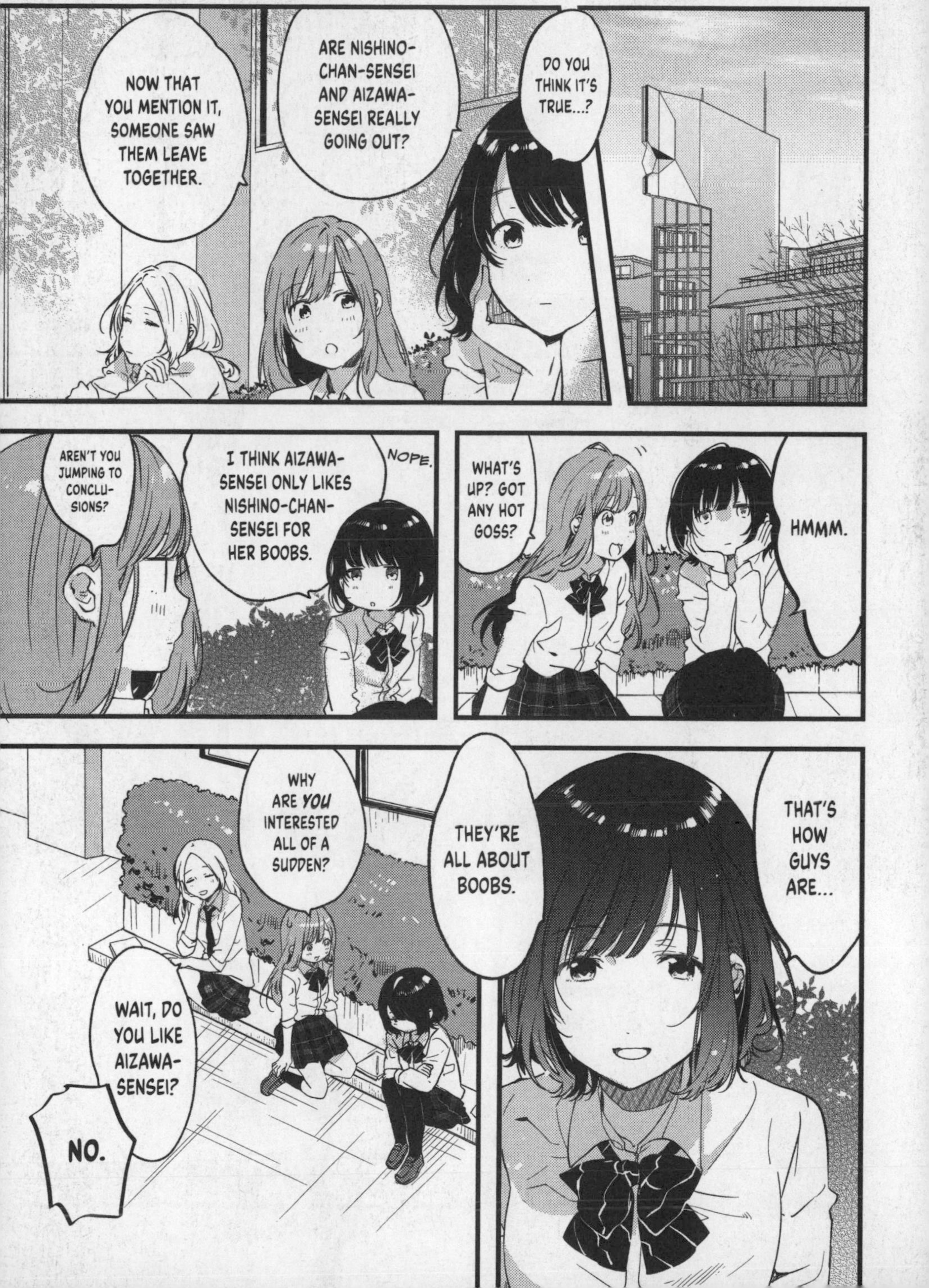
DO YOU THINK IT'S TRUE...?
ARE NISHINO-CHAN-SENSEI AND AIZAWA-SENSEI REALLY GOING OUT?
NOW THAT YOU MENTION IT, SOMEONE SAW THEM LEAVE TOGETHER.
HMMM.
WHAT'S UP? GOT ANY HOT GOSS?
NOPE.
I THINK AIZAWA-SENSEI ONLY LIKES NISHINO-CHAN-SENSEI FOR HER BOOBS.
AREN'T YOU JUMPING TO CONCLU-SIONS?
THAT'S HOW GUYS ARE...
THEY'RE ALL ABOUT BOOBS.
WHY ARE *YOU* INTERESTED ALL OF A SUDDEN?
WAIT, DO YOU LIKE AIZAWA-SENSEI?
NO.

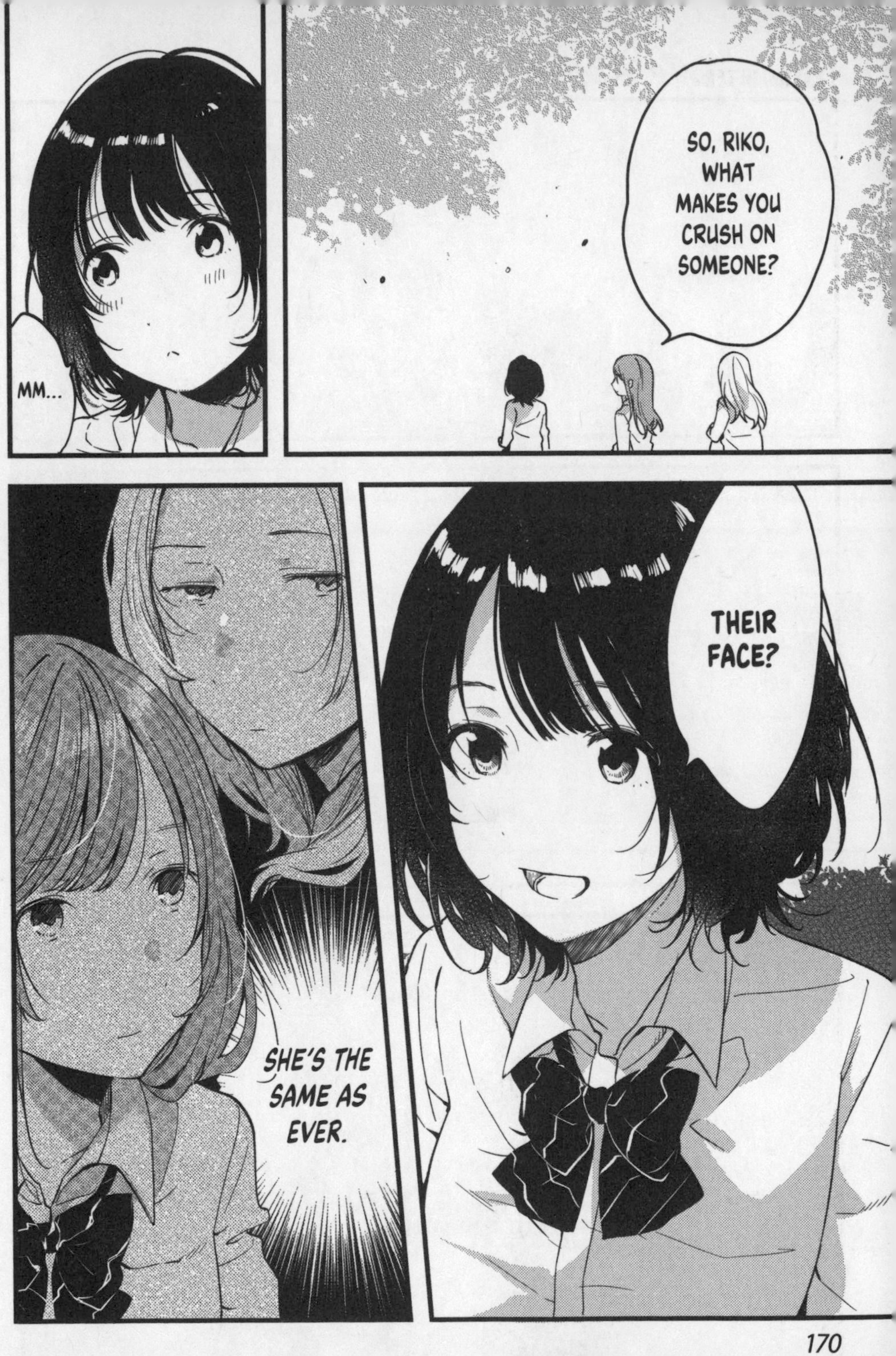
SO, RIKO, WHAT MAKES YOU CRUSH ON SOMEONE?
MM...
THEIR FACE?
SHE'S THE SAME AS EVER.

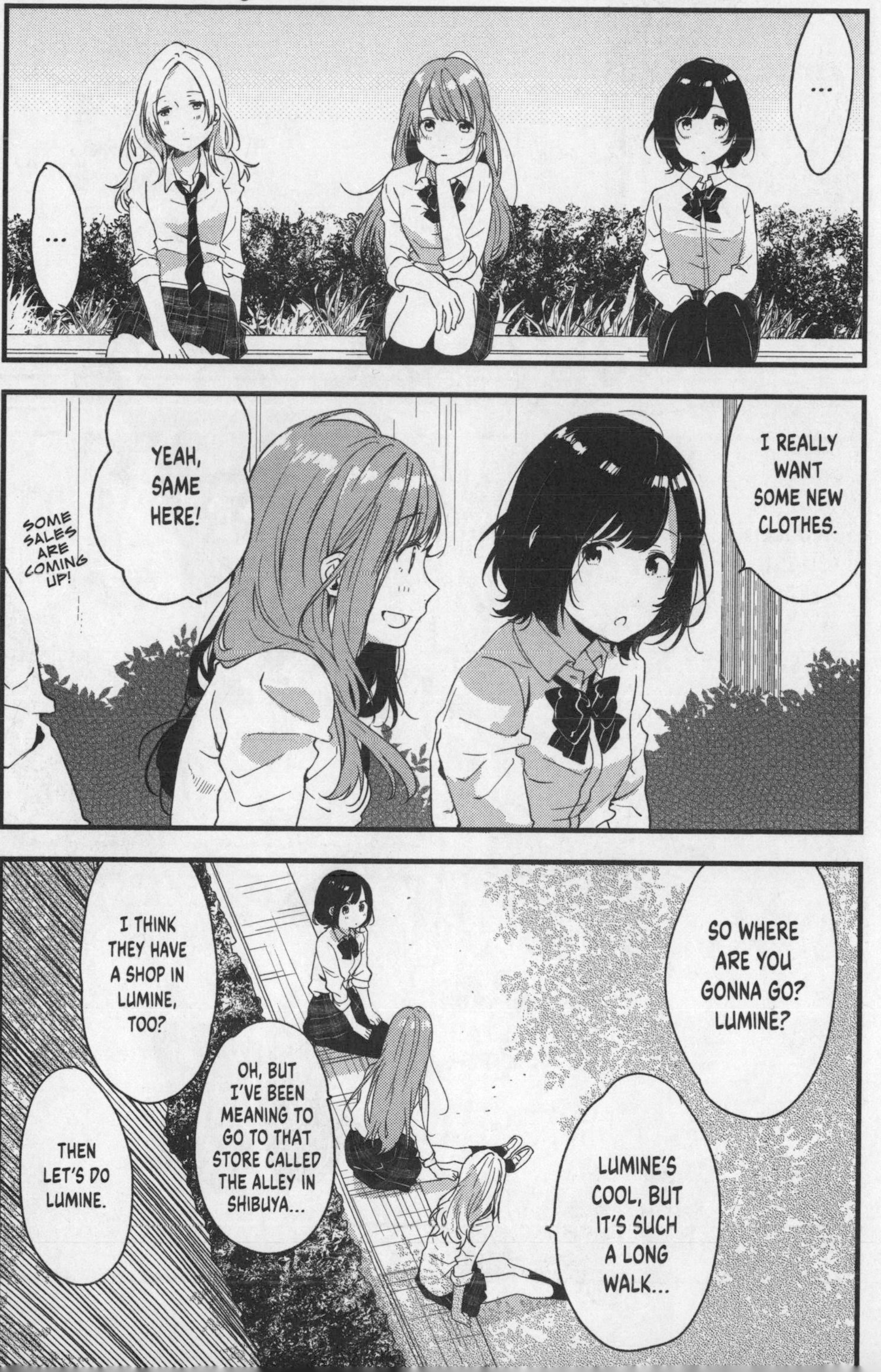
...
...
I REALLY WANT SOME NEW CLOTHES.
YEAH, SAME HERE!
SOME SALES ARE COMING UP!
SO WHERE ARE YOU GONNA GO? LUMINE?
LUMINE'S COOL, BUT IT'S SUCH A LONG WALK...
OH, BUT I'VE BEEN MEANING TO GO TO THAT STORE CALLED THE ALLEY IN SHIBUYA...
I THINK THEY HAVE A SHOP IN LUMINE, TOO?
THEN LET'S DO LUMINE.

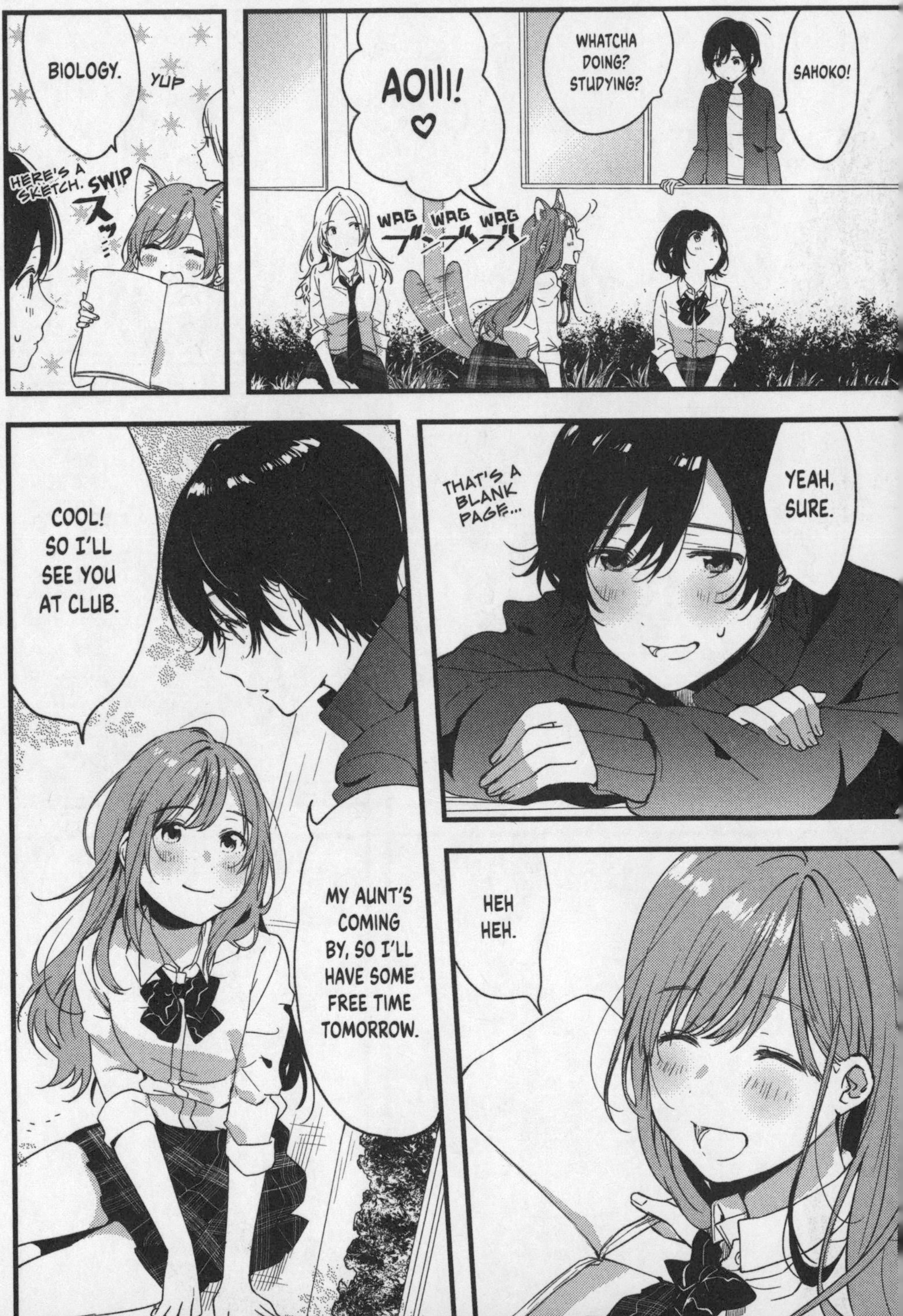
SAHOKO!
WHATCHA DOING? STUDYING?
AOIIII! ♥
WAG WAG WAG
ブンブンブン
BIOLOGY.
YUP
HERE'S A SKETCH.
SWIP
スッ
YEAH, SURE.
THAT'S A BLANK PAGE...
HEH HEH.
COOL! SO I'LL SEE YOU AT CLUB.
MY AUNT'S COMING BY, SO I'LL HAVE SOME FREE TIME TOMORROW.

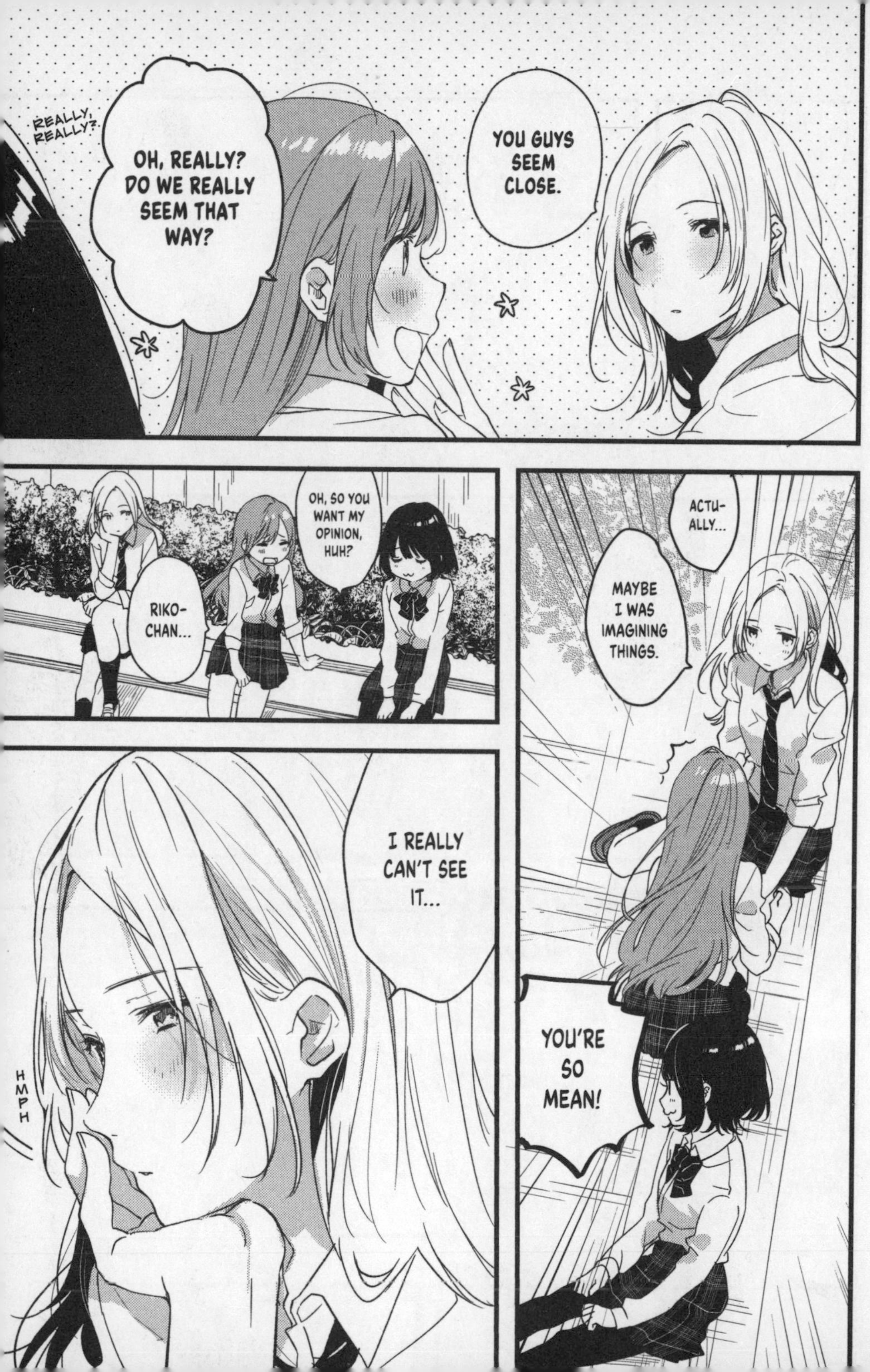
YOU GUYS SEEM CLOSE.
OH, REALLY? DO WE REALLY SEEM THAT WAY?
REALLY, REALLY?
ACTU-ALLY...
MAYBE I WAS IMAGINING THINGS.
YOU'RE SO MEAN!
OH, SO YOU WANT MY OPINION, HUH?
RIKO-CHAN...
I REALLY CAN'T SEE IT...
HMPH

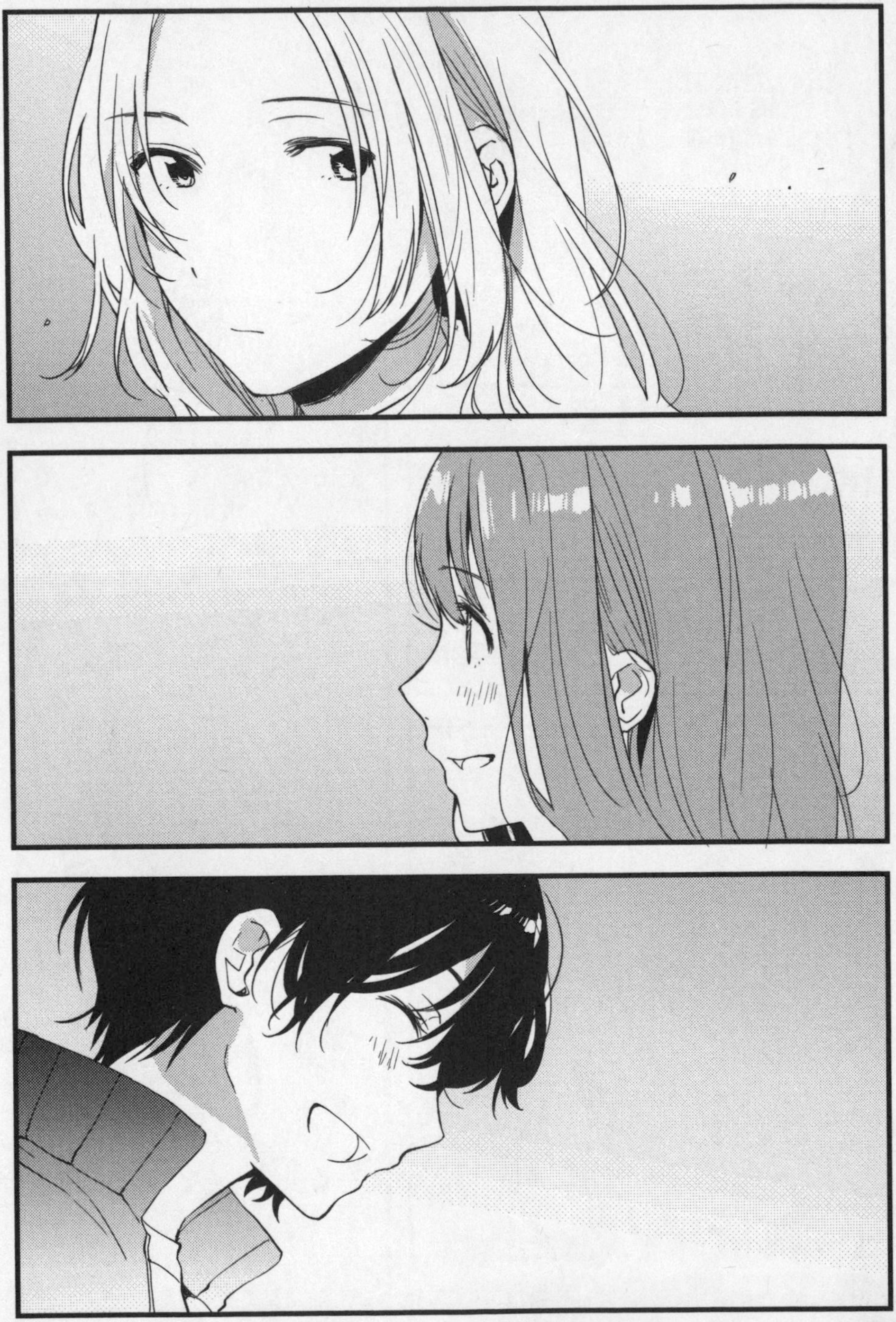

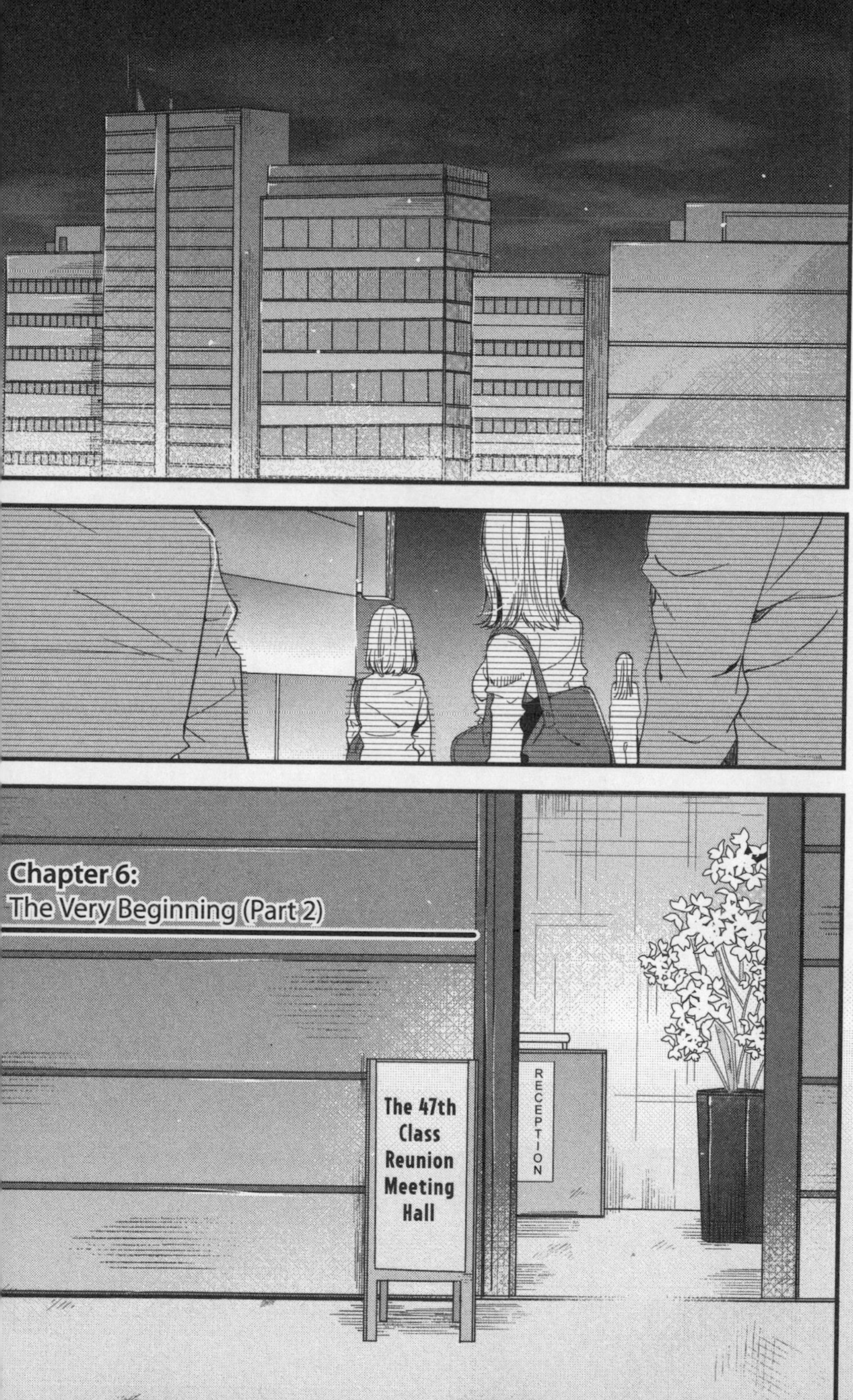
Chapter 6:
The Very Beginning (Part 2)
RECEPTION
The 47th Class Reunion Meeting Hall

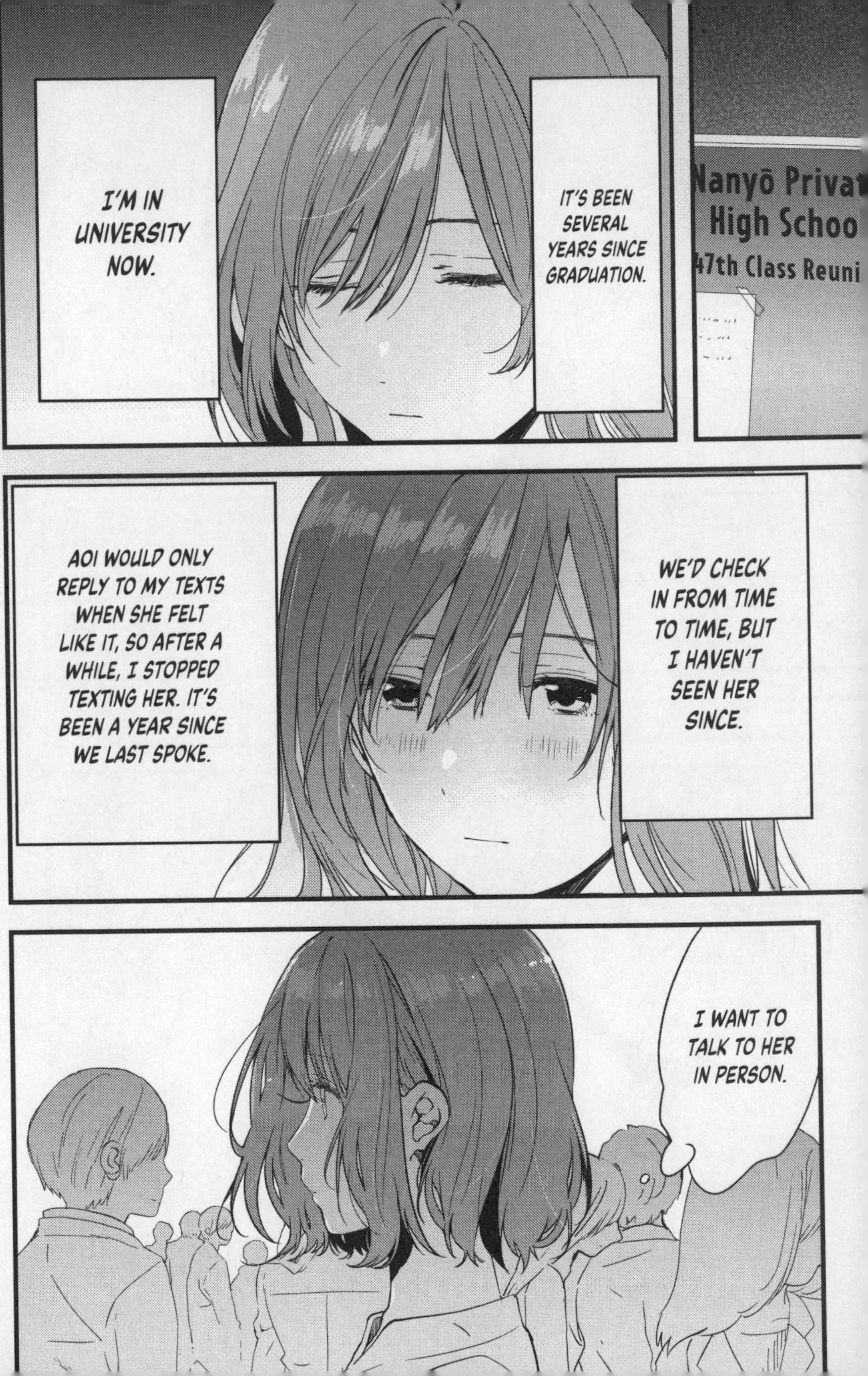
Nanyō Privat
High Schoo
47th Class Reuni
IT'S BEEN SEVERAL YEARS SINCE GRADUATION.
I'M IN UNIVERSITY NOW.
WE'D CHECK IN FROM TIME TO TIME, BUT I HAVEN'T SEEN HER SINCE.
AOI WOULD ONLY REPLY TO MY TEXTS WHEN SHE FELT LIKE IT, SO AFTER A WHILE, I STOPPED TEXTING HER. IT'S BEEN A YEAR SINCE WE LAST SPOKE.
I WANT TO TALK TO HER IN PERSON.

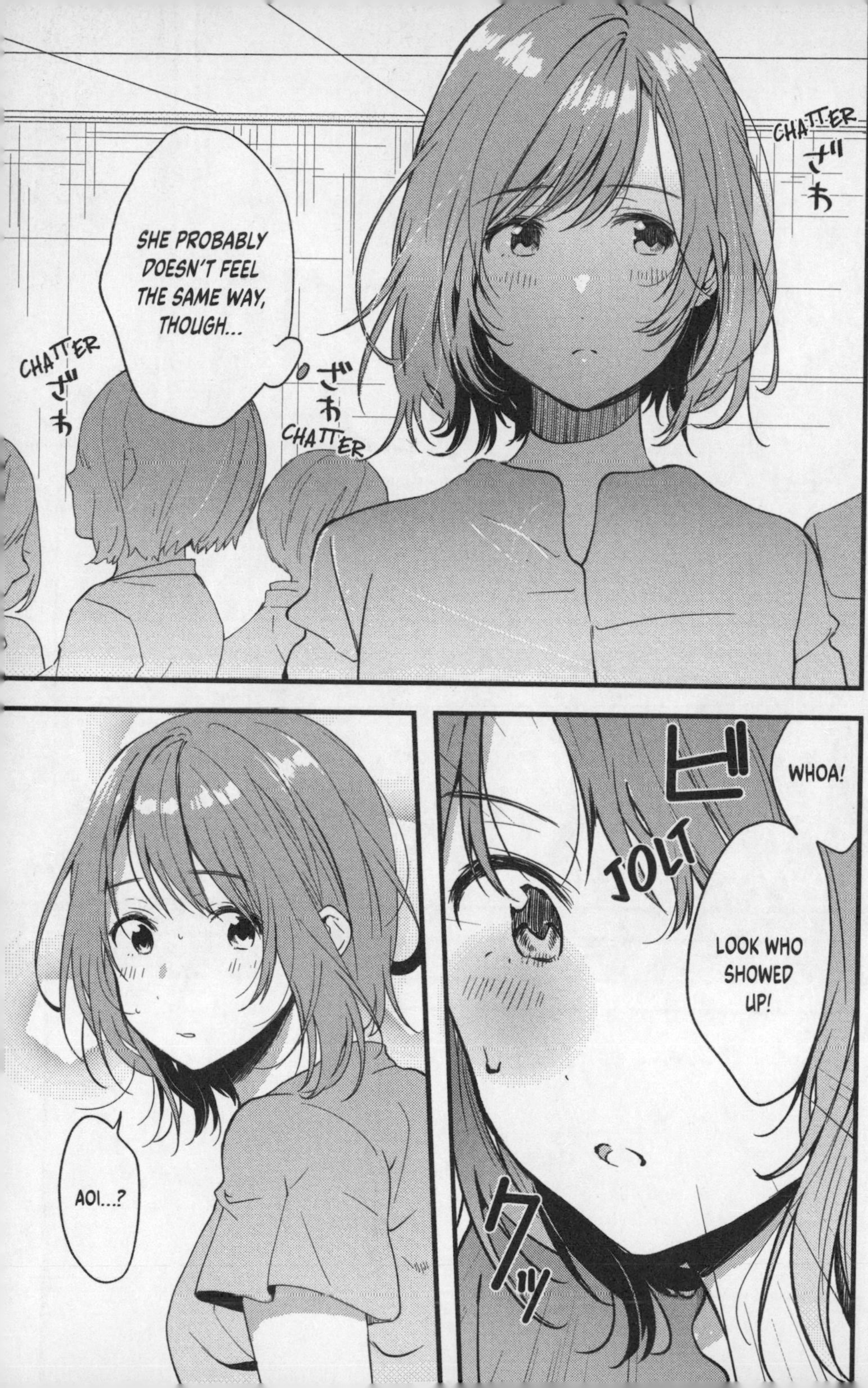
CHATTER
ざわ
SHE PROBABLY DOESN'T FEEL THE SAME WAY, THOUGH...
ざわ
CHATTER
CHATTER
ざわ
ビ
JOLT
WHOA!
LOOK WHO SHOWED UP!
クッ
AOI...?

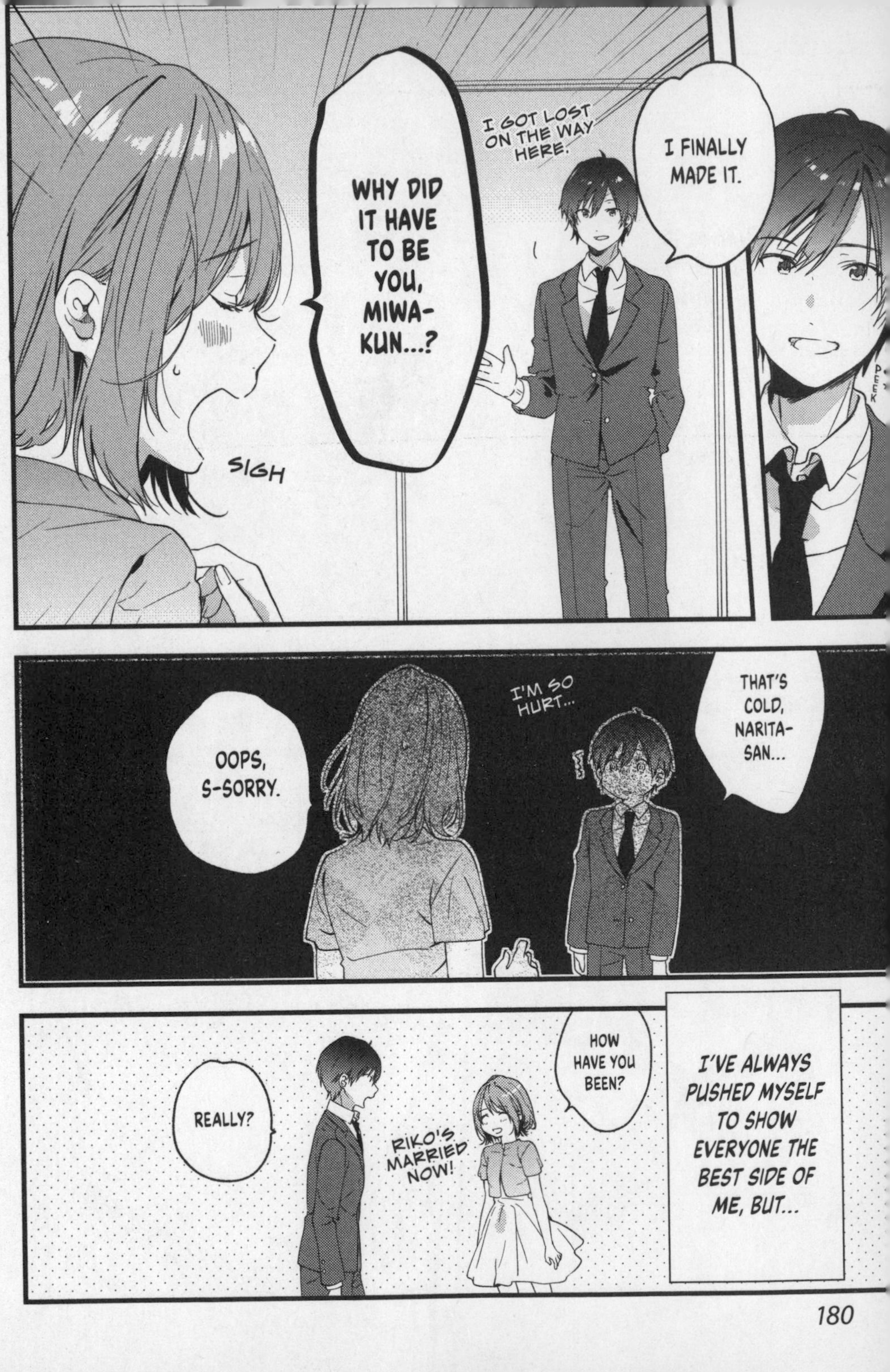
I FINALLY MADE IT.
PEEK
I GOT LOST ON THE WAY HERE.
WHY DID IT HAVE TO BE YOU, MIWA-KUN...?
SIGH
THAT'S COLD, NARITA-SAN...
I'M SO HURT...
OOPS, S-SORRY.
I'VE ALWAYS PUSHED MYSELF TO SHOW EVERYONE THE BEST SIDE OF ME, BUT...
HOW HAVE YOU BEEN?
RIKO'S MARRIED NOW!
REALLY?

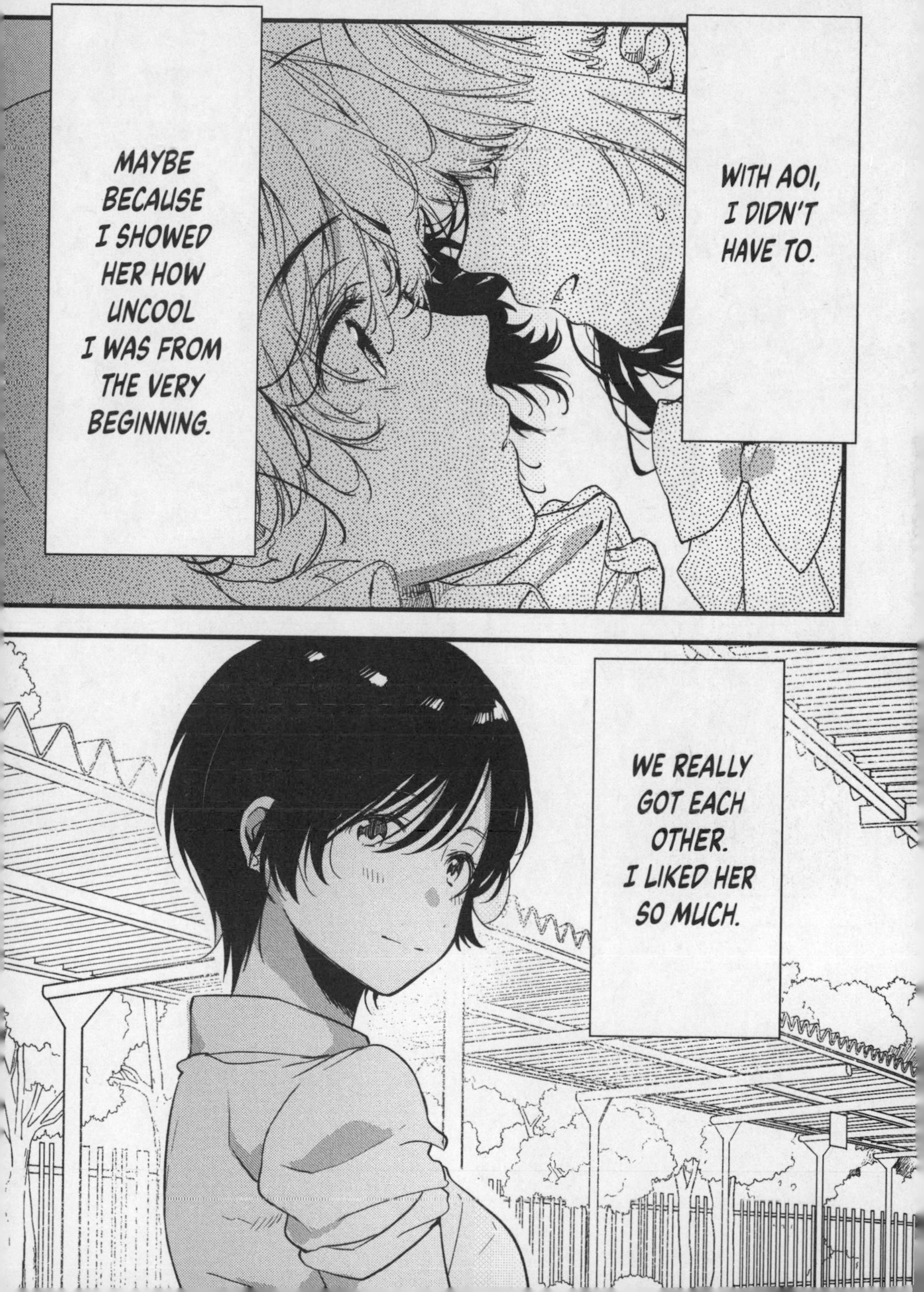
WITH AOI, I DIDN'T HAVE TO.
MAYBE BECAUSE I SHOWED HER HOW UNCOOL I WAS FROM THE VERY BEGINNING.
WE REALLY GOT EACH OTHER. I LIKED HER SO MUCH.

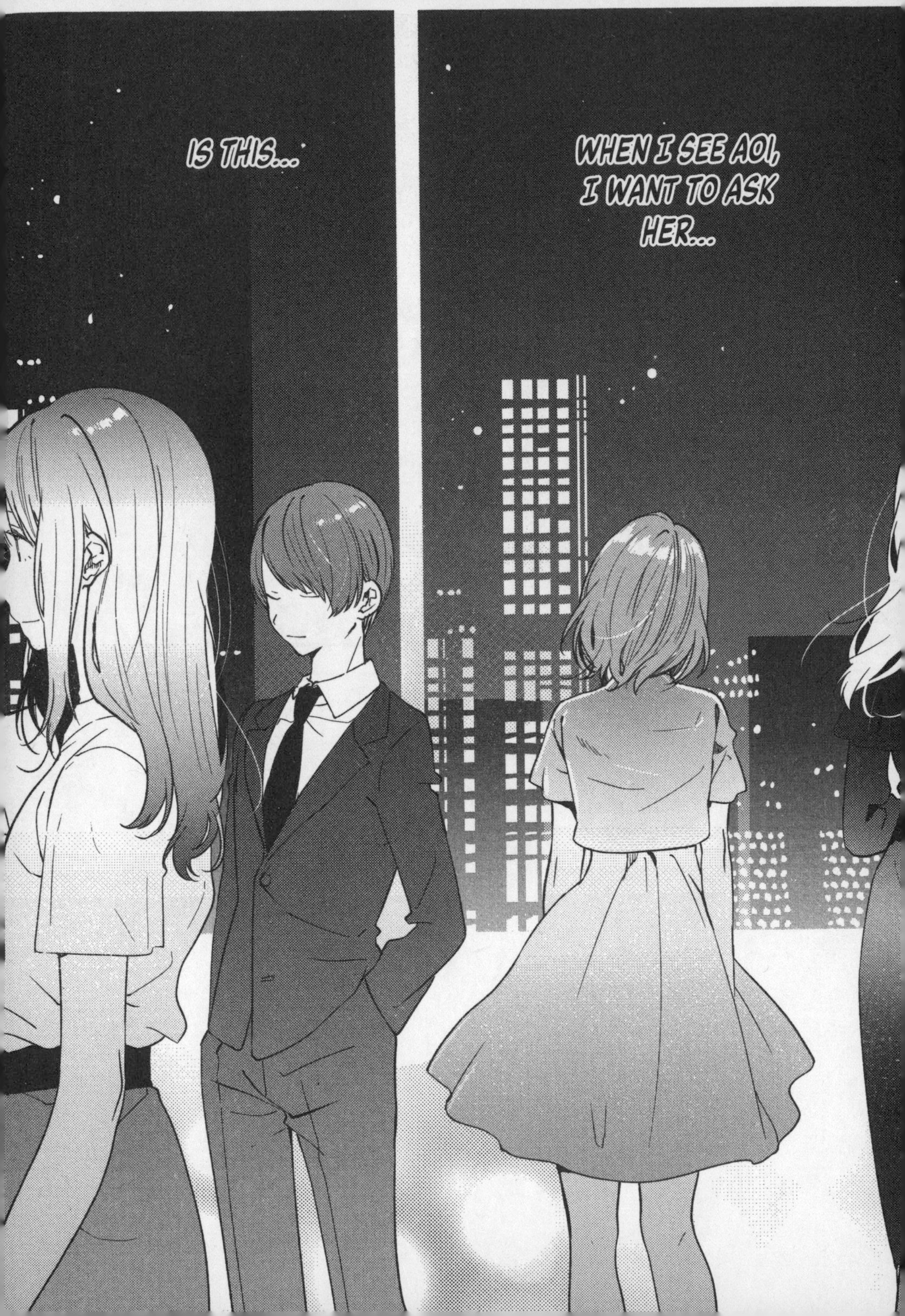
WHEN I SEE AOI, I WANT TO ASK HER...
IS THIS...

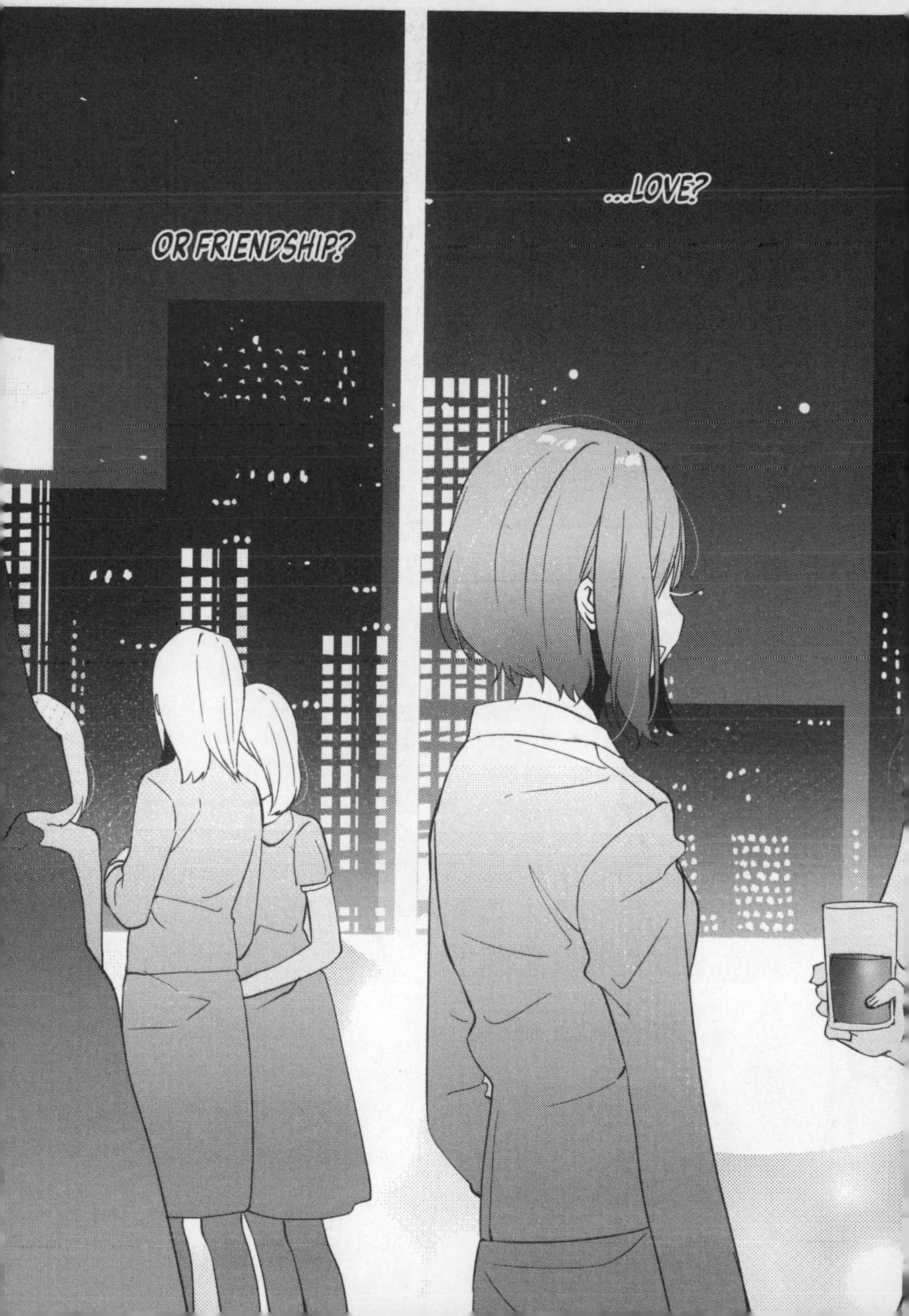
...LOVE?
OR FRIENDSHIP?

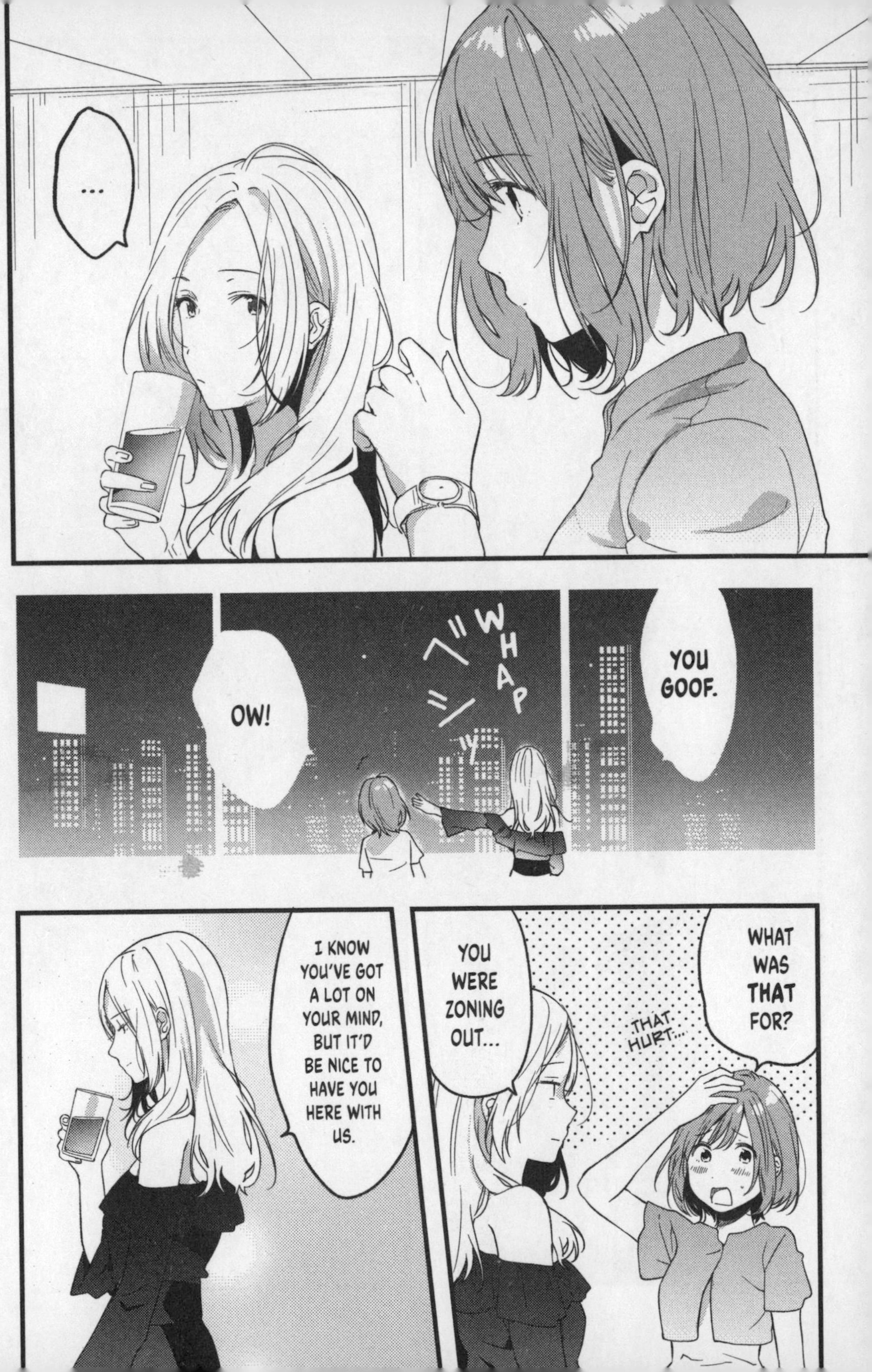
...
YOU GOOF.
WHAP
OW!
WHAT WAS **THAT** FOR?
THAT HURT...
YOU WERE ZONING OUT...
I KNOW YOU'VE GOT A LOT ON YOUR MIND, BUT IT'D BE NICE TO HAVE YOU HERE WITH US.

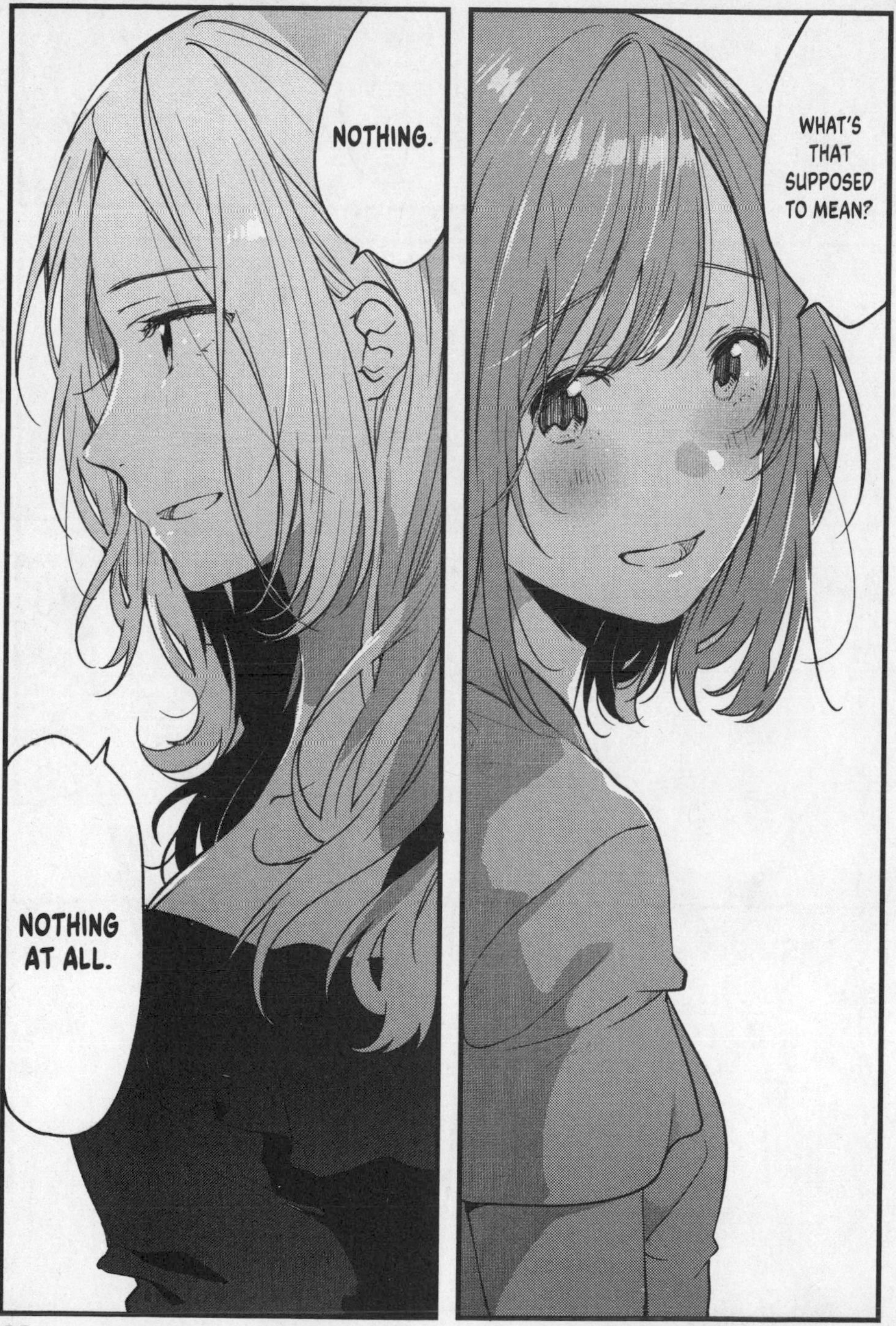
WHAT'S THAT SUPPOSED TO MEAN?
NOTHING.
NOTHING AT ALL.

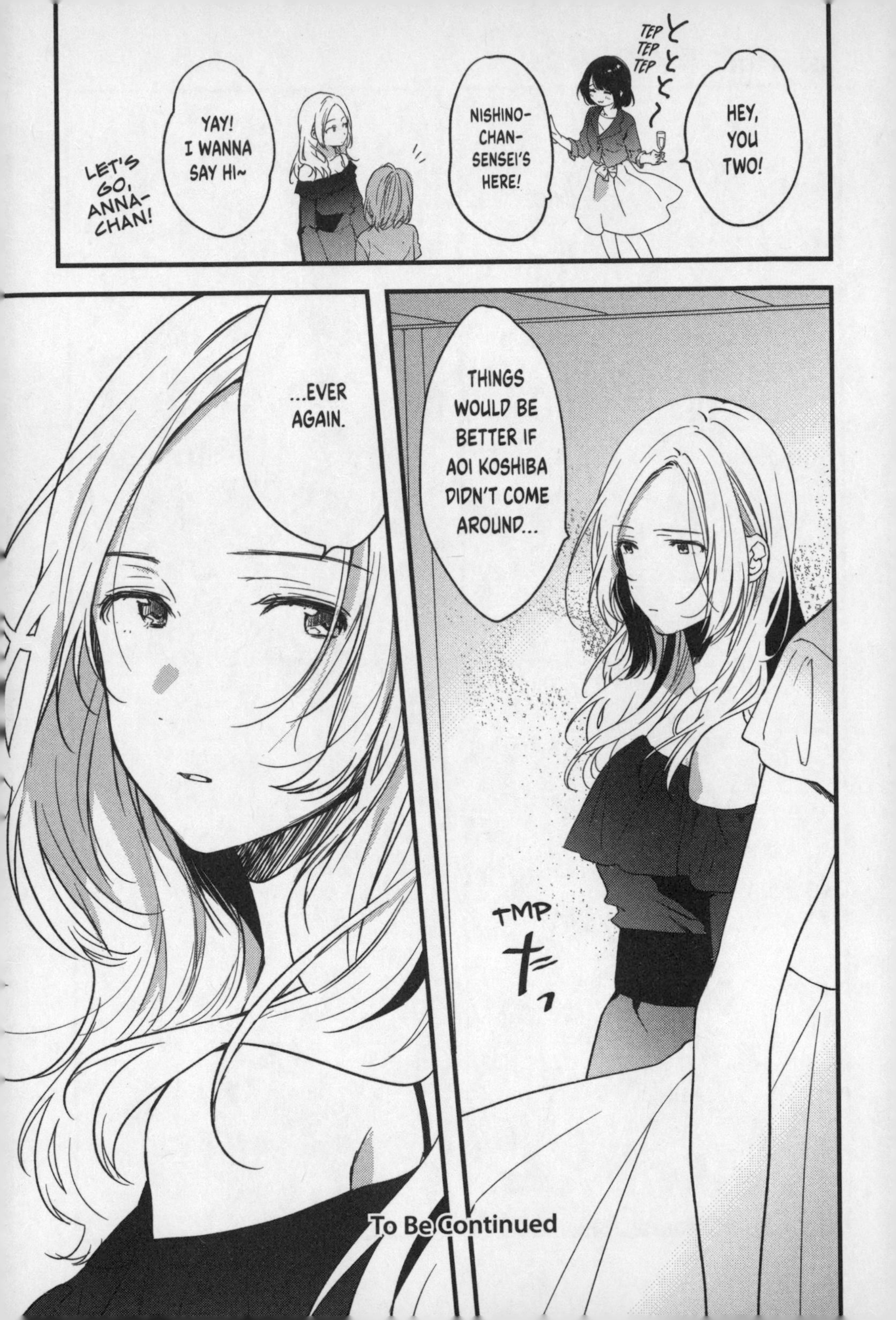
HEY, YOU TWO!
TEP TEP TEP
とと〜
NISHINO-CHAN-SENSEI'S HERE!
YAY! I WANNA SAY HI~
LET'S GO, ANNA-CHAN!
THINGS WOULD BE BETTER IF AOI KOSHIBA DIDN'T COME AROUND...
TMP
たっ
...EVER AGAIN.
To Be Continued

CHASING AFTER *Aoi Koshiba*

Winter, Third Year of University

This story began with the character drawings for Sahoko and Aoi, coupled with the theme, "the woes of youth." But how far it will go, and how closely we'll follow that, no one knows. It's a whole new world, so I hope you'll come along for the ride!

Hazuki Takeda

The relationships and feelings in this story are quite fluid and difficult to express. I look forward to depicting everything thoroughly and properly, all the way through. So join us, and thank you for reading.

Fly

CHASING AFTER
Aoi Koshiba

Yuri Is My Job!

miman

JOIN US FOR AFTERNOON TEA WITH EQUAL PARTS YURI, ROM-COM, AND DRAMA!

Hime is a picture-perfect high school princess, so when she accidentally injures a café manager named Mai, she's willing to cover some shifts to keep her façade intact. To Hime's surprise, the café is themed after a private school where the all-female staff always puts on their best act for their loyal customers. However, under the guidance of the most graceful girl there, Hime can't help but blush and blunder! Beneath all the frills and laughter, Hime feels tension brewing as she finds out more about her new job and her budding feelings...

KC KODANSHA COMICS

"A quirky, fun comedy series... If you're a yuri fan, or perhaps interested in getting into it but not sure where to start, this book is worth picking up."
— Anime UK News

Acclaimed screenwriter and director
Mari Okada (*Maquia, anohana*) teams up
with manga artist Nao Emoto (*Forget Me
Not*) in this moving, funny, so-true-it's-
embarrassing coming-of-age series!

When Kazusa enters high
school, she joins the Literature
Club, and leaps from reading
innocent fiction to diving into
the literary classics. But these
novels are a bit more...*adult* than
she was prepared for. Between
euphemisms like fresh dewy
grass and pork stew, crushing on
the boy next door, and knowing
you want to do that *one thing*
before you die—discovering
your budding sexuality is
no easy feat! As if puberty
wasn't awkward enough,
the club consists of a
brooding writer, the
prettiest girl in school,
an agreeable comrade,
and an outspoken prude.
Fumbling over their
own discomforts, these
five teens get thrown
into chaos over three
little letters: *S...E...X...!*

O Maidens in your Savage Season

Anime
out now!

Mari Okada   Nao Emoto

KC
KODANSHA
COMICS

The slow-burn queer romance that'll sweep you off your feet!

10 DANCE

Inouesatoh presents

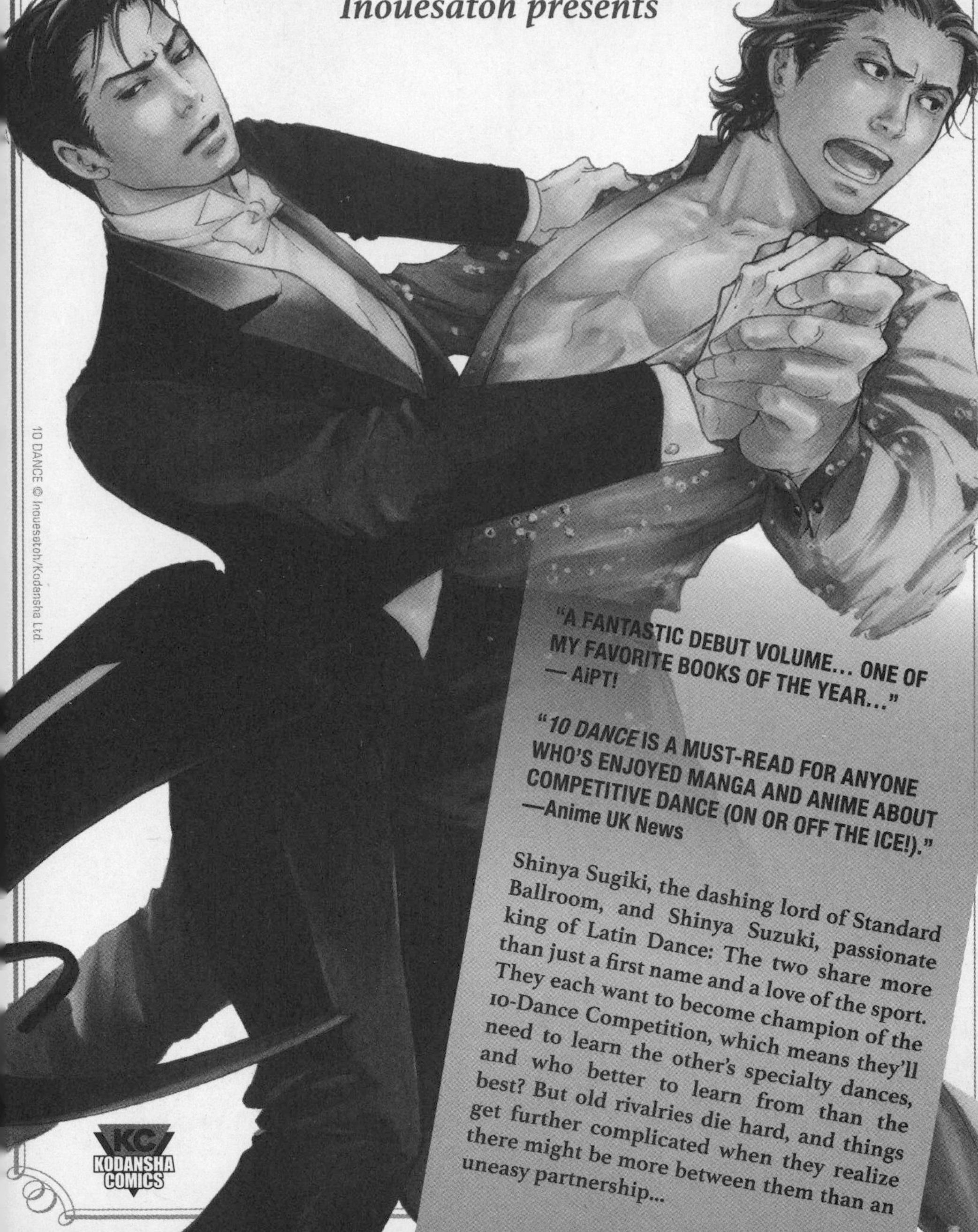

"A FANTASTIC DEBUT VOLUME... ONE OF MY FAVORITE BOOKS OF THE YEAR..."
— AiPT!

"10 DANCE IS A MUST-READ FOR ANYONE WHO'S ENJOYED MANGA AND ANIME ABOUT COMPETITIVE DANCE (ON OR OFF THE ICE!)."
—Anime UK News

Shinya Sugiki, the dashing lord of Standard Ballroom, and Shinya Suzuki, passionate king of Latin Dance: The two share more than just a first name and a love of the sport. They each want to become champion of the 10-Dance Competition, which means they'll need to learn the other's specialty dances, and who better to learn from than the best? But old rivalries die hard, and things get further complicated when they realize there might be more between them than an uneasy partnership...

KC KODANSHA COMICS

"I'm pleasantly surprised to find modern shojo using cross-dressing as a dramatic device to deliver social commentary... Recommended."

-Otaku USA Magazine

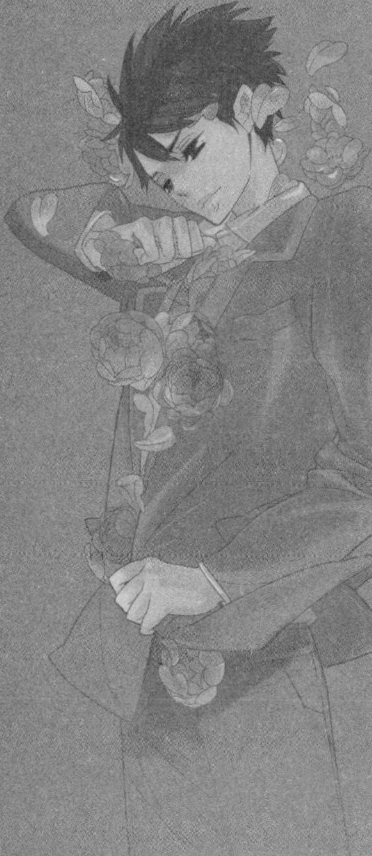

The prince in his dark days

By Hico Yamanaka

A drunkard for a father, a household of poverty... For 17-year-old Atsuko, misfortune is all she knows and believes in. Until one day, a chance encounter with Itaru-the wealthy heir of a huge corporation-changes everything. The two look identical, uncannily so. When Itaru curiously goes missing, Atsuko is roped into being his stand-in. There, in his shoes, Atsuko must parade like a prince in a palace. She encounters many new experiences, but at what cost...?

PERFECT WORLD

Rie Aruga

A TOUCHING NEW SERIES ABOUT LOVE AND COPING WITH DISABILITY

An office party reunites Tsugumi with her high school crush Itsuki. He's realized his dream of becoming an architect, but along the way, he experienced a spinal injury that put him in a wheelchair. Now Tsugumi's rekindled feelings will butt up against prejudices she never considered — and Itsuki will have to decide if he's ready to let someone into his heart...

"Depicts with great delicacy and courage the difficulties some with disabilities experience getting involved in romantic relationships... Rie Aruga refuses to romanticize, pushing her heroine to face the reality of disability. She invites her readers to the same tasks of empathy, knowledge and recognition."
—Slate.fr

"An important entry [in manga romance]... The emotional core of both plot and characters indicates thoughtfulness... [Aruga's] research is readily apparent in the text and artwork, making this feel like a real story."
—Anime News Network

KC KODANSHA COMICS

A Kodansha Comics Trade Paperback Original
Chasing After Aoi Koshiba 1 copyright © 2019 Hazuki Takeoka/Fly
English translation copyright © 2021 Hazuki Takeoka/Fly

Published in the United States by Kodansha Comics, an imprint of
Kodansha USA Publishing, LLC, New York.

Publication rights for this English edition arranged through
Kodansha Ltd., Tokyo.

First published in Japan in 2019 by Ichijinsha Inc., Tokyo.

ISBN 978-1-64651-186-0

Printed in the United States of America.

www.kodanshacomics.com

9 8 7 6 5 4 3 2 1
Translation: Alexa Frank
Lettering: Paige Pumphrey
Editing: Haruko Hashimoto
Kodansha Comics edition cover design by Adam Del Re

Publisher: Kiichiro Sugawara

Director of publishing services: Ben Applegate
Associate director of operations: Stephen Pakula
Publishing services managing editor: Noelle Webster
Assistant production manager: Emi Lotto, Angela Zurlo
Logo and character art ©Kodansha USA Publishing, LLC